To Jerry,

THE POSTMAN
Sydney to Alaska by 105cc motorcycle

Honourary member of the
Garbage Run Gang,

All the best for the
adventures ahead
Nathan & Dorothy
10/5/18

NATHAN MILLWARD

ISBN 978-0-9572297-3-0
© Copyright 2015 Nathan Millward, All rights reserved.
See www.nathanmillward.com for more information on my travels
Published by Dot Publishing
Printed by Books Factory

For those who are lost and still looking

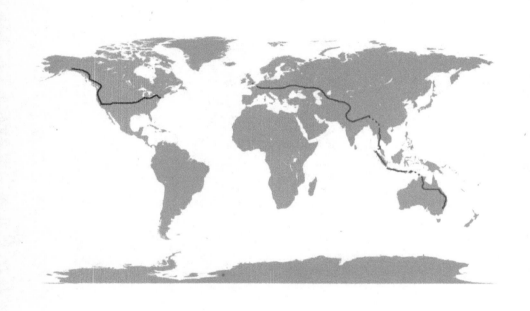

This is a compendium of my two books; The Long Ride Home (also known as Going Postal in Australia) and Running Towards the Light: Postcards from Alaska. I always felt they were both part of the same story; hence now joining together to form one book: The Postman.

PART 1

THE LONG RIDE HOME
SYDNEY TO LONDON

Prologue

This is the story of my motorbike trip across the world. It took place from January to September 2009, on a little Honda called Dorothy. She's a brilliant bike, painted red, the colour of speed, though she herself is not very fast. One time we hit eighty-five kilometres per hour and almost crashed with excitement.

I say 'we' because it's me and her. The two of us, who one day hit the road and never turned back, not until we'd ridden 35,000 kilometres in nine months, through eighteen countries in a single pair of basketball boots and with gloves that seldom matched. But that doesn't matter.

The road knows no fashion sense and neither did we. We were just riders, of no fixed abode, pushed on by the most incredible urge just to get there, the other side of the world. Leaving on a whim, no planning, no preparation. Just go.

But this journey doesn't start with a motorbike, or even the open road. No, as you might well expect with a story of this nature, it begins with a woman, who for the sake of this book we shall call Mandy.

If it wasn't for Mandy there would be no adventure, no Dorothy and certainly no story to tell. There would just be me, in an office cubicle somewhere, looking out of the window knowing there's something else out there but not having the faintest idea what.

I met Mandy in Sydney, at speed-dating of all places. She was the beautiful blonde with good style on table six. I was the scruffy Englishman on a working holiday visa with dirty glasses who came over with a bottle of beer; and the first thing she said was, 'Where's mine?'

It wasn't the best way to start the three minutes we had together, but it couldn't have been that bad, because at the end of the night she ticked my box and I ticked hers.

We went out a few days later and just clicked, connecting in a way that at times felt as though we were held together by a bungee rope, pulling apart as far as we could until we shot back together with a bang.

To me she was a challenge, strong-headed and stubborn... about me she probably would have said the same. Yet we both hung on in there, through the good times and the bad, the worst of which was when we were on opposite sides of the world for five months, because if there's one thing guaranteed to get in the way of a good relationship, it's a visa.

In fact, it was during that five months apart, me in my native England, Mandy in her adopted home of Australia, that I came up with the idea for this trip.

It's flying, you see. I hate it. And so when I finally accepted that life on the other side of the world really wasn't much fun without her, I figured rather than fly back to Australia, I would ride there by motorbike instead.

I had three reasons for thinking this to be a good idea. First, I like motorbikes. Second, I like travelling. Third, a friend of mine called Thomas Wielecki once told me how a big motorcycle trip like this can change you. He never said how or why or in what way, just that it happens. And I quite liked the sound of that.

Immediately I went out and bought the perfect machine for the trip. It was a Honda C90, painted baby blue, a step-through. It cost five hundred pounds and whilst I realise that was a far cry from what Ewan McGregor and Charley Boorman were going around the world on at the time, it was the most reliable bike I could afford. And the colour matched my eyes.

From there I began to research exactly what documents I'd need and the route I would take. From England, through Europe, Turkey, Iran, Pakistan and India, then across to Thailand and down through Malaysia and Indonesia, until finally Australia, and Mandy's doorstep.

For a while it really seemed like I was going to give this thing a go. I told my parents, I told my friends, who all thought it was ridiculous, but I was adamant I was going to do it, right up until the point at which I asked my nan what she thought. Her advice was that if I wake up in the morning and still know it's the one thing I want to do, then go off and do it. But, she said, if you wake up with the slightest hint of doubt, then maybe it's not the right thing after all.

I woke up the next morning and it didn't feel right. I couldn't possibly wait however many months I assumed it would take to ride across the world before seeing Mandy again. I had to see her that minute, that second, so I gave up on the idea to ride across the world on a motorbike, quit my job in London, booked a ticket and flew back to Australia the following week.

'What are you doing here?' Mandy asked the day I surprised her on the ferry she took to work. 'I've come here for you,' I said, the Opera House now in view (I'd not told her I was coming, just in case she told me not to).

And so began an eight-month period together in Sydney, back in the place where it all began. Great times: holding hands, walking on the beach, the waves at our feet. Going back to Australia was the best thing I ever did. The only problem was that in my haste to get there I'd only been able to get a tourist visa, so ended up working cash in hand, making sandwiches in a café for a Greek man named Spiros. I even tried medical testing but got turned away for not having a permanent address.

It wasn't then an easy time for either of us. Mandy wanted stability, knowledge of a future, some nice living room furniture; all I had to offer was leftover lasagne from the café and the troubles of an uncertain situation. But we tried, dear lord we tried; we tried to the point at which we surprised ourselves that we were still, well, trying.

Then the whole thing came crashing down the day I went to ask Immigration for an extension on my visa. To that they said, 'No, it's time for you to go, be gone in no more than twenty days.'

And that's where this story begins.

Chapter One
Sydney

I sat in the centre of Sydney waiting for the lights to turn green. In the reflection of a shop window a familiar image was staring back at me. It was typically English — collared shirt, big teeth, bad hair, terrible combat shorts. But then I looked down at Doris, the decommissioned 105cc Australia Post bike I was sat astride, and felt instantly cool again. She was red, like they all are, with four semi-automatic gears and an orange milk crate strapped to the back. I gave her a gentle rev, just a tickle. The light turned green. Go.

Flat out in first, the speedo firing like a rocket until the moment I clicked her into second and on the wave of acceleration continued, past Town Hall and down the hill beyond. Pedestrians ran for their lives, darting left and right in a bid to get out of the way of this flying red machine. Third gear now, past Darling Harbour to our right and the Powerhouse Museum to our left, traffic streaming in every direction, the pair of us blaring down the centre, eyes alert, spider sense tingling: don't you dare step out, don't you dare pull out.

On to the freeway now, dodging the traffic on the inside lane, over the brow of Anzac Bridge and down the other side. I loved this bit of the journey, flat out at seventy-five kilometres per hour, weaving between cars and lorries until hard right at the bottom then up the hill towards Rozelle. Nothing less than full throttle, Doris's 105cc chest beating as though it was about to explode and the pair of us squeezing between cars and buses as they waited at the traffic lights. At the top of the hill we turned right down Darling Street and jinked through a series of narrow side streets, always riding the racing line and not braking for the house until it was almost too late.

'How did you get on?' Mandy asked as she greeted me at the door. 'Not good,' I said, 'I've got to be out of the country in twenty days.'

I took off my helmet and gloves and followed her into the house. The corridor was cool and dark compared to the bright roaring light outside. My old Converse boots made the floorboards clatter as they led a familiar trail through to the kitchen at the back of the house, where the back door was open and the heat of a Sydney summer's day came blazing in.

We sat down around the kitchen table and drank a cup of tea. If I tried to write the words to accurately reflect the mood at this moment the page would be blank, because for a while we sat in silence, nothing much to say but, 'What are you thinking?' And the other one saying, 'I was just thinking how shit this all is.' The other one nodding and then sipping their tea.

Though if we were being completely honest, there was probably a part of both of us that day that saw this as a blessing in disguise. It simply hadn't worked out. My plan to come back and make things work had failed.

Love certainly wasn't the problem. There was plenty of that. It was more the background to it, the uncertainty, and the visa. We just wanted to let the relationship breathe and develop at its own pace, without the pressures of an uncertain situation. Yet everything we tried seemed to fail, every door that momentarily opened again slammed shut. And the longer I had to work in the café, the longer the uncertain situation dragged on, the harder it became. We even talked about marriage, but were reluctant to have it seen as something done for a visa, though in fairness, it wouldn't have been just for that.

Mandy was the person I never realised existed. The one that smashes your defences to smithereens and leaves you completely exposed. You are revealed for all that you are and all that you are not. Sometimes that was painful but sometimes that was nice. I guess she was my mirror and

I was hers. Often the reflections were so ugly we would try to look away, but when the person you care so desperately about is the one holding the mirror that's not something so easily done. So you look and you see yourself, warts and all. And strangely that was addictive.

The options now were few. The lady at Immigration had explained how I could fly to New Zealand and come back again as that would automatically grant me another three months tourist visa, but that would be the last of them, and from there it would have to be home regardless. We thought about this but concluded it would just be more of the same, and we were too tired for that. The only other option was to enjoy the twenty days we had remaining together and then I would go to the airport, say goodbye and get on the plane and fly home to England with the return ticket I already had. Hard as it was, we accepted that this is what we needed to do.

And that's probably what would have happened, had it not been for Mandy, who suggested that maybe I should ride a motorbike home instead. Of course I'd told her of my original plan to ride the C90 from England to Australia and sweep her off her feet when I got here, including my reasons for wanting to do so, but not for a minute did I think she would present it as an option that day, because I certainly wasn't going to.

'No chance,' I answered. 'For a start I don't have the time, I don't have the money, and on what, Doris? She'd never make it.'

No, it was a stupid idea, one not even worth thinking about. In the space of twenty days I'd have to prepare the bike, sort out all the visas and other documents, buy and pack the equipment, then ride almost 5,000 kilometres across Australia to Darwin where I knew a boat would be able to take me to East Timor. All that in twenty days. It wasn't possible, and I explained so for three main reasons.

First, the lack of time. I calculated that at Doris's seventy five-kilometre-per-hour maximum cruising speed we would need at least two and a half weeks to ride to Darwin, with a day at that end to sort out final details and get her on the boat. Twenty minus seventeen, minus one, equals two. That's how many days we would have to transform me and Doris into a pair of sturdy explorers ready for a ride across the world. A book I once read advised allowing at least a year to prepare for such a trip. Two days. That's all we would have.

Second, the lack of money. The café didn't pay me much and scribbling down numbers on a piece of paper confirmed I had around $2,000 left on one credit card, $3,000 on another, $1,000 in cash and I was still owed a few thousand dollars for some work I'd done on the side. That made $8,000 of accessible funds. I didn't know if that was going to be enough, and in truth had no real way of knowing. I could only guess at how long it would take and how much I'd need to spend along the way, based on the calculations I'd made the first round, when planning on coming the other way.

Thirdly, the state of Doris, the 105cc motorbike that wasn't quite a moped but looked like one anyway. She was a Honda CT110, or postie bike as they're known in Australia, as all the postmen use them to deliver the mail. As a private individual you can only buy them second hand, after the postal service has finished with them, as I'd done with Doris, paying $1,400 on eBay and collecting her from a man who lived up the coast.

Not many weeks later she began making a strange noise from the engine, hence why she was booked in to see a mechanic the following week. Her back wheel was also missing a spoke, her headlight didn't always work, she leaked oil, and one of the exhaust guard mounts had broken off and was held on by wire. She was alright for the city, but I wouldn't want to have ridden her much further than that.

If those three reasons weren't enough, there was also the small matter of it being the wet season in the north, my parents' known opposition to the idea, my lack of mechanical skill, not to mention that after Australia we were talking about riding a 105cc semi-automatic postie bike across Indonesia, Malaysia, Thailand, Nepal, India, Pakistan, Iran, Turkey and Europe, on a route that, while well-trodden by overland travellers, is still by no means an easy, safe or predictable one, especially without any planning.

Yet Mandy was right. One way or another I had to leave the country in twenty days, whether by motorbike, or on the return air ticket I already had. And the more I thought about it as we stood in her kitchen that day, the more I thought, 'Yeah, she's right. I do need to do this because if I don't I'll find myself in later life forever wondering why I didn't set off on a motorbike that day.' I mean, how many times does life present you with such an opportunity? No commitments, nothing to go back to, no job, no kids, no mortgage. The only thing I had in my life was her. And she was the one telling me to do it.

But it wasn't just that. In a way I didn't know where else to go or where else to be. If I flew home to England people would ask what I was doing there and why things hadn't worked out in Australia. I didn't really want to answer those questions or face the reality of it myself. It hadn't worked out because... me, us, the situation. I don't know, maybe it was never meant to work out; two peas from very different pods.

Now it was a sense of wanting to disappear, get lost, embark on a journey and undertake a terrific challenge, to clear my head, to sort things out, in the hope that things would somehow be easier, be better, I would be better, when, or if, I ever made it to the other side. And so the motorcycle idea suddenly had a new purpose to it, a point, to escape and to find, to get lost in the world for a while. And I didn't need much more convincing than that.

With that I put my head in my hands and took a deep breath. Was I really capable of riding across the world on such a small old motorbike, after only two days of planning, with no clue as to whether I had enough money to make it, with no back up, no support, no mechanical knowledge, no proper equipment, nothing organised, just my own hands and my head? I didn't know, I just didn't know. But I knew I had to try.

With that, I cut the rope and fell.

For the next two days we scribbled a dozen lists and ran the length of Sydney ticking them off. I bought a cheap tool set from Bunnings, some spare oil, a set of instant tyre inflators and a huge aluminium box from Supercheap Auto to bolt on the back.

Neighbours Pete and his son Louis helped drill and fix the box to the rear rack. Mandy donated her pocket knife and sleeping bag; her house-mate Sal bought me a waterproof map of Australia on which we worked out the best route — up the east coast, not the red centre — while her boyfriend Matty set me up with a pair of welding gloves to ride in. They were beige, with blue piping around the cuff. Another friend, Rohan, came over later with a spare pair of gloves; these were leather with silver metal studs.

After that I rode to the army store on York Street to look at hunting knives, camping equipment, tents, that sort of thing, none of which I had a budget for. Instead I bought a three-litre water pouch and a second-hand roll mat from a charity shop for a couple of dollars.

For true bargains I hit the cheap Chinese store near Central Station, buying scissors, a money belt, bungee ropes, not to mention a sewing kit which I thought I might need. I stopped at the chiropractor's in Bondi to treat my sore back that had bothered me for years, then on to the café, where I'd already resigned, to say goodbye. I don't think they believed me; no one believed me. Not even me!

The next morning I rode to Glebe market to pick up some last-minute things. As I was putting on my helmet I saw Kevin Rudd, the then Prime Minister of Australia, get out of his car and go inside a bookshop across the road. I considered this to be an omen, and so followed him into the bookshop, asking his bodyguard at the door if Mr Rudd would mind signing my helmet as I was riding to England the next day on a postie bike and I needed all the luck I could get.

The Prime Minister of Australia was mildly baffled by my disturbance as he looked at books at the rear of the store, but obliged nonetheless, writing upside down on the back of my plain white open faced helmet; 'All the best, K. Rudd, P. Minister.' I walked away chuffed, until I realised I should just have asked him for a visa.

I double-checked what documents I might need before cancelling Doris's appointment with the mechanic as there was no time to have her looked at before setting off. The shipping company told me there was a cargo boat leaving Darwin for East Timor one day before my visa expired. To compensate, I reduced my riding time to sixteen days and made a mental note to ride like the wind, as ships to East Timor only sailed every ten days and if I missed that one then I'd be in deep trouble with Immigration.

I bought a five-litre jerry can from the BP garage on Darling Street, tightened Doris's chain with my new tools, had a few farewell drinks in the back garden with a group of good friends from my time in Sydney, and that was it, planning done. Leave the next morning.

The alarm clock blew early, around 6am. It was a strange moment waking up that day. The smell of adventure in the air, a pile of bags to be packed in the corner of the room, and Mandy lying beside me, who I would soon be leaving behind. The pair of us had remained completely numb throughout all this, neither of us willing to acknowledge that I would be gone that day.

'It'll be alright,' we'd continued to tell ourselves, which I imagine is quite a normal thing to do in circumstances such as these; you know, about to ride a 105cc motorbike across the world. We ate a breakfast of toast and Vegemite; the last time in a long time that we would both be sat around the same kitchen for a while. We didn't have a plan for the future; we were just going to wait and see.

From there it was a case of pack this, fold that, room for this, no room for that. The aluminium box was mounted wrong so we had to go back to Rohan's workshop to borrow tools to drill four new holes and tape up those that were wrong. By the time we made it back to Mandy's house (the place I'd been living) it was 11am and I was already three hours late getting on the road.

In the back garden I bungee-roped the milk crate on top of the box to carry oil and spare petrol cans that were now brimful. Everything else went in the lockable aluminium box, or, like my tool kit, roll mat and flip flops, strapped haphazardly to the outside. I gave Doris one big rock to make sure nothing fell off. It did.

A bright bolt of sobriety struck me as I manoeuvred her from the back garden to the launch pad out front. The weight was stacked far too high and even in a straight line I struggled to keep her upright. This didn't fill me with much confidence, but it was too late to worry about it now; I had to hit the road, time was ticking away and that boat out of Darwin now left in just over two weeks' time. The bike had to be on it, and so leaning this way and that, I guided us around the corner and parked outside the house, where by now everyone had gathered at the gate to witness the departure of the person they expected to be back in time for dinner that same night.

But who could blame them? On my feet I wore a brand-new pair of blue basketball boots, on my hands the beige welding gloves donated by Matty, across my chest a white T-shirt reading 'Canada' (because that's where Mandy's originally from), on my legs a pair of cargo trousers to go with the skateboard that had recently been crushed beneath the wheels of a bus on Oxford Street, while on my head sat a bulbous white helmet, which despite being signed by Kevin Rudd still made me look like Marvin from *The Hitchhiker's Guide to the Galaxy*.

Then there was Doris, a clapped-out Honda CT110 with a spoke missing in the back wheel, an oil leak with no traceable source and a clatter from her engine that sounded like stones going round in a dryer.

'Clatter, clatter, clatter,' she went as the shocked neighbours looked on, wondering where the English guy next door was off to. But for once even her headlight was working and her back tyre hadn't gone flat. The pair of us looked like real bags of shit that day. But we'd done our best in the two days we'd been given and now we were ready to see if determination alone really was enough compensation for everything else we lacked.

Mandy joined me at the kerb, the hardest day. This was it, after all that'd been. Where would I be if it wasn't for her; not sitting here in Sydney, that's for sure. The sky above wouldn't be an Aussie blue but an English grey. I wouldn't know Doris and I wouldn't now have a story to tell. As Doris purred beneath my knees the tears rolled down our cheeks. See you in a thousand weeks.

With that *The Long Ride Home* began...

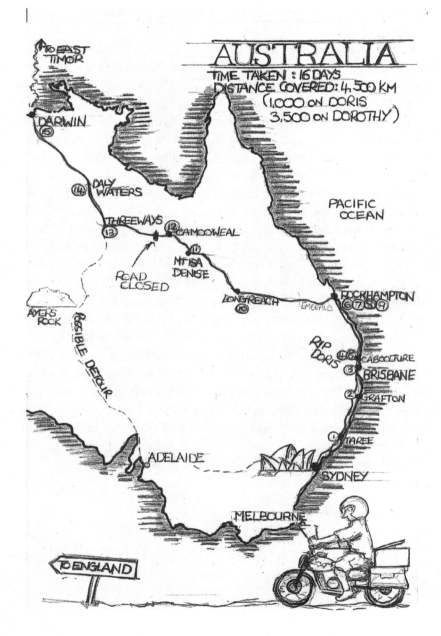

Chapter Two
East Coast of Australia

This then was it, no turning back, ride as fast as I dare, the wind in my hair and the sun beating down. It really was the most baffling of all days. I couldn't tell you what I was thinking, a bit of everything I suppose. Happiness, sadness, fear, excitement, doubt, freedom. Doris beneath me, roaring her poor little head off as she struggled to tug all that weight along. But cope she did, for as the arch of the Harbour Bridge rose above our heads we were already up to seventy kilometres per hour and even passing some traffic along the way.

'Where's he off to?' I imagined the drivers of the cars thinking as I shot by with my head on the handlebars to keep the slipstream low. And then they would have read it, scribbled in felt-tip pen along the side of the aluminium box: 'From Sydney … to London.' Oh how they must have laughed, and I could have laughed with them, because it really was an absurd situation. Did I really think I could make it across the world on Doris? Well, I was going to give it a damn good go.

In many ways, this first stage of the journey across Australia was going to be the hardest test of them all. So much ground to cover, so little room for things to go wrong. I'd based all my calculations on a ride I'd recently made to Canberra for the Summernats car festival. I'd done that distance of 250 kilometres in six hours and rode back the same day. So already I knew that twelve hours in the saddle would take me approximately 500 kilometres, figuring this would give me plenty of time to reach Darwin and take care of any mishaps that might happen along the way.

One thing's for certain, that moment you realise you've drifted away from the safe shore is terrifying and truly liberating in its brutal extreme. It suddenly hits you: you're on a motorbike with every single thing you own in boxes on the back, and you don't know where you're going to sleep that night or where you're going to eat or where you're going to get fuel. You don't know who you're going to call if you break down; every kilometre you cover takes you one step deeper into the unknown. You can read about it and you can hear the stories of what it's like to do such a thing, but suddenly being thrust into that position with barely any time to let it all sink in was like a cold bucket of water to the face. I mean, what does it involve, what does it take? I was so naive, so unprepared in so many ways, but this was my life now, a life on the open road.

And no more a place will you ever be in charge of your own destiny as out here. The sense that everything that follows is of your own doing, of your own organisation, decisions and shortcomings. Maybe that was the appeal; how everything depends on those two hands resting on the handlebars, the right one with the throttle to the stop, the left one largely redundant as on this bike there was no clutch. But your life, your future, your sanity, it all hangs in the balance now, no certainty to any of it. That's what I mean by terrifying, because of course you doubt whether you're really capable. Of course you worry that you don't have it in you or that something is going to go terribly wrong.

What had worried me most in those two days of packing was that I might have second thoughts after I'd hit the road — what if I wanted to turn back? What if I realised just what a big mistake I was making? A bit like setting up your own business or walking down the aisle, I suspect.

It was then some relief to find that as the road opened up and the towers of Sydney slid further and further behind I felt nothing but the urge to just keep riding, to see how far we could get, to give it everything I'd got. I knew turning around wouldn't solve a single thing, so I put my head down and when a tear reached my lips I would lick it, because it really was a hot day and I needed the fluid.

As for what Mandy was going through right now I'll never truly know.

I imagine as I turned the corner and disappeared out of sight she would have walked back up those steps and into the house, perhaps making a tea and sitting down at the same kitchen table where only a few days prior she gave me the confidence and conviction not to fly home but to ride home instead. After all that had been, she was still thinking what was best for me. I would miss her, and I hoped that she would miss me.

***

My route from here to Darwin was going to be a simple one. Up the coast to Rockhampton, at which point I would turn left along the Capricorn Highway and through the Outback, join the Barkly Highway and then at Threeways junction turn right for our final run along the Stuart Highway into Darwin. Two turns in over 4,500 kilometres.

I considered going up through the red centre, given that the distance was slightly shorter, but was keen to ride the coast, to see the sea and smell the salt air, to pass through the beautiful Byron Bay and follow the path so many backpackers in this part of the world tend to tread, something I'd never found time to do in all the time I'd spent in Australia.

To now be entering such a world on a motorbike was an incredible feeling; the sun on my face and the wind buffeting us about. There is no interface, just man and machine, no glass, no sound but the engine you sit astride and the rumble of the tiny tyres on the road.

I'd ridden and driven the road just north of Sydney a few times before, but today it felt different; it felt like it had no ending and that if I put enough trust in it, it would take me all the way to the other side of the world, of course having to cross a couple of seas along the way.

I still wasn't quite sure how I got to England from here. I wasn't thinking that far ahead. It would be a case of one day, week and country at a time. For now though, as the sun began to set, it dawned on me that I never did go back for a tent.

I had a roll mat and a sleeping bag but nothing to put them under. That left me to consider the other options, and passing signs for the town of Taree, 300 kilometres to the north of Sydney, I thought there must be a caravan site or motel here. And sure enough, the Twilight Caravan Park had a vacancy sign twinkling in the dimming light. I swung off the road and down the gravel drive, bringing Doris to a stand-still and entering reception, where I was immediately told about the road.

'It's closed,' said Ray, the owner, as I paid for a caravan he was letting me have cheap. He said far up north, deep inside the Northern Territory, the rain was so bad that the road had been completely washed away. The road was now impassable, and the chances of it opening by the time I got there were slim. I couldn't believe it at first — one road between Sydney and Darwin? But it was true.

As we studied the map on his wall, I asked about alternative routes, Ray pointing towards Adelaide and suggesting I turn back and go that way, up through the red centre. It was a detour that would add at least 1,000 kilometres to the distance and probably give me no chance of making that first boat.

It wasn't a tough decision because I knew if I turned around and went back via Sydney I would stop off there and probably never get going again, hanging out with Mandy the remaining few days before catching the plane home to England instead.

I didn't want to do that. I wanted to do this. So I knew in my mind that whether that road opened or not I was just going to keep riding and let fate decide whether I was going to make that boat or not. If the road opened in time, then we would make it; if it didn't, then we wouldn't. That night I ate KFC while studying the map with Ray on the bench outside the caravan. Then I went to sleep. My first night on the road.

The next morning brought rain as well as my first puncture. I was in Coffs Harbour, buying cream for my saddle-sore backside when it happened. 'No problem,' I said to myself, spreading my new tools across the floor of a supermarket carpark. I thought I had everything I needed; spanners, screwdrivers, pliers… a big hammer. The one thing I didn't have were tyre levers. I'd thought about buying a pair back in Sydney, but decided I could do the job with the screwdrivers instead, which turned out to be like trying to open a tin of beans with a spoon.

After an hour wrestling with the tyre beneath the blazing sun I still hadn't managed to get the tyre off and was close to giving in and turning back, something Mandy on the telephone suggested might be a wise thing to do. Shortly after, a man named Dave showed up.

Dave was a wily old bloke, thin as a rake, wearing a dirty white T-shirt and a dark blue baseball cap pulled low over his weathered face; the appearance of a salty old sea dog. Dave had been driving by in his beaten-up Holden jalopy and seeing me struggle pulled over and asked what the matter was. When I told him about the tyre levers he said he'd be back in ten minutes and went home to fetch a set of this own.

It turned out Dave had backpacked home from London to Sydney when his dreams of being a rock 'n roll legend had bitten the dust back in the sixties. He thought I was stupid even thinking of going through Iran and Pakistan, even though he'd come through Afghanistan and loved the place and the people. I listened intently but didn't take too much notice; to me those countries were still so far away that I couldn't even comprehend the thought of me and Doris ever making it that far. Getting out of Australia was going to be a hard enough task in itself.

In the end it took two hours, three failed attempts and a trip to the local bike shop for more patches before the repaired wheel was back on and we sat down on the grass with the cold beers I'd bought in celebration.

We talked all sorts of rubbish, like two old blokes passing time in a bar. After the storm of the last few days it was nice to sit for a minute, hearing Dave explain how I should wrap my legs in cardboard in case a snake jumped up and bit me. I really liked the bloke. He'd had dreams and ambitions and I admired how he'd made the transition to regular family life without any hint of bitterness, no regrets.

I covered just 300 kilometres that second day on the road, arriving in the rural town of Grafton where I spent another night in a caravan, this one costing forty dollars for the night. I know that doesn't sound a lot, but to try and stretch my money out as far as it would go I had worked out a budget of just twenty Australian dollars a day, or around ten English pounds. That would have to cover food, fuel and accommodation, and while that would undoubtedly not be enough for the journey across Australia, I hoped by the time I made it to Asia that would be plenty.

Money was the least of my concerns right now however, as by this stage, I'd still not told my mum!

As far as my parents were concerned I was still in Sydney trying to sort out my visa. I knew if I'd have told them in advance they would have said, 'Grow up, settle down, get a job.' It was the law of their generation, and they would have made me feel so guilty that I might very well have listened. Not because I do what my parents tell me, but because I find it very easy to let other people's fears talk me out of doing things I want to do. And I often think that's all advice is: other people telling you why they wouldn't do it, rather than understanding why you should.

That night I sent them an email from my laptop using the free Wi-Fi in the local McDonald's. I explained how my idea to ride across the world on a motorbike was finally happening. I explained what it meant to me, and how taking a plane wasn't an option. I told them I accepted every risk and how they shouldn't worry about me, this was something I wanted and needed to do and nothing, not even their words of sanity, were going to stop me. I finished with the line, 'I love you,' something we don't often say in our family because we're too shy to say it. And so the situation was rather liberating. All the protocol and tradition of our family had gone out the window. I could say what I thought because, why not, I'm on a motorbike and might get wiped out by a lorry in the morning. So say it now, say it while it matters. Say it while you still can.

After that I sent a group email to friends and acquaintances back home. For me, this marked the point of no return, as announcing to the world that you're going to try and ride a 105cc motorbike from Sydney to London leaves a huge amount of room for embarrassment should you ever fail, or quit. I imagine in such circumstances there will always be those people who will say, 'I told you so,' and have a good laugh at your expense.

Perhaps I shouldn't have sent this email, not telling anyone until we were much further into the trip. But I figured I could use the fear of losing face to fan the flames if the fires ever burned dim. I know we shouldn't worry about what other people think, but I did, I do.

The next morning the phone rang; it was Mum, hysterical. 'What the hell are you doing?' She screamed before I'd even had chance to say hello. I was outside a bike shop buying tyre levers at the time. Now I had to take my ear away from the phone, mum not exploding in an angry, violent way, just in a, 'I'm your mother and I spent too long in labour to let this happen,' kinda way.

Dad thought it was brilliant — at least that's what I gathered when I spoke to him briefly. But what else could he say? He was the one who got me into motorbikes in the first place, taking me and my brother Jason down to an old quarry for us to tear around on a little 50cc moped.

I was probably five at the time and not very good. I always remember approaching a corner and not bothering to turn or to stop; I just kept on going, shooting straight on with Dad chasing after me shouting, 'Brake Nathan brake!' When he finally caught up with me he said how close I'd been to hitting the barbed-wire fence. He was right, but in my mind I wasn't aiming for the fence, I was aiming for the lane beyond. I guess now, all these years later, I was about to find out to where it might lead...

With Mum back on the phone, I managed to reduce her fury to a simmer, explaining how there would be no turning back and how she shouldn't worry, that I would be alright. 'Fine,' she said. 'Well just be careful and if you need anything just ring.' With that we said goodbye. It was incredible really. My parents get an email with news of their son riding across the world on a 105cc wotsit, they ring in hysterics and within five minutes are offering to do anything they can to help. The best parents in the world.

Not that they could do much to help with our third problem in as many days. It was Doris, making a louder knocking noise than ever.

I knew it hadn't been wise setting off from Sydney without first taking her to a mechanic, but in the same way as not telling my parents until after the event, I knew if I'd have had her looked at I would have been faced to accept the reality; that she was far from being up to the job. And I didn't need to hear that. It would only have cast doubt on my mind. That's why I'd shut my ears to the noise, said, 'Sod it,' and off we'd set.

Now though I couldn't ignore her rumblings any longer, I had to have her looked at and properly prepared for the journey ahead. Fortunately,

I knew just the place. In the Queensland town of Caboolture, an hour to the north of Brisbane, there was a shop specialising in the type of bike that I was riding; the Honda CT110.

I'd found them on the internet during those few days of planning, deciding it a good idea to call in on the way past. It was one of the reasons I'd chosen this route over coming up the red centre. My plan then was to have Doris looked at, fixed up, and be back on the road by midday at the latest...

The shop was owned by Joe, a tall genial man, early fifties I'd say, wearing a collared short sleeve navy shirt, matching shorts and a pair of black boots and socks. He ran the place with his good friend, Katrina, the pair of them surprised to see me sat on their doorstep when they came to open up that day, their shop on an industrial estate on the outskirts of town.

Having explained the problem, Joe came outside to take a look at Doris, asking me to fire her into life, and there she sat, clattering louder than I ever did hear her. 'Doesn't sound good,' Joe said, 'Could be your bottom-end on its way out.'

I asked Joe if she might make it to Darwin. He scratched his chin and said she might. He told me a story about a guy who tried riding up to Cape York on a postie bike when the same problem occurred. I asked what happened and he said it blew up before it got there. That sort of answered my next question but I asked it anyway; 'What about England, Joe, will she make it to England?'

Joe stopped scratching his chin and looked at me funny. 'Mate, you've got no chance!'

Joe was a patient man and if he thought I was a plank he didn't show it. Instead he presented me with three options. The first was to rebuild the existing engine, probably taking five days and costing $400.

'I don't have that much time,' I told him. 'Alright, what about if I fit a reconditioned engine?'

That was going to take a couple of days and cost $700. That sounded better and it looked likely that I was going to do that. Then the bastard laid a turd on my toe by making a third and final suggestion that burrowed deep beneath my skin and gave me no choice but to consider it. And that was to trade Doris in for one of the more reliable bikes he had in his showroom. At first I laughed and said, 'I don't think so.' But while he went off to serve another customer I had a look anyway.

There were rows of machines just like Doris, all decommissioned postie bikes waiting for new owners to ride them around the city and sometimes farms. They're tough, tiny little things, modified for Australia Post to carry the extra weight of letters and parcels. It was on one of these that my friend Thomas Wielecki, had ridden all the way around Australia on a shoestring, and in telling me the story had, through many twists and turns, led to this, me being here, on the same type of bike, about to try and ride it across the world.

I stopped at one bike and admired it. As well as the standard five-litre fuel tank beneath the seat, this one also had an extra eight-litre tank from a motocross bike mounted in the step-through, a set of huge orange panniers sacks like those the postman uses, a tent rack above the headlight, a handlebar brace, heavy duty tyres, heavy duty chain, and a sheep skin seat cover that was just like sitting on a cushion. She looked so much tougher than all the others, like a proper motorbike. Not only that, she was in perfect condition, almost like new, and that was with 40,000 kilometres on the clock.

'Why don't you take her for a spin?' Joe asked.

This was dangerous. I'd dropped by to get my bike fixed, not to buy another one. Yet from the very first moment I sat on that bike I knew I had to have it. The engine was so smooth and with all the additional equipment it felt like a much sturdier machine. It was almost as though someone knew I was coming, on Doris, and had purpose-built the perfect postie bike for riding across the world. And deep down, as much as I wanted to deny it, I knew there was no chance of her making it all the way to England. I had to be serious about that, and honest enough with myself to accept it, because to do otherwise would be reckless.

Back at the shop I did false sums to convince myself I could afford it. Joe said he'd give me $700 trade-in on Doris, leaving me another $1,700 to find for the new bike. By this time it was late afternoon, so I said I'd sleep on it and get back to him in the morning. I borrowed a tent that Joe had kicking around his shop and attempted to put it up on a campsite not far from his shop. But whether one of the poles was missing or I just didn't have the knack, I could get the blasted thing to go up so took a ride to Kmart in town, buying a simple two-man tent for forty dollars.

That evening I sat with my laptop in the shaded area of the campsite kitchen, recording a video diary about the events that had unfolded so far. I faced a real dilemma.

I still didn't know if the road across the Outback was going to open in time or not. It was a fifty-fifty chance judging by the weather forecast and I knew that if it didn't open in the next week or so, then buying a new bike would be a huge waste of money because I'd have to abandon it to get back to Sydney and catch the flight home the day my visa expired. However, if the road did open and we made it to Darwin in time, how long realistically could Doris continue without needing serious repair or replacement? Not very. And so in many ways it would be pointless to ride her any further whether the road opened or not.

The next morning I handed Joe my credit card.

'Are you sure mate?'

'Yep, let's do it.'

I spent the afternoon in the Transport Offices trying to register the new bike. Not being an Australian resident I had to put my address down as Joe's bike shop. For a while it looked like it might not be possible. I had to cancel the existing registration, get a refund on that, then register the new bike in my name with a new number plate so that I had enough time to get to England before it expired.

While I was doing all this, Joe and his team were getting the new bike ready back at the shop, giving her a last once over and removing the aluminium box from Doris and bolting her to the back of this one. By the time I made it back to the shop she was all set and rearing to go, mid-morning of Day Eight, just over 1,000 kilometres covered, 3,500 to go in just the eight days remaining. It was going to be close.

'Thanks Joe, you guys have been great,' I said as I saddled up and fired the new bike into life.

'No worries mate, now you ride safe and let us know how you get on.'
'Will do,' I said, as I revved the engine for take-off.
'By the way,' Joe hollered after me.
'Her name's Dorothy.'

Chapter Three
Across the Outback

The story of Dorothy is an interesting one. In 2004 she began life as a mail delivery machine around the suburbs of Queensland. Three years later, after 30,000 kilometres, she was retired from service and, like all other postie bikes, sold off at auction. Hers took place in Brisbane, where she was bought by Joe to sell in his Caboolture shop.

Not long after, a man named Colin walked through the door. Colin was fifty-six years old, had just spent two years sailing around the Queensland coast in his yacht, and was now after a new challenge, one not on water but on land. His search for this new adventure somehow led him to the doorstep of One Ten Motorcycles — Joe's shop — where from a line-up of identical machines he picked his new travelling companion.

With big ambitions for his new machine, Colin immediately kitted her out with all the things he thought she'd need to tackle the vast Australian Outback; an extra fuel tank, soft seat cover, tent rack, heavy duty tyres and inner tubes. With that done, the pair of them started with a two-week trip west to Canarvon Gorge, where Colin's new motorbike was said to be faultless. Their second outing was even longer, a four-week ride up to Birdsville and then on to the Flinders Ranges, Broken Hill, along the Darling River and on to Bourke and Brisbane, a 4,500-kilometre trip on which the only thing that went wrong was two bolts falling out of the front mudguard mount.

Colin was said to have developed quite a bond with his bike — he would talk to her as they rode along — and it was with real sadness when the day came for him to part with her, Colin deciding he needed something bigger, more powerful, selling this little Honda back to Joe, who once more put her up for sale in his Caboolture shop. That was the end of 2008, not many months before I would burst into that same shop, desperate for a solution that would take me all the way to England.

The name Colin had given the bike I subsequently picked out from line-up that day: *Dorothy*, after his favourite character from a *Wizard of Oz*.

***

I felt a little guilty leaving Doris behind. She may not have made it all the way to England or even as far as Darwin, yet this was a bike that at a moment's notice had transformed herself from city hack into world explorer. She's the bike I'd picked out of the crowd on eBay. She's the one I'd put a nervous bid in for and fretted over as the auction expired. She was the bike I'd caught the train to Newcastle to collect. She was the bike I'd thrashed around Sydney, gone to work on, showed off on, fell off of. She was my bike, and I was leaving her behind. To rot on a farm, because that's all Joe said she was good for.

Now I'd bought Colin's old motorbike; Dorothy, or Dot for short. It was stupid really; if that road didn't open I'd be stuck with a credit card bill for a machine I'd have to try and sell before I was kicked out of the country in two weeks' time. The sensible thing would have been to carry on with Doris and ditch her if the worst happened. I wouldn't have lost a dollar then. But I had to be realistic: I needed a bike that was going to give me the best chance of making it to England. And that was Dorothy.

I was no mechanic. I could change oil and now felt confident fixing a puncture, but I didn't have the first idea how to check the valves or the timing or the carburettor. I'd always been interested in motorbikes, but had never learned how to fix them or take them apart. All I hoped for the journey ahead was that I'd meet plenty of people more capable. And if I didn't, then I guess I would just have to learn, and learn very quickly, because at this stage I couldn't have imagined what it must feel like to be riding through a place such as Pakistan and have your bike breakdown and not have a clue how to fix it.

Some people may wonder why I didn't buy a better bike when I had the chance. Why did I get another postie bike and not a BMW or something a little bigger? The truth is I couldn't afford much else. But also, define better. Postie bikes are notoriously tough, they're reliable and while they lack performance, this trip was always going to be about endurance, not speed. And to be honest, a postie bike quite suited me, perhaps a better reflection of my character than anything else. A bit steady, ponderous perhaps, and that Dot was out of her depths would serve as a nice reminder that I was too, trying to ride a postie bike where no other had gone before it. Though that's not entirely true.

By this point I'd been in touch with a couple from Perth who were attempting to do the same thing (ride from Australia to the UK on a postie bike), but with two of them on the same bike, with all their luggage as well! I found that incredible; Colin's old motorbike was already loaded to the gills and unable to carry much more, and yet there was their little bike, exactly the same but carrying an extra person.

The last I'd heard, the couple was already in Thailand, taking it slow, with me hoping to catch up with them along the way, and no doubt race them across the finish line. Oddly, the name of this guy was also Nathan. He was the same age as me, on the same bike, and even interested in the same musical instrument, made only in Switzerland and called a hang. The similarities were uncanny.

For now though I had to get back to my trip, and the next thing I needed was a document called a Carnet de Passage. This is the paperwork needed to take a vehicle abroad and works just like a passport. Stamp in, stamp out; the idea being to stop you selling your vehicle for profit while in a foreign country. Back in Sydney I'd called the RAC, the people who administer it, only to be told the document usually takes four weeks to process. However, if I was to apply for it in person at their branch in Rockhampton, a town 1,600 kilometres north of Sydney on the east coast, they might just be able to do it in a week.

It was to Rockhampton I was heading now, pale skin burning in the blazing sun as I followed the liquorice strip of a coastal road as it dipped down to the water's edge, before twisting back inland through tree-lined canyons.

It was great fun, waving at the European backpackers touring the east coast in rented camper vans, pulling in at the free Driver Reviver tea stops, where you'd get chatting with families heading up to the Gold Coast in their Falcons and Commodores. That's the great thing about travelling in Australia. Every hundred kilometres or so there's a stall giving away tea and biscuits for a donation to the Rotary Club or whichever charity is running it. Some people would give me sandwiches or bits for my bike, like tie-wraps; it was just a good experience.

As for Dorothy, she was proving to be a god-send. With the extra petrol tank I could ride further — at least 330 kilometres between fill ups — and with the seat cover do so in more comfort and for longer periods of a time. The tent rack over the headlight helped balance the weight, while at the rear the huge orange pannier sacks swallowed all my gear and proved much more manageable than the milk crate, which I'd now disposed of.

To say she was the same make and model of motorcycle as Doris she rode completely different. She felt more firm and stable, more like a proper motorcycle, though strangely a little slower, happiest, I soon found, cruising at 65kmh, unlike Doris, who had seemed more eager to sit at ten kilometres more, thought that's probably why she'd gone wrong.

To give an idea of how fast we were travelling, I passed a hitch-hiker with his thumb out trying to hitch a lift. I passed him at such a speed that I had time to make eye contact and smile, pointing back to the huge box on the back of the bike and him grinning in acknowledgement that there was no room for him to sit. I carried on for the next two hours, riding as fast as Dorothy would go and not even stopping for fuel. Then up ahead I see that same hitch-hiker, still with his thumb out by the side of the road. I rode past grinning, as he grinned back. The tortoise had just overtaken the hare.

I wouldn't laugh for long however, not when I arrived in Rockhampton thinking it was Thursday night, when it fact it was Friday, and that meant the offices of the RAC wouldn't be open for another two days, not until Monday morning.

I was angry with myself for making a mistake that would cost me three valuable days, but soon simmered, seeing it as a bit of relief that I could take a moment for it all to sink in, the past week such a whirlwind as it was.

I found a campsite down by the river of this cowboy town, the place famous for its cattle, its streets built in a grid with bars down back alleys and signs warning of alligators around the edge of the campsite, though I never saw sign of any.

I began the weekend by laying all my belongings on the ground and working out what I needed and what I didn't need. I had three jumpers, nine pairs of underpants, eight T-shirts, three pairs of shorts, two pairs of trousers, two pairs of Converse, flip flops, a big bag of tools, spares that Joe had given me, then a whole mound of electrical equipment: ten inch laptop, a Canon digital SLR camera, helmet camera, mobile phone, iPod, charger, batteries, cables and wires... travel adapters, documents, sleeping bag, tent, roll matt.

I'd pretty much packed everything I owned the day I left Sydney and clearly I wouldn't need all this. I threw half of it away and thought of things I didn't have and hoped I could manage without: first-aid kit, waterproof trousers, a towel, soap, stove, and torch. The rest I threw back in the sacks and aluminium box and closed the lid. There was no order to any of it.

One of the other jobs I had to do over the weekend was arrange some travel insurance. My existing policy didn't cover me for 'motorcycle touring' and I was nervous of riding uninsured given how in France a decade earlier I'd skied into a tree and broken my femur and pelvis, needing a helicopter to airlift me off the mountain. The bill for that was astronomical with it fortunate that I had good insurance to pay for it all.

Given the scale of this trip I didn't like the idea of being without it, and with my dad on the case he soon found a company that would cover motorcycle touring and also didn't mind that I was already outside my home country when taking the policy out. At $500 it wasn't cheap, but then neither was the Carnet de Passage when I went to the offices of the RAC to collect that on Monday morning.

Nine-hundred-and-fifty Australian dollars, about five-hundred and fifty English pounds, just for the document needed to take a $2,400 motorbike abroad. Fortunately I'd anticipated such a fee, and in a way considered myself lucky, because with the cost based on the value of your machine, had I been riding a big BMW or anything else equally expensive then the bill for the Carnet could have run into thousands. It did trouble me however to think that if the road didn't open in time I'd just wasted $500 on the insurance, close to a thousand on the Carnet, not to mention the $1,700 I'd paid for Dorothy.

To add to that worry, the Carnet was going to take at least a week to process and no way could I wait for it here. I would have to have it posted ahead, to Darwin, where I hoped and needed to be in just over a week's time. The only problem was I didn't know anyone in Darwin; I'd never been. That's when I remembered the telephone number written on the back of my Australian map. It was put there by a woman I'd met at one of those tea stop a few days prior. I'd got talking to her and her partner on one of the picnic benches, where they'd explained how they had a son up in Darwin and how if I needed anything then I was to give him a call.

It was his number written on the back of the map and so I dialled it now, explaining my predicament and asking him if it'd be okay. 'Of course it was going to be okay,' he said, adding that his mum had already warned him about the English guy who might be calling in need of assistance. He gave me his address and I passed it on to the counter staff at the RAC who'd done absolutely everything they could, above and beyond, to make sure I got that Carnet in time. All I had to hope was that by the time I made it to Darwin, it too would be there waiting for me.

***

With that sorted, the only thing left to do was hit the road. This was now 4am pre-sunrise, Tuesday 20th January 2009, twelve days after my appointment with Immigration, nine days after leaving Sydney aboard Doris, my visa expiring on the 28th, the boat leaving on the 27th. I'd ridden 1,600 kilometres, had 3,000 to go, still with no certainty if the road 1,000 kilometres west of here would be open or not. Otherwise I had everything I needed, a new bike, a Carnet, my travel insurance. The wet season was upon us. When it wasn't raining it was stinking hot. The flies were getting thicker, the Outback stood before me and all I could do now was ride with everything crossed, for the future, both short term and long. Just ride…

Cutting through the silent, sunless morning, the world was dark, empty and desolate. The temperature was perfect and with only us on the road the sense of solitude hit hard for the first time. I suppose others would call it loneliness, but wherever we fell on that continuum I adored it. Just to be alone with your thoughts as the dark strip of highway stretched out ahead, the only noise of Dot's little engine thrumming softly away, and my iPod providing the soundtrack.

I was listening to David Gray, *New Day at Midnight,* track twelve. It seemed a fitting soundtrack to the moment the sun came up from over the horizon. You knew it was coming when the mirrors began to glow. There wasn't any warmth yet, just dim light building and stretching along the horizon until it exploded over the top, lighting up my helmet like a bulb.

For the rest of the morning I'd watch it rise from behind until it was above my head, making my face red and my body sweat. And then fourteen hours later it would set, gone for another day. What an incredible realisation of scale, that me and Dorothy were so insignificant in all of this, just a tiny ball of moving metal parts and pieces of pale sun-burnt flesh. If we crashed tomorrow, that huge ball of fire would still rise and fall just as it always had. And still the music would play.

At the town of Emerald, 270 kilometres in from the coast, I encountered a group of Aboriginal kids as I sat eating my lunch outside of a bakery. They were barefoot and inquisitive, wanting to know about the bike and where I was going. I explained to them as briefly as I could before riding off. I was scared of them, but why? All they wanted to do was talk; they were friendly, full of curiosity. Why had I been so rude? Was it because of the things I'd heard, like the trucker who told me that, 'All they do is fuck and breed?' Or was it those I'd seen in Sydney, drunk, shouting, that had made me nervous?

For the rest of way to the town of Mount Isa (the last main town before the road closure) I tried to figure it all out. I knew it wasn't rational, but like the poisonous spiders and snakes, people had warned me about Aboriginals. 'Don't go near them, they might bite.' But these hadn't, and neither had the others I met later near Tennant Creek.

So why had I listened? Why hadn't I judged the kids for who they were? Instead I'd been taken over by the same irrational feelings as the trucker. I didn't understand these people; they looked different, acted different, and instead of being curious I'd been afraid. Now I was a little ashamed.

Rain fell. Deep dark clouds would wait for us on the horizon, hoping the road would take a detour around them but it never did, always leading me into the very eye of the storm, at such point I'd put my shorts and flip flops on; the rain as warm as it was. At one point, so much rain had fallen that the highway between Winton and Cloncurry was almost completely flooded. For a while the road was closed and around all the travellers stood, swatting flies from our faces in the searing heat, wondering which one of us was brave enough to try crossing the flooded road first.

A 4x4 took the gamble, making it through the deep brown water and giving hope to those that followed. I pulled up at the edge of the tide behind a couple of young teachers, Brody and Sarah, on their way home to Mount Isa. They offered to put Dot in the back of their ute and carry her across. It was kind of them but it would have felt like cheating.

I watched instead as they crossed gingerly in their flat bed ute before rolling up my trouser leg and ensuring everything was sealed tight. The water looked like it would reach the top of my knees, and it did so, Brody reminding me to keep it moving and not to let the bike bog down.

It was terrific fun and from one flooded stretch of road we arrived at another and another. There must have been a dozen in total, Dorothy crossing all of them with good grace and dignity; not even a splutter.

On the other side of the flood waters I once again bumped into the teachers at a service station where both of us had stopped for fuel. Brody asked if I'd like to crash at their place in Mount Isa that night and given the sight of the black rain clouds on the horizon. I didn't hesitate, arriving two hours later, dripping wet on their doorstep having been caught in the biggest monsoon of the trip so far.

Their house was wooden and built up on stilts beside the overflowing river. I stored the bike in the garage below the house and went upstairs to where their house-mate Jason was cooking spaghetti bolognese. After a week and a half eating finger food and banana sandwiches it was real nice to eat with a knife and fork again, then have a shower, drink a beer, watch some TV, until I drifted off on the sofa and woke the next morning in a daze.

Having thanked the teachers I rode into Mount Isa town centre in search of the tourist information centre in order to get an update on the road, the closure now only a hundred kilometres up ahead.

When I finally found the right building I approached the lady on the information desk nervously. This was the moment of truth. Make or break. 'Is the road to Darwin open?' I asked with trepidation, part of me not wishing to know the answer.

'Yes my dear, it opens to light traffic in the morning.'

I sat down in the café and ordered a pot of tea. Mixed emotions I suppose. In a way I now wished the road had stayed closed, then I would have had my excuse to go back and spend the last few days in Sydney with Mandy. Instead it opened, and on I had to go.

A lady by the name of Denise brought the tea over. She was pleasant and cheerful, perhaps in her fifties and like an old aunt most of us once knew. The pair of us got chatting, about the road and where I was going. I explained the nature of the trip and how I came to be sitting at one of her tables that day.

After a while she disappeared and came back with a $50 note. She handed it to me. 'By the sounds of it, you're going to need this more than I do.' I didn't know what else to say, but 'Thank you,' and deeply meant it.

Before leaving, Denise returned with some advice. She said, with complete sincerity; 'If you ever find yourself in danger and in need of assistance, just ask the angels and fairies, and they shall come.'

In any other circumstances I might have considered her completely crackers, but right here, in Mount Isa visitors centre, somewhere in the middle of Australia, a 105cc motorbike parked outside that I planned on riding to England, I wished to believe in angels and fairies as well. In fact, I probably already did. Dave was one. So too Ray. Joe another. How many more might I meet between here and England? Quite a few I hoped.

The road opened the next morning and off I went, 1,500 kilometres (900 miles) to cover in just three days. The hours passed and the sun soared. We passed the point at which the road had been closed, the hole in it — now patched up — was massive, like a bomb crater. We rode on. Hour after hour. Face burning red, one of Joe's old T-shirts tied across it, my nose in the armpit, flies in my eyes, hardly any traffic here. You wave when you see someone else on the road. Signposts point to communities down dusty tracks. Who the hell lives out here? How did the early settlers ever cross this place? Nothing, and I mean nothing, around. Only the birds in the sky, the bush and the desert and the sense it will never ever, not for a minute, come to an end.

Then you would arrive at a homestead; an oasis in the desert. These were places, sometimes as much as 250 kilometres apart, where you could buy fuel, food and accommodation. Often there was nothing in-between but emptiness. This was certainly the case at the Barkly Homestead, where I ate a burger in the café, served by a stunning English girl who told me how she lived out here having passed through as a backpacker and fallen in love with the homestead owner, the pair of them now married.

Other travellers lived out here as well, mainly English and Irish girls, who I would ask why and they would often explain how the homestead served as a retreat from the wider world, their lives much more manageable here than out there, and I could well understand it. I could see the appeal. They were escaping. And in a way, so was I.

Even for me this place was perfect. So much space to breath and to think, to reflect and try and make sense of things. No distraction, no noise, no commotion, just an endless swathe of desert and hours of time in which to cross it.

I thought much about what had led me to be here and the decision to do it. I thought much about Mandy and what she would be doing now, and how she would be feeling, now the dust had settled and all that remained were the memories and the questions over how things had worked out, or hadn't worked out.

It had been a tough time in Sydney. We'd tired each other out, drained one another completely. Neither of us could figure it out, why things were as complicated and difficult as they were. It was so frustrating, soul destroying in every way, trying to fathom what was going wrong, why our lives together were so complicated and harsh. It shouldn't have been. It should have been simple given the feelings we had for one another.

I guess then that this was me running away from it all, taking the opportunity when I had it. A break for freedom perhaps, or simply just throwing in the towel, figuring the best thing for me to do right now was disappear, channelling all the frustration and anger at the road. But as well as this, I also rode with hope, hope that somehow, in the future, things between us would all work out, with it my belief that an adventure such as this needs this push, as well as this pull, if you are to avoid getting stuck in the middle.

By this stage I was riding 14 hours a day, from sunrise to sunset. The most distance I covered in a day was 650 kilometres. I ate whatever and wherever I could. Every fuel stop was a race to get back on the road. As for the places I slept I was still at this point too nervous to do anything but pitch the tent on a designated site, paying handsomely for relative safety.

I realise I could have found somewhere out in the wilderness for free, but I liked having people around and being in sight of civilisation. Maybe things would change once I got my confidence up, but for now I was still quite a nervous, apprehensive traveller. Though learning fast.

At the Threeways Homestead we turned right, joining the Stuart Highway, noses pointed towards Darwin. Full tanks, empty stomach, red face, watery eyes, determined watery eyes. A couple in a car I'd been leapfrogging ever since Mount Isa pulled over some distance ahead and flagged me down, handing me a slice of fruit cake and a cup of coffee from their flask. They sat in their car, I was stood beside it, Dot to my left, and other than those three things there was nothing else for miles around, only a dead dingo, rotting in the road.

The couple in the car told me the road up ahead might also be closed because of the rain. I listened, but didn't much care. By now I was a lightning bolt of determination, prepared to swim with Dot on my back or flap my wings hard enough to fly us both over any obstacle.

I stopped to help a young soldier whose truck had broken down. I met another women at a food stop, from Canada, who had come to Australia for the Olympics and now almost a decade later was still here, no intention to go back at all.

On the TV screen in a cafe I watched the inauguration of Barrack Obama, thinking nothing much had changed, only the shade, while later that penultimate day the rain was so fierce it drove me from the tent and into another caravan, this one at Daly Waters, where in the morning before heading off I caught the end of some religious programme that told the tale of a man who questioned where God had been during the tough times in his life, as when he turned around he saw only one set off footprints in the sand. I thought what nonsense, we undertake these journeys alone, until I went outside only to see Dorothy's tyre marks in the dirt.

Then it came, Day Eighteen. This was the big one, the final 589 kilometres all in one go: more sun, more rain, more flies, more pies. The road was arrow straight, dead north, along the Stuart Highway, passing tatty towns and villages, Aboriginal men sat by the roadside drinking grog from paper wrapped bottles, petrol pumps in the middle of nowhere, signs to national parks, no time to see those, holiday homes, the town of Katherine, buying bananas and bread to make a sandwich, sand in my eyes, a dry throat, sore limbs, sun soaring overhead, the kilometres fading away, a constant 65km/h, the last stretch, the final push, sign posts beginning to count us down, from 200 kilometres to a hundred, to ninety, to fifty, to twenty, to ten, to one. And then there it was.

Darwin.

Sunday 25th January, 2009, around the same time most people would be settling down for their evening dinner, me and Colin's old motorbike sauntered through the city gates, two weary travellers on the point of collapse, her with a bald tyre and in desperate need of fluid, me in a frazzled-eyed state with buttocks I could barely sit on. There was no champagne or party girls, just quiet, sombre relief. Eighteen days after my appointment with Immigration, two days before my visa ran out, just over 4,500 kilometres covered, we'd made it, alive, on a different bike, having navigated flooded plains and sticky situations by the faintest of margins. Though we weren't out of the woods just yet.

The next morning I went over to the stranger's house to collect the Carnet I hoped would have arrived by now. The stranger's name was Carl, a family man living in a rough suburb, with a guard dog that bit my ankle and made me bleed. He told me the documents still hadn't turned up, something that made me panic because without a Carnet I wouldn't be able to put Dot on the boat, and if I couldn't put Dot on the boat, then I couldn't leave the country before my visa expired the following day.

I asked Carl to call me if anything arrived and rode back into town to find a doctor to give me the necessary injections for travelling through Asia — rabies, malaria, hepatitis and typhoid — plus a tetanus jab for the dog bite.

The next day my phone rang, it was Carl; 'Sorry mate, it's still not turned up.' I was crestfallen. After all that effort getting to Darwin in time it looked like we were going to be thwarted by a document delayed in the post. I called the shipping agency to see if there was anything they could do. The ship had been delayed a day. We were still in with a chance. Breathe… stay calm. The Carnet just had to turn up in the next morning's post.

And it did.

With that I took Dorothy down to the docks, left her in a warehouse ready to be loaded on the cargo boat, then raced back into town to book my flight to Dili, the capital of East Timor, leaving the following morning. I would be one day over my visa, something Immigration thankfully didn't object to.

This last night in Australia I sat alone in the park, watching a group of homeless men collect food from a charity van. As I did so I felt a strange sensation of having more in common with them than anyone else in Darwin that night. This sensation scared me more than anything else, more even than my flight to East Timor the following day, because seeing these men made me realise that once you've cut the rope you can never be entirely sure just how far you're going to fall. And on that sombre but exciting note, I wished Australia, and all I cherished there, goodbye.

Now, for the rest of the world.

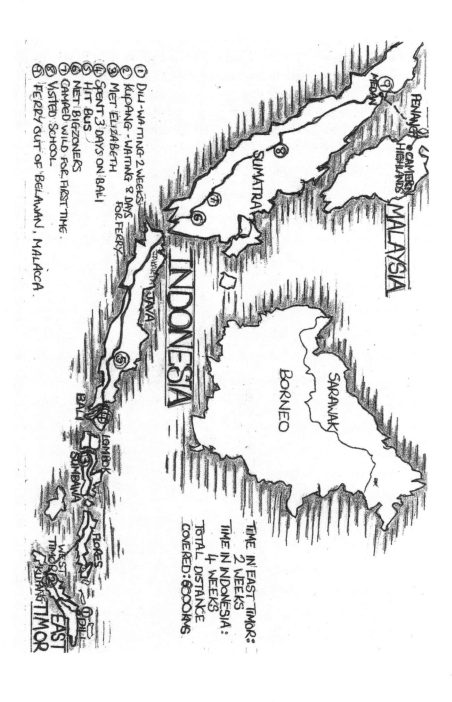

Chapter Four
East Timor

Landing in East Timor — two hours by plane to the north of Darwin — was terrifying. I'd never been anywhere in Asia before and due to the speed at which I'd had to ride across Australia I'd had no time to do any research or arrange anything in advance. I just landed, at 7.30 in the morning, with no map or guidebook, no accommodation booked or clue as to what I was going to do for the week I would have to wait for Dot's cargo boat to show up.

It left me with no other option but to bury my head in my hands and pull everything tight as a swarming crowd of men gathered around me in an attempt to take me somewhere in one of their taxis.

On the flight over I'd sat beside a man who had warned me about all this. He was born in East Timor and on his way back from an oil drilling course in Darwin. He told me about the country's violent past, how it was once a Portuguese colony and quite peaceful until 1975, when it was abandoned and then immediately invaded by the Indonesians who swarmed across the border from West Timor. In the 25 years that followed as many as 100,000 East Timorese died due to murder and starvation.

This period, the man told me, only ended in 1999 when the United Nations intervened, forcing the Indonesians back over the border into West Timor. A fragile peace had remained ever since, the UN still needed to enforce East Timor's new found sovereignty.

The British government advises people not to go there, but I had to, as it was on my way to England, and the only other option would have been to go directly from Darwin to Singapore, missing East Timor and Indonesia out completely. And that too would have felt like cheating.

Now at Dili airport I must have sat with my head in my hands for fifteen minutes or more, no clue what I was going to do or where I was going to go.

Suddenly I was alerted by a minibus that pulled up outside the terminal doors to my left. I realise how this might make me sound but when a group of white people clambered out I felt a huge wave of relief. They grabbed their bags and came into the airport building, seemingly to catch a flight out of here, leaving a middle aged woman — the driver of the minibus — to turn on her heels and walk back out of the building, towards her stationary white van.

I grabbed my things and rose to my feet, scattering the men around me and darting for the door and the path that the woman had taken. I caught up with her just as she was clambering through the driver's door of her vehicle. 'Excuse me,' I said, as I stood in the burning sunlight behind her. She turned around and caught me with her eye. She looked startled to see me there, in my scruffy combat shorts, white 'Canada' t-shirt and Converse boots. I explained my predicament and wondered if she knew of the guest-house I'd heard about, somewhere in the city. She smiled, 'Hop in my dear, I'm driving right past.'

The lady introduced herself as Jill, an Australian in East Timor helping kids with malnutrition. She told me how she had re-mortgaged her own home in Australia to fund the construction of a new facility to help the children. She reminded me of Sigourney Weaver from *Gorillas in the Mist*; tough and firm, and now tearing down the broken road that ran from the airport straight down to the centre of Dili, the capital of East Timor.

We passed all sorts of things I'd never seen before; this was Asia, with chickens in cages, men sat on curb stones smoking cigarettes, mopeds loaded five people high, things being carried on heads, the smells, the sights, the sounds, the commotion. In my head I just couldn't fathom any of it out. To me it was an alien land. And to think it was only two hours north of Darwin.

Jill asked what I was doing here and I told her. She looked aghast. She was a mother herself and couldn't imagine how my mum must have felt hearing the news that I was going to attempt such a thing. She told stories to suggest the island was a terrible place. The murder and the atrocities, people being mugged and beaten. To be passing through it on motorbike would be suicide.

Jill told me more about her work on the island and how badly the children in the remote villages were suffering. In fact, in the very seat I was sat in she had in the past few days carried the body of a young girl who had died of malnutrition. This wasn't a joke any more.

We finally pulled up outside a big metal gate with barbed-wire across the top and along the perimeter walls. Beneath it hung the sign for the Dili Smokehouse, a name I recognised from my brief search on the internet the night before I flew out of Darwin.

'This is it,' Jill said, as I shuffled in my seat, knowing any second now I would have to evacuate the safety of her minibus and face the chaos outside.

Jill gave me her business card and told me where her clinic was in case I wanted to stop by and lend a hand. I grabbed my bags, thanked her once more and slammed the door. She sped off, tearing down the hot dusty road, leaving me stood there, blowing weakly in the breeze.

'Welcome to East Timor,' I thought to myself.

I walked through the open gate and down the driveway, passing beneath a narrow archway that led into a leafy courtyard, painted many vibrant colours and well shaded from the sun. There was no one around, only plants, until a short woman with a big toothy smile and glasses appeared at the bar in the corner.

The lady asked what I wanted and I wondered if she had a bed for the night. She smiled and asked if I had a booking. I shook my head. Fortunately I was in luck; the place — despite being the only hostel in town, or even on the island — was far from full, with the door she led me through revealing a glut of empty dorm beds.

The room was faded pink, with the windows boarded up and at least a dozen beds. She told me it was ten American dollars a night. I accepted this and suggested I would be here for over a week. The woman introduced herself as Rita and said that would be fine. I breathed a sigh of relief and threw my things up on the top bunk, careful not to fall as I clambered up the steps because in a country such as this, where our governments advise us not to go, any travel insurance you have is null and void. If you crash and burn you're on your own, and given what I'd said before about insurance this worried me a little, even though there was nothing much I could do, only be careful.

But if I had taken the risk then so had several others at the hostel. Also staying there was Faustoe, a lively backpacker from Italy who had travelled the world and conquered every women he'd met along the way by the sounds of things.

Darren was less brazen, from Singapore and wearing glasses and a shell suit. He looked like he was dressed for badminton and quite out of place, yet he too had come alone, simply out of curiosity, to see the place having heard about it on the news.

Mal was even more laid back. He was a dread-locked hippy from Perth, working in a quarry back in Australia, a job he didn't particularly like, but it was necessary, he conceded, to finance his love of travel.

Other 'adventure' motorcyclists were also staying at the Smokehouse; a Russian man on a big Honda who never said much and in fact was quite rude. More friendly were two German motorcyclists, Oliver and Willy, who were only in their early twenties and together had travelled the length of the world, the pair of them starting in Germany and working their way along the same route I was going to take. They were now heading to Australia, happy to tell me all about the world I was about to encounter.

I could see when I told them about my intentions, on Dorothy (still to arrive by cargo boat), that they didn't have much faith in my choice of machine. This bothered me, but also gave me incentive, to prove such perceptions wrong; that you don't need a big bike to do something like this, that any machine will do.

Also German were the cyclists, Sven and Caroline, the pair of them pedalling around the world on two steel framed push-bikes. They had already crossed South America and Australia, and were now heading the same way as me back to Europe.

They told how, across Australia, they'd had to tow a trailer for all the water they needed for the 250 kilometre gaps in civilisation. They also had the most romantic story, explaining how they met not many months before Sven was due to undertake the global trip on his own. He set off as planned but only made it a few weeks in before realising he missed Caroline too much and so turned around and cycled back. He waited a year for her to prepare and finally they set off, around the world on push-bikes together. It certainly was an interesting gang of travellers.

***

The Smokehouse in which we all slept was a fascinating place. At night the brothers and cousins and distant relatives of Rita, who all slept on mattresses on the lounge floor, would sit up watching VHS porn; they'd even do it during the day time. But nobody minded, it was just part of the place's charm. There was a filthy kitchen and equally grotty toilet block, surprisingly with hot running showers, and even plumbed in toilets.

There were though some odd stories about the place however; men with knives apparently trying to get in at night and Rita's brothers having to fight them off. We didn't know if this was true or not, but it all added to the sense of unease, that you were in a place that not always you felt like you belonged.

For food we'd always go to the open-air Indian diner next door. Rats would run around your feet and you could see straight through to the filthy kitchen where the food was prepared in giant vats. The food though was delicious, especially the dosas we ate for breakfast; folded over batter with veg curry in the middle, washed down with spicy chai tea, costing just a few dollars. The American dollar was the main currency here in East Timor, ever since the UN had stepped in.

The only other place I ventured those first few days was over the road to a run-down building with a bank of computers connected to the internet in a side room. The computers were relics from the past and the connections hit and miss.

I tried my best to update my blog and send message of my arrival to those concerned. Friends back home still couldn't believe I was doing this, offering messages of support and surprise. Of course I was still in regular contact with Mandy, using Skype we even managed to speak on the phone. The conversation was strained. What do you say when one of you is running as fast as they can away from the other? Not much.

Finally, after two days tethered to these two places, I thought it time to face the rest of the city. I laced up my boots and dropped my penknife in my pocket. On my iPod I played *Bitter Sweet Symphony*. I was Richard Ashcroft, get the hell out of my way... when in reality I tiptoed down the driveway, past the barbed-wire fence, until I had no choice but to step out onto the street.

The pace of it hit me. Mini buses burst at the seams with passengers, some even hanging on to the sides, the driver signalling his intention to pull over by blowing a horn, the sound of which was like that used to announce a scene change in the old Batman TV series with Adam West. It went, 'De-le-de-le-de-le-derrr...' People jumped off and others dived on. I walked past with my head down low, trying not to make eye contact with anyone.

What struck me as I wandered further were how nice the houses would have been before they were either shot at, burned down or blown up. Some were just charred remains; others were still quite pretty. I cut through one estate, walking past a refugee camp — just a canopy of make-shift tents — and found myself down on the waterfront, where the flags of foreign countries fluttered above a monument.

If you ignored the stranded bottles, the pieces of blue foam, the random sandal, the driftwood and the soft drink cans it would have been a beautiful beach, arching the length of a city similar in size to Darwin. At the far end of it was a statue of Jesus perched high up on the cliffs — a reminder that the faith here was predominately Catholic until the Portuguese left in 1975, the Indonesian military in West Timor streaming over the border almost immediately after.

I walked further, past the battered ships moored up at the docks, where the cargo boat carrying Dot would arrive in less than a week's time, then on to a spot where teenagers sat on the sea wall kicking it with their heels the way bored teenagers do the rest of the world over. They wore trainers and fashionable jeans. Some waved and said hello. They were friendly, welcoming; they wanted to talk but we couldn't understand one another so well.

Women selling water would smile and the men chopping coconuts would offer me one. Boys with bags of mangoes tied to long sticks balanced on their shoulders would hassle me to buy some. One kid followed me for an age until I finally relented and bought a bag. I took out my knife to cut a bunch from his stick, his eyes opening with surprise. Strangely, this seemed to bring me respect and his friends relented, leaving me alone after that.

By the side of the road I also met Richard from Australia, who explained to me how he was here to see if he could set up a fair-trade coffee processing plant, as East Timor was currently selling raw beans to other countries, which then made all the money, and profit, on the processing. His plan was to set up a facility so that could be done on the island instead. The country certainly needed the money.

The buildings, the roads, the infrastructure — it was all in ruins. And yet there'd be five electrical stores on one street and brand-new scooters parked outside most of them. Richard explained that a lot of the money came from relatives working in Europe or America, sending money home to their families.

By far the oddest sight on my walk around the city was the platoon of Australian soldiers, in full combat gear and armed with rifles, casually walking down the street towards me. I stood on the opposite side of the road in my flip flops and shorts, not wishing to stare, but not able to help it either.

They looked at me and I looked at them. It was just so surreal. I didn't know if they were being over cautious or I was being foolishly brave. But to consider, only the year before my passage through the country, joint assassination attempts had been made on the President, José Ramos-Horta, and on the Prime Minister, Xanana Gusmao; the whole country divided, between those who want the Indonesians to return, and those who wish for them never to come back.

I read of such things in a book titled *A Dirty Little War*, written by an Australian journalist by the name of John Martinkus, who witnessed first-hand the bloody withdrawal of Indonesia soldiers and militia back in 1999, the book lent to me by an English lady who was trying to establish a bookstore in town. I sat and read it on my bunk bed, dumb-founded to think that in the city I'd just walked through so many atrocities had been committed less than a decade before; babies having their heads smashed against rocks, women raped, men tortured, all because Indonesia didn't wish to honour the country's new found independence.

No doubt I heard about all this on the news at the time but probably paid no attention; just another war-zone in a far off land, no relevance to me so why should I care? Now I was here, in the thick of it, and all of a sudden it felt so very real.

To keep the peace and help the country stand on its own two feet the United Nations were now here in force. Moving along every road and parked outside every restaurant, shop and bank, or so it seemed, were new Toyota 4x4s, painted white with the organisation's initials in blue down the side.

Many of the international aid agencies were here as well, including the Red Cross and Oxfam — they, too, were in brand-new Toyotas. In fact, the Japanese manufacturer was doing such a good trade in East Timor they'd built a huge glass-fronted dealership on the road to the airport, next door to the wooden shacks in which the local people lived.

Of an evening, the staff of these organisations would drink imported beer and eat steak in the restaurants and bars they'd built along the seafront to cater for them. No locals ate in them; prices were too high, the same as you'd pay in Australia. In here you'd get talking to the sons of the UN envoy, to the foreign soldiers, and to those working for the aid agencies who lived in secure compounds throughout the city, often with drivers and maids. I found out that they were all on maximum pay whenever our governments advise against visiting the country.

The cynical side of me saw this as being quite convenient, because to look at, it seemed as though these people were all on something of a jolly, while telling the rest of us to stay away. Then you pick up the local magazine and read how the UN needs more money, in the billions, for their operations around the world. Given what Jill had been prepared to do to build her clinic, I couldn't help but think if they all bought second-hand Toyotas and stopped spending all their money on imported booze, the money might just go a bit further.

Yet there was certainly something about the place; a presence, an unease, that I still struggle to put my finger on. Sometimes it felt like paradise, as though those UN personnel weren't needed at all. And then at other times you could understand why they were here — you sensed something, a crackle in the air, a ripple of turbulence in the fabric of the city.

The locals were friendly and none approached me with any ill-intent, but when I asked them about the past or for opinions on the state of the country they turned away. I sense they were careful about what they said, but with Indonesian informants probably still in the city it was perhaps no wonder. If you were drunk on that imported beer you probably wouldn't notice anything wrong at all. But to me it felt like a city still quietly simmering.

One afternoon a strange man appeared at the hostel. He had a thick moustache and ponytail. Rita said she knew him and they chatted a while before he made his way over to me. The man was friendly, in an overly inquisitive way. He wanted to know about my camera and my laptop, details about my trip. He wanted to take my picture, which made me worry because, I mean, why would he? All sorts of theories ran through my mind and I withdrew from the conversation.

I began to wonder if he was an informant of some kind, sent to check me out after I'd naively, and stupidly, put 'journalist' as my profession on my visa application, as the job I'd quit in London to go back to Australia in the first place was as a road tester on a car magazine and I thought it sounded better than sandwich maker.

Jill, who I visited at the clinic, said I might be pulled in for interrogation as a consequence of this admission. I'd brushed that off as being too dramatic, yet in that book I'd been reading it had stated how journalists had been targeted and killed during Indonesian times. When the man with the moustache returned the following day and suggested that I go with him into the mountains to visit his relatives I made my excuses.

What unnerved me most was the poster for the missing Swedish backpacker hanging on the hostel wall. He was last seen in East Timor two years before, vanishing without trace. It made me aware of my own vulnerability; how you could disappear in the blink of an eye and no one would ever know. Having declined the man's invitation I spent the rest of my time in East Timor, holed up in the Smokehouse, waiting anxiously for the cargo boat with my bike on it to arrive.

Mal thought I was overreacting and said it could be the anti-malaria tablets making me paranoid. The doctor in Darwin had warned me that the tablets could have that side effect, but it was so hard to tell whether it was the drugs or the realisation of where I was and the scale of what I was aiming to do that was finally catching up with me.

After all, Australia had been a long hard slog in a familiar land. I knew the culture and I understood the language. Now I was in East Timor, the toe of Asia, looking north-west up the leg of Indonesia, questioning whether I could do this. And if I was uncertain of myself at this early point, what about when I reached India, Pakistan and Iran? How would I cope in countries with reputations as fearsome as those?

From this point on I would have to overcome the fear of being alone on a bike in a foreign land. I'd have to overcome the fear of not knowing how to fix my bike, of not knowing if I had enough money to finish the trip, of not knowing how long it would take, of not knowing how I would cross Indonesia, of not planning anything in advance. There was so much I didn't know, and yet for all that I had a sense that I was on the right path, doing the right thing, in the right place. There was no doubt or indecision, just fear, and I think that's the right way round.

Fear you can face, but doubt and indecision — that's not a nice place to be. Treading water, going nowhere while your mind ties itself up in knots. I didn't have that out here, just a simple challenge, to ride as hard and as far as I could, to find out what Asia was like for myself and see if one day I would make it to England. This was my challenge now and all East Timor had done was hit me with the danger of it, the reality.

Already I'd met people already doing similar things and realised for the time being I came up short. Yet I'd tried the food and realised it wasn't too bad. I'd seen the roads and knew that with more care I could survive. By now I also knew that such endeavours come at a price. And what you gain with one hand you lose with the other.

There are consequences to a trip like this. You are forced to make a choice, to leave something or someone behind. Most of all, you are made to question yourself and confront the things you don't like most about yourself. And not all the time are you happy with how you answer.

Would we make it all the way to England? I still wasn't sure. The man at the Indonesian Embassy, the day I went to collect my tourist visa, insisted I wouldn't be able to take my foreign motorcycle over the border into West Timor (part of Indonesia). I argued with him, presenting my Carnet de Passage and telling him of the other couple on the postie bike who had passed this way just six months prior.

But he was adamant; my bike would not be able to enter Indonesia. And if that was the case then the only way around would be to put her on a boat back to Darwin, then another one to Singapore, and fly there myself. No way could I have afforded to do that. The trip would have been over. But I remained optimistic, racing down to the docks the day Dot's boat finally arrived, intent on finding out for myself whether she could cross into West Timor or not.

Chapter Five
Dili Onwards

It had cost $300 to ship Colin's old motorbike from Darwin to East Timor. It was a simple process, taking her down to the dock in Darwin where she was measured and then eventually rolled into a container and sailed across the Timor Sea. I would have travelled with her, only they don't allow passengers to travel on the cargo boats, hence why I'd needed to fly. This was something I would have loved to have avoided, my fear of flying born out of the lack of control you have up there, at least that's what I believe.

Your life in the hands of someone else, leaving you to just sit there, hoping nothing bad happens because if it did then I couldn't imagine anything worse than in that moment of free-fall, thinking of all the things you should and could have done in life, because now it's too late to put things right or learn from your mistakes. Your time has come, and now it's gone, though this is perhaps a fear of regret, as much as it is of flying.

Back in Dili I finally tracked Dot down to a cargo depot on the outskirts of town. It was set amongst the jungle and stacked high with big metal containers resting in the dirt. None of them looked like they'd been moved for years. In a portacabin by the entrance I found a man in charge who examined my papers and led me outside to where he assembled a team of labourers, the lot of us marching down the yard to a blue container in a long line of blue containers.

The labourers cranked open the door and the light shone in. All I saw were pallets of food and other bits, doubtful my bike could have been in there at all. Pallets were dragged out one by one, still no sign of her. Then from the shadows I caught a glimpse of a headlight, a bright orange pannier sack, and there she was, the old Australian postal bike from Caboolture. It was good to see her again.

We spent a few days riding around Dili – just getting used to the roads – even heading out with Mal, Faustoe and Darren, who rented scooters from a nearby petrol station, owned by an Australian man of East Timorese dissent. These were better times, riding as a group, heading east along the coast, past gorgeous beaches and across arid savannahs. As we rode along the kids in villages would come out and try and hi-five us, making a fuss of us every time we stopped.

We rode that day up the coast to the second city of Baucau, a place once said to be the last stop on the hippy trail way back in the seventies, when the overland route from England to Australia was said to be more common.

There wasn't much in Baucau now, only old buildings from Portuguese time, a UN base on the outskirts of town, a cheap café where we all had a plate of noodles, washed down by cans of cheap cola, before finally heading back, riding through the outskirts of Dili in darkness, the wooden hut houses illuminated by candlelight and feeling like you'd stepped back into another time and place. It surely was a majestic evening. I shall never forget the smell of smoke from fires that hung heavy in the air.

I hung out with the guys a few more days, wondering if, before crossing into West Timor, I ought to do a lap of this eastern half of the island in order to do justice to my visit here. I worried that when would be the next time I would find myself here with a motorbike and time on my hands to explore the place? I calculated that I could make it all the way around East Timor in three days and then cross into West Timor and planned on doing just that.

Yet as I rode out of town heading east, rather than west, it just didn't feel right. Whether it was the fear I still had of the place, or simply the sensation of riding in the opposite direction to England, my instinct told me I was doing the wrong thing, going in the wrong direction. So I turned around, rode back past the Dili Smokehouse — where earlier I'd said a heartfelt farewell to Rita and the other residents — making haste towards the border with West Timor instead.

The road now was spectacular, pinned in tight between the jungle and the edge of the ocean. Small villages were dotted every few miles, their houses made of wood with a dirt floor outside on which children played. Other children were on their way to school, dressed impeccably in their uniforms and continuing to try and hi-five me as I passed.

On the beach to my right were houses made of sand, a huge dome of it with a wooden doorway and animals tethered up outside. I really wished to stop and take some photographs, but I still felt very uncertain about this, as though I would be intruding and bringing undue attention to myself. I think I preferred to try and remain incognito, though that was impossible given the way the local kids would spot me, stop, and then wave.

A few hours into the journey I passed a signpost pointing to the village of Maliani. I remember reading in the book how it was here that five Australian journalists were executed as the Indonesians invaded in 1975. This was a sobering reminder that whether I'd imagined the threat of the moustachioed man or not, the events of that year were real.

People had died and for the next twenty-five years had continued to do so. The Indonesians were now long gone. But very soon I would be crossing into the country into which they'd fled following UN intervention in 1999. From here I would be on my own. Just the road. And a penknife in my pocket.

I should then have been scared to enter West Timor (thankfully the man at the embassy had been wrong), yet crossing the border — marking the start of Indonesia — was like putting heavy bags down after a trip to the supermarket. That sensation when you've carried them up the drive and through the door and the handles are hurting your hand and you can't wait to get to the kitchen so you can at last rest them on the floor and shake the numbness from your hand.

That's what I felt like leaving East Timor; as though I'd just let go of the baggage. I waved at every West Timorese person I saw. I stopped for photos, bought petrol from the roadside in little glass bottles. I felt great; the paranoia was lifting. Then I got to Atambua, the town I intended spending that first night, and once more the weight of the situation hit me like a brick.

Riding into town, a man on a moped began to follow me. I tried to shake him off through the back streets, but when I stumbled upon a hotel he pulled up right behind me. I looked at him nervously as I climbed off the bike and gathered my things. He walked in circles, pointing at me and my belongings and laughing with the other men who had gathered.

I wanted to tell them to go away but I feared that would make things worse. This, after all, was the town in which three UN staff had been murdered back in 2000, the militia that had caused so much carnage in East Timor fleeing here once sovereignty had been restored. I asked the name of the man who had followed me. He said it was Adi. I wrote this, and his number plate, down on my arm, before heading inside to see about a room.

I was given a room around the back of this tatty hotel, paying six dollars or so for it. It had no sink or shower, but I could park Dot right up close to the door. By chance, there was a French couple staying in a room across the way, in their fifties and travelling through to East Timor by local bus.

That evening I sat and shared a cup of tea on their balcony, copying some of the maps in their travel guide into my diary and writing down the names of the major towns so that I would at least have places to aim for. Travelling without such maps and guidebooks didn't bother me, I just figured that as long as I rode away from the sun as it rose in the morning, and then towards it as it set for the day, then I would be going in the right direction.

Besides, I think deep down I just craved a pure adventure, free of all protection, and to have a map and a plan is to take some of that element away. In a way, this was me against the world, and all the challenges that came with that. In essence, I had a lot to prove to myself, and perhaps to other people, this desire possibly stemming from the worthlessness only a relationship of this nature can make you feel.

Another strange thing happened that evening. One of the guards who had been at the border crossing into West Timor earlier that day checked into a room across the courtyard.

I asked him what he was doing there and he told me he was staying at the hotel because the water pipes had burst at his own house. It seemed an unlikely story, this all now too much of a coincidence for my liking. First the moustachioed man, then Adi, and now him. I felt like I was being followed.

That night, after a timid walk around the streets in search of food, I dragged the mattress close to the door, chained the bike to the fence outside and balanced a beer bottle on the footrest as a crude booby-trap. If it fell in the night then I was armed and ready with the hammer and penknife that I kept on the pillow beside me. Thankfully, by sunrise, nothing had been disturbed.

Over breakfast, the French couple gave me a different type of anti-malaria tablets so that I could get off the Lariam. Was it this that was making me paranoid, or did I have a genuine reason to be suspicious? The answer came just a short while later, when, on the outskirts of town, having stopped at a phone shop to buy a local sim card, a familiar face walked into the canvas roofed shop. It was Adi, though clearly trying not to be spotted, his head lowered and trying to look the other away.

'Are you following me?' I asked. He shook his head, but I knew he must have been.

Outside I checked the registration of this bike with the one he was on the previous night. They didn't match; he was riding a different bike. I don't know why, but this small detail filled me with terror.

I fired Dot into life and for the next eight hours, all the way to the ferry port in Kupang, rode like the raging wind. I stopped for nothing or no one. I rode as though I was being chased by a large black dog, glancing over my shoulder, looking for traps up ahead; spotting people on mobile phones by the roadside and worrying that they were somehow coordinating my downfall.

Dorothy had never travelled so fast. I didn't slacken the throttle one bit, racing along the jungle roads as fast as I dare, taking corners flat out.

My eyes piercing the horizon. Adrenaline racing through my veins. I was scared, hoping only that once I made it to Kupang I could hop on a ferry and be shut of Timor for good.

Disaster. The ferry had sailed that very morning and there wouldn't be another for exactly two weeks. My heart sank. The error was in me thinking that a daily ferry service was running between the Indonesian islands, but because of the rough seas those ferries had been cancelled and it was only the big ship, the fortnightly service, which was still in operation. That wasn't the only problem.

In enjoying the thrill of the chase I'd only applied for a one month tourist visa, when it would have been possible to get a visa for two months. The German cyclists, Caroline and Sven, had advised me to get the latter, but I had ignored them, believing a month would be enough. Now I wouldn't have a month.

By the time the ferry sailed in a fortnight, I would have just two remaining weeks to cross the vast expanse of Indonesia, from one end to the other, before making the crossing to Malaysia. Worst of all; there was nothing I could do, only find a place to stay, and wait.

***

Kupang, the capital of West Timor, was a busy, chaotic place, much like Dili, only without the presence of the UN and aid trucks. If you were to compare the two cities to people you would say Kupang was the bully, and Dili was the bullied. There was just more bravado, more front, and more confidence here in Kupang. The people were far less weary of approaching you, everywhere you went kids would call out, 'Hey mister,' almost as a taunt.

Apparently, Kupang was once a busy tourist town, but after the direct flights from Darwin were cancelled, travellers no longer came here, bypassing it completely and flying directly from Darwin to Bali. The only people passing through these days were those on their way to Dili, of which there didn't seem very many.

I tried a few hotels, but one was a brothel and the other one was closed.

I remember reading in the French couple's travel guide about a cluster of hostels and a bar down by the waterfront so headed there. I was still in panic mode, half expecting to come face to face with Adi. In my mind he was everywhere.

On the last road before the sea I found a small motel ran by a man named Mike (his adopted Western name), who showed me to a basic room where I collapsed on the bed and shut my eyes. For the next few days I came down with a horrible fever. I was achingly cold with a cracking headache and no strength in my bones. I ate biscuits and drank fizzy pop, bought from a wooden shack across the road.

Mike invited me to his father's funeral in a week's time. I thought that odd, but maybe that was custom. I did my best to decline without seeming rude. I thought why would he want me there, I'd never even met the man, and obviously never would.

My strength recovered, I spent time at the bar across the road from the motel. It was owned by a man named Edwin, in his fifties, who to me resembled Morgan Freeman.

His bar only had two walls, the other sides looking out across the ocean. It was built on the edge of the cliff and served as a hub for travellers, Edwin a hive of information, with a computer hooked up to the internet which you could use for free. I emailed Mandy and my parents with an update. They were worried sick. But I was hanging in there.

Days came and went. I visited the dock to see if there were any update on the ferries. The seas were still too rough, with it a huge effort booking the bike on to the fortnightly ferry. She would have to be winched aboard, the cost extortionate and no clear way of going about this. I wandered the streets, eating nasi goreng — a fried rice dish — from wooden stalls parked in the shadows.

It was one day when taking a stroll that I spotted a girl up ahead who didn't look to be from around these parts either. I caught up with her and shouted, 'Hello.' She spun around, startled to see me, and together we walked the rest of the way through the city. She was Australian, here in Kupang for a year to conduct research on local tribes for her university project. She'd only arrived that day and still nervously trying to adjust. I thought her incredibly brave. And she wasn't the only one.

Back at the motel a girl by the name of Anne had arrived. She was from the Czech Republic, in her early twenties and travelling this part of the world completely alone. She explained how her Catholic family had disowned her following her decision not to practice the faith. That had been her catalyst and from there she'd took off, travelling the length of Indonesia by local transport, now planning on crossing to East Timor and then flying on to Darwin.

A month or so later Anne emailed to tell me how she'd hitch-hiked all the way to Adelaide with an aboriginal man who'd picked her up by the side of the road, and now she planned on riding around Australia on a motorbike. She was as crazy as they come, and useful for me, making me realise that it was about time I grew a pair of balls.

Finally, after what felt like a lifetime in Kupang, came good news; Edwin informing me that the local ferries were sailing again after a break in the weather. He said that if I went immediately down to the docks then I might just be able to make the one that sailed that very afternoon, and if I made that one it would mean that I had three weeks, not two, to ride across Indonesia.

I packed quickly, apologising to Mike for not being able to attend his father's funeral that evening — because in truth I would have gone — and made haste along the short coastal road to the dock. The road was flooded in places but the bike powered through just as she had in the Outback, dropping down the hill to where a battered wooden jetty cast out at ninety degrees to the shore.

At the end of the jetty was a rusting metal ship already being loaded with vehicles and goods. I had to buy a ticket from the counter and then follow instructions to see the two policeman sat in an office just back from the water's edge. They took my ticket and the only way to get it back was to pay them a bribe of around $5, which I reluctantly did so, because I just wanted to get the hell out of there.

With the ticket back in my hand I threw a leg over the saddle and charged along the dock towards the ramp and onto the boat that swallowed me whole. After almost a month on the island of Timor —

East and West — this was it, time to leave, set sail for the next island, Flores, then make my way across the rest: Sumbawa, Lombok, Bali, Java and Sumatra, before crossing to Malaysia in less than three weeks time. The race once more was on.

Chapter Six
Leaving Timor

The boat was to take eighteen hours and sail through the night. It was two decks high, about the size of a local swimming pool and once painted white, though now riddled with rust. I'd parked to the left of the vehicle deck at the end of a long line of brand new scooters. The only other vehicle onboard was a battered red truck parked in the middle, loaded with all sorts of boxes and products, covered by a tarp. Nearby were dozens of cages of chickens, most of them with barely any feathers and in a terrible state, clucking loudly. I never realised it at the time but there was a passenger deck upstairs. It would have made no difference, I was determined to stick with the bike, as a lot people were lurking around, and well, to be honest, I just didn't trust them.

There was one man who bothered me more than any other. He was short and stocky, with his hair dyed an odd shade of strawberry blonde. He looked at me through piercing dark eyes and stood too close for comfort.

Before the boat had even sailed he was hanging off the handlebars, blowing smoke in my face and asking too many questions, too many times for me to feel at ease with him. Like Adi I wanted to tell him to go away, but I thought it best to simply humour him, smiling politely and ignoring him as best as I could. But still he would return, with more questions, more cigarette smoke. I was intimidated by him and made a note to avoid him when we reached the other end.

My other companion that night was a woman curled up beneath a blanket, sleeping against the wheel of the truck. She must have had flu or something, because every minute or so she would clear her lungs of green sticky phlegm and spit it across the deck, or blow it though her nose onto her fingers, which she would then flick in whichever direction she fancied. It went on through the night. Sinus Night. The whole deck covered in her snot.

I lay between Dot and a row of other scooters, on a wicker mat I'd bought off an old lady aboard the ship for a dollar, being bothered by the man, being disgusted by the women, trying to get some sleep. The floor was cold hard steel.

At the dock the next morning a crowd of local sellers jumped the boat before it had even landed, like pirates swinging aboard a rival vessel. I panicked and dropped Dot against the line of band new scooters. The first one wobbled and if that had gone down then so would all the rest, just like a stack of dominoes. Thankfully, the line of bikes remained stable, allowing me to hoist Dot back upright and take a seat.

I fired her into life and through the crowd we waded, struggling to lose my sea legs as we hit dry land and almost fell off as the ground was no longer swaying on the ocean swell. I kept an eye out for the man with strawberry blonde hair. He was nowhere to be seen. And with that I was gone.

***

The plan from here was to ride to the nearby town of Ende, just a few kilometres along the coast, where I hoped to meet up with Caroline and Sven, the Germans on the push-bikes who happened to have caught the fortnightly ferry that I missed that day back in Kupang. They had been staying at a hotel in the town ever since, with it my intention to find and stay with them that night.

I made my way along the coastal road, stopping for petrol on the outskirts of town, a long line of scooters queuing for the pumps, their riders' eyes turning to greet us with a stare. I filled Dot to the brim and paid with the currency I'd withdrawn from the cash machine back in Kupang. Thankfully my cash card still worked out here.

Ende itself was a maze. A grid of dusty streets and two-storey buildings, gangs of youths sat on street corners watching intently as I rode by. It was late morning and extremely humid. I rode around in circles, flagged down by a policeman who wanted to check the bike's details, and then stopping at the sight of a white man who stuck out like a sore thumb. He was French, working for a charity on the island and direct in his appeal for me not to trust anyone.

This was advice I'd heard quite often, though always from people who'd never been beyond their own doorstep. This man had lived here for years, making the advice more credible and I paid attention to it. He knew of the hotel I was looking for and sent me off in the right direction. But I never found it. I just rode around and around in ever increasing circles.

By now it was midday. I was on a strange island, in a strange town. Still with no map, no guidebook. No idea where I was going to stay that night. But all I felt was the most incredible urge to hit the road and just keep on riding, because it was on the road that I felt most confident and reassured in what I was doing.

In the sky the sun had come up from my right, so I decided if I headed left, to where it would set, I would be travelling in the right direction. No safety net, no nothing. The simple task of riding was all that I had to do. And that day me and Dorothy did it. Pounding the road with the ocean to the left and the pyramid mountains of Flores rising all around. It really was a stunning island, any trace of civilisation hidden neatly by thick banana leaves, the mountains pyramid shaped, like green blocks of chocolate Toblerone.

The people in the villages I passed through wore dusty sandals and shorts, with tops made by Reebok or Adidas, or more often than not declaring their following of an English football team. Even the man who'd stamped my Carnet way back at the East/West Timor border had bellowed, 'David Beckham, Wayne Rooney, Michael Owen...' the only English words he'd known.

But I'd known no Indonesian either, and in fact I was finding the language not much of a problem, realising how little of communication is actually done through the spoken word at all. As long as you smiled and was humble and laughed and didn't expect any English skills from people then you were fine. Soon my name became 'John', because few of them could pronounce the word 'Nathan' (Nat-han, Nay-fen, May-fen).

It was now that I thought back to those Aboriginal kids in the Australian Outback and how scared I'd been when they'd approached me outside the bakery that day in Emerald. Slowly I was realising that I couldn't have carried on like that, frightened of everyone that was different to me. I had to relax and in doing so accept that no way was I going to travel half way across the world not trusting anyone, as the Frenchman and so many others had advised me not to do.

I thought, 'I have to trust them, because if I don't then what kind of miserable journey will that be?' Isolated and alone. Lost in the world with no friends, whereas when you accept you have no enemies either then why not relax a little and go with the flow, like a twig in a river, which, in many ways, is all I was on this endeavour; not totally powerless to steer my course, but not completely in charge of it either. Was I brave? No. Foolish? Perhaps. Determined? Definitely.

As the sun began to set for the day I still didn't have a clue where I would be sleeping that night. Of course I had the sleeping bag and tent but I wasn't brave enough to use it here in Indonesia, not yet anyway. Besides, with dense jungle either side of the road, and houses built between any gaps, there was nowhere I saw fit to erect it. Fortunately, after another hour riding in the rain, I happened upon a town buried deep in the bowels of a forest basin. It was a carpet of wooden buildings, the low-watt lights giving it dim illumination and there me and Dorothy sat, up on the rise, looking down upon it, no clue as to it's name or its location on the island. I sensed I would find a bed there, and thankfully, I did.

I checked into one of the small tourist hotels on the way into town, taking a room on the ground floor. I threw my things on the bed, sat down on the stool, looked in the mirror, rubbed my eyes with my hands and let out a big sigh.

It was only a day ago that I'd left West Timor in a hurry. So little time had passed since then, yet so much had happened. Ferry, spitting bitch, shifty eyes, marauding 'Hey misters', my realisation that it's not all that bad. Recording a video diary that evening I sang *Always Look on the Bright Side of Life*.

Later I ate dinner with a group of backpackers on a guided tour from Bali, now only three islands away. They were so happy and relaxed, on holiday with the hope of seeing the volcanic Kelimutu lakes and doing some diving off one of the great beaches I'd no doubt raced past in a state of blind panic. Their calmness and sense of confidence compared to mine led me to conclude that mood is entirely a response to circumstance, and not location.

I say that because while they were still sinking beers in the restaurant and having a great evening, I went back to the room and had a little cry. I guess I felt swamped by things, as though I'd got nothing left to give and was tired of being on edge. I wasn't having fun at this point, which is a stupid thing to say; in a gorgeous part of the world on a motorbike not having to work. What could be so bad about that? I suppose the joy of solitude I talked so fondly about in the Outback had now been replaced by loneliness.

I thought of Mandy. She was now two hours time difference behind. That would mean she was not long home from work. She might have driven or she might have used her push bike. Dinner would be on, a stir-fry or a chicken wrap. While it was cooking she might be hanging out the washing or talking to her house-mates in the back garden. Being a teacher she might have had some marking to do, or some lessons to plan. She'd do this in her bedroom, lying on her bed, with a glass of wine perhaps, maybe with the telly on. Outside it would be sunny and bright. Traffic would be calming. Sydney would be settling down for the night, just as she would be doing in her bedroom now.

I wished I was there. To massage her back and stroke her hair. Make her tea if she fancied one. Listen to her snore as she drifted off. If only we could live in the world nostalgia creates. If only that world existed.

The next morning I found necessary distraction in a twelve hour day on the road, the destination Labuanbajo, a port town on the very western tip of Flores. I knew from here I'd be able catch a ferry to the next island of Sumbawa. The road to get there was tight and twisty, a roller-coaster of hills that would have us slowly ratchet to the top before blazing down the other side. Then it would flatten, passing between fields where rice was grown.

Cows were tethered by the roadside, chickens dangled alive from racks on the back of minibuses. I overtook flat out at sixty-five, Dorothy just perfect for the roads around here. I never asked more of her than she could deliver. We were perfectly suited for each other, and as the journey progressed, I began to talk to her more and more.

What I liked most about this stage of the journey was the way in which time seemed to slow down when you made eye contact with the people in the villages we passed through. I might be doing fifty kilometres per hour, but still, I would look at the old man sitting in the shade and he would look at me, and in that split-second it would feel like we'd connected, our eyes engaging in dialogue, telling the other what we were thinking, and perhaps even what kind of people we were and whether or not we pleased to see the other or not. Time would once again speed up and the same thing would happen with the next person, and the next. I must have met a thousand people a day that way.

For the following few days I rode and caught ferries from noon until sunset. I stayed in whatever place I could find, ate at roadside stalls, while writing the name of the next town on my hand and showing it to locals in order to find my way.

It was certainly a better time, the hours I was riding really allowing me to see Indonesian life through all stages of the day. First thing in the morning I'd see villagers stretch and yawn as they got out of bed. I saw mothers cooking breakfast and serving it up on big wooden tables outside. Children in uniform would walk along the side of the road to school. This being a Muslim country the call to prayer would sound, and then people would go to work, in the rice fields or in the tiny wooden shops that stood in front of many of their homes.

The full heat of the sun would then cook the day. Around lunchtime the families, especially the men, would sit under wicker huts, just talking, snoozing, losing, playing card games. If this were Spain, they'd be having a siesta. And then the late afternoon would come, more work would be done, children would return home and play badminton in the dirt outside their homes before eating dinner around that table again. Mother and father, brothers and sisters, aunts and uncles, all digging in. Then the boys would take girls out on scooters and come roaring past me and Dorothy as we drifted through, fascinated by the life people lived out here, so calm, so tranquil, so leisurely by the appearance of things.

Somewhere in the middle of Sumbawa (the island after Flores) I stopped in a town with a military base to buy a map. I quite liked the idea of having one now, if only to acknowledge the sights I was missing along the way.

At a small stationery store I was told by the attendant that he didn't have any maps, but his sister-in-law, who was Australian, might be able to help. I thought to myself, 'There can't really be an Australian living out here, we're too far off the beaten track?'

I followed the man, weaving down the back alleys on our motorbikes, eventually pulling up outside a square wooden house, where sure enough, inside was a true-blue Australian; Elizabeth, from Melbourne.

She emerged from the house wearing a long red traditional Indonesian dress and told me a lovely story about the man she'd met in Bali and later wed. Now she lived here, in a world I thought looked quite lonely, a prison perhaps. But she seemed happy, with her new found family around and her satellite TV broadcasting shows from back home.

Elizabeth said Bali was less than a day's ride away and that I wouldn't need a map. We sat and drank tea and talked about Australia, the country we both missed. I think both of us enjoyed the brief companionship that afternoon. Two strangers in a foreign land who happened to meet quite by chance.

'Nice to meet you,' I said as I waved goodbye and made my way back through the alleys and rejoined the main road.

From Sumbawa I crossed to Lombok, enjoying the most wonderful ride through the darkness behind a man on a moped who knew the road like the back of his hand. I ate at McDonald's in the capital city of

Mataran, stayed the night in a cheap hotel that gave me bed bugs, the next morning taking directions from a man riding a mean looking motorbike and sidecar, and was once again astounded by the bravery of others I met on the road.

Three Austrian girls had ridden rental scooters from Bali, with bulging backpacks strapped to their bikes, while an Australian girl was doing the same, on her own, having told the rental shop she wouldn't take the bike off Bali, and then proceeding to take it all the way to Flores. So brave. So alone.

I too arrived in Bali, the oasis in the Indonesian island chain that I'd been waiting for. I knew here I would find some respite, even if it was only for a day or two, feeling myself blow a big sigh of relief as the ferry docked on the east coast town of Lembongan. I stayed there that night in a gorgeous wooden guesthouse overlooking the beach.

The Australian girl on the scooter was also staying there and to save money we shared a bunk, her top, me bottom. Though don't get any funny ideas. She was ginger and I had wind. And in the morning we went our separate ways, her heading north along the coast, me heading west to Kuta, the main tourist town on the island, and certainly a place I didn't much care for.

Maybe it was the contrast with the rest of what I had encountered in Indonesia, but to me it resembled the gaudy seaside towns of England, only beneath a brighter sky. The place was full of tacky bars, naff market stalls, fast food joints and branded surf shops. It seemed to be the place where Australians came for their winter vacations, the town devoted to them, in the same way somewhere like Benidorm or Magaluf is geared towards the British.

It was sad however to see the memorial to 222 people who had died in the terrorist bombings of 2002 and 2005. You could sense where the conflict might have come from: Traditional Islamic islands either side, with Buddhist Bali in the middle, where everything and anything seemed to go. Obviously a bomb is no way of solving things, but sadly, in some ways it had succeeded; tourist numbers were down on what they were before.

I stayed in Kuta just a few hours, having Dot's oil changed at a small garage for a few dollars — careful to check it was genuine as I'd been warned much of it out here was fake or reconstituted — before being told about the town of Ubud, a few hours to the north, where things were said to much calmer, and quieter.

I followed the road there, fascinated by just how much of the craft for sale in the island's shops was actually made here. In row upon row of workshops I could see statues being carved from wood or crafted out of pot, while the arc of a welding gun lit up dark dens where designs of steel were being made.

Again, I wanted to stop and take pictures but still didn't feel confident doing such a thing. It was for this reason that most of my pictures so far were either of me, or Dot, or me and Dot together. By this time I'd started doing handstands for the pictures. I don't know why, perhaps it was just a reflection of my improving mood.

Ubud, once I'd found it, was exactly what I needed; calm and tranquil, the kind of place my parents might have liked. There were Hindu temples and divine old buildings, surrounded by lush green rice fields cascading down the ledges cut into the hills. Set amongst this were the boutique hotels and cute little cafés, the craft shops, the bustling little markets and the Jalan Monkey Forest from which monkeys came out to play on the road.

I stopped a couple of foreigners walking in the street. They were American backpackers; young and full of beans — and piercings — telling me about a great little guesthouse perched up on top of the hill, overlooking the rice fields, with incredible views all to yourself. I thanked the Americans and rode on, following the directions that they had given me.

It was only a small guesthouse when I found it, family owned, the father showing me to a room that was clean and had a bathroom with a hot shower and patio that overlooked his beautiful garden. It was something ridiculous like six dollars a night and perfect in every way. I took off all my clothes, had a long shower — the rest of the way it had been cold water from a ladle — lay on the bed, then sat on the patio drinking the pot of strong Indonesian coffee the mother had brought to my room.

It had been almost a month to the day that I'd arrived in East Timor. In that time so much had happened, so much fear and pressure had been felt. To get to the other side of Indonesia I still had so very far to travel, across Java and Sumatra, still maybe another 3,000 kilometres to be covered in around two weeks. I would be hard pushed to make it, but for the next two days, I took a much needed breather.

I'd wander down into town, taking my laptop and sitting in a café drinking glass after glass of ginger tea. In a bookshop I found an old Lonely Planet guide for Indonesia, printed back in 1995. It was much cheaper than a new one and figured I would make do with fifteen year old information. In its battered pages I read of the Agung volcano, not far from Ubud, which I visited the next day, circling its rim and then dropping down into its centre. It was like landing on the surface of the moon, so black and dusty, it last erupting in 1963 and still active, occasionally belching smoke, though now with villages and sporadic homes built right inside the very crater. It wasn't as extreme as it sounds.

But it was nice to play around, setting up the timer on the camera and catching me and Dorothy in action, crossing the jagged stones, the conical of the volcano towering like a cliff top all around. I stopped at a thermal spa but turned back when I saw the price. That was the only thing with Bali, it was very touristy, even away from the main tourist areas.

Often when I stopped I would be hassled by a herd of kids or a lone old man, trying to get me to buy items such as postcards or carved wooden elephants. After the innocence of East Timor, the people of Bali just seemed so desperate.

As frustrated as this sometimes made me I could understand it in a way. So much investment had been made on the island through the nineties, the building of brand new shops and facilities to cater for the swelling tourist trade. Then the bombs came and no longer did so many tourists.

The income the locals now relied on was gone, or had at least dwindled. The ugly face of the tourist trade perhaps, and how it sweeps through in cycles, building up hope and then knocking it flat when the markets change. It made me wonder if Bali would have been better not getting into it in the first place, though I guess that was just its fate, being as pretty as it was. I just hoped East Timor didn't go the same way, as that would be a shame.

Though, if there's one memory that will always stick with me from Bali it's that of the food I ate the day I made my way to the port where I would catch a ferry to Java. It was a dish called bakso, something I'd eaten before so knew it to be a soup dish, with noodles and congealed balls of chicken floating on the surface. You'd buy it from men pushing little wooden carts down the road. They'd make it fresh and drizzle in all sorts of spices and bits of chopped herbs to give it a kick. It was dirt cheap.

The one I had this day featured a special ingredient. It was long and thin and grey in colour. When it was offered to me I thought what the hell and nodded my head. With that the man took out his scissors and 'snip snip snip', cut the long dangly thing into the soup. The texture was like tubes of pasta and the taste was pretty strange. I later learned it was intestine. Yum.

Chapter Seven
Java, Indonesia

The rest of the journey across Indonesia was a time of lonely highways and strange encounters. We had to ride harder and longer than we had ever had to ride before. We had more ground to cover, less time to do it in, and on roads more treacherous than any we'd encountered so far.

Those across Java were dense with trucks and other heavy traffic; those across Sumatra were remote and in a terrible state of repair. Along them we had accidents and crashes, we bent things, lost things, taught English at a school, climbed a temple, pitched a tent in the wild, and by the end of it had the biggest battle of them all trying to find a way of leaving it all behind.

It all began with a bus heading straight towards us. It was my fault, riding in a day dream and not giving much thought as I pulled out to overtake a slow moving Toyota people carrier to my left. This put me in the centre of the road with nowhere to go, when a bus suddenly came hurtling around the corner, also in the centre of the road. I was doing over sixty kilometres per hour, he must have been doing the same.

Instinctively, I swerved in as tight as I could to the people carrier to my left and braced myself for a head on impact. The oncoming bus missed the front of the bike by a whisker, whooshing down the side of me until it clattered the pannier rack on the right hand side.

The force of this threw me against the people carrier, the gap between the two vehicles in the split second they passed so tight, so compact that me and Dorothy had no choice but to stay upright, my shoulders ricocheting off the vehicles either side, the pair of us bucking wildly, like being caught in a fast-moving vice.

In the blink of an eye it was over, shooting out from the gap, wondering what had just happened. I didn't stop, and the other two vehicles didn't stop either. I kept on riding, thinking it best to make some distance on it all, and then come to rest.

When I finally pulled into a petrol station I clambered off the bike and took a look down her flanks. The heavy metal framework supporting the orange pannier sacks was mangled on both sides, bent completely backwards and twisted, the welds being torn apart. I dread to think what a mess it must have made of the panel work on the other two vehicles, both racks covered in their paint, which must have acted like tin openers down the doors of the two vehicles.

It had been a lucky escape that day. If we had have gone down we'd have been under the wheels of both vehicles and that wouldn't have ended well, especially out here where hospitals are so few and far between. I often wondered what would happen if I had a bad accident in a place such as this, but really, it didn't bear thinking about.

By this stage my parents had posted me out a GPS tracking device, but after a few false alarms and the hassle of having to keep it charged I turned it off and left it in the bottom of the panniers. After all, the idea of a trip like this is to go off-radar for a while, not be permanently on it.

Finding places to stay was always tricky on this leg of the journey, this being a road less travelled. The hotels were always for locals, in small towns, with no one who spoke English. It was always dark, and often raining, when I arrived. The owner would sign me into their huge ledger, taking my passport and visa details and entering them neatly into this giant tome of data.

I'd then be shown to a grotty room, where often all night I could hear people coming and going, doors banging, men and women too. I think most of those places were really brothels. One place wouldn't have me because I was foreign; another asked if I wanted a lady sent to my room. 'No thanks,' I said, 'I'll take care of myself tonight.'

That's why I was glad when finally, after more than two months on the road, I felt confident enough to use my tent. Of course there are no campsites in Indonesia, and barely anywhere to put one up because there are so many homes built single-file along the roadside, but one evening, feeling brave, I found a dirt track that ran out of sight to an abandoned rain shelter in the corner of a field. When no one was looking I darted down the track and lay Dorothy on her side beneath the shelter and covered her with branches.

I sat listening to the traffic passing by on the road. The sun was setting over the fields. I didn't have any food, or stove, or torch, or pillow, or even a roll mat having thrown the original one away all the way back in Darwin. All I had was a bottle of water and a bag of chewy sweets. And then the storm came.

With the rain thrashing down and the lightning tearing through the sky I crawled into my tent, used my jumper as a pillow and gripped the knife. I had no internet, no telephone. No one in the world knew where we were, just me and the bike, beneath a canopy, in a remote Indonesian field watching the sky illuminate overhead.

More rain fell, the smell so sweet I wish I could have bottled it and sprinkled it on this page. You could say I was doing this to save money, but really, deep down, I was enjoying this moment of isolation, of being shut off from the world, and my responsibility to it. Nothing could find me out here. Not even my mistakes. Instead I performed cartwheels in the rain.

To think I used to be scared of the dark. Not many weeks before setting off on this adventure, me and Mandy had gone camping to a spot just north of Sydney. It was a national park with a place to put your tent right down by the river. The car was parked a five minute walk away, down a lane with woods on either side. I had to go and get something from it late one night.

I ran the whole way there, and back again. I thought any minute now something's going to come out from the woods and get me. 'You big pussy,' she said when I got back to the tent. It was true, I was. And yet a couple of months later, here I was, camping out alone in the Indonesian woods. Perhaps I was the monster lurking in the forest now.

I didn't get much sleep that night, even after the rain had stopped. Every noise I heard I would sit up, feel for the knife and peek outside to make sure there was nobody about. I dread to think what I would have done if there had been a face or a shadow. Near damn shit myself I suspect. But when I knew there was nothing but the night outside I would lie back down and drift off to sleep, waking as soon as the first rays of light scratched the tent and made my eyes dazzle.

Opening the tent zip and stepping out into the wilds of Indonesia was a great feeling. Part of that was the realisation that I carried with me everything I needed to survive. After this night I felt I could turn to the wilderness whenever I needed a bed.

For breakfast, I would stop at the little wooden shacks by the roadside for a blazingly strong coffee and whatever the lady happened to have in the pot. Sometimes these places were beside petrol stations, sometimes they were in lonely little villages, where at around 7am, I would see a family sitting down to breakfast and having stopped I would be invited in to join them.

After the food I would fetch my Lonely Planet guide from the aluminium box, showing the faces that gathered around where I had been and where I was going. These were my favourite days, not seeing a fellow tourist or westerner for a week or more, just me, Indonesia, and its people, some of whom helped fixed my punctures for free, others who just simply made a fuss, and raised my spirits when they were low. It was a tough yet rewarding slog through their country.

Riding at such a pace, doing fourteen hours a day, not stopping to see the tourist sights, just trying to make a deadline, there's a worry that you won't actually see or experience anything of the countries that you pass through. But I was so focused, so alert, that I don't think I missed a thing. And I did make time for interactions when I thought it worthwhile.

In one village, while eating lunch at a small stall, I was approached by a young student who asked if I could give a talk at his school, which was just around the corner. Warily I agreed, going on to spend the next three hours speaking to various classes and having lunch with the headmistress, who told me I was the first passing foreigner to have ever accepted an invitation. It was perhaps for this reason that I was mugged like David Beckham, by the girls in white veils, who took my photo and giggled, even if I did, or because I did, look and smell like shit.

It was also around this time that I began to names some of Dorothy's ancillary components, even some of the gear I wore. I did this to pass the time, perhaps to counter those moments of loneliness that crept up on me from time to time.

The aluminium box on the back was named Phil, the orange pannier sacks either side were called the Cheeky Girls, while the extra petrol tank was named Linford Christie, and my tent Mr T.

To my gloves I gave the names Phil and Grant, the Mitchell Brothers, while my helmet was named Dave, as everyone's got a mate called Dave. The two water bottles were Simon and Garfunkel, whilst the bike lock Joe gave me back in Caboolture was named Esther Rantzen, as I figured no one would mess with that. Clearly the road does something to your mind after a while.

Of course, at times I wished that Dot could go a little bit faster, but once you've accepted that 65kmh (40-45mph) is as fast as she's happy to cruise at, it's just a matter of doing the hours, which at those speeds just never seems to tire you out.

Given stops for fuel and food, I would work on an average of covering fifty kilometres an hour, so if I knew that day's ride was 400 kilometres, I would guess at it taking me around eight hours.

I would break the distance down into chunks, aiming for the next town, and then the one after that, doing it all day, until suddenly, what do you know, you've ridden the whole length of an island!

That was certainly the case with Java (crossed in five days), and Sumatra (crossed in seven), where at the first petrol pump on that latter island I emerged from the restroom only to find a dozen bikers, dressed in black leathers, circled around my bike.

I didn't know who they were or what they wanted, but approached as calm as I could, greeting them politely. Up close they were far less intimidating; a mixture of guys and girls, of university age, curious to know more about my presence here.

It turned out that they were a bike gang, travelling from Jakarta to attend a motorcycle rally in a nearby Sumatran town. They called themselves the BigZoners, their motto, 'Keep Brotherhood Til Die.'

They made a fuss of me and Dorothy, inviting us over the road to a cafe for a coffee. I thought why not and around a little table we all gathered, a stack of helmets beside us, everyone leaning in to hear about where I'd come from and where I was heading. We ate deep-fried snacks and drank more coffee. It was now midday. I had to get going, but was asked if I wanted to ride with them to their friend's house a hundred kilometres or so away, as they were stopping there that night and meeting up with a load of other bike gangs that same evening.

I was welcome to stay with them and carry on the next morning. It felt like a tough call, as ideally I needed to make more progress that day, but I thought it can't be too often that you get to ride with an Indonesian bike gang called BigZoners. So I nodded my head and said that would be nice.

I was told to go in the middle, with five bikes in front of me and five behind. I expected them to fly fast and have me and Dot pedal hard to keep up, especially given their power advantage. But they were a bunch of dawdlers, taking it steady, with a real formality to the way the group rode.

I felt embarrassed as they fired up their sirens and forced other vehicles to pull over and let us pass, as though as I was a real-life VIP. Some of these road users were okay and smiled, others looked annoyed, one man even gave us the finger. This made me feel very conspicuous after such a long time doing my best to blend in and travel beneath the radar.

The best part was the pothole avoidance system. I'd been talked through it by Roda Dua, the self-styled leader of the gang, the idea being that at the front of the pack he would stick the relevant leg out to indicate which way he was swerving to avoid a pothole. As soon as he did that, the man behind had to do the same, and back the signal was expected to flow, like a motorised Mexican wave, until all eleven bikes were safely around the pothole.

It worked perfectly at first, the line of bikes moving like a snake between the various ruts, but then the road surface got so bad that both my feet were off the pegs trying to indicate to the man behind me which way to turn, so when I did finally hit a pothole it was my bollocks that took the impact as they slapped against the petrol tank like balls against a bat. I gave up after a while and picked my own way through.

When we arrived at their friend's house we all stripped off our helmets and riding gear and took turns to have showers from a bucket and ladle. The main room of the house was full of family photographs, coffee table, and trophies on the mantelpiece. It was home, just like any of ours might be. I don't know why this surprised me, it just did.

The owner, who's name I never caught, brought out what looked to be a short branch of a tree that he explained was passed down from generation to generation, and poisonous, though only if dropped and broken. It was something to do with a tiger that defended the house against evil. Much of it was superstition and folklore, there wasn't really a tiger, but it was interesting to see how tradition still plays a part in modern Indonesian life.

That evening I was asked to ride pillion with Roda Dua, something I wasn't keen on doing as it meant leaving Dorothy behind, but I obliged, if only to be polite, the lot of us riding into the town where thousands of other bikers had gathered. It was an incredible sight and sound; the dark streets lit up by all those headlights and the place feeling so alive.

Around midnight we were sat on stools in the corner of a park, eating noodles from a stall, glad that I'd made the decision to spend some time with my new found motorcycling friends. The only embarrassing moment was when they asked if I remembered all of their names and I had to confess that I couldn't. Names were never my strong point. Thankfully they didn't hold it against me, deciding the next morning to make me and Dorothy honorary members of the BigZoner motorcycle gang.

I was asked which membership number I would like and chose thirty-three, the number I had on my motocross bike when I was ten. This number was adhered to a metal plaque, bolted to the back of Dot. She also received a beautiful yellow bell to go on her handlebars and a whole load of stickers. I was given a jacket with the gang's logo on the back. I also received a helmet bag and a pair of waterproof trousers.

As a symbol of my appreciation, I left them with the number plate I'd removed from Doris having carried it with me all the way from Caboolture, a memento of the first 1,000 kilometres we covered together. Strangely it carried a lot of sentimental value and it was a big deal for me to leave the spirit of her behind. But I wanted them to have it all the same.

Before leaving I sat with Roda Dua on a couple of stools outside the house, sharing stories about our two countries and doing our best to compare them. He told me about crime in Indonesia and how there isn't much about. He said if a burglar is caught, he will get a beating from the community he stole from. If he, or she, is caught doing it again, then they're in big trouble, the possibility of them being beaten to death.

Same goes for anyone who commits murder, with the police often deciding not to get involved and allowing the community to deal with the perpetrator as they see fit. As a result, crime here was low, a real fear of the consequences, quite unlike what we know back home. It was strange then to hear Roda Dua express his desire for his country to be more like ours.

In many ways I couldn't blame him. He'd see our iPods and airplane tickets taking us to all these places, and from that it would be easy to conclude how life in England, and other parts of the Western world surely must be wonderful. Then he'd ask about our health system and I'd have to tell him how, 'yes, it's free,' and also about our welfare system, giving money to those not able to fend for themselves.

We talked about the gear I was carrying — the laptop, the helmet camera, the SLR camera — and he asked how much I'd paid. You could read it in his face, when I told him, that he assumed I was rich, and I guess I was, compared to him. I tried explaining that as a percentage of our wages it's not so much. Which of course made him think we all get paid like millionaires in the West.

To try and convince him that his world wasn't so bad, I told him about the level of crime in our country, not to mention the massive problem of homelessness, especially in Sydney and London, which was something he just didn't believe.

I explained that to afford these iPods and flight tickets we have to work tirelessly in offices, factories and cafés, and that, if we ever lost those jobs and couldn't swiftly find another, we would no longer be able to afford to pay the massive mortgages and debts most of us have, leaving us in big trouble because our societies and families are fragmented, unlike here in Indonesia where they still seemed very much unified. About our happiness I tried to explain that by comparison our faces are often very glum.

But I could tell that he didn't want to believe any of that. He saw England and the Western world as the model his country should aspire to. That was his dream for Indonesia. And by the sounds of things the transformation had already begun.

Credit cards were being embraced by those living in the cities. As a result, young people in particular were getting into the sorts of financial trouble anyone would if one day they were suddenly able to purchase those things that for so long had been beyond their reach. Using my credit cards to pay for much of this trip I was in no position to criticise. It just seemed sad that their aspirations to become a 'better' country were leading them up a path that might not lead to a place as good as they imagined.

I just wished he could have seen, as I saw, the ways in which we could learn things from his country. I loved that a real sense of community spirit prevailed, that people did still eat together and watch out for one another. And that they were able to welcome strangers into their homes without fear or judgement, as they had done with me. I loved how simple their lives were, how they worked for themselves, how they were self-sufficient, how they dealt with criminals. And yet, having said all that, I still wouldn't trade places and move to Indonesia, and that, maybe, was his point after all.

From there it was back to the road, riding non-stop as hard as I could in an effort to arrive at the very northern tip of Sumatra (the port town of Belawan) before the visa ran out. The roads, as I said, were terrible, non-existent in places. I even had some problems with camping.

For a second night I slept wild, beneath another abandoned shelter — this one on stilts — down a steep slope a stone's throw from the road. I had no problem riding down the slope, but it rained in the night and the next morning the ground was too muddy to get back up. It was still dark, jungle all around, and as many times as I tried I got halfway up and then either ran out of power or grip, or both, slithering back down.

Finally I gave up trying, dumped all my gear at the bottom of the slope, then dragged Dorothy to the top, inch by inch. I was knackered and covered in sweat and mud by the time we made it. I repacked all my gear and put on my helmet, but I just couldn't get her to fire into life. Clearly she was flooded from all the time she'd spent on her side.

I changed the spark plug, but that didn't work, neither did swearing. Then, from nowhere, a local gentleman on a scooter appeared. He stopped and tried to help but he couldn't get her going either. He motioned me to get on the bike and for what seemed like a mile this poor old man in sandals pushed me and Dot as hard as he could, until finally, she cleared her lungs and burst into life. This man-fairy then got back on his bike and rode off. And that was my fondest memory of Sumatra.

Chapter Eight
Strait of Malacca

The ferry from Belawan (at the tip of Sumatra) to Penang (on the west coast of Malaysia) would only take foot passengers, with no motorcycles or other vehicles allowed. It wouldn't have been so bad but I only discovered this after a man with many promises — a ticket tout — had told me otherwise and, as requested, I'd spent a good hour stripping the bike of all the panniers and draining the tank of fuel in preparation for the ferry's arrival.

I gave the fuel to the crowd of men stood around, becoming increasingly excited at the thought of finally leaving Indonesia behind. It had only been three weeks since we'd shared the ferry with the Spitting Bitch, though it had felt like a lifetime. Now I just wanted to move on to Malaysia. That's when the captain came ashore, took one look at the bike and said, 'No motorcycles.' I could see it myself; there was no way of getting her aboard.

There were no cargo boats either, none that anyone knew of. That left me standing at the docks, looking out across the water wondering where exactly I was going to go from here. The gentlemen I gave the fuel to laughed as I bolted everything back on the bike and wheeled her outside into the sunlight. 'No bensin,' they said, pointing at my empty tank and laughing because from here back to town they assumed I would have to push.

With that I turned the fuel cock to reserve, petrol gushing from the standard tank hidden beneath the seat and into the carburettor below. They'd not realised that the bike had two tanks and that I'd only drained one of them. With that Dot fired into life and the pair of us rode off, not quite as daft as we looked.

It was a short lived victory. Riding into town I felt the weight of the situation fall upon me. My Indonesian visa expired the next morning and the likelihood of being in Malaysia by then was slim. To make matters worse, the port town of Belawan was a sinister place, not one I wished to linger in.

I parked the bike in the shadows and walked along the main street. It was mid-afternoon, still very hot, still very dusty and with so many motorbikes still swarming about. Men with pedal taxis lounging in the shadows called out, 'Hey mister, where do you go, where you from?' I smiled and pointed up the road towards the internet café I'd seen on my way through. There I hoped I might find some answers online.

Searching through the pages of Horizons Unlimited, a website populated and read by people riding across the world on motorbikes, as I wasn't the only one, I found reference to a local man named Mr Monte. Someone travelling this way in the past claimed he'd hired this man to take his motorcycle across the same stretch of water on a cargo boat.

This was as good a lead as any, paying the owner of the internet café — a friendly woman with a teenage daughter who was offered to me as a wife. As beautiful as the daughter was, I needed a boat, not a bride, so politely declined and rode back towards the docks, determined to find this mysterious man named Mr Monte.

As I rode along I tried to muster some courage, having developed a trick for doing this; bracing my arms against the handlebars and screaming through gritted teeth; 'COME ON! COME ON!' Over and over again, until I was full of adrenaline and rage.

I barged back into the nest of vultures who I'd given my petrol to earlier, asking, no, demanding, to know if they'd heard of this Mr Monte. I was met by a wall of blank expressions. It was as though this man had never even existed, which left me feeling more desolate than before. I felt so brittle, so broken. But I had no choice but to hold it together, because breaking just wasn't an option right now.

Finally, one of the men took pity on me, suggesting that I go and see the harbour-master on the top floor of the main ferry terminal building. I found this man — elderly, with white hair — in a long open room, the late afternoon light flooding through the open windows, the view beyond of the ocean I was so desperate to cross.

The harbour-master was a kind and patient man, having me explain my predicament, something I did by repeating the word Honda, revving my right fist as though it was an imaginary throttle, before moving my other hand like a fish and pointing in the direction of Malaysia. He grasped my issue in an instant, clearly able to sense my desperation, and so having poured me a tea, led me down to another office where he introduced me to three men: one young, one old, one fat.

The three men were pleasant, suggesting I take a nap on the bench while they talked amongst themselves. I was incredibly tired but couldn't sleep, staying awake as the harbour-master came and went. It was as though the cogs of an almighty wheel were slowly beginning to turn.

I sat wondering what would happen next, before all of a sudden the door burst open and through it pushed Forest Whitaker from *The Last King of Scotland* — at least that's who he looked like.

You could sense he was the boss immediately; stout and full of menace. He shook my hand — stiff and firm — and once more I did my fish to Malaysia gesture and he demanded I follow him outside to where his moped was parked beside mine. 'Follow me,' he said, speaking a little English.

We set off across the docks; a labyrinth of huge warehouses joined by a network of lanes and alleys that the pair of us were now hammering along, the masts of ships towering high above. This being a Saturday there was no one else around; no vehicles, no people, nothing in this huge sprawling dockland, other than me, riding Dot, following a moped ridden by the Last King of Scotland, the sun still baking hot.

Finally, he turned up a ramp and onto a platform, disappearing through an open door that led into a huge empty warehouse in which we stopped and got off our bikes.

We climbed a set of stairs into a glass fronted office overlooking the warehouse floor, our bikes parked below. The Last King of Scotland turned and stared me straight in the eyes.

'I take motorcycle to Malaysia for one million rupiah,' he said with little room for negotiation. I calculated that to be almost sixty English pounds, over a hundred Australian dollars, which out here was a huge sum of money. Clearly he'd sensed my desperation and priced accordingly.

'When?' I asked.

'You leave motorcycle here and it will go to Penang in three days.'

He said I should get the passenger ferry, sailing the same day as the bike, and meet it there. I nodded my head and gave him the cash. It was all the money I had. But I had no other choice but to accept his offer, though I didn't have a great feeling about any of it.

I asked for a receipt. 'Not necessary,' he said, and that was that. I took all my electrical gear and a change of clothes from Dot's panniers and stuffed them into a rucksack and left everything else I owned in the lockable aluminium box on the back of the bike. I gave her one last glance as we rode away, me on the back of Forest Whitaker's bike, frightful I might never her see again. He dropped me off in the centre of town and went on his way. Trust, you've just got to trust.

There was nowhere really for me to stay in Belawan, apart from a seedy motel near the docks, leaving me to catch a minibus into Medan, the capital of Sumatra, only an hour's ride away.

In the three days I was there I managed to be tricked into buying dinner for a group of local students who befriended me. We all went for dinner one evening and at the end they handed me the bill, as though that had been the ruse all along. I was apocalyptic with rage and made them pay half. I didn't like being taken for a ride, especially as until that point they had seemed like genuine friends, and out on the road, alone, such things are to be cherished.

Finally, I caught the four hour express ferry to Malaysia, paying the fine for overstaying my visa by three days (US$60), and hoping Dorothy would be waiting for me at the other end.

It was a nervous taxi ride, dashing down to the docks the second I arrived, only to be told the good news, that my bike had arrived. But there was bad news as well, for she was being held hostage, and that to get her back would mean paying the same fee again to the agent on this side of the Strait of Malacca, a word, which, coincidently, is the Greek word for wanker.

I paid this Mr Lim another one million rupiah, being told that I shouldn't have paid a thing at the Indonesian end. That made me a little bitter, as well as temporarily mad, but it didn't matter, as we'd just ridden what turned out to be 6,000 kilometres across Indonesia, in three weeks, catching ferries, hitting buses, falling off several times, eating intestine. And now we were in Malaysia.

Good progress.

Chapter Nine
Malaysia

Arriving in Malaysia was the moment at which the wheels could finally come to a stop. There was nowhere for us to be, no visa to rush for, no urgency to be anywhere. And for two months and 11,000 kilometres I'd not experienced that before.

During that time there'd always been something, whether it was getting up and riding every day, or waiting for Dot's boat to arrive, or even just the unease I'd felt in East Timor; there'd always been something to do or focus on. Now there was nothing; this fourth country of Malaysia sprawled out in front of us and I could go off in any direction I wanted, at whatever pace I pleased.

And that was strangely daunting. Because now I had options, and with options come decisions, and with decisions come indecision. So I wasn't exactly sure what I was going to do. I could have ridden down to Kuala Lumpar, or even carried on to Singapore. I could have visited the tropical islands off the northern coastline of Malaysia. Or I could have skipped Malaysia completely, riding straight into Thailand to make progress on our long journey to England.

Admittedly, having to choose between those options wasn't such a bad position to be in, but it did make me wish for another deadline and another place we had to be, because then the decision would have been made for me.

While trying to make up my mind, I spent a few days recuperating in Penang, an island half a mile from the coast and connected by either bridge or car ferry. It was in Penang that the ferry from Indonesia had docked, not realising at the time the island's popularity as a package holiday destination, with a pearl of purpose built resorts strung along its shoreline. Of course, I wouldn't be staying in any of these. Instead, I found a cheap guesthouse in the main town (George Town) on the southern end of the island.

This was also the island's commercial centre, an eerily lit weave of strong stone buildings, a remnant of the country's British colonial past, though now with signs to China Town and Little India, as these were the outside influences now.

Many of the backpackers to Malaysia visited the island. In fact, it was the most amount of foreign travellers I'd seen in one place since leaving Darwin, now just over six weeks ago.

I didn't feel like a backpacker though, I felt like someone who'd just crawled out of a hedge-bottom, and was now stumbling to my feet with twigs in my hair. Watching the new arrivals shuffle nervously about in the street made me realise just how much I'd acclimatised and adapted to my surroundings. After all, I'd been like that myself, probably worse, back in East Timor, cowering with my head in my hands at the airport the day I arrived. Now I walked with a weary knowledge of the world and an acceptance of its nature to scare and to thrill.

It was a nice feeling in that sense. I felt like I could just stand with my two feet on the spot and survey the world around me rather than cower from it as I'd previously done. It had been a steep learning curve coming through Indonesia and, while at times I hated the place and the hurdles it posed for me, I was now grateful for the test it had set. It had made me stronger and educated me in the rules of travel, and survival and fending for myself.

Most of all it had taught me to live with uncertainty and to no longer fear it or worry about the things you can't have a hand in shaping. I think in a way that's the only skill, if you want to call it that, that you need for a journey such as this — just a willingness to live an uncertain existence.

I just wish I'd taken more photographs of the places I was passing through. It's not that I was afraid of my camera being stolen, more that I just never felt comfortable taking it out and aiming it at the people I was passing. I know some would ask you to take their photograph, but for the most part I couldn't help but wonder if the camera gets in the way, almost acting as a barrier to your interaction with the world around you, because you're seeing everything through a lens, and not face to face.

The images I did take I was now uploading to Facebook and to the website my brother Jason had set up. With patchy internet connection through Timor and Indonesia I couldn't do this very often, nor could I send many group emails which I always liked to do as it was a distraction from the riding. Most of the time I'd try and make the emails light-hearted, poking fun at my situation, even during the tricky times. Sometimes I'd fail in doing that and send one explaining how I really felt, like when I was in Flores with a tear in the hotel room.

I'd sent an email that night saying how things weren't great and how I was having a hard time and I'd had a few responses saying, 'Cheer up, look where you are, stop moaning.' And that really was annoying, as I thought, 'What do you want me to do; lie and pretend everything's perfect?'

In that sense, I became increasingly aware of a strange dynamic to my personality. I realised just how much of it was an act back in the real world. Sometimes pretending to be someone you're not. Out here on a motorbike, meeting strangers who don't speak your language there's no need for any of that, so I was allowed to act much more naturally.

If I wished to be grumpy and solemn then I could be. If I wanted to be loud and excited I could be that as well. But then when you go to write an email you think, 'Well should I write it as 'me' on the trip or 'me' outside of the trip?' Sometimes, for people back home, it must have been like getting an email off a complete stranger.

They wanted to hear from the person they knew, or thought they knew. After figuring this out I'd always pretend and enjoy the rest of the time free to be whoever I liked.

Had this been me in isolation, things might have been plain sailing right about now. But it wasn't just me, it was me and Mandy, still trying to maintain something, trying to keep the pair of us together throughout all this, or at least not come to the point of silence.

And there is no doubt that it is the person who is left behind that suffers most in a situation like this. They are the ones with the routine and the time to sit on the porch drinking their wine just wondering if a motorbike is going to come around that corner having decided to turn back. They are the ones who feel the distance growing bigger, who feel the silence of the empty inbox that goes on for days and days, who wonder why you haven't called, who wonder where you are, and what you're doing as you're camped out in the Indonesian wild.

Thankfully, our concerns of never seeing each other again were unwarranted, as it had been decided that in Bangkok we should meet up, Mandy flying out for a visit, spending a week with me and Dorothy and, I don't know, doing whatever it is that two people do. We still didn't know how this would end, whether the two of us as a couple would ever work out — still two peas from very different pods — and yet still so addicted, so unable to leave the other one alone.

Perhaps it was about time we went our separate ways and moved on. But the heart isn't so easy to over rule as that. And if it insists that you should pine for one another, then no sense of sensibility will ever be able to overcome that. For whatever reason, for whatever purpose, we had stuck up an incredible bond that night at speed-dating, and already it had changed both our lives forever. Now I was just really looking forward to showing her my world. And sharing it.

My main problem in the meantime would be money. By now my mum had emailed in great panic over the state of my finances after she'd been brave enough to open one of my bank statements. In her words, 'It was time to come home.' That was perhaps her general worry as much as anything else, and I knew I couldn't do that, not now, not having come this far and having placed so much importance on the completion of this thing.

All I could do was extend my overdraft and make a call to the bank to up the limit on my credit card. I also had a great friend from university called Paul Taylor, who right from the start had offered to lend me some cash if I ever fell short. I emailed him from Malaysia and asked if I could borrow a bit to tide me over until the money came through. Self-sufficiency went out the window; I now had a back-up crew. Though in a way I always had; I'd just never realised it.

At the beginning, as I crossed the Harbour Bridge, I claimed that my destiny was in my own two hands, but over time I'd accepted that it wasn't, not entirely anyway. Instead, it was in the hands of the many people who had already helped me along the way. The men who had fixed the road in Australia, the captains of the ferries who took me from one Indonesian island to another, the man who drove me to Darwin airport at 5am to catch my plane. They are the cogs that make all this happen.

Now I had Paul to thank, a friend who'd worked solidly ever since leaving university to put some money together so that he was able to lend a hand when one of his friends set off across the world on a motorbike without enough money. And for that I shall be forever grateful. Just as I was to the mechanic I found in Penang who gave Dorothy a tune up for free.

It was the baker next door to the guesthouse who had directed me to him, drawing a map and warning me that this man was very selective about the bikes that he worked on. He might help me out, but then again, he might not.

Navigating the town's back alleys, I pulled up outside his workshop, stacked floor to ceiling with motorcycle parts. The mechanic, a white haired man in his sixties — a mechanical Mr Miyagi — took one look at Dot and was immediately smitten.

He'd never seen such a thing. 'From Australia?' He gasped, recognising the engine and some of the other components fitted to the bikes he fixed in Malaysia. Of course he would work on her, and in no time at all he'd set the valve clearance and cleaned the carburettor and sent me down the road for a test ride. She felt brand new again, the postie bike that had just brought me 11,000 kilometres from Caboolture. What an incredible bike so far she had been.

Now the pair of us was itching to get back on the road, any road, wherever it might take us. We joined the highway out of Penang, a modern thing with multiple lanes and a surface more smooth than any we'd encountered for a long time. This was better, hugging the hard shoulder and being able to saunter along, looking at sign posts, trying to figure out which way we were going to go because I'd still not decided.

It was just one of those days when you make it up as you go along. I saw a sign for Kuala Lumpar and for a moment I thought about that until I realised I didn't want another city, as nice as I'd heard this one to be. I wished for a bit of peace and quiet instead, somewhere to put my feet up and grab some fresh air before pushing on to Thailand.

Thankfully I'd heard of just the place; an area of Malaysia just north of Penang called the Cameron Highlands. It was here that the nation's tea was grown, vast fields of it, high up in the hills where the air would be cooler and the pace of life much more relaxed. Having spotted the sign for the town I headed in that direction, pausing briefly at the McDonald's at the bottom of the hill for a burger, tasting so good after my diet of intestines and other such things the past few months.

Then it was up, up and away, climbing out of the flat lowlands and following the road as it twisted like a snake around the mountain, the air becoming crisper and cleaner with every turn, fields of tea flashing by on either side, tourist coaches overtaking me on the race to the top.

The main town of Tanah Rata consisted of one long main street, threading a path through a deep green valley, with walks to the waterfalls that tumbled all around. It reminded me of an alpine village, except there were no ski slopes or any snow, just the atmosphere associated with it; very relaxed, very touristy, and with a Starbucks of all things, where a cup of coffee was the same price as a night in a dormitory bed in the Kang Travellers Lodge on the outskirts of town.

It was a ramshackle place, down a littered lane, a graffitied wall outside and steps up to the main floor where I found people from all over the world lounging around. There were even some travellers from Iran, who gave me their address and told me to drop by on my way through (was I really going through Iran on a motorbike?).

On an evening a group of us would huddle around a roaring fire in the yard behind the hostel, not drinking beer because it just wouldn't have suited the mood. Instead we bought boxes of flavoured tea and sat sipping that instead. If we were feeling especially extravagant we would buy a bunch of bananas and a bar of chocolate from the shops down in the town and cook them up in some tin foil and eat it as a pudding, chatting our way though to 4am until finally we all walked like zombies to the dorm and got up the next morning to do it all again. Often we would watch a movie, something appropriate like *Into The Wild*, hoping on a better ending to our adventures.

It was during this time that I realised just how much I enjoyed meeting people on the road. It's almost as though the awkwardness of the introductory process is completely removed, because you might only have that one conversation and never see each other again. It allows you to be totally frank and honest with each other — no searching for thoughts or what you think is the right word; you just say what's on the tip of your tongue. You seem to find out so much more about each other that way as well. Equally, if you want to sit in silence in the corner and get drunk on the vapours of your mind, then you could do that as well.

Finally, after a week in the Cameron Highlands, I woke one morning to find everyone in the hostel had vanished. All of the people I'd been hanging out with had suddenly disappeared, whisked away on the tourist conveyor belt that looped around this country and many more wherever the tourists roam. That left the hostel very quiet and empty, a shell of the place it had been before; a reminder that mood is often a consequence of circumstance, not location. I made a mental note to make sure that I was never the last person to leave a place again.

As I loaded Dorothy with all my gear I thought about going on a mad dash around Laos, Cambodia and Vietnam, but deep down I didn't have the heart or the energy for it; I didn't have the money either. And in all seriousness, I didn't think it wise to go off gallivanting down side roads when Dot still had 20,000 kilometres or more left to go.

I certainly didn't want her breaking down a distance from England equal to the length of the detour I made just so I could check out a temple, or even look around Singapore. My gut was telling me to move the trip forward, get to the next country where in a few weeks' time Mandy's aeroplane would be landing. With that decision made, I kicked Dot into life and headed for the border.

Chapter Ten
Malay-Thai Border

The mountain road was much faster on the way down, tea fields flashing by either side, and even on the skinny tyres, bought in Indonesia for less than five dollars, Dot handled the corners with confidence, rolling from left to right and happy to lean as far as I dared push her, which wasn't very far to be fair, but it was just a nice place to be riding, dipping down through the clouds and staring out to the green earth below.

The temperature warmed the closer we dropped to sea level, and off came the clothes, back to the shorts and shirt, sleeves rolled up to the elbow. I should be grateful that I never crashed dressed like this as I would have been skinned alive.

The intention now was to cross the Thai border that afternoon and cover a couple of hundred kilometres on the other side before nightfall. It was wishful thinking, as not long after joining the smooth highway I felt the rear end skew about and the wheel make direct contact with the ground. I ducked off the highway and down the slip road of a motorway service station, coming to a stop in the carpark at the bottom.

Ahead of me was a petrol station. Above was the shade of a tree, to my left a line of food stalls and some seats where people sat watching as I jumped off, swearing in frustration, turning the air blue before lifting the back end of my motorcycle up on a brick and getting out the tools.

I'd had enough punctures by now to know the procedure, though still found the whole process an ordeal. Take off the axle bolt and two rear brake caliper nuts, knock out the axle with a hammer, lean the bike on her side to allow the wheel to fall out and from there it's just a case of fixing the inner tube, or replacing it with a new one, then putting it all back together again and inflating the tyre.

A passing group of smartly dressed business men stopped to help, and in no time at all we stood like proud parents as Dot rested on her mended wheel. We took photos, shook hands, waved goodbye, only for me to turn around, ready to ride again, and find the tyre had once more gone flat. Then the rain came, and you could just tell it was going to be one of those days.

Back on the road I'd never seen it rain so heavy, not even in the Outback during the 'wet' season. Every time a lorry overtook it would cause a bow wave that would come rolling towards us with such force that I would be sodden — my eyes and face so full of water — and the bike would judder to suggest she wasn't coping with the bombardment so well either.

I threatened to pull off the road a couple of times and find a place to put up the tent, but there were too many people and houses about. Gone were the little lanes to views over rolling hills. The world around here was flat and mostly agricultural; sometimes industrial, too. At least the water was warm and the waterproof jacket and trousers the BigZoners had set me up with were doing decent jobs of keeping much of the rain out, even if the Converse boots and gloves — now mismatched having lost an opposing pair — were not.

I made it to the border. It was now almost nightfall and the rain eventually slowing to a trickle. As Thailand doesn't recognise the Carnet de Passage, foreigners travelling to the country with their own motorised vehicle are instead issued with a temporary import slip, covering them for thirty days.

At the bottom of this form, in small print, just below the signature, it reads that if you aren't out of the country within that period, then you'd be issued with a fine of 420,000 Thai baht. This was the equivalent of $15,000 Australian dollars, and given that I would need to be in the country a little longer than thirty days, I was relieved to hear that you could have it extended at any of the border stations around the country.

As for a place to stay that night, the border guard advised me to sleep in Hat Yai, the first major town I'd come to, an hour's ride or so away. This would be interesting, as the city, and in fact the whole southern region of Thailand, has a travel warning against it due to the sporadic fighting that takes place there.

I later found out that it's a secret war, waged by Muslims in the region who claim to have had land taken from them by the Thai government. Almost a hundred civilians had been killed in bomb blasts over the past few years, with several detonating in Hat Yai alone. Given the unrest in East Timor, I wasn't as fazed by this as I might have been, figuring that if I kept my head down then things would be fine.

What alarmed me most was that on the road leading into the city there must have been a hundred bars, all decorated brightly with neon lights, and the trend, as far as I could see it, was to have a throng of scantily clad girls gyrating around outside, trying to lure people in, for sin of course.

I'd heard Thailand could be that way inclined, but this was more vivid than I'd expected, being told later out how this road in particular was popular with Malaysian businessmen, popping over the border on 'business' trips, though there weren't so many out this night. The bars looked empty and the girls looked bored.

What they must have thought as I passed by, seeing a white faced man with a growing beard on a little red bike, heading towards Hat Yai at midnight, being met by patrolling armoured vehicles, coming the other way.

Having reached Hat Yai and eaten street food in a busy part of the city, I went and found the only hostel in the vicinity. It was down a side street, up a flight of stairs with a scowling attendant who reluctantly showed me one of the rooms.

It was off a dark creepy corridor, much like those in an American high school horror movie, and while I'd slept in far worse places I just didn't want to that night. 'No thank you,' I said, as I walked back down the stairs, through the door and out into the empty moonlit street.

There was no traffic about, only the sound of silence. Had I been a smoker I would have lit one now, taking a drag as some cool blues music played inside my head. An old newspaper would have tumbled across the street, a distant dog would have barked, steam would have risen from a vent in the wet empty black road. I didn't need to sleep, I needed to ride, through the night. 'Phuket Dorothy, that's where we'll head.'

I rode back through the town and out along one of the main streets, stopping at a local convenience store, which must surely have been the only one for miles around to be owned by a middle-aged Englishman from Yorkshire. He had a Thai wife and had lived here for many years.

I couldn't quite believe it at first; it just seemed so random. It was late night in Thailand, in a city deep in the country's south, and I was in a convenience store owned by a man who once lived in the same county as my parents, who was able to draw me a map of the area because I didn't have one, who served me coffee and engaged me in interesting conversation.

Weighing all that up, I deemed him one of Denise's fairies and quite possibly a figment of my imagination, because he couldn't possible have been real, could he? I carried on my way, the fairy's map strapped to my petrol tank for guidance.

Out on the open road, well shut of the city, I squinted to see in Dot's dim headlight. Our route was north-west, passing through the cities of Phatthalung, Trang and Huai Yot, on our way to Phuket. I guessed it to be a distance of four hundred kilometers, the plan to get there in time for breakfast.

At times like these, if the tank didn't run dry, if I didn't get hungry or need to take a pee, I think I could have ridden forever and ever, because it was just such a great sensation; that feeling of getting somewhere, of covering ground, especially at night with no one else around. It felt like I had the whole world to myself, as though I was seeing all the things everyone else was missing while they were tucked up in bed.

There's a golden rule of adventure motorcycling that says not to ride at night because of the danger. But what about the beauty and the magic that comes alive at the witching hour? I'll accept any risk for a little taste of that.

The only problem of course is tiredness. By 2am I could feel myself drifting off, my chin hitting my chest until I snapped back to life and returned to my side of the road. Eventually, I had to accept the danger in this and began looking for a decent spot by the side of the road on which to pitch my tent.

The best I could do was a bus shelter in the middle of nowhere, riding Dot inside it and laying the wicker mat I'd bought back on the ferry from Timor to Flores (the one with the Spitting Bitch) across the bench.

I set my alarm to go off forty-five minutes later and was surprised when it seemed to wake me five seconds later, finding it quite disorientating to wake up on a bench in a bus stop in the middle of southern Thailand, not able to see a thing in the thick black night.

I rode until I felt tired again, sleeping in another bus stop, waking up to the sight of the rising sun and the world around me, beginning to stretch and yawn as a new day was begun.

I'd never thought much about my passage through Thailand, I'd certainly never felt the need to visit the place in the past and thus far it had been just another name on the map. But already I could feel myself beginning to like its vibe. It was more modern and orderly than Indonesia, the people perhaps more relaxed, yet at the same time it wasn't quite so stilted and orderly as I'd found Malaysia to be. I could sense I was going to enjoy my time in Thailand immensely.

Clearly however I was never going to make it to Phuket, not this morning, not in this state. Instead I settled for a town called Krabi, pulling into its waterfront streets after almost twenty-four hours on the road. I was completely knackered and looked quite disgusting. Worse of all, in that moment I realised that I should have purchased mandatory third-party insurance for riding in Thailand back at the border with Malaysia, now a fourteen hour round-trip back in the direction from which I came.

Having asked around I realised there was nothing else for it but to ride back and get it, which I did reluctantly, the very next day.

Times like these I really wish I'd done a bit more planning.

Chapter Eleven
Thailand

Looking back, that night on the road from Malaysia to Thailand was one of the highlights of this whole adventure. I may have had punctures and needed to grab a little sleep in some pretty odd places along the way, but to be on the road at midnight in a strange land was simply magical. Alone in the world, just a headlight piercing through the inky darkness, no real clue as to where we were going, just riding, covering the miles and doing the distance in the same way we'd been doing all the way from Sydney, setting ourselves targets and clinging to the hope that if we keep on riding then sooner or later we'll get there.

In that sense it's not that different to how we live back home, telling ourselves if only we can make it to Christmas or to the end of term, or to pay day, then everything's going to be alright. Short term goals; that's what was getting me across the world.

As for Krabi — that first place I stopped at in Thailand — it was in a beautiful spot, right where the river joined the Andaman Sea. *The Beach* and *The Man with the Golden Gun* were filmed just a short boat ride away. Even if I hadn't known that, I still might have guessed it given those familiar-looking tower blocks of stone that grew from the earth and up from the ocean floor.

At times, when they were lit in silhouette, the cliffs and rock stacks gave the impression of a city skyline. Were it not for these structures the world around would have been completely flat. There were no hills or even any tall trees, just clusters of jungle, sitting below a sky of vivid blue.

What I also liked about Krabi was the way in which it was a town for Thai people that just so happened to have facilities for foreigners, and not the other way around. At night an ocean of food stalls were set up on the banks of the river, the whole world, or so it seemed, sitting down on little red stools to eat cheap Thai food, like pad thai noodles, fresh and fragrant, cooked in big woks by women with chubby faces and even broader smiles.

The air hung heavy with the most incredibly smell, the air crackling with the soul of so many people sat down by the river on a warm sunset evening, eating delicious food for a dollar and ordering another bowl if you fancied one.

The hostel I stayed in was on the road along the waterfront. It was only a small place, in the same row of buildings as the travellers' bookshops and cafés and other guesthouses. The wooden-walled room cost a couple of dollars a night. There were no windows, only a single bare light bulb swinging above an old spring bed. It was more like a shed. But I hardly spent any time in there, preferring to go for a stroll around the bustling market in the centre of town, or walk along the waterfront saying, 'No thank you,' to the men trying to get me to book a boat ride.

Of an evening, the owner of the guesthouse — a large, scary looking woman who one day knocked Dot over and was nice to me after that — would allow me to wheel her inside the small restaurant, clearing the tables and chairs to make room for my motorbike, so she would be safe at night.

Keith was staying at the guesthouse too. He was ex-military and in his fifties, telling some incredible stories about his army days and more recently those he'd spent on the road.

I asked him if he ever considered moving home to England and settling down, to which he said he didn't have a home. I felt sorry for him in a way; I guess everyone needs a home, even if sometimes we're not always entirely sure where it is (where you were born, where you feel you belong, where your heart is?).

Keith spent his time going backwards and forwards between India,

Nepal and Indonesia; living off his pension, telling stories to strangers like me and Will, an eighteen-year-old English lad who wasn't sure if he was enjoying his first experience of backpacking or not.

He'd considered going home early, which I think is a natural urge your first time away from home. I know I'd been the same when I'd done a skiing season in France at the age of eighteen (the time I'd broken my leg). The sense that with so much at home, why would you possibly want to be out here alone?

It was a tough time then for Will. I felt for him; perhaps he came for answers, and like the rest of us only found more questions. To cheer him up, the pair of us relented and went off on a boat cruise; five islands in a day, offering us the opportunity to masquerade as proper tourists for a change: snorkelling, eating packed lunches, that sort of thing. The boat was especially cool — narrow and wooden, with seats facing each other and a flapping red canopy overhead.

The captain stood at the back, operating what looked to be an old diesel engine from a lorry with a propeller mounted on a long drive shaft. It was smelly and noisy, quite in contrast to the stunning water world through which we were cruising, those pillars of rock casting shadows all around.

I'm not sure any of us found our '*Beach*' that day. Whether we were looking for it in the right place I'm not so certain. After all this time on the road, something told me it's not a place made of sand, but instead only exists as a place inside your head.

The next day I reunited with Dot and rode out to the nearby Tiger Temple. I'd been told that if you had the patience, and the sweat, to climb exactly 1,237 steps, then you would be rewarded with the same vantage point as the three-storey high statue of Buddha that had been built at the summit.

I climbed, taking an age and having to use my hands to haul myself up as monkeys slid down the handrail like kids down a banister. The steps were steep, chiselled roughly into the rock and giving way to sheer drops. After an hour or so I made it; podgy, unfit, beetroot red, like Rocky shadow boxing at the top of those Philadelphia steps.

I stood and looked out at the sea and the land now so very far below. Such a great view from up there, the place so calm and peaceful, no one else about but a groundkeeper sweeping the dust from the tiled floor that surrounded Buddha's feet. The summit of this pillar of stone was a great place to stand and think, first about jumping off (in the weird way that high places always make you do), and then about what it must have taken to have built such a thing. I suspect it starts with people brave enough to climb it, strong enough to carry the rock to the top of it; skilled enough to build on it. Then you need people persistent enough to finish it, devoted enough to climb it for daily prayer, and also tolerant enough to let people of different faiths visit it for free.

I watched a plane flying overhead. Maybe it was the altitude making me mental, but I stood there thinking, 'We did that… humans.' Conceived, designed and built a flying metal tube that shuts the door on one world, hurtles down a runway, takes off, defies gravity, serves you a meal, shows you a movie, brings you beer and some nuts, then nine hours later or whatever it is, lands without exploding in a totally different part of the world where everything you know has been turned on its head.

The same device then scoops up a load of people wanting to go the other way and gives them the same sensation, only in reverse. Riding that sort of distance on a motorbike sure did make me appreciate how cool that is.

A few days later I arrived in Bangkok, just as that year's political protests were erupting. A news bulletin told of policemen killed, bullets fired, vehicles set ablaze. Kevin Rudd, the man who'd signed my helmet back in Sydney, had cancelled his trip to the city and advised everyone else to do the same. He said it wasn't safe, something me and three German backpackers gave much thought to as we sat just down the road from the protesters, drinking a beer on the pavement outside the guesthouse we were all staying at.

We couldn't believe he was talking about the same city, one that we were able to walk through and enjoy without any hassle, the protesters in their hundreds of thousands, but causing no bother, to us at least. In fact, just around the corner from the protest, celebrations for Thai New

Year — Songkran — were being held. And of course you saw no pictures of that on TV.

It was fascinating to see for myself just how much the media twists things, in order to create a sense of drama and keep people fixated perhaps. If anything, this gave me hope for the road ahead. Pakistan was now looming ever closer on the horizon. Every time I turned on the television another bomb had gone off and more people had fallen to the turmoil there. The newsreaders told me the Taliban were surging, that their 'army' might take over Islamabad within a few weeks.

To think I was intending to ride through there on a postie bike was a little harrowing, but I had great hope that the reality would be the same as the one I'd experienced in Bangkok; that I would get there and find that the media had exaggerated the situation and that people there were no different to the people I'd encountered elsewhere on my travels, and that, if I kept my head down, I would have no trouble at all quietly passing through. Beyond Thailand, beyond India, I guess I would find out for myself.

For now though, I was really growing to like Bangkok. I may sound naive, but I expected it to be an ugly, polluted city, made up of shanty towns and quite primitive, flooded with women on their backs firing ping pong balls for men to catch. But it wasn't like that at all. The main centre was full of huge glass-towered shopping malls with names of all the Western stores we might recognise. I saw expensive German cars and even a Lamborghini.

Not being an economist I couldn't quite figure out how, with such a weak currency, they could afford to build and buy such things given some of it would have to be imported. The traffic fines surely must have helped — the police stopped and fined me and Dorothy twice, for various things, but mainly because we were riding like a pair of maniacs.

The city's backpacker scene was largely confined to just one road, Khao San, closed off to traffic and chocked full of stalls selling cheap t-shirts, jewellery and counterfeit CDs. You had to be careful walking along it. Sellers would ask if you wanted to buy something or go in a bar and you'd say, 'No, next time,' and carry on walking. When you walked back later that day they would have remembered your face and say, 'So you come in now?' And you'd have to make up some other excuse.

At either end, men would stand beside their tuk-tuks making popping noises to suggest they could take you to one of those ping pong shows, or to any place you wanted to go, as long as you didn't mind stopping at a dozen tailors and jewellery stores along the way, the drivers making their money through commission on anything you might buy from those shops.

This is why I stayed in a guesthouse a twenty-minute walk away from Khao San, in an area called Thewet, along the river, out where families — and the rioters — lived.

It was a great place to see typical Thai life. The guesthouse fronted on to a square with a market in the middle and houses and shops around the edge. Next door was a tiny alcohol merchant's with men sitting outside on wooden crates playing draughts and chequers and sinking beers, while across the road an old woman with a hunched back lived amongst the garbage she collected and recycled for money.

At night a van would pull up across the road. A white haired man, notoriously drunk, would cook up the best noodle soup from a pan mounted on the back of this vehicle. He'd bring it over in a bowl to the blue plastic seat you were sitting on in the middle of the pavement as the sky fell black and the tree-lined street grew largely still.

The neon flash of a tuk-tuk would scream past, a pink taxi perhaps, boys on scooters, for sure. I was no longer seeing such places from behind the visor of a speeding helmet; I was now within that world, breathing its fragrant air, eating its food, meeting its people. This was an element of the trip that I'd not anticipated when I'd set off, but I adored it now because I got to see the soul of a city, and not just its sights. I stopped feeling like a traveller, more like a local instead.

Somewhere around Bangkok, as I was riding along, a teenager pulled alongside me on his scooter and began to ask me questions. He barely knew any English, but was curious to know who I was and where I was heading. We chatted as best we could as we rode side by side along the highway. Eventually the teenager, who's name was Egh, raced off into the distance, the pair of us having ran out of things to say. A short while later he was up ahead, parked beneath a shelter, keen for me to pull over as I approached.

I came to a halt, wondering what the matter was, and with that he removed his jacket and gave it to me, motioning how it would prevent my arms from burning in the midday sun. It was a gift, from a Thai teenager, earning US$200 a month in a factory, to a Western visitor with a camera, worth four times as much.

Later, stopping for lunch at a stall on the road between two towns, I got up to pay and the lady serving pointed towards a man getting into a black four-wheel drive. It took a minute to work out what she meant — that he had paid my bill — and by that time all I could do was watch him drive away, with no time even to say thankyou.

I've since read how it's part of Thai culture to give a gift to strangers, which explains things. But still, it makes you feel incredibly humble, and even guilty, for receiving gifts from people who might not have as much as you. Perhaps in other ways they do have more than you, and that's why they can afford to give. I liked Thailand a lot. It had a kind soul, and seemed to be so full of fairies.

I just wish some of this generosity had rubbed off on the man at the Pakistan Embassy in Bangkok the day I went to ask him for a visa. The first thing he said was, 'You have to apply for a visa in your own country.'

'That's England,' I said.

'Then that's where you have to go,' he replied.

'I can't fly to England just to get a visa and then come back.'

He was adamant; I'd have to. I said there must be another way, and he told me, 'No, go home.'

I had no answer to this and was prepared to do so if necessary, calculating the budget implications of a flight home to get a visa for Pakistan, then back to Thailand again. I certainly couldn't abandon the trip because of it, I'd come too far and invested too much into it. This wasn't about getting home, this was about getting home by motorcycle.

Thankfully, his colleague told me there might be another way, explaining that if I went to the British Embassy in Bangkok and got them to write a letter confirming they had no objection to me going through Pakistan, then I might just be able to save myself the airfare to England and back.

Leaving Dot's saddle bags at the hostel, I was able to race to the embassy through central Bangkok traffic in record time. It was like an arcade game, flat out everywhere we went, squeezing between the gaps in the traffic and racing the brightly coloured taxis and doing anything we could to keep the racing line.

I would be dressed in my shorts and flip flops, much like the other scooter riders in the city, and at the traffic lights we would all sit, revving our engines, looking across at each other and up at the towering buildings and the endless concrete jungle. Then the light would turn green and off we'd all shoot, one giant mechanical mass of motorbikes swarming through the city streets.

You could have the best adventure flying into Thailand, picking up a local rental bike for a few pounds per day, riding it around to your heart's content. You wouldn't need any of the documentation or hassle that I was having on this trip; you could just take off, ride into Cambodia and Laos as well, maybe even Vietnam, which is a little trickier to get into with a foreign vehicle, but possible.

I'd met a Scottish traveller who'd done just that on a Minsk motorcycle he'd bought here, taking it through the jungle and camping wild, living with the locals and riding endlessly until the bike finally stopped and he abandoned it somewhere, catching a bus back to Bangkok. I was fascinated to hear how easy it was, and cheap. It's clear you could ride in so many directions and camp every step of the way.

I slept in some odd places myself during my time in Thailand; on those park benches the day we crossed from Malaysia, also behind hedges at the side of the road, even on Phuket beach, being told by a local man to keep an eye out for the prowling ladyboys.

My favourite spot of them all however was at a national park called Khao Sok, just north of Phuket. I stopped there on the ride north from Krabi to Bangkok, riding down a long avenue of tourist facilities, before reaching the jungle at the end and putting up the tent beside a little stream, beneath a canopy of trees.

Having arrived early in the afternoon, I went for a walk along one of the trails, the path so narrow and the jungle so close. It was dark and eerie in there. On the trees were nailed warning signs for wild elephants and on my feet I attracted half a dozen leeches. They're persistent things, having to cut them off with my pocket-knife as they grew ever bigger from the blood they were draining from my feet.

I met a German couple experiencing exactly the same problem, the girl having to drop her trousers and the husband scrape them off after they'd somehow got up her trouser leg. From there we walked together, the couple explaining how they were in Thailand for a month, exploring the country by local transport and clearly having a good time. Walking together, we discussed our lives on the road, the ups and the downs, and then at the end of the trail we went our separate ways, never to see each other again. The sad realities of the road; say hello, and wave goodbye.

***

Back in Bangkok, the British Embassy was an interesting place. As far as I could tell, the room was split into two groups. There was the group of older gentlemen, sitting with younger Thai women who I assume they were hoping to take home as their wives. The second group were youths who appeared to have lost their passports after getting drunk the night before, and now they were panicking about how they were going to get home.

Some of the latter group were real scumbags, swearing at staff, becoming aggressive and just plain rude. I was being judgemental, just as they had every right to be about the hairy bastard in the corner muttering something about a visa for Pakistan.

Finally, I was told that the letter of non-objection to me travelling through Pakistan would be ready in a week, though in no way, shape or form would the British Government take any responsibility for my trip. I would be on my own, through thick and thin.

That realisation was pretty sobering, as in the waiting room I'd watched the BBC News highlight the plight of 500,000 Pakistanis displaced by the fighting. It worried me to see that, but not to the point of having second thoughts; it was more a case of looking at the images and thinking, 'I hope that's all calmed down by the time I get there.'

There was an inevitability to it now, as though as long as Dot held together then we'd be going to that place on the news, where the people were being killed. I was resigned to that, almost attracted to it because I was curious to see it for myself.

The route I planned to follow ran along the southern corridor of Pakistan, from Lahore to Quetta, and then on to the first city in Iran, Bam, which had just been struck by an earthquake. For the last 600 kilometres in Pakistan the road would lead through the bandit land of Balochistan, a dry desert region, well beyond government control and in tribal hands.

There, I could expect to be given an armed military escort as the risk of being kidnapped is so high. Armed police even hang around your hotel room overnight, or they may prefer you to sleep in their compound, whichever is safest. The system isn't fool-proof. In the months leading up to this point, a French traveller had been taken from his 4x4 and not seen since, while a Polish contractor had been executed after being abducted from his workplace near Peshawar.

At the Pakistan embassy in Bangkok, the man examined my letter of non-objection and still said no, insisting that it wasn't worded correctly. I argued with him, making a nuisance of myself. I had to; if I'd walked out of the embassy without a visa that day, I really would have had to fly back to England to get a visa to come back — that's how determined (desperate?) I was to complete this task of riding across the world. Finally he asked, 'What bike are you on anyway?'

'A 105cc Honda post bike,' I said.

He looked up from his paperwork. '500cc?' He asked, not hearing me right.

'No,' I said, 'ONE-HUNDRED-AND-FIVE-cc.'

This made him laugh. 'That's ridiculous.' To which I nodded. 'I don't get you people,' he continued. 'Why do you live like this, why don't you go home and get a job?'

I said he sounded like my mother and he laughed again. Then he asked for my passport and US$200 and told me to come back for my visa the following morning. I was getting a ten-day tourist visa for Pakistan, at a notoriously difficult embassy, all because of Dot's tiny engine capacity.

It was another stroke of good fortune, something that had been happening the whole way from Sydney. Whether it was the help of Denise's fairy, the signature of Kevin Rudd or perhaps just simply that once you put yourself out there good things happen, and you meet good people along the way.

The world is clearly not as bad as the TV news would have us believe. And on that positive note, I headed to the airport to pick my visitor up.

Chapter Twelve
Thailand

I didn't quite know what to do or say as Mandy walked through the arrivals lounge. Just smile, say, 'Hi, how are you?' And give her the biggest hug, feeling my eyes start to water and my insides turn to mush.

I'd missed that hug, and when I closed my eyes I could feel all the turbulence of the past four months just drain away. And what a contrast: me, hairy and scruffy; her, manicured and neat. Beauty and the beast, walking through Bangkok airport, hand in hand. She looked stunning, and I was nervous; I think we were both nervous, because it had been so long. But after a few minutes it was just like old times, like being back in Sydney again.

I thought it would be a nice surprise to pick her up on Dot — that way she could see what it was like to travel by motorbike. I'd even rustled up a spare seat and planned on emptying the contents of her giant rucksack into the panniers and then somehow carrying the rucksack on the bike as the pair of us rode along the main highway, back to the guesthouse, about an hour's ride away.

Given the fact that she'd just got off an eleven-hour flight and it was gone 10pm by the time her flight landed, she humoured me really well. But then it became obvious that her gear wasn't going to fit, and it looked like she was about to kill me, so I suggested we get a taxi instead. 'Yes, what a very good idea, Nathan,' she said. Poor old Dorothy had to stay at the airport overnight, having to return the next day to fetch her.

We sat in the taxi holding hands. It was pink, the seats were vinyl, I remember that. Mandy was wearing blue denim shorts, her hair in pigtails. I was in combat shorts and wore a tatty black cap I'd bought in Malaysia. We looked out at the city as we approached it, night time. The neon lights burning the darkness away. Skyscrapers drew our vision up, other taxis flew past in the outside lane. We'd been fleeced on ours, paying far too much, but it didn't matter. Tonight it was irrelevant.

We smiled. Squeezed hands tighter. So surreal. So brilliant. God, I missed being with her. As good as Dorothy, her surrogate, might have been at conversation on the long lonely roads, it wasn't the same. And so, with Mandy here, I'd found my '*Beach*'; it was right here in the back of a Bangkok taxi.

We didn't really have a plan for the holiday. At first we thought about catching a train up north to Chiang Mai, but as the carriages were cancelled due to those political protests in Bangkok, we devised a plan to ride south instead, along the coast to where we could catch a ferry to the island of Ko Chang.

In preparation, I stuffed the sheepskin seat cover with jumpers and used bungee cords to strap it to the rack on the back of Dot. Mandy could fill one pannier, while I had the other for tools and a few clothes. She would use my helmet, while I wore a plastic one bought from the supermarket for seven dollars. Her feet would have to rest on the straightened pannier racks, something that was awkward, but we managed, just like that other couple — Nathan and Aki — had been doing all the way from Perth. They were now in India. I admired them even more.

Finally, we hit the road, weaving through Bangkok traffic until we found the road out of town.

So far Thailand was easily my favourite place I'd passed through on this trip, with it hard to imagine how life at this moment could have be any better. Astride a brilliant bike, in the middle of a great city, heading to the beach, with Mandy on the back, her arms around me and her head resting on my shoulder. If you could pause life and live in the same moment forever and ever — *Groundhog Day* — then this would be my moment.

One of the best things was how I'd long since taken all this for granted; a motorbike through a foreign land with no clue where I was going and every road and place a new one. It was my day job. I got up and did it without even thinking. Now I had someone who was new to the concept, and who was excited by the possibilities of the endless road. This made me buzz as well, which was a curious thing.

Travelling for so long on my own I'd noticed how, after a while, I began to flat line, and cruise along emotionally neutral as there was no point in being happy or sad because there was no one there to witness it. Now it all came flooding back. Those arms tightening around my waist, the sun getting hotter, Mandy talking to me over my shoulder, asking where we should eat, and how we're doing for petrol, and how long until we get there. We just needed a soundtrack, maybe Canned Heat, *Going up the Country*.

In a city we passed through along the way we got caught up in the carnage of Songkran, the New Year festival involving endless water fights and clay being smeared on faces, whether you wanted it smeared on or not.

The festival had been taking place across all of Thailand, even in Bangkok, just down from the protesters. Youths in trucks now tried to drench us as we weaved through lines of traffic that had been brought to a standstill. It's great for a day, alright for two, but this being the third day of celebrations I was keen to stay dry, so I tested Dot's agility, two-up, weaving between gaps in the traffic, all the while trying to use other vehicles as shields from the water that locals were determined to throw over the foreigners on the motorbike, for fun of course.

We made it to Pattaya, halfway to Ko Chang, staying the night in a hotel in the centre of this seedy beach-side resort. Despite the tropical surroundings, we rowed that night, just about the situation and where it went from here. It was more frustration than direct attack. Mandy, rightly, just wanted some certainty, about what was going to happen at the end, where we both might be. Normal questions that needed to be asked. I struggled with them, because I had no answers.

I didn't know how much longer this journey was going to take; it was already taking much longer than I'd anticipated, even though I was doing it as quickly as I could. It was also difficult with Pakistan looming on the horizon. I struggled to see beyond it. I saw it as my nemesis, the one that I had to face and hope for relief at the other end. I was fatalistic, and also realistic. But knowing more than ever that I couldn't skip that stage, or turn away from it. In setting off I'd put myself on a path, and I felt I had to follow it all the way through to the end, or else never know where the road might take me. It didn't help that I was still riding away from her, and her life. The route, sadly, wasn't circular, unless I went full circle.

Catching the ferry to Ko Chang the next day we rode around the island to Lonely Beach, the quietest beach. We stayed there well over a week, doing nothing in particular, just swimming and eating cheap food beneath a huge pagoda overlooking the sea, sitting on cushions, relaxing with a cold drink. Mandy had brought me a tube of Vegemite and so we had that on toast every morning with a cup of tea.

We were staying in bungalows right on the beach-front. They were on stilts and consisted of just one square room, with a bed in the middle, a mosquito net overhead and a partition wall with a shower and toilet behind. For safekeeping, I hung my SLR camera on the back of the shower door, went for a swim, came back, had a shower, forgot about the camera. And it never worked again.

That night we got drunk, which was the worst feeling in the world, because all this way I'd needed to be totally alert and watchful for everything, in front of me and behind; I had to be. Now I couldn't sit up straight or see properly, and the sense of vulnerability scared me. I didn't drink after that.

In the nights that followed we sat on the bungalow steps instead, listening to the sound of the crashing waves in the darkness, Mandy telling me about the things I was missing: our friends who were getting married, the parties they'd had in the back garden, the days in the park, the movies she'd watched, the good times she'd had, in Sydney, a place I still, deep down, considered my home.

I missed it more than ever now. I looked at the reality of where I'd been the last four months, in dirty hotels, in danger, fourteen-hour days on the road. You think the world waits for you while you do these things, but it doesn't, it moves on.

Despite my need to finish the trip, we talked about me flying back to Sydney with her instead. There was a chance I could get another tourist visa and start again, try again. Who knows, maybe with better luck, and greater conviction, something good will happen, and I will find a way to stay.

I thought about it; abandoning Dorothy, out here, in Thailand, and flying back with Mandy. But I was scared. What if it didn't work out, what if I ended up in the café again, waiting to be kicked out? And if I did get a permanent job, with sponsorship, would I resent Mandy for being the reason I never finished what I started?

Irrational, perhaps, but at the time I told myself that I needed to finish this if it was ever going to work between the two of us. Why I thought this trip was the answer to all my problems I'm now, with hindsight, not quite sure. It had become my obsession, to reach England by motorcycle.

We headed back to Bangkok on the eve of Mandy's flight home. She took the bus because I had to detour down to the border with Cambodia to renew Dot's temporary import slip as it expired in a few days and I didn't want to be landed with that huge fine. Mandy then would arrive in Bangkok before me, returning to the same guesthouse we stayed at before. I was on the road all day, playing catch-up, racing as hard as I could, excited, because I knew that when I opened the guesthouse door that evening there would be Mandy, lying on the bed, or in the shower, or ready to go for dinner. And that was just the best feeling, the best of the whole trip, because in this crazy world of motorbikes and roads across the world, this was a taste of normality, of how life should be. And could be. If only I had the nerve, and the will, to abandon this and go back and try again.

I couldn't.

Saying goodbye at the airport the next day was horrid. I got a taste of what it felt like to be the one being left behind. It was as if the roles had been reversed and I was being left to my routine while Mandy went off and lived the exciting life. And now, as I stood against the glass partition at Bangkok airport, watching Mandy go through Customs and security, turn and wave and then disappear from sight, I had a very uneasy sensation that I might not ever see Mandy again.

With that I turned around and left, eyes full of tears, catching the bus back into the centre of Bangkok, looking out the window at that familiar skyline, thinking of the journey ahead and the events that had just taken place. I can't begin to imagine what Mandy must have been thinking up in the air, staring out the aeroplane window, looking down at the same skyline as it slowly disappeared from view, perhaps thinking it's finally time she got on with her own life, and moved on.

A week later, she did.

Chapter Thirteen
Over Burma

The road wasn't going to get any easier from here, mainly because there wasn't one. I'd reached what you might call a dead end, being in Thailand with Burma to the west and China to the North. Burma you can't ride through as it's still a military dictatorship and in no way shape or form will they allow anyone to enter at one end and exit from the other. You can fly into the capital of Rangoon and spend a fortnight touring the designated tourist sites, or you can enter overland for a day, but not with your own vehicle.

As for China, the situation is even worse. To travel through the country on a foreign motorcycle, or any foreign motorised vehicle for that matter, you need a local guide to accompany you at all times. The cost of this can be as much as $200 a day, and as I would need at least a month to cross China it was just something I simply couldn't afford. That left me with one option; put the bike on a plane and fly it over Burma.

It had been an easier process than I had anticipated. I simply found a freighting agent in Bangkok, got a few quotes, told them where and when I wanted the bike go, filled in some paperwork and then, a few days before the flight, took her down to the depot to have a wooden crate built around her.

I'd read in advance that to save money the trick is to make your bike as tiny as possible; that way the box is smaller and so is the cost. With that in mind I stripped her of the handlebars, pannier racks, foot pegs, engine guard and even her front wheel until she was no bigger than a bicycle. It had cost around five-hundred American dollars, with all the removed parts squeezed down the gaps inside the wooden box.

The sky that night I flew to Kathmandu was menacing, full of thunder and rage. I sat by the window and watched the violent streaks of lightning tear a hole in the purple haze. The rays of sunlight were streaking through the clouds I could see down below. It was an epic sight, a reminder that up here we're not in charge, we're just bodies in metal tubes suspended in the sky, and if we were to fall from it that night, in the grand scheme of things, it wouldn't be such a big deal.

I wasn't then so afraid of flying tonight. Perhaps now, after the separation that had just occurred, I found solace in my acceptance that you can never have done enough, been enough, seen enough. Lived enough. There will always be something else to chase. And in a strange way, I found contentment in this, and also tears. I guess this was the reality of life, not just of flying.

***

Arriving in Kathmandu, I took a taxi to my guesthouse in the centre of the city, amazed by the altitude of the place, the Himalayas all around, the air already noticeable thin. I had just enough time to dump my luggage in the room, have a shower and take a quick look around before heading back to the airport having received confirmation that the bike had also arrived.

On the way there I filled a couple of coke bottles with petrol, as to put her on the plane I'd had to empty her tanks — which I'd actually done this time — before being directed to the offices of the cargo terminal, where I had to present all my documents, have the Carnet stamped and then head down to the warehouse itself; a huge hanger with a gate outside where a man approached and offered to be my 'fixer'.

Having become frustrated with such things in the past I waved him away, only for the security guard at the gate to insist I hired him or else he wouldn't let me in.

I was annoyed by this but also grateful, as what followed was a network of chaos and bureaucracy I never thought imaginable. As I stood in the centre of this hanger, my eyes adjusting to the dim light, the heavy air of cigarette smoke hanging all around, my man dashed around for well over an hour, having me follow him to tiny offices at the end of long dim corridors where officials sat at desks and had me sign documents and confirm details before sending me on to the next.

At one point, I took a seat at a worn old table beside an old man who seemed totally disgruntled that I was there, in his country at all. 'What are you doing here?' He barked, with no interest in how I answered. Finally, I was presented with a slender wooden crate that didn't seem big enough for a motorbike at all.

A man with a crowbar began levering at the lid, forcing the wood away from the nails as if he were opening some ancient artefact discovered in a tomb.

When the lid came off I saw my bike, wrapped head to toe in cling-film and mounted on a strong wooden base. Together with two men from the crowd we lifted her from the base, sitting her down on the warehouse floor. Without chance to stop them, the two helpers began bolting her back together; fixing the front wheel, and the handlebars, whilst I stood back and watched. From the two cola bottles I filled her main tank with petrol before rolling her outside and into the sunlight.

There was a large yard outside the front of the hangar, in the centre of which we came to a stop. By now a large crowd had gathered around, asking questions of power and price; low on both accounts.

I inserted the key and twisted it to the right, watching as the neutral light turned a brilliant green. With that I made sure both fuel and choke were on, before pulling out the kick-start and placing my now tatty Converse shoe upon it.

I took a deep breath, the moment of truth, after her flight from Bangkok, now 1,400 miles to the east, I wondered if she would start first kick as she had been doing all this way. The crowd fell silent, watching on, perhaps in dismay. And then;

Kick … and kick … and kick … and kick … and … Nothing.

I tried again. Kick … kick … kick … and kick. Still nothing.

This went on for five minutes or more, beginning to wonder if she was putting it all on, an act, to make me look stupid in front of the swollen crowd who by now were restless, wishing – like me – that the damn thing would start.

Finally, they motioned for me to put my feet on the pegs and hold on tight, as they were going to give me a bump start.

By this stage of the journey I'd read a book called *Zen and the Art of Motorcycle Maintenance*, a famous motorcycling book that recounts the tale of a man recovering from a nervous breakdown and the journey he takes on his motorbike with his son on the back. I liked the book very much, all except for the bit where the author defines his bike as nothing more than an assembly of metal and bolts, governed entirely by science and reason.

In the early stages of the trip I might have agreed with him, but now, having come so far, I was less inclined to believe such a thing, convinced I could feel the bike ageing, finding the best way to cope with the difficult conditions she was going through.

That's why I had to believe those farts and whistles and bad days she had were not caused by the air mixture or something else rational, but were instead the result of her mood, or her period, or other things unfathomably female.

And so … down the ramp we sailed, neutral now, then first, right fist to the gutter, a cough and a splutter. And there, in the warm afternoon sun, she lived.

Chapter Fourteen
Nepal

I'd actually been advised not to fly into Nepal, the online community suggesting it much wiser to fly to Bangladesh instead. The worry is that Nepal can often run out of petrol, leaving the pumps completely dry. It was a consequence of the ongoing political situation within the country, left-wing Maoists now in power having sacked the old monarchy and sent them into exile.

Just as you could feel in the streets of East Timor, here was that same sense of unease and nervousness, almost as though the nation was expecting more riots to flare, barricades to block the roads and the petrol pumps to run dry once more.

In preparation, the pumps were guarded by policemen with riffles who patrolled up and down, the queue for the pumps often out on to the road.

I was staying in the centre of the city, in the tourist district of Thamel. This was a labyrinth of lanes and alleyways, dark and eerie, with guesthouses tucked away in corners and rows of cramped little shops selling climbing gear, guided tours and anything else the backpacker might need for their assault on Everest. Local kids ran amok barefoot, some of them clearly high on drugs, holding up clear plastic bags to their noses and taking great drags of hallucinogenic air.

As you passed them by they would bother you to buy some, or for you to give them spare change. Having told them to go away they would follow you until you darted into one of the many shops for a moment of peace from the street, which by 10pm would fall almost completely silent, Thamel a nervous place to be out walking late at night.

It seemed Thailand had lulled me into a false sense of security. Back there I felt confident and increasingly assured of my ability to navigate through these foreign lands. But that illusion had been destroyed by my movement to the next country. Perhaps it revealed my state of mind to have been a well-crafted act, one that simply hid my nervousness beneath it. Or just maybe it was the doubt creeping in, and the questions, and the realisation of what was happening here, choosing to do this and not go back. Of finding this road across the world in the first place, rather than finding a way to stay in Australia.

I guess it was a time when the question of, 'what if?' reaped its destruction on my mind, playing out scenarios of how things could have been, should have been, if only I'd have made different choices in life. Instead I was here, in Kathmandu, alone, vulnerable, and scared. And still with over 15,000 kilometres left to go.

Of more pressing concern was my debit card that had been lost to a cash machine in the city. I called the bank in England who informed me that my account had been hacked, by someone in Poland of all places, and that all of my cards had been cancelled with new ones issued to my address in England. At the time I had just ten dollars in my wallet and no way of getting any more.

I called home and spoke to my dad, who raced down to the Western Union depot near our home and wired out a bundle of American dollars for me to survive on the next few weeks. People have since advised me how it is wise to carry a reserve of American dollars somewhere upon your bike or person, and I would say this is a great idea. Such things you learn from experience.

I used some of the sent money to equip Dot with a new rear tyre and a change of oil. The owner of the guesthouse I was staying in told me of a motorcycle spares shop on the road just down from the old King's Palace. The shop was a small place, on the side of a busy street, discovering it to harbour that familiar smell of oil and leather, a range of gadgets and accessories hanging from the wall.

The man behind the counter spoke some English and was amazed to see my old bike, as once upon time they used to sell the same model in Nepal and the owner of the shop had owned one. He said he had met a few people travelling across the world on motorbikes and to me he asked how I was affording it.

Embarrassed, given the conversation I'd had with Roda Dua of the BigZoners back in Indonesia, I told him of my credit cards and overdrafts, that being all I had the day the opportunity came along. To this he smiled. He could see how that would make sense and I was relieved by that.

The man had a selection of tyres, one of which was like those fitted to a motocross bike, perfect I reasoned for my passage along the anticipated rough roads of India and Pakistan. I also purchased a litre of engine oil, before heading outside to where it was now raining. The man asked where my wet weather gear was, to which I replied that I didn't have any, cursing the day I posted home the waterproof suit the BigZoners had given me, thinking it wouldn't rain much west of Thailand.

'Wait there then,' said the man, darting back into his shop and returning soon after with a brand new waterproof jacket and matching trousers. 'I want you to have these,' he said, handing me them and insisting I try them on for size.

They were perfect, I even liked the colour, a shimmering purple-pink. 'Thank you,' I said, not quite sure what else to say, before riding off into the steaming traffic, where men crossed roads with sofas on their heads as overloaded trucks and buses swerved around them.

Over the next few days I wasn't sure what to do with myself. There was no rush to leave Nepal and I didn't feel any particular haste to enter India either, especially given the terrible stories I'd heard about the danger on the roads there. If anything I reasoned it would be nice to have a break from my blind pursuit of England, and all the trouble it had caused me. As cruel as it might sound, I also wanted a break from Dorothy. I'd spent every day with her for so many months and I thought how nice it would be spend a little time out of the saddle.

By chance I met a group of three backpackers — Nicolas, Sophia and Maria — who were heading out for a hike around the Annapurna Circuit, a walk that would take two weeks and cover 259 kilometres. I've never been much of a walker, and completely ill-equipped for such a long hike, but thought it a nice idea and so joined them at the start of the Circuit, not too far from Everest base camp.

I left the bike in a hotel yard having knocked on the owner's door and asked him if, for a couple of days of my budget (around £20), he would be able to keep her safe while I disappeared for a few weeks. It was callous really, abandoning her beneath a flimsy cover in the backyard of guesthouse which didn't have any guests and was in a place I couldn't have imagined many people wanting to stay either.

At any other time I would have been worried sick about her, not abandoning her in the first place, but on this occasion I was just glad to be free of the responsibility to ride her for a while. And this would be a new challenge, a huge walk, through beautiful scenery with good company and plenty to distract my mind and test my muscles, alien things that hadn't really had much exercise since the day we rode out of Sydney, apart from my right wrist of course.

It is probably why from the outset that I found it such hard work. The start of the trail was a bouncy bridge across a raging river, then turning sharp left, to follow the flow of water as the trail made its way up a steep gorge, sometimes the steps cut into the side of the rocks and the ground rough underfoot.

Through the sole of my Converse I could feel every pebble, my back already throbbing, though to counteract that, the views around were spectacular. It was a world absent of motorcars or industry, just mountains and valleys and a dome of beautiful sky, our four shadows passing through it with rucksacks on our backs and few words spoken as every last breath was being used for exercise. The target was to walk nine hours a day if we were going to cover the distance in the recommended time.

The villages we passed through, accessible only by foot, were all hanging off the edge of cliffs, or buried deep into the rock. They all had little wooden stalls selling water and chocolate that gradually increased in price as the altitude went up.

In the peak season of October and November this would have been crowded with walkers, but May being very much the low season we were almost the only people on the circuit. This meant accommodation in the little wooden guesthouses along the way was free, just as long as you ate breakfast and dinner there. The showers were always freezing, the rooms just as cold and stark, but Christ, to wake up in a room overlooking a gorgeous waterfall halfway up a Nepalese mountain is surely worth a little suffering.

Though what would I know about that? On one particular steep and craggy climb we watched a trail of men carrying building materials on their backs. Their strength was incredible, walk a minute, rest a minute, along the narrow ridges and steep inclines, delivering their goods to the city at the top of the mountain.

I found it utterly baffling. Why would you build a city up there, ten days walk from a road and only accessible by foot or by air? I don't know if it's testament to man's tenacity or his stupidity. Every single can of Coke, every single bar of chocolate and brick and shoe and door knob had to be carried to the top of the mountain by this team of worker ants. The risk was incredible.

Referring to the village kids who pestered us for pens and for money, I said to Nicolas how nice it would have been 20 years ago before it got like this, to which he replied, 'Think what it'll be like in twenty years time.'

He was right. In my mind I pictured a giant revolving escalator looping the mountain on which you'd be able to sit in a comfy armchair, being brought drinks and food by your guide who casually points out the ridiculousness of the past when such trails were once walked, now ridden, by the new wave of tourists from China and India, once those markets come alive. But who could blame the lazy for wanting to see this. It was spectacular in every sense.

I just wish my mind had been better in tune with what was around. The further I walked, the steeper the terrain became, the more I realised that actually, this wasn't for me. I shouldn't have come. I already had my challenge and had neither the endurance nor patience to take on another one. More than ever I just wanted to get to England, to see if I could, to get it over and done with, as strange as that might sound. And being out here, on this mountain, wasn't achieving that, it was wasting time and energy; at least that's how I saw it back then. I told myself how I could have been in Delhi already, sorting out my visa for Iran. Then I worried about the bike I'd abandoned. If she was stolen or vandalised, then all of this would have been in vain. The journey would be over and I didn't know what I would do.

On the evening of day two I explained to the others that the Annapurna Circuit just wasn't for me, accepting that if I turned around now I wouldn't have so far to backtrack, accepting that the farther you venture into something the harder it is to go back.

I woke early the next morning, leaving a note to say goodbye, before making haste back down the trail to where, nine hours later, I found the bike, just where I left her, beneath a sheet in the back yard of this random guesthouse.

The aluminium box had been left in the manager's office, along with my riding gear. I thought about staying in the guesthouse that night as it was already past six in the evening, then thought, 'No, let's get going, I need to feel some movement again.' Besides, the hotel had a strange atmosphere, as though it was a front for something more sinister. Or maybe it was just my negative vibe.

It was certainly a murderous road, weaving down mountains and out along the valley floor. Once the light had gone I could barely see the edge of it, only the shadows and the subtle outline of people, who just seemed to meander along the road, not bothering to move for the traffic that was howling towards them through the thick black night.

I felt the first flecks of rain, then sheets of it, making me ever more grateful for the rain suit now keeping me warm and dry.

By 10pm we had made it to Pokhara, the second largest city of Nepal, where a long main street led you down to the edge of a lake, this being the place where all the tourist infrastructure was built. I found a cheap hotel and crashed for the night, waking the next morning with diarrhoea so violent I wasn't able to leave the hotel room for a week. This absence of movement just about finished me. Though there was plenty of movement of the other kind.

Chapter Fifteen
Indian Border

The road to the Indian border was the hardest of them all, not because it was too rough, or bumpy, of which it was both, but because I just didn't want to be there. The feeling was one of guilt, for being out here, for doing this, for not finding a way to stay in Sydney, for not going back, for having my parents worry, for taking Mandy for granted. It was other things as well, like hearing my nan hadn't been so well — nothing serious, but weakening, through age, Mum updating me on her condition and me feeling as though I should be there, how that should be my priority, not this stupid adventure.

Such a thing had happened before, the first time I was in Australia, when my Granddad Stan had died and I wasn't there, neither for the final moments nor for the funeral. You convince yourself you can't be there, that you have to live your own life. Then you think about other people's needs and feel utterly selfish.

The prospect of riding at least another 15,000 kilometres, through places such as India and Pakistan, now filled me with dread. I thought about flying back to Australia to try and make amends, I thought about quitting completely and flying to England. But I didn't have the will power to make a decision to do either. I went with the easiest option instead; carrying on, riding through the south of Nepal, between the valleys and the villages, swerving around people who continued to meander in the road.

Maybe it was my mood or the unsettled political situation, but of all the places I'd ridden, Nepal was the one where I sensed it wouldn't be a good place to break down. Not because I thought I might be in danger, more likely that I wouldn't be helped (though I probably would have been).

It was late in the afternoon when I made the final approach to the Indian border, the road lined with a thousand trucks, all parked bumper to bumper. I didn't know if they were waiting to cross or whether they were just, waiting. I rode past them trying to psyche myself up, 'COME ON COME ON,' I forced through gritted teeth, it not having quite the same effect as it had back in Indonesia when trying to find that boat to Malaysia.

Some of the stories I'd heard about riding in India didn't help. Apparently, with the way that the Indian compensation system works, if you are struck by a vehicle once, you are likely to be struck twice to make sure you are dead, because the fine for killing someone on the road is less than if you maim them. Likewise, if you hit and kill a cow or a child don't stop, go straight to the police station, because some say the locals would attack you in retribution.

I was frightened, and as a result, just couldn't bring myself to cross the Indian. Instead, I turned around and began riding back the way I came, back into Nepal. It was now around 5pm and I just didn't know what to do, my indecisiveness had returned. I had another go at the border, getting close to it and then turning back again. I just could not bring myself to cross it, though I knew I would have to; just not tonight. I headed instead to the little town of Lumbini, apparently the birthplace of Buddha, which I knew was maybe forty kilometres down a road running parallel to the border. It was a dusty, dark, truck-infested road.

This town consisted of just one dishevelled street that was dark and eerily silent. Being on the tourist map for its temples and monasteries, Lumbini had a scattering of guesthouses on either side of the road. I chose one that would allow me to roll the bike inside reception. The bedroom was on the first floor and filthy, the sheets seemingly not changed for months. I laid the wicker mat from East Timor and a sarong I'd bought in Bali on the bed as a base cover and went out, across the road, to a restaurant still serving food.

On the balcony I talked to some travellers about Iranian visas. By coincidence most of them had tried to get one, or knew someone else who had. All had failed. The simple truth was that at the time the Iranian government didn't like the British, thanks to our meddling with their politics in the past, and there just wasn't anything you could do about that. Not being able to get an Iranian visa would be a huge problem, because Iran was on my route to England and there weren't that many ways around it.

The next morning I woke, still not wanting to cross the Indian border but knowing I had no choice. I rolled Dot out onto the dusty street, slugging back a chai from a stall by the roadside, then on we went, zapping past those lorries and finally succeeding in making it to the border, where an officious Customs' officer made life hell. Things were photocopied, and I had to run between buildings in the blazing sun, all the while my bowels feeling like they were about to explode, bunged up on Imodium, the flood gates about to break.

I was relieved, but not in that sense, when finally I could pass beneath the arch marking the border. A metre into India I was ordered to stop beside a desk and dismount, presenting my passport and visa to a man in the shadows. The world around me was chaos. The man in the shadows pointed me to the Customs house across the crowded road.

I dodged lorries and cycles to get there, bursting through the door and into a long narrow room. A man in military uniform addressed me in English. He asked about the nature of my business. I told him I wanted to ride across his land and into Pakistan. He looked incredulous. I looked incredulous.

He opened a giant tome of data, a storehouse of information on all foreign machines that had passed this point in the past. Dot's details were now entered, making a record of this moment until the end of time. This was 2 June 2009; we had covered almost 18,000 kilometres and it was our 142nd day on the road.

And what a road now, spearing south of the border, Nepal disappearing behind us, the barren hot land of India sprawling out ahead, because for once the man-made divide meant something to nature as well. This was the point at which the moist foothills of the Himalayas levelled out and shot flat and straight with barely a single thing growing from the earth. The air was immediately hotter and drier, the temperature almost fifty degrees.

The colour of the world around was monotone, a dusty red haze hanging in whichever direction you turned. I didn't imagine this openness, this vastness of India. But I wasn't surprised to see evidence of the road toll I'd heard about — the wreckage of vehicles littered the roadsides. In one place, two lorries had collided head on, their cabins evaporated. There was death in that, had to be.

But stopping for my first snack warmed me to the people. It was a stall serving food and quickly my visit drew an observant crowd. Children from the village came swarming, standing around curious about everything I owned, especially my helmet camera that was now strapped on with tape as the clips had long since broken.

I sat at a table, all eyes on me. This was like being back in the deepest depths of Indonesia again, just mingling, hanging out, trying to explain myself and tasting the local food, which was good, especially the tea, or chai as they call it, which is sweet and hot. One child invited me to look around his nearby village, but I declined, regretting it immediately when I saw his hurt expression. I just felt I needed to keep on moving.

Having spent the night in a hotel in the first main city of Gorakhpur, that southerly road eventually led me to Varanasi, where on the first night in this holy city, as I was walking through its network of alley ways, or ghats as they're locally called, a gang of men came towards me with a dead body on their heads. The men were singing and chanting.

I stood to one side to let them pass, when, without warning one of the men grabbed my arm and insisted I join them. I had little choice, being dragged beneath the body, not really feeling the groove, or the mood, then thinking, 'Sod it,' throwing my hands in the air and letting out little yelps as I danced wildly with my mourner mates down this Indian back alley. The men shook my hand and carried on, taking the body down to the banks of the River Ganges where it was soon to be burned.

It's a religious thing, Hindus believing the burning of a body by this holy river takes them one step closer to somewhere, someplace, hopefully better. The ground on which it's done was no bigger than a tennis court and ran down to the water's edge, anywhere up to six bodies being burned at any one time. Each had its own fire pit, with it said that it takes up to three hours for a body to burn.

No women were allowed to observe, the belief that this is no place for undue emotion. Instead the men simply stood around, watching their friend or relative turn to ash. Tourists were allowed to watch as well, though not take photos, unless you paid the 'attendants' a decent bribe. Strangely there was no real smell, perhaps because beforehand the bodies had been rubbed with scent.

Not all bodies were burned however. If you were to die from a cobra bite, or as a child, or from leprosy, or whilst pregnant, or as a holy man, you are already deemed 'pure', and therefore did not need to be cremated. Instead, the body was wrapped in fabric and rolled into the river to decay. You could take boats to the opposite river bank where these bodies would wash up and be eaten by wild dogs. Other bodies would float on the surface of the water and bang into the side of your boat as you bobbed along.

You'd imagine such things would gross you out, yet oddly you just accepted it as the way of life out here, something to observe and not pass judgement on because to an outsider we perhaps have some bizarre, maybe macabre traditions and activities as well. The only thing that might make you wince was the way in which the river, filled with rotting bodies as it was, was also used as the local bathtub.

Each morning thousands of men would descend the watery steps in their loin cloth underpants and bathe in the soupy green water, swilling it about their mouths and scrubbing their bodies clean. Others would be washing their clothes, or their animals, soap suds frothing across the surface. Some would be teaching their children to swim, others preying in it, playing in it, splashing around as those bodies continued to float on by.

Initially this disgusted me, until it dawned on me that I was the ghoul who got up at 4am to take a boat ride up and down the river to watch these people and take photos of them with my camera. And I wasn't the only one; a dozen boats or more also sailing silently by. Imagine it from the point of view of those in the water; like opening your shower curtain every morning to see a different stranger waiting to take a picture of your penis.

But sometimes it was hard to feel much sympathy. Every time I stepped from the guesthouse door I could guarantee that someone would be there to try and sell me drugs, clothes or postcards. And 'no' never meant 'no,' not here. 'No' meant 'maybe,' so all the way along the river's edge I would be followed until I'd get really mad and tell them to fuck off.

Then I'd feel bad, because all this way I'd been conscious how, as a traveller, you are an ambassador for all other travellers, and the impression you leave affects how locals respond to the next person to pass through. That's why it really riled me to see people being rude to locals. It sets a bad precedent. And yet here I was, in India, telling someone to rudely get lost. One man trying to rip me off defended himself by saying, 'You can't blame us for trying.' To which I responded, 'Then you can't blame us for getting pissed off when you do so.'

Though in many ways, it was these encounters that made the time with the other backpackers so special. On the top floor of the Shanti Lodge, where the seats of the rooftop restaurant overlooked the city on one side and the river on the other, dozens of us would sit, backpackers from all over the world, bitching about the things that had happened to us that day and cheering each other up before we'd put on our crash helmets and thick skins and venture out for another dose. Because that's what it was; love and hate, pleasure and pain. I hate it, yet I want to see what it's going to throw at me again. And it was through those shared experiences that I made some real good friends in India.

One day down by the river I met a Frenchman named Bernard, who told me an amazing story about how he'd spent the last three months walking the length and breadth of southern India. No buses, no cars, nothing, just his own two feet. He lived on a dollar a day, sleeping by the side of the road, ostracised even by the Indians for being too poor.

He was an interesting man, on a journey, one he said was now complete and that it was time for him to go home. He must have sensed that there was nowhere left for him to walk, and now his flight home to France was leaving at the end of the week. I was jealous in a way; to think I could be home in nine hours as well, as simple as getting on an aeroplane.

I threatened to send many emails to Mandy attempting to explain, trying to make amends, but by now she'd told me she needed a break completely and that I wasn't to contact her at all. And I didn't, because I had no answers, no solutions to all this. So I saved my emails in 'draft,' before heading back to the street in the forty-eight-degree heat, slowly falling into a trap of not being able to bring myself to leave this place. My enthusiasm for everything, for all this, was in the gutter, sailing by, being chewed up and digested by the holy cows until it drizzled out into the Ganges and was flushed completely away. I wished to be anywhere but here.

Sometimes I wonder if that's what I told myself however. Because there was another side of me that recognised how easy it made things being shut away from the world like this. I existed at times in total isolation, and that made life much lonelier, but also much easier. Perhaps I convinced myself I was better off out here, that way my actions and decisions couldn't do any damage to anyone, only myself. Perhaps that's why I'd enjoyed the night in the Indonesian wild so much. No one knew where I was and in my mind that meant I had no existence beyond that shelter. And without any existence I didn't feel any responsibility towards anyone or anything; total isolation, but also total freedom. Can you live like this forever, and would you want to? I still wasn't sure. Travelling perhaps not the remedy, but the curse.

In the end it took me ten days to escape Varanasi. I even tried putting the bike on the train so as to avoid the 1,000 kilometres of dangerous road between here and Delhi. I got as far as buying a ticket at the station and draining Dot of her fuel as instructed. But then I was told I would have to strip her completely bare of all her panniers and the aluminium box and I just couldn't be bothered with all that faff. Besides, once more it would have felt like cheating. Instead, I retrieved my fuel back from the stranger I'd given it to, poured it back into the tank, fighting to keep my place in the queue at the refund counter where men piled on each other like a rugby scrum. One man pushed me in the back and didn't like it when I pushed him back. But I was mad at this point, through with it all.

And yet in a strange way I quite enjoyed that four day journey from Varanasi to Delhi, the highlight not being the Taj Mahal, as impressive as that was the day I stopped in Agra, or the giant Hawaiian I had all to myself in the nearby Pizza Hut. Instead it was the moment in the middle of nowhere when I was disturbed from my toilet break in the bushes by a pair of local men who pulled up on a motorbike and greeted me like old friends. They brought their hands to their mouths to question if I was hungry. I wasn't at the most trusting point in the trip, but I thought what the hell, why not.

I followed them for several kilometres until we pulled up outside what resembled a long decrepit cow shed. There was no door, no windows and the roof was in tatters. This didn't look much like a café, something that made me suspicious, checking where my knife was as I followed them through the opening in the wall. Eight beds were laid out before me, all steel and void of mattresses.

Laying on them were men who looked weary and hot. One was a holy man, dressed in orange robes, and smoking, yet all smiled and greeted me as I walked through the door with my helmet still on my head. I'm not entirely sure who they were, but I concluded that this must be a rest house for drifters making their way along this desolate dusty road.

In the corner was a young man cooking fresh food in huge pans on a red-hot kiln. I had one portion, then another and still more came. It was a thali with rice and chapatti. I even drank the water from the well, which I didn't think I should do, but what the hell. This was an experience I needed because, rightly or wrongly, I'd developed quite a negative impression of India and of Indians. Too many had tried to trick me to think anything else. This though was a timely reminder that there are plenty of good people out there, even if sometimes you have to travel a bit further to find them.

When I offered to pay, the man wouldn't dream of it. I thanked them all, and carried on my way. A great memory: the day I became an Indian drifter on the long dusty road to Delhi.

Chapter Sixteen
Delhi

The backpacker zone of Paharganj was exactly where the map said it was, right at the heart of Delhi, opposite the train station where people arriving for the first time would be told they needed to take a tuk-tuk and so jumped in and rode around for half an hour before being dropped off a few hundred metres down the road from where they originally got in. It was a popular scam and symbolic of the place you were about to enter. One long corridor of peddlers, meddlers, bandits and vagabonds, stretching a kilometre or more in length and lined with shops and food stalls and cows that you must swerve around as you ride at slow speed along the dusty street.

Dark alleyways led off in every direction, the buildings leaning in at the top to trap you should you ever try to fly away. Hostels were scattered amongst them. These were creepy places, with no safe place to leave your bike except chained to a gate, which is what I had to do with Dorothy, leaving her to choke on an air of stale piss, contributed by the men using the open urinals lashed to the side of the streets. You can walk past and pat the pisser on the back if you like; just hope they don't spin around and shoot you in the back. A dirt and rock floor covers it all, so when it rains the whole place turns to mud and makes your trousers brown.

I kept seeing the same poor guy, Swedish going by his appearance, who was always completely off his face on drugs. He had sores all over his arms and sat rocking on the pavement, mumbling to himself. I thought about helping him, but decided not to get involved, realising in that instant just how self-absorbed, and selfish being a lone traveller can make you. Looking out for just yourself and no one else. And so I stepped around the man, leaving him to rock backwards and forwards in the gutter.

For food I ate in the local cafés with their torn filthy fake tile floors, broken seats, chipped tables and vats of food at the front, slopped into metal trays. The food was always good, and cheap, at less than a dollar for a thali; a mixed tray of rice, dhal, pickle and chapati.

Outside I'd buy a kilo of mangoes at one of the wooden stalls and guard myself against the pickpockets. Three boys working together: one walking across my path and stopping, which made me stop. As I did so a second boy came from behind and went for the wallet I had in my trouser pocket. I spotted him just in the nick of time and chased them away. I thought about grabbing one of them and taking him to the police, but they would have beaten him black and blue.

You have to watch the water as well. So many of the bottles you buy in shops or from stalls had a small hole in the bottom that looked to have been resealed with heat to leave a messy plastic scar. Fake spring water, perhaps; but how? If they were refilling bottles already used then the seal on the cap would have been broken, and yet these 'fake' bottles had a seal, so if they could re-create a seal why the need for the hole? And if they couldn't re-create a seal what were they doing with the original water they drained out of the crude holes they were making in the bottom of the bottle? Drinking it themselves, using it to flush the toilet? None of us could figure it out. It was all just part of the charm of spending time in Delhi, and India in general.

Of course, there are nice parts of India, even of Delhi. Connaught Place was one of them; a huge circular series of buildings, like a stone doughnut, built by the British and with a park in the middle. It is here that the Indian middle classes park their Mercedes cars and go off browsing expensive clothes shops, bakeries and bookshops. There's also a McDonald's, a KFC and a Pizza Hut.

Waiting weeks for my Iranian visa to come through, I used to go down to Connaught Place almost every day for a soft-serve cone in KFC. I'd often eat it upstairs, on the chairs, beneath the air-con and listening to MTV. It always fascinated me, these parallel worlds created by the fast-food chains. The furniture, the food, the uniforms, the taste, the smell, the mood, the music, the atmosphere — it was the same here as it was in England. Or Australia. Or any other KFC anywhere else in the world.

I remember arriving at the city of Mataram back in Indonesia, finding a McDonald's and sitting there eating my burger while the Lighthouse Family played *Ocean Drive* over the radio. I was seventeen again, doing my A-levels, naive about all this, naive about the world beyond my own little bubble. Back then I used to stare out of windows or walk down lonely lanes wondering what else is out there; now I felt as if I knew. The world is out there. Just that the fast-food chains have beaten me to it.

Then it was outside, into the oven that would melt my ice-cream if I brought it out with me. I'd sometimes sit on the grass, always being bothered by men wanting to clean my ears. They had metal probes which they'd dab with cotton wool and offer to test to see how dirty my ears were. One time I let a man do it, and he fished out the biggest wad of wax. He probably had a box of it up his sleeve, or jabbed it in the ear of his dog. Or maybe my ears really were that dirty.

Another man, presentable and smart, began talking to me on the way back from the bank. He said he was going back to his shop, and that he was catching a rickshaw and he could drop me off. I dropped my guard and climbed in, spending the next hour being hauled around various clothes and jewellery shops. He was on commission, being paid if I bought anything. Daft fool; me, not him, for falling for it. I told him to go away and he chased me down the street...

The same street I would later bump into Keith again, the army guy from Krabi in Thailand. That might sound quite surprising given the scale of the earth, but to be fair, the paths that travellers take is so narrow you find yourself bumping into familiar people all the time. We had a drink together, with Keith telling me more stories about his lonely life on the road. I realised there and then that I didn't want that; being in my fifties and still on the road. No abode, no place to call home, no one waiting for me to walk through the door and give me a hug or even a bit of earache.

I'd prefer that to not having a door at all.

It actually scared me to think that that might happen, that I might never be able to lay down roots, to be a tree in a garden and know only that space, sharing that place with someone who matters. It terrified me to think I might always be looking for the next adventure, still wanting to catch the next trade wind, explore, dream, discover, as Mark Twain might have us chant, while the people around you are moving on, settling down, growing up, standing tall. I think this was the greatest fear of mine; that this trip wouldn't be the end, instead that it would be the start. And then those people would truly be gone.

It's why I always responded to those people emailing with dreams of taking off and leaving it all behind by advising they should take no notice of me, that they should instead value what they have and cherish, whatever it was, even if it's just a coffee down at their local café. Because yes, a life on the road can be triumphant, liberating, spectacular in all its freedom. I've not known freedom like it before and at times I loved it. It gave me strength, it gave me clarity. But it can also be confronting and ugly and destructive. By now I'd realised there are sacrifices to be made in all this and often you struggle to convince yourself that it's worth it.

For the time being I'd been to see the man at the Iranian Embassy. A large white building on a nice estate; they always are. My optimism was piqued, I felt a twinge of good fortune and hope. I could feel Denise's fairies fluttering about as they made their way to have a nice word with the man on the desk.

'Come on, let him through, don't make him have to find another way. He needs that visa, please don't say no, please don't say no.' My turn. I could feel it, sense it, yes, he's going to say yes. But instead, 'Sorry, there will be no visas for Americans, Canadians, Australians or... British,' confirmed the man on the other side of the counter.

The Americans and British were refused for political reasons, the Canadians for being America's neighbour, while the Australians were temporarily banned because some Indian students in Melbourne had been beaten up in what apparently were racist attacks. A butterfly swings its fists in Melbourne, causing a tornado at the Iranian Embassy in Delhi.

Clearly those idiots doing the bashing would have had no clue what impact their actions had, but still, if you're reading this can you please stop beating up little Asian kids? Thanks.

I rode away from the embassy feeling like one of the characters in the *Dungeons and Dragons* cartoon back in the eighties, desperately seeking a way out of this strange fantasy land I found myself in, but never quite managing to find it. Quit, turn back? No, not now, there has to be another way; over, under, around? Any way round? Has to be another way around Iran. Must be. Find it. We must find it, because no way are we flying home or turning back now. We can't do that. We will not do that.

I turned to the internet and asked the world for advice. The contributors on Horizons Unlimited and ADVRider; a site I was posting a blog to, came up with numerous suggestions.

'What about a boat from Pakistan to Egypt?' Said one man. 'How about you and Dorothy on a plane north to Kyrgyzstan and then across Russia,' said another. 'What about a flight straight over Pakistan and Iran from India to Turkey,' said my worried mother trying to talk me into the quickest path home.

They were all ideas involving wheels off the ground or Dorothy on a boat. 'No. No. No. On the land Dorothy, that's where your wheels have to stay, on dry land.' I hated looking at the map and seeing the gap between Bangkok and Kathmandu; it felt like I was cheating and I didn't want another gap.

This left only one option: China.

As mentioned before when dealing with the issue of Burma, the problem of passing through China is huge. It's as though the government don't want foreigners entering the country with their own vehicles, perhaps for the reason that there are things that they don't wish for you to see. As a result, the Chinese make it as expensive, time consuming and problematic as possible. And it works. Few people go through China with their own vehicles, and when they do it's usually in big groups because that way the costs involved are shared between them.

The main burden is that you have to employ a local guide to accompany you the whole way. I'd read that this can cost as much as US$200 a day and take an age to organise. One online commenter suggested instead that I skip all this and smuggle myself and Dorothy over the border with the aid of an unsavoury character I might happen upon in a Pakistan bar. I'll admit to thinking that sounded quite romantic, me and Dot crawling beneath the strafe of Chinese searchlights, but I didn't have the confidence to do such a thing. Even now I was still a modest traveller, keen to keep as low a profile as I could.

I contacted an agency that specialised in taking foreign vehicles into China. David was in charge — I'd heard his name mentioned before — his agency reported to be the best. In my email I asked how long it would take to do the paperwork and how much would it cost to dip into China and head west. David responded straight away, explaining how it usually took three months to organise. I replied to say that my visa for Pakistan expired in just under five weeks, so really I needed to enter the country before then or else I would have to re-apply for another visa, and after the experience, not to mention cost, at the Pakistan embassy in Bangkok I didn't fancy my chances of being so lucky next time around. To all this David said that this was cutting it fine, but still he might be able to help.

And the price? I had to sit down for this one: US$2,200 for a seven-day crossing, including guide and hotels for the night. My mouth hit the deck, my tongue unfurled across the floor and someone stood on it, making my eyes pop out. I'd heard it was a lot, but that was more than Dot had cost, a quarter the price of the original budget for the whole adventure. I couldn't afford it; by now my finances were in dire straits. The trip was costing far more than I'd ever imagined; buying Dot, the Carnet, the flight over Burma. At this stage I could not afford to ride through China. Then came a stroke of good fortune.

Back in Bangkok I'd posted out a batch of eighty personalised postcards to various media outlets around the world in the hope of getting some coverage, and possibly commission to write something about the trip. There been some response, the Sydney Morning Herald in particular asking for 500 words on the trip so far. For this they paid me a few hundred dollars and having sent it off never thought anything more about it.

Then one day in India, as I passed through the town of Khajuraho (home of the erotic temples), I received an email from a publisher who had seen the story in the Sydney Morning Herald, thought the trip sounded interesting and wondered if I might be keen to write a book. I was excited by this, having considered that I might like to some day. Best of all they were going to pay me an advance on signature of the contract, a figure more than enough to cover my entry into China and keep me on the road a little longer.

Thinking back, it was crazy how it all just melted together; the trouble in Iran, being told about China, David being able to get me in before my Pakistan visa ran out, the book deal to pay for it. At so many stages the whole thing threatened to implode and become improbable and now there I was, sitting in an Indian internet café, dumbstruck by it all.

My whole trip had been turned on its head. I'd always thought it would go Pakistan, Iran, Turkey, then along the southern coasts of Europe: Greece, Italy, Spain, France. And now, because of the Iranians, I'd be seeing a whole different side of the world: China, Kyrgyzstan, Kazakhstan, Russia, Poland, Ukraine, Germany — a colder and much longer route, but perhaps true in what they say, that all roads lead to home.

There was just one problem. To go this way would mean riding over one of the highest roads in the world; the Karakoram Highway (KKH for short), which reaches a peak of 4,693 metres (15,397 ft) as it threads a path from Pakistan to China over the Himalayan mountains.

At those sorts of altitudes an engine will struggle for lack of oxygen, as will its rider. The simple fact was that Dot might not have the power to climb such a height, and that really worried me because if she couldn't conquer the KKH then I could be stranded in the north of Pakistan with a visa about to expire and no idea what to do next.

To make matters worse, the road sweeps up past the Swat Valley, an area where the fighting between the Pakistan army and the Taliban had been at its most fearsome.

This was no place to be conducting altitude experiments. I needed to put myself and Dot through our paces in a much safer environment. Fortunately, in the north of India, I'd heard of just the place: Kashmir.

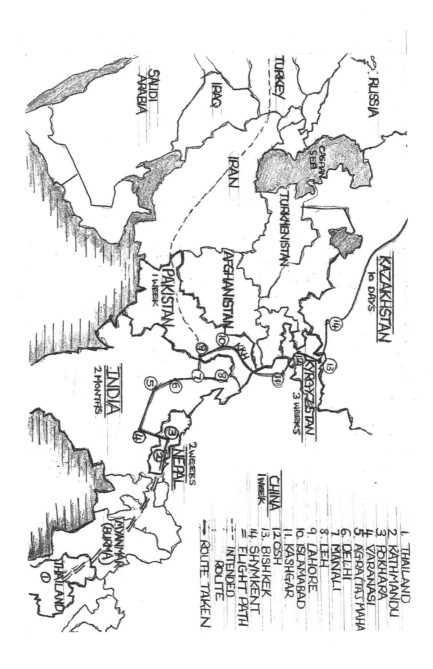

Chapter Seventeen
Indian Himalayas

The Manali to Leh Highway is the second highest road in the world and, with a maximum elevation of 5,325 metres, is even higher than the KKH. It is 479 kilometres in length, takes two days to pass and is only open between June and September because of the terrible weather that affects it. It's in the very north of India, in the region of Jammu and Kashmir — the area fought over with Pakistan — and takes you between the two towns in its name. If me and Dot could manage this, then we'd ride with optimism into Pakistan. If we couldn't make it, well, we were screwed and the deposit I'd just paid David to start the process of getting into China wasted.

In preparation, I'd posted home the aluminium box and the orange postie sacks and replaced them with a set of throw-over fabric panniers I bought from a Delhi motorcycle market. This would lighten Dot's load and make her more agile as the weight would be carried lower down. It was also in anticipation of Pakistan, where I wished to travel more discreetly. I'd also bought a foot pump and had a man in Delhi service and wash her so now she shone as bright as I ever did see. But it wasn't to last. The 400-odd kilometres from Delhi to the start of the road in Manali was a mud bath. Recent rains had swamped the road, big lorries and buses had churned it to sludge. By the time we arrived in town we were covered from head to toe.

I rested in Manali for a few days, meeting many foreigners riding around India on Royal Enfield Bullets. That was the trend. Fly to India, buy a vintage bike for a few hundred dollars and ride it around until you sell it and fly home. Hardly any of the riders wore helmets and most were on a bike for the very first time. As you can imagine, there were some nasty accidents. The cool confidence of youth I suppose.

The point of staying in Manali was to acclimatise to the altitude, as the air here was already thin, causing both me and Dorothy some breathing problems. There was a hill in the centre of town that both of us struggled up, and this was only at 1,950 metres. We would be going two and a half times that height. It didn't bode well, but we did what we could to enjoy Manali while we were there.

A few of us went to a waterfall just outside of town. It was a beautiful spot, the water seeming to appear from a point a mile in the sky. Then splash, a clear pool at the foot of it in which travellers from all around the world were swimming. Oddly, there was an old women stood up on a rock to one side, screaming at us and waving her arms as if indicating for us to move. We ignored her, thinking she was crazy and carried on. Then the most almighty sound from up above, to where we looked, spotting an object at the top of the hill that was now tumbling down, faster and faster. We could see now that it was a tree stump, the old women clearly signalling for us to evacuate the water before it came crashing down.

Every bounce sent the stump in our direction. It looked huge now, as big as a car, demolishing the scenery and other trees as it came hurtling down (it turned out they were felling trees at the summit). Many people froze with fear, not knowing which way to run, or which way the stump was going to tumble. The group split and raced off in different directions, all except for one poor girl who just stood there, terrified, looking straight at it, until a second before it flattened her she bolted, tripping over a stone and falling in the water as she did so.

This enormous tree stump missed her by a metre, coming to a stop in the water beside her. She stumbled to her feet as white as a ghost and shaking. It was genuinely the closest I'd ever seen to someone being killed.

On the way back down the trail we warned those climbing up it about the falling tree stumps, to which these people looked at us as though we were crazy, in the same way as we'd looked at the old woman thinking the same.

With that we were ready for off, the road from Manali to Leh — a passage through the Himalayas — simply to see if we could climb it or not. It was a task that for once didn't involve a visa or bureaucracy or anything else complicated. This challenge was simple; to make it to Leh in the hope that in doing so we would gain confidence ahead of our passage through Pakistan.

Things got off to a great start; the initial climb was gentle and smooth. The road surface was asphalt and steadily it wound its way up through little wooden villages, twisting in and out of narrow streets that reminded me of being in the Alps. The shape of the valley landscape was like a giant three-dimensional 'V', fallen flat, with the road somehow climbing the point at which the two lines met.

Before long the road became steeper, rougher and muddier. You could feel the temperature drop with every turn and soon you were looking out over lethal drops, with no safety barriers and barely room for two vehicles to pass. I rounded one corner only to find a string of tourist buses and trucks on their way to Leh, all taking it in turns to try and claw their way up a horrible muddy slope. Many of them were stuck up to their axles and going nowhere.

Not wishing to suffer the same fate, I arced my way past and nailed the throttle, paddling desperately with my feet, Dot's back wheel slipping and sliding before catching traction and slowly rewarding us with progress, the road going on and on, up this mountain, seemingly forever, all the way to the top.

I could feel the altitude affecting her more and more. Instead of third gear I'd need second, instead of second gear I'd need first. The road now was like a skipping rope curling around and back on itself as the side of the fallen 'V' grew steeper and steeper. The roadside drops were killer, with no barriers or warning.

A truck had overrun on its way down and had its front wheels right over the edge. Men were unloading it to try and balance the weight, while other trucks attempted to drag it back onto the road. Another truck was

152

on its side having clearly clipped a bump in the road and tipped over, the margin between it coming to a rest on the road and on the cliff far below not more than a foot or two.

At 3,978 metres you come across the first pass, Rohtang La. This is a flat, treeless tablet of land and the first resting point after eighty kilometres of riding. There were little stalls selling tea and snacks. I sat and sipped a few cups, my head starting to throb from the altitude. Judging by the amount of traffic this was a popular route for the trucks and the tourist buses, but still it felt like a world of extremes, as though none of it was a given; that your survival on this road wasn't to be taken for granted. Strangely, it reminded me of the remote homesteads in the Australian Outback and the way they would harbour a great energy that would help propel you to the next one.

Beyond that first pass the road descended along a stony, rutted causeway. Picking up speed was dangerous but also irresistible. Dot being so light and nimble she simply skipped across it all. I'd stand up on the foot pegs and let her back-end do what it liked, weaving in and out of the ruts and bumps. It was great fun and much easier than going uphill.

I stopped on a hairpin corner to admire the view across this vast mountainous landscape. As I did so a youth on a motorbike pulled up alongside me. He had a head of fiery red hair and turned out to be German, only eighteen years of age and going by the name of Sascha. He told me how, in the previous week, he'd had a nasty accident involving an Indian man who had almost been killed. This was now Sascha's second bike after the first one was written off in the crash.

He sat and smoked a spliff, telling me how, after India, he's off to Vietnam to visit the granddad he'd never met before. He was a cool guy, the pair of us deciding to ride the rest of the way to Leh together. His 500cc Enfield of course had more power than Dorothy, but she had the agility and that made the pair of us quite evenly matched.

It was just nice to have company, to ride as a pair, even though it annoyed the hell out of me to keep having to stop so he could smoke another spliff. I don't know how he was managing to ride straight. But he'd just get back onboard and bomb along with his wild red hair flapping in the breeze. Together we squeezed past the chugging lorries and waved at the teams of workers who toiled endlessly to repair the road. Many were women and children, by the roadside chiselling rocks. It made us feel guilty for riding past, having such a blast.

Wild rivers ran fast across the road, sweeping off the edge and into the abyss below. Most had been quite easy to cross and barely worth a mention, but one in particular was sinister, the water deep and raging, the road surface beneath it just a bed of jagged loose rocks.

We stopped to watch a truck pass through it and held our breaths as we lined our bikes up, picking the most appropriate line and then gunning it. The water came up to our knees, threatening to wash us over the edge. Somehow the bikes caught traction and we scrambled out the other side and stood dripping on the spot. We whooped and hollowed before carrying on.

From there the road became tougher, steeper and rougher. It was brutal, but gorgeous, an awkward contrast that made me want to stop and turn back, but also ride on to see more of it. Every so often there'd be a little village with food stalls set up in the palm of mountains. The accommodation out here was little tent communities, operated by Tibetans or Nepalese for the few months the road was open. The plan was to cover the near-five hundred kilometre distance to Leh in two days, staying in one of these tent communities along the way.

By 5pm on that first day we were only just starting to climb the second pass of Baralacha La at 4,892 metres. This was a real test for Dot. Every kilometre she'd stall through a lack of oxygen and therefore power. Eventually she would fire up again and go a little further, but then cut out again. I was concerned, as we were quite a way from anywhere and by this stage my hands were bitterly cold. My feet were worse, sodden from all the waterfalls and not helped by the fact I was only wearing one sock.

I'd lost the other somewhere on my travels and now, with snow towering in banks along the roadside, and Converse soaking wet, I could feel the day losing its heat and the deep chill of night fast approaching. It definitely wasn't the best time to get another blasted puncture, but that's exactly what I got.

I cruised to a stop on a patch of gravel just off the road, just short of 5,000 metres. An old building with no roof and no floor was buried in the snow nearby. Sascha was nowhere to be seen as he was riding faster than me and was probably already a good few kilometres ahead.

I took out my tools and with shivering hands and feet set to work. By now I'd done it half a dozen times or more, but this time, whether it was my numb limbs or the disability of panic, I just couldn't do it. My efforts grew worse and worse until finally I conceded that I would be spending the night in the old building, with just a tent, no sleeping bag, no stove, no food, only a bit of water, wearing only one sock, and the temperature would be well below freezing.

That's when I heard the sound of a motorbike. As it drew near I knew it had to be an Enfield; the moment Sascha burst around the corner one of the most joyous of my life.

It was the sight of salvation. And of raw joy, of which I can't imagine you could ever replicate. It existed only in a moment such as this. And if we're going to believe in fairies, then this ginger-haired German was the biggest one of the lot. He'd spotted I was missing and stopped to wait. When I'd not shown up he'd come back looking for me. He now jumped off the bike, grabbed the tools and began fixing the puncture as I sat there pathetic. So cold, so damn cold.

With the puncture finally mended we remounted and took to the road, the pair of us now completely alone out here, in this vast wilderness, no other traffic, only a scenery of shimmering snow.

As darkness fell I tucked in behind the Enfield as the headlight was brighter and the road ahead pitch black and bumpy. I couldn't feel my hands; my feet were numb. Dot was almost dead. We were just lucky it was downhill, allowing us to free-wheel. If it had been uphill, with her cutting out, it would have been hell.

Into the night we kept on riding, taking it steady; a frightening time along a rutted muddy road, strewn with rocks and even more of those sudden drops into the abyss. Finally, two hours later, we stumbled upon one of the Tibetan encampments, a dozen tents buried deep in the cup of this barren mountain land.

We pulled off the road at 9pm. It must have been minus ten degrees. No one else was here but the hosts; three Tibetan men, huddled together in their tent with a roaring fire and drinking hot cups of sweet chai tea. We ate a plate of food around the stove and slept in one of the tents, under a triple layer of blankets. The bikes were outside, broken and shivering. Our bodies were inside in the same state. This was riding in the starkest wilderness and it had taken its toll.

The next morning when we finally crawled from under the covers and wrapped up as warmly as we could, we finally witnessed our surroundings by daylight. A violent palm of rocks. Raw, sinister bleakness. No mercy from nature. There was wind and there was snow. There was bitterness, there were wet gloves and shoes and a sock. I wrapped my feet in plastic bags to keep them dry, put my Converse boots over the top of them and wore all the clothes I'd got.

Dot was in a worse state than any of us. She would barely start and, when I did get her going, she would move a metre before stalling again. She was frozen stiff, dead, or close to it. I kept firing her into life and trying again. Finally, she mustered just enough strength to build some momentum and from there it was simply a case of slowly coaxing her back to life, though it was clear she was on the verge of packing up.

I said as much to Sascha, explaining how it was probably best that I turn around now, thinking it best not to go any further because when I made it Leh I was only going to have to turn around and ride back again. I explained how I must preserve her engine for Pakistan.

To all that Sascha turned around and called me 'gay'. I didn't care, call me that; I rode off in the opposite direction, towards Manali, a day's ride away, while he went off the other way, towards Leh, until five minutes later I thought, 'Bollocks to this, I'm not having a ginger-haired German calling me gay.' So I turned around and, riding like a maniac, managed to catch him up, more determined than ever that me and Dot were going to prove both him and me wrong.

That was a tough day. I was frantic for Dot. So many times she would die and come back to life. We met a couple of British bikers on Royal Enfields who had a fiddle with her carburettor and promised that would improve her — but it didn't.

On some of the slopes, she would have to sit in first gear for kilometre after kilometre, the speed down to fifteen kilometres per hour. If the road took even the slightest dip, even if just down the other side of a bump, I would 'hump' her to help build that little bit of momentum, hearing the revs rise slightly.

If I could get her into second gear with some revs behind her, then she would be alright. But getting those revs, that was impossible. So through this wilderness she was tortured in first gear, for hour upon savage hour. But she never gave up, just kept on screaming.

The only reprieve was a plateau that must have been thirty kilometres in length. It was almost like a giant table top, smothered with sand, mountains all around to stop the sand blowing off. At times along here Dot touched fifty, her back end slewing through the sand. I imagine on something like a big BMW you'd be at the mercy of the machine, and be intimidated by that fact. Instead, on little Dorothy, I just kept the throttle open and only a few times considered the consequences of coming off in skateboard trousers and salmon pink waterproof jacket at such speed, on such a rough surface, so far from medical assistance.

Then it was on to the biggest challenge of them all, the road's highest point, Taglang La, at 5,325 metres. This was hell. Utter, sheer, endless hell. Dot in first, screaming in agony, my head feeling like it was going to explode from lack of oxygen, the muddy unpaved road seemingly going on and on forever, a vicious drop-off to the side, trucks coming the other way, snow beginning to fall, the wind howling, the speedo down to ten. It was endless torture for both of us, yet we kept catching glimpses of the summit, knowing that if we kept pushing and riding then we would eventually make it, no matter how long it would take and however much pain it caused. We *had* to make that summit, even if we both collapsed at the top.

And finally there it was; the top of the world. Colin's old motorbike, bought from Joe at One Ten Motorcycles, ridden 25,000 kilometres on this adventure alone, now here, having conquered the second highest road in the world with no modifications, with me as a rider, and the weight of all my gear, standing at 5,238 metres.

She'd done something truly spectacular. She'd punched well above her weight, and with that I was genuinely, humbly, proud, because by now Dorothy wasn't just my motorbike carrying me across the world, she was also my companion and friend; she was what stopped me from feeling so alone on this journey. Because by now I'd realised how life is a bit like a see-saw in a park — it only works when you have someone sat on the other end. And that 'person' in the seat opposite me right now was Dorothy, the 105cc motorbike that had just climbed to the very top of the world.

***

It was a great feeling rolling into Leh later that day, almost as though we'd survived a great disaster, though me and Sascha somehow got separated in the traffic and I never saw the ginger haired fairy again. As for Dot, she was in quite a state. Her front forks were weeping oil, the mad rush to change the tyre at the top of the mountain had left her rear axle threaded, her front brake cable was stretched and she even struggled to make it up the hill in the centre of town.

I took her to a mechanic who told me her piston was shot and she needed a new one, which he didn't have, though I didn't believe him anyway. I tried tuning Dot myself and ended up with the carburettor in pieces and had to phone Joe, back in Australia — time zone permitting — to have him talk me through the process of putting it back together again.

During this time I was staying in a guesthouse down a back lane with friends I'd been running in to much of the way through India. Nancy (Swiss) and James (English) were travelling around India on a Royal Enfield having purchased it in the southern Indian city of Pondicherry, then riding it up through Delhi, to Rishikesh — the place where we'd first met — and now up to Manali and Leh as well. They argued like cat and a dog but were a great couple to be around, I liked them very much.

Then there was Jayme and Kristen, a couple of Canadian girls I'd met in Delhi, our journeys through India shadowing one another's and now bringing us all together here, where the pair of them took pity on me, buying me a thick pair of woolly black socks for the return journey back down to Manali.

The lot of us hung out for a few days, meandering into the town and sampling every cake in the coffee shops. Leh was busy with travellers, the pace much more relaxed than the rest of India, almost as though it wasn't part of India at all. The traveller's uniform was baggy cotton trousers and all manner of brightly coloured tops, Leh clearly the scene of the modern day hippy.

One of the days we hired a couple of extra motorbikes and headed out to a monastery on the outskirts of town, the others going off to take photos of the monks while I stood and looked over the valley, enjoying a bit of clarity. Later we rode up to a giant statue overlooking the town, sitting with our legs dangling over the side as the sun came down. A beautiful memory of a beautiful time, though I was a little on edge throughout all this, Jayme quite rightly calling me a curmudgeon. Little wonder really...

From here, the plan was to ride back down to Manali (which I did with Nancy and James on their bike Excalibur), rest a night, then enter Pakistan on the very last day my visa would allow it. From that moment on, I would have ten days to ride up the spine of the country, along the KKH, to where, on that tenth day, at the border with China, I would meet Abdul, my Chinese guide. I would then be in China for seven days, cutting a small corner of it, a distance perhaps of no more than 1,000 kilometres.

From there I would enter Kyrgyzstan, a country I'd not really heard of until the detour took me that way. Here, I would plan the next stage of the detour that was taking me up and over Afghanistan instead of beneath it. I calculated the detour was going to add at least 3,000 kilometres to the total journey length, and in terms of time, a great deal. It'd already taken six weeks trying to arrange this alternative to Iran. Our last ride into England would be met with an autumn chill at this rate.

As for Pakistan, the country of immediate concern, I'd received an email from my cousin Jane who worked with a girl who was born in the country. The friend had told her it really wasn't safe for me to go, and how even she, as a national, wouldn't go there herself. More bombings had been reported on the news and there'd still been no sign of the kidnapped Frenchman.

In preparation I emailed my Hotmail and Facebook login codes to Paul and put him in charge of sending out the final word should it not come from me. I even emailed Mandy, just to say hi, and possibly goodbye; what the hell. Say it whilst you still can.

The other guys on the postie bike, Nat and Aki, who I'd been in contact with — hoping to meet up in India but never finding mutually suitable dates — had decided not to venture beyond India and were instead deciding on another route.

I couldn't blame them. I don't think I could have crossed into Pakistan with someone I loved on the back either. I respected them for having the courage to make that decision because I'm certain it must take more courage to stop and turn back than it does to carry on. Is it only the coward who continues to run? I often wonder.

Chapter Eighteen
Pakistan

It's not said with any intent to sound dramatic, but in the build-up to Pakistan I'd given much thought to the prospect of death and what that would mean and what that would feel like. Where would it take me, what would I see? Do you see blackness, for example, do you see nothing, but what does nothing look like? I just couldn't get my head around it. And I guess this is the one time on the trip I wished I'd been religious. Because if I had been, I'd have ridden towards the border with the belief that should the worst happen I would simply go to a better place and carry on, that it wouldn't be the end, just part of the process of life. But not being a religious person, all I saw was the end. And that scared me.

But I think it's necessary to consider such things as part of the preparation. Because you do need to know that what you're about to do is worth the risk. And of that you need to be absolutely certain, because I couldn't imagine anything worse than being at that border and feeling unsure of your conviction to cross it.

You need to know with every bit of confidence that there is no alternative to this, that this is the only option you have and that you must take it or forever wonder why you didn't. I spent many hours thinking of the consequences of the situations I might find myself in; of kidnap, of bomb blasts and torture, but none of them scared me as much as the thought of turning away from this challenge and flying 'home.' There was never any question or doubt about riding into Pakistan, not at any point, and I'm grateful for that or I would have struggled otherwise.

And so Pakistan, here I go. Riding along your highway, heading to Lahore, what do you have in store? The first thing I saw were boys pulling wheelies on motorbikes no bigger than Dot. They were good at it, too. With their friends sitting on the back, as the front wheel touched the sky, they would nod at me and I would nod back.

The road was smooth and straight and all around hung the humid dust of a dry barren landscape. Brittle wooden buildings rose from the ashes, and if anything there was less litter and general clutter here than there'd been in India. Also much less colour; the world was drab in comparison, with none of the vibrant fabrics worn by the men and women on the other side of the border. The typical outfit was the salwar kameez — like a baggy pair of pyjamas — in sombre colours to match the drab earth.

The road continued straight. It wasn't far from the border to Lahore, perhaps forty kilometres. I kept my eye out, the most alert I'd ever been. Curious, nervous, worried, alive, so damn alive. Bottle this, this can be my opium. But you know, for all the worrying, this wasn't so bad. I saw Caltex petrol stations, I saw the familiar fast-food chains of Subway and KFC. I saw roundabouts being built and a city little different from all the others I'd encountered along the way. It had the same buzz, the same sweat, the same dreams being dreamed as anywhere else. And when I asked for directions people still took time to help me and point me in the right direction. There was no communication problem either; English spoken in Pakistan was the best I'd encountered in Asia so far.

At the traffic lights I sat staring at the mass of motorcycles, their riders all in their salwar kameez, their feet in brown leather sandals, their hair neatly gelled and some with thick black moustaches.

No one wore a helmet and their bikes were all the same: Honda CD70s, the CD standing for Cash Deposit, which was written down the side as though some kind of boast. Some had wheeled benches rigged to the back, acting as taxis. They belched out noxious black smoke, but moved slowly enough for me to weave between them, those new saddle bags clearly not keeping my profile low, as I still stuck out like a sore thumb. I was just glad I hadn't covered Dot, as I was going to, in black tape as part of an attempt to make the pair of us more discreet, because all the bikes in Pakistan were the same red as Dorothy.

I found the place I intended to stay in Lahore — the Regale Internet Inn — down a back alley, the walls of which were strewn with posters and graffiti written in Urdu. This was the place where almost every overland traveller to Lahore stays, recommended by the Lonely Planet guide, something I didn't usually like carrying for the way you can find yourself religiously following its advice, but for Pakistan I thought its knowledge might come in handy.

The man at a street café had pointed out the entrance to the inn, an inconspicuous single door leading to a dark set of steep stairs. I climbed them, my eyes adjusting to the light and slowly focusing on the familiar world of temporary beds and pillows with occupants that changed with every passing day; this one now serving as my momentary sanctuary from the world.

Having dumped all my gear on a bed in a dark dorm room, I climbed even more steps to the rooftop, four floors up, where I stood and looked out at a stunning view across the chaotic city below. Naively, I thought I might be the only person daft enough to be here, and yet there were almost half a dozen of us staying in the guesthouse that day.

Andrew and Amelia were an English couple in their thirties, travelling around the world in an old Toyota Landcruiser. They too were struggling to get a visa for Iran, but rather than commit to going through China, had decided instead to enter Pakistan to give it one last shot at the Iranian Embassy in Islamabad. If that failed, then they would have little choice but to consider going up through China as well.

Daniel was an Englishman in his late twenties with a shaven head and an easy-going manner. He was driving a Toyota HiLux around the world. His next destination, he said, was Afghanistan, something we said was suicide, though to this he simply stretched his hands behind his head, leaned back, and as casual as you like said, 'I'll be alright.' And we all shook our heads and laughed because he probably would be.

He was certainly an interesting guy, not giving much away about his reasons for being out here and wanting to do such a thing. He was just here, and that was his plan, and that's all we needed to know. Daniel wore a salwar kameez, just like the local Pakistani men, and had one outfit spare that he kindly gave to me as disguise for the road through the perilous north.

The last person to arrive that day was Michel, a Dutchman, in his thirties, tall and slender, riding a big BMW R1200 GS from Holland to Nepal, the bike at least twice the size of Dot. Michel was also very quiet and unassuming — he was just here, in Lahore, as though he'd popped out to the shops for a pint of milk. His route had brought him down through China and over the KKH, the route I would be doing in reverse and so he talked to me about it, telling me it was fine, which was reassuring.

He also excited me with talk of the countries that lay beyond, like Uzbekistan and Turkmenistan, which sounded another world entirely. I couldn't have imagined riding through such countries the day I'd set off, or in fact the day I'd sat with Dave, fixing that fist puncture way back in Coffs Harbour. But then again, I couldn't have imagined riding though Pakistan either.

Today though there was just something very comforting about that group at the hostel in Lahore. Usually I would feel the odd one out in a hostel, being the guy on the motorbike with the beard riding across the world. Sometimes I felt like I didn't always belong with the other backpackers, or have much in common with them, as our trips were so different.

This is what sometimes contributed to my loneliness; that I didn't have much contact with people of my own nature. But here, around that table, I'd found a nice place to belong, to sit and talk with people in similar situations and going through similar things. We'd all turned to the road for various reasons, escaping from something, or running away, for want of a better word.

We tried once more to talk Daniel out of his plan to ride through Afghanistan, but there was no point. That was what he was going to do and no way were our fears, or even his own, going to stop him going ahead with it.

In a way this frightened me, because in him, and in me, I could see how it escalates. Almost every day you feel like you've reached your limit and then something happens — you feel you have to push yourself just a little bit further, a little bit harder. It's almost as though you start your journey with the string on your kite nice and tight. You're nervous; you don't want to fly it too high. Then, every time you face a danger you're forced to let out a little more string. As the danger grows and the journey continues, you let out a little bit more string and up the kite goes, higher and higher. Every time it happens you think that's as high as your kite will fly, until the next time, when you realise you have all the string in the world. And that means one day I will probably want to ride through Afghanistan as well.

**

As I wound out the throttle and watched Dot's needle flicker past seventy, I kept seeing signs for Islamabad. I couldn't quite believe it; I was in Pakistan, that place I'd seen on the news so many times in the months leading up to being here. The Taliban were said to be surging faster than ever, and yet to be here you would never know it. For all the worry and the build-up, it was just another place on the map. Another bunch of people with different customs and traditions and yet the same fundamental basics of humanity — family, health, wealth and a peaceful existence — that make all corners of the world seem so familiar once you get past the visual. And so I relaxed and just cruised along, staring out to the dry bush land and half finished construction projects, just as I would have done anywhere else in the world. I didn't ride any faster. I didn't ride with any more fear. This was just a road, and for me now the road was the most predictable, orderly place I knew.

Of course, with no more than ten days in the country there are only so many conclusions you can come to. That's what you realise about travelling; it's just a snapshot of a place, capturing a brief moment in time and space that can never be repeated. You could return the following year or even the following day and get a completely different experience of it, depending on who you meet and what situations you encounter. But of

Pakistan I got a good vibe and really didn't feel a need to worry. Maybe the missing Frenchman had felt exactly as I did, right up to the very moment he was taken away at gunpoint. But it served no purpose worrying about such things. Still, the biggest danger to me was the traffic on the road, not the bandits beside it.

As for Dot, she wasn't running quite as crisply as she did the day I rode her out of Joe's shop in Caboolture, yet she gave me no reason to doubt her ability to take me to England or even over the Himalayas for the second time. She certainly didn't need a new piston as the mechanic up in Leh had thought, and as for all the other problems it was almost as though she'd cured herself.

The front brake still worked despite the stretched cable, the rear axle was still held in place by the threaded bolt, the front forks still held up — despite the leak which I'd topped up — and the shoelace I'd tied around the headlight bracket to stop it rattling was holding up nicely. When Michel had told me how his bike would have to be shipped home if it suffered any serious problems, I realised more than ever that I was riding the right machine.

**

Islamabad, the capital of Pakistan, really surprised me having arrived there later that day. Given what I'd seen on the news, I imagined it to be almost in ruins, like Dili or Kathmandu. In fact, being purpose-built in the sixties, it reminded me of Milton Keynes in England, or Canberra in Australia.

The streets were set out on a grid, with space made for parks and a huge mosque at the northern end, green hills all around. Expensive German cars drove along its streets, people sat out at pavement cafés. There was a huge bookshop, and a Honda dealer. If the Taliban were coming, I certainly didn't see any evidence of panic, just the occasional military checkpoint which I imagine is quite normal. The only thing that looked out of line was the machine gun emplacement, trained on the gate of the tourist campsite on the outskirts of town.

I'd not seen it at first, entering the leafy yard at the invitation of the ground-keeper who hurried across the grass to greet me. Then, out of the corner of my eye, I caught sight of a wall of sand bags a short distance away, resting on them a big machine gun, at least 30 calibre, manned by a soldier, with a nest of army tents behind him. Clearly they were there to protect the tourists passing through town.

Having crossed the line of sights, nodding to the gunman as I went, I set up my tent on the acre of grass that resembled any other campsite I'd slept on in the past. There were trees to give shade, picnic tables and a mandatory filthy toilet block.

The soldiers shared the facilities. In the morning you would meet them at the urinal, guns slung over their shoulders. I desperately wanted to take a picture looking down the barrel of the main gun at the entrance, its sights set on my bike. But I dare not ask them. I wish now that I had.

Andrew and Amelia were also at the campsite, having driven up from Lahore that same day to take one last shot at the Iranian visa. We all wandered around Islamabad together, me and Andrew in our salwar kameez, Amelia with her head and shoulders covered out of respect. We had no bother at all; in fact, when I entered the Honda dealer inquiring about replacement parts, the owner brought me a tea, sat me down, wrote me his contact details on a piece of paper in case I found myself in trouble, and at the bottom added the line, 'I love foreigners.'

He seemed genuine enough, though I did wonder if it was an obligation of faith, and not self will that had him write that, though it was charming nonetheless.

That night Amelia cooked us all beans and bread from the back of their 4x4. Their vehicle was an incredible thing. On the roof was a fold-out tent with ladder leading up to it. Inside was a fresh-water pump, a fridge and a shelving unit for all their gear.

They'd bought all sorts of things on their travels; rugs from India, paintings from other parts. My camping equipment was pathetic by comparison. But I didn't mind. I'd reached that point where I was happy with just petrol in the tank and some clue as to where I was going. I didn't need much else. Just follow the road. The rest had fallen away. Even my blog and website had been put on hold. They can be quite draining after a while, an obligation, which people begin to expect you to fulfil.

In a way then I was pretty naked now. I didn't have any problems, well, nothing I really worried too much about. It was no good worrying about Mandy; she was gone. Moving on. Back in Australia, a world away, nostalgia still at play.

If only … why didn't I … I should have … I could have … I must not make the same mistakes again. But I know I probably will.

**

Dorothy and I were now on the KKH, starting just north of Islamabad. We had four days to ride 800 kilometres to the border with China, where we would meet our guide, Abdul. It was a plan of military precision that just so happened to have been blessed with good luck and timing, for the day my Pakistan visa expired aligned perfectly with the earliest date David at Stan Tours told me I could cross into China. If they hadn't have aligned, it would have caused quite a hassle, and could have involved applying for another Pakistan visa, but, as things had turned out, there was no problem at all, and our only responsibility was to make sure we were there, at the Chinese border, on that date.

Near the town of Abbottabad, where Osama Bin Laden would later be discovered and killed, I stopped in one village to ask an elderly man if I was heading in the right direction. No sooner had the engine stopped running before he had yanked me from the bike and insisted I sit in the shade while he fetched me a glass of tea. Other men and boys from the village gathered around, curious to know where I was heading.

As I was trying to explain myself, the elderly man removed a steel-toothed comb from his pocket, removed my cap and began dragging the comb through my tangled hair. I'd not brushed or cut it since setting off as there was no need to, hiding it instead beneath the cap. I allowed him to do it, if only to be polite.

When he was done he asked if I had any whisky. 'No,' I said, asking what the local policeman would say if he was caught with such a drink.

'Nothing,' he said. 'Not as long as he got a drink as well.' I laughed. It might have been a different religion and way of life, but it still shared the same inclination towards insubordination and simple pleasures.

The road from there began to climb the shallow valley. It really was beautiful out here; quiet, green and peaceful. At one point, a car pulled alongside me, the window winding down and a head leaning out. For a second I thought it was someone wishing me harm, but instead the head smiled and shouted something spoken with a broad English accent from the north.

As we slowed down to a crawl, the man explained how he lived and studied in Manchester and was in Pakistan visiting his relatives up here in the mountains. He asked if I wanted to have dinner with them and to that I agreed, following their car to a tiny village, not far from where the massive earthquake struck in 2005, killing a staggering 87,350 people, something I still can't quite comprehend.

The house was just off the road, up a hill to the right, a stone wall surrounding it and a gate through to a yard with the main house to the right and the guest quarters to the left. The men of the family all sat in here, around a spread of food set out on the floor; trays of various curries, dhal, breads and rice. The women of the family were nowhere to be seen. Only the student — who's name I sadly now don't remember — spoke English, meaning that he had to translate for those asking questions. The food was delicious, we ate it with our hands and then relaxed with tea.

By this time it was 4pm and I was asked if I would like to stay the night. I considered the offer before conceding that there was too much daylight and kilometres to cover before calling it a day. I thanked the family and said goodbye, riding a few more hours along lonely mountainous roads, before finally coming to a rest at the town of Besham.

Andrew and Amelia had travelled up here for a look around a few weeks before, telling me how it wasn't the nicest of places and that I'd be better off finding somewhere else to stay. Amelia said she had felt threatened by the mood of the town, even inside their truck. Fortunately, on the edge of town was a Government operated compound promising safe haven for the night, with a chain of these facilities found throughout rural Pakistan.

From the main road I turned down the drive, stopping at the security gate where guards approached with Kalashnikovs. The man in charge insisted they search my luggage, something that meant all of my gear had to be strewn across the floor for the whole world, and the boys of the village, to see. Only then was I allowed to carry on my way, down the driveway to the fenced compound at the bottom of this long rocky drive.

There was a choice of two guesthouses, both of them built of concrete and resembling nuclear bunkers. I chose the one with the room for just under ten dollars. It was a young boy who bartered with me, no older than ten or eleven years of age, but already a shrewd businessman.

He showed me to a room, one that not so long ago must have been his, given the cartoon jungle wallpaper and tricycle in the corner. I unloaded all of my gear while he made me a pot of tea, drinking it in a secluded little garden which had its own table and chairs. The air was still, the night calm, the sun long gone and the sight of the stars in the sky above drawing my vision up. Steep red cliffs rose all around. It was strangely silent, not even the sound of a truck could be heard because even they don't travel at night due to a fear of banditry.

I took out my diary and wrote some notes, distracting myself with the things that I had on my mind, which always would catch up with me whenever the wheels failed to turn. It turned out to be a terrible night. I was up most of it with sickness and diarrhoea. It was perhaps the food that had changed, from largely vegetarian cuisine in India, to the meat based meals of Pakistan.

Stalls would sell kebabs on the street. Mutton was commonplace and then for desert the street cafés would have huge vats of lassi, a sweet yoghurt drink, which you bought in bags and while obviously warm, still tasted really good. The best food we found however was back in Lahore, at a department store with a supermarket in its basement, stocking a full assortment of English goods, from Heinz Baked Beans, Kellogg's cornflakes, Cadbury's chocolate, and best of all, Bass Shandy in a can. I imagined my toilet trouble now was down to the lamb.

After little sleep I left early the next morning, riding through Besham at first light. You certainly wouldn't want to break down around here, the town marking the start of the KKH's worst section, running for a couple of hundred kilometres alongside the infamous Swat Valley, once hailed as the Switzerland of Pakistan and once popular with tourists, though now said to be in the hands of the Taliban. As a result, foreign cyclists passing this way are forced to travel by bus for their own safety, while those on motorcycles are given police escorts to ensure their safe passage.

I wasn't given one at all, being stopped at the remote checkpoints to have my passport details taken down before being allowed to ride on alone. The road was mountainous, empty and stark. I'll admit to being a little nervous, especially when the local kids tried to poke sticks through the front wheel as I rode past, or leapt out from behind boulders, I'm sure with the intention of frightening me into riding off the edge of the cliff.

If anyone tried to kidnap me, my plan, I reasoned, was to ride straight for them, dodge some bullets and leap over the top, Steve McQueen-style. Or more likely surrender to the first shot. But I'm serious, I really did think I could escape capture if they tried. In my mind nothing could stop me. At times like this I felt like an unstoppable wave, which I suppose is necessary to help you push though the trepidation you might otherwise feel.

I stopped in one village for a drink. It was a middle-of-nowhere place; jagged mountains all around, sand coloured single-room houses on one side of the road, hills running down to a river on the other. The shop was in a courtyard. I got the sense I was being watched as I entered and parked. Movement in the shadows, eyes looking on. In the shop, the owner slammed my can of cola down on his counter so hard he damn well nearly smashed it. I picked up some biscuits and he jabbed the price into a calculator with such venom that he almost broke that as well.

I stood outside in the scorching sun, slugging back the fluid, tearing at the biscuits; I didn't feel welcome here. It happened at another stop a few hours later, where a couple of boys were prowling around as I drank my tea. They were squaring up for a fight. Six months ago I would have wilted in the heat. Now I stood my ground; I was ready to go. Fight, not flight.

But in a strange way, this is what I enjoyed most about the country. Whether they loved you or hated you, the people of Pakistan weren't afraid to show it. That meant you always knew where you stood. In India and Nepal you were never sure if people were talking to you because they were friendly (or curious) or because they wanted money from you.

In Pakistan I never got that impression. In fact I liked being ignored and snubbed, because it meant I could ignore and snub people in return, rather than have to act polite. I'm glad then that not everyone followed Islam's mandate to welcome all guests, especially those from a foreign land. It gave the interaction I had with people a certain authenticity. One mechanic even refused to mend my puncture and just turned away. I respected that. And in a way didn't blame him. He had every right to hate me, especially given what was happening to his fellow tribesman just over the border in Afghanistan, being bombed by the British as they were at the time.

As for the scenery of the KKH, what is there to say other than it is a road through mountains so tall and so powerful in their explosion from the earth that you can only hope they don't come alive and smash you. There were three levels to it: at the very bottom the raging river had cut a deep trench and ploughed violently through it, the flow powered by the summer melt. Above that was the plateau, green and fertile, on which the road ran. Here crops grew, people lived and the moisture from the soil would cool me as I rode through. Then straight up, almost vertical, rose these savage-looking mountains. It was staggeringly beautiful, but at all times I had to keep both eyes on the road. Because up here you wouldn't wish to fall from that.

Chapter Nineteen
China

It had been a nervous climb up and over the highest point of the KKH, the 4,693-metre Khunjerab Pass. At the last town in Pakistan there was no unleaded petrol and I didn't think I would have enough fuel in the tank. A delivery was being made the next day and the owner told me to wait until then, but I couldn't, I had to cross into China that same day. All I could do was set off along the hundred-kilometre stretch of mountain road and hope I had enough fuel to get me to the top, at which point I could coast down the other side into China. Thankfully, just as I was preparing to leave, one of the guards from the Pakistan Customs house came running out with a cola bottle full of petrol he'd taken from the building's generator. It wasn't a lot, but enough to confidently power us to the summit.

The border between Pakistan and China is at the top of the world, with a huge stone arch to mark it. Just beyond that you get to the first Chinese checkpoint, a wooden hut, set amongst the mountains. It was incredibly cold up here and my head pounded from the altitude. I hoped Abdul, my guide, would be here but I couldn't see him.

I was ordered by the Chinese soldiers instead to dismount and take all my gear into the shed for inspection. I emptied my panniers and rucksack on to the table and watched as the guard inspected it all meticulously. I suspected they were looking for drugs, though they seemed more concerned with my laptop, memory cards and camera. They took these off me, as well as my passport. One of the soldiers spoke a little English and explained that my gear would have to be inspected at the main Customs House, 130 kilometres further along the Friendship Highway; Chinese irony at its best. There I would get them back.

I was not allowed to ride that distance alone; instead being ordered to sit and wait until a tourist bus also making the journey was ready to leave and we would all go in convoy.

On that bus was a Swiss man, also named Sascha, who was about my age and a crane driver by trade. He told me he'd been hiking solo in the Pakistan mountains, going off for days on end, camping in the most desolate spots, with no form of communication or anyone to make sure he returned. His next move was to try and sneak into Tibet, which is an incredibly difficult thing to do given how strictly the Chinese control the movement of foreigners there. He was a cool guy, full of spirit, living his life to the full. He stood and smoked a cigarette, while I played with my black and beige gloves.

Finally, the bus was given the green light to start its journey down the Friendship Highway, the soldier with all of my belongings jumping aboard and instructing me to tuck in behind. Unsurprisingly, it soon transpired that there was no way a 105cc motorbike could keep up with a minibus at 4,500 metres, especially not with a ferocious headwind such as it was this day.

Our convoy swiftly developed an accordion like motion. They'd speed off, I'd fall behind, they'd slow down, I'd catch up, they'd speed up, I'd fall behind, and so on. This infuriated the bus driver, not to mention his Chinese and Pakistani passengers onboard, Sascha the only westerner on the bus. I couldn't blame the others for getting irate; it was late in the afternoon, they just wanted to get to where they were going, not wait for the silly foreigner on his motorbike.

At one stage, the bus pulled over, allowing me to pass, before tucking in behind me. It then came within an inch of our tail light, as though the driver thought his presence there was going to somehow grant us extra speed.

I hated it being there, the bus filling my wing mirrors, and so I waved furiously for it to pass. Still it pushed. Still I waved. Until eventually it overtook, every face on board stuck to the side windows urging me to speed up. I looked across at them, still doing fifty, still being battered by the wind, still so very cold, still so very worn out in the middle of the Himalayas, and I yelled back at them with all my might: 'I'm going as fast as I can you fucking cunts.'

After three hours and one of the hardest, least fun rides of my entire life, we made it to the Customs House, a square shaped, formal building on the outskirts of a small town called Tashkurgan. As I dismounted, the soldier from the bus approached with a motorcycle tyre that I recognised as the one I'd bought in East Timor. It had fallen off Dot somewhere along the highway, the bus driver stopping to pick it up, something I was grateful for.

I'd bought that tyre in Dili, used it for 5,000 kilometres or more, and when I finally replaced it just couldn't bear to part with it and so had carried it all this way as a spare. Strange how attached you get to the things you carry, even something as inanimate as a tyre. I reattached it to Dot and gathered my paperwork, ready to enter the building. It was now, finally, that a man with a clipboard approached and introduced himself as Abdul.

Abdul was a stout man, not tall, with a moustache and decent grasp of English. Poor Abdul had been waiting there all day and it was now almost 8pm. But for the riding over a mountain pass, but for waiting two hours for the bus, but for the 130 kilometres riding it behind it, I might have been there sooner, as it was, we weren't and he had no choice but to wait, because he and his paperwork colleagues were being paid $2,200 to do so.

I still couldn't figure out why I needed him and why China imposes such rules. If I was to fly there and buy a local bike I could have ridden it around the country until my heart's content, but because I was bringing in my own vehicle I needed a guide and all the paperwork that goes with that. And with the paperwork there was a problem.

Some of the bike's identity numbers didn't match those given on the forms I'd faxed through to the agency in China, and because the art of bureaucracy is so precise here they wouldn't release the bike and instead impounded her overnight. Which was fine, no big deal. I could handle that. I just needed to retrieve all the gear that had been confiscated back at the first checkpoint.

I was given my passport, then my laptop, but not the bag it went in. Finally I got the bag back, but not the memory cards. I complained. Finally I got the memory cards back and climbed into Abdul's car thinking that was everything, until one of the staff opened the door and handed me the external hard-drive I didn't even know had been taken. It would have been funny, had I not been so tired and weary.

The following morning I returned to the Customs House with Abdul. There, we learned that I was being made an example of by the Chinese Government. Our case had gone all the way to the top, not just to the local government, but the central government. I didn't get it. I was bringing my bike in for seven days to cut the corner into Kyrgyzstan. I wasn't moving here, setting up business or wishing to stay. But no, it seemed the Chinese wanted to show how welcoming they were by letting me through, even though there was a glitch with the paperwork. It really was a farce, one in which I never really knew what was going on.

Abdul I feared spoke in half truths, and I didn't like that sense of being in the dark. All the way from Sydney to China I'd been the one responsible for everything. It had been just me, dealing with the paperwork, negotiating with authorities, learning how to overcome the language barriers and all the other issues surrounding international travel. Now it was all in someone else's hands. I thought I might like that for a change, but I didn't. I didn't like relinquishing control, relying on other people, because to them it's just a job, it doesn't matter so much. To me it was everything.

With Dot finally liberated, I saddled up, assuming Abdul would have to follow me; that, after all, was the reason I was paying the money. Yet he told me to ride ahead, and that he'd catch up with me a little later, as he was faster than me and he couldn't bear to travel so slowly.

I rode off, bemused, but just happy to be riding again, the road threading between more mountains, past gorgeous lakes and through canyons where a whistling wind blew. It was so cold I had to put every single item of clothing on. I stopped only for a military checkpoint, where I thought I'd be in trouble for not being with Abdul. But there was no problem at all, being waved through, having first been told me off for taking photographs. After five hours of riding and still no sign of Abdul, I stopped in a village to buy some food. Only then, an hour later, did Abdul finally catch up.

He said there had been a problem with his car and that it kept breaking down on him. I struggled to hide my frustration. I'd come all this way alone, always riding at my own pace, and now I had to wait for the person I was paying two-thousand dollars for the privilege of riding with.

But I didn't blame Abdul; actually I felt a strange empathy with him, as though both of us were muddling through some tricky times that day, so I went along with it and tried to help him fix his car every time it stopped, which was every mile. There we'd stand by the side of the road, our heads under the bonnet of his Mitsubishi, both of us incompetent, pulling at leads and trying again while Dot perched on her stand behind. Finally, Abdul called his mate who came out on a little red tractor and towed his vehicle the final distance into Kashgar.

As we crawled behind it, passing through the now flat, empty landscape, I looked down at my mismatched gloves, one still beige, one still black, then in the wing mirror at my reflection: a bundle of hair and tired, blood-shot eyes. I looked old; this journey so far of seven months and 27,000 kilometres had taken its toll. I had sun spots, my beard was wild, so was my hair; I had to wear a cap under my helmet to keep the hair out of my eyes.

Dot was looking equally ragged, starting to show the effects of being ridden over the Himalayas two times, yet still plodding on with nothing more than a regular oil change and an occasional service. She dropped a bit of oil, but nothing much to worry about. We certainly must have looked quite a sight pulling into Kashgar that day: a tractor towing Abdul's stricken 4x4, the foreign vagrant riding his little red motorbike behind.

I was going to be there for four nights before being escorted to the border with Kyrgyzstan, the accommodation included in the price I'd paid for the seven-day transit through China. I would have preferred to have carried on riding, just to keep the wheels turning, until I saw the luxury of the place I would be staying and soon changed my mind.

The Seman Hotel was set in its own grounds, a horseshoe of buildings with a garden in the middle. The room had a trouser press, satellite TV, a bathtub and an ornate ceiling, which I observed from the comfort of my bed. I soon added a few contrasting touches: my spare tyre in the corner, my dirty clothes on the chair and a litre of oil by the sink in the bathroom. I had power, I had light, I even had a woman ring me at 10pm and ask if I wanted a special 'massage', the name of the hotel clearly quite appropriate. I declined and had a bath instead, enjoying this period of luxury, and Kashgar itself, which was a modern, clean city, though with a very strange split to it.

In this westerly region of China is an ethnic group called the Uighurs. They have rounder, more European faces and eyes, compared to what we stereotypically think of as the Chinese (the Hans). The Uighurs are mainly Muslim, and once ruled this part of the world back when it was called East Turkestan — Abdul was a Uighur. Then, in 1949, China made a claim on the land, sending a flood of Han people into the region and creating the source of the simmering tension that had recently flared up into violent rioting.

From all accounts the recent rioting had been brutal, with 200 dead and 1,000 injured, one man apparently eating his dinner outside a restaurant when, without warning, he was beheaded by the rival side. The streets were now patrolled by the Chinese army, their trucks parked in long lines with soldiers nursing machine guns. Anyone taking a picture of the soldiers had their cameras confiscated and were heavily interviewed by the police.

Abdul dropped into the Seman Hotel every now and again on his electric motorcycle. These were strange things, with huge, white, sharp-nosed fairings and neon graphics that made them look like laser guns. They might have been props from *Back to the Future* or *Battlestar Galactica*. A lot of people had them here; plugging them into the mains and off they went.

Abdul took me to the hospital on his. It was my leg, the one I'd broken skiing into a tree ten years before. It had been a good accident: flat out down a black run, going too fast, slipped on ice, carried on sliding, unable to stop, off the side of the piste, mid-air, hit a tree, crash-landed, broken femur and pelvis, helicopter ride off the mountain, operation, bone infection, one year in a wheelchair. I'd been lucky, real lucky.

In a way it was this accident that spurred me on to do things, before I lost my mobility or did it again. Now it was playing up, the fracture site swollen and sore. It was painful to walk on and I began to worry. I think it was the rough Himalayan roads that had taken their toll.

Credit to Abdul, I only mentioned it in passing and without any encouragement he took me straight to the main city hospital. This was an experience alright; a world of total chaos, yet, like the road system in this part of the world, it just seemed to work. We queued at one counter, bought our ticket for an x-ray for ten dollars, went upstairs, wandered around the wards looking for a doctor, then finally found two of them, who sat me on a bed beside a pile of bloody bandages from the last patient.

When they saw the results of the x-ray they told me the fracture site was looking weak and that the three tiny metal clips that had been left in from the original surgery should be taken out in the near future before the leg broke again.

The doctor advised I rest ten days before going any further. I crossed into Kyrgyzstan the following day.

Chapter Twenty
Kyrgyzstan

The Kyrgyzstan border was a desolate place, nothing around but rocky hills and an empty bleakness. The wind was howling, the road was broken — this was the wild.

I approached the soldier guarding the barrier and as I did so he clasped his fingers to form a gun and pretended to shoot me. When I stopped, I could see he was grinning, his mouth full of gold teeth, his eyes maniacal. Compared to the Chinese border post I'd just left behind, there were no big buildings or towering pillars of bureaucracy, only a caravan of wooden huts with a man at a window who glanced at my passport before giving it back. He didn't want to see the Carnet or even check my bike.

Had he done so he might well have spotted the oil leak that by now had worsened. I'd noticed those few drops of oil back in Pakistan, thinking nothing of it but gradually it had grown worse and was now almost a constant trickle, leaving a pool of black fluid wherever we'd been stood. This made me panic, as all of a sudden, the most dependable element in this whole adventure, Dorothy, wasn't in such a good way.

Irrationally, I saw this as the end, the moment it all would come to a halt, still some 8,000 kilometres from England. But what did I expect of her? She'd ridden through some incredible places, been forced up mountains she had no right to climb. She had come back from the brink, several times. Now she had three more days to ride before we made it to the Kyrgyzstan capital of Bishkek, where I hoped I could get her fixed.

Through desolate landscape we pottered, a ridge of snow capped mountains to our left, rolling green hills to our right; the only signs of human life being the circular animal-skin tents, called yurts, housing the local nomads who lived out here in the wild.

Sometimes they stood alone, other times in little clusters. Children played in the wilderness around. Horses and other animals were tethered nearby. An old Soviet 4x4 vehicle would be parked outside, and always, with absolute certainty, the family's ferocious dog would see me sauntering past and set off in chase. Their speed was incredible, and even riding flat out, pushing Dot to the limit over the wild bumpy road, leaving a trail of oil behind, we still struggled to escape.

On one occasion my sunglasses fell off my head mid-chase, the dog snapping at my heels and me thinking no chance am I stopping to pick them up now. The dog can have them.

It made me wonder how the family I'd met back at the border had managed. They were French and travelling by push-bike. The two adults had a bike each, their luggage bolted to the side in huge red waterproof sacks. Attached to each of their seat posts, almost like a tandem, were the bikes ridden by their children, who were no older than five and six. They'd travelled like that all the way across Kyrgyzstan, on these terrible, winding, bumpy roads, past these vicious dogs, and were now about to do the same across China.

I'd met some brave, crazy travellers on my way, but this family, they were the bravest and maddest of them all. How they carried all their camping gear and clothes for the kids I'll never know. But it just went to show that adventures didn't have to come to an end the day you have a family.

I arrived in Sarry Tash, a lonely outpost town three hours into my journey from the border. It was built at the point at which three roads met; the one that had led me there, the one that I would be taking to Bishkek, and a third road that journeyed south to Uzbekistan.

The town was once a trading post on the drug smuggling route and not a big place — probably a two horse town — with a scattering of weathered wooden homes dotted either side of the main junction.

Children in woolly hats played in the dirt, a broken vodka bottle lay on the ground, an old petrol pump dispensed gasoline and a tiny wooden café stood across the road.

I walked inside and asked the lady at the counter if I could have a coffee. A young girl entered the café a little later, perhaps twelve years old, asking if I needed a hotel for the night. This being mid-afternoon I reasoned against it, only to feel the ache from my bones and instead concede that maybe I should.

It wasn't a hotel but her family home, a plastered single storey white building with rotten blue window frames and a barn outside in which the bike could be stored safely. The girl managed to communicate the price and how that would include food. Her parents weren't around and so I was put in the side room, staring at the ceiling until they came home and looked disapprovingly at me, in a way that would suggest they were happy to have the money but not necessarily my company.

I was fed a dinner of vegetable noodles, whilst in the main room next door I could smell that they were having meat. My bed was a layer of blankets on the floor. Bright coloured blankets also hung from the walls, whilst the toilet was down the hill, in a corrugated iron shed, just a hole in the floor. I couldn't wait to get out of there the next morning, making me realise just how much I appreciated my own space on an evening. It allows you to relax after a long day on the road.

It was colder than ever that day, Dot struggling the way she had on the way to Leh. These were desperate days, stopping to buy engine oil from stalls by the roadside in order to keep her level topped up, while the road not once eased off, more rocky and rough as it traced the edge of a ravine to where small villages were built high up on cliff tops.

Stopping to take a picture of the bleak empty landscape I was approached by a man on a horse who climbed off and insisted I take to the saddle. We didn't go anywhere, just sat on the spot looking down at Dorothy, shivering below. The man suggested he would like a copy of the photographs I'd been taking of him and his horse, and once again I had to explain that's not how it works, wishing to pack a Polaroid for such occasions next time round.

The rest of those three days to Bishkek involved sleeping behind hedge bottoms, being chased by more wild dogs, climbing up over mountain passes with long dark tunnels at the top, Dot's headlight barely able to register as the old German cars, most commonly driven in these post-Soviet parts, came roaring past within a whisker of my right ear.

Several times on stopping I was offered a bowl of fermented mares milk, known locally as koumiss, which was difficult to swallow given its bitter taste, but anything to be polite. I stopped off in the town of Osh for some lagman noodles, passing gorgeous lakes along the way. Despite the worry over the oil leak these were good days, as they always were when my only challenge was to get somewhere. Still, when we finally made it to the capital of Bishkek, I could have kissed the ground with relief.

***

In Bishkek I met a fellow traveller in the street who told me about Sabrybek's Guesthouse, a place at which I would be well advised to stay. I found it down a leafy side street, not far from the city centre and right opposite the German embassy. It was once the home of a famous Kyrgyz author and had since been passed down through the generations, now in the hands of Sabrybek himself. He was a man in his fifties with wild white hair and father to a baby named Denise, a real demon child, that would crawl about the garden chasing a litter of kittens, which, if caught, would either be dunked in a bucket of water or have their necks squeezed until they had to be rescued.

Sabrybek's brother also lived in the garden, in a shed with his wife, the pair of them always wasted on vodka. The place had one toilet, one shower, and the beds were just pieces of foam, or if you were lucky, you got a proper mattress. It was a real rustic place, but one with a very pleasant and welcoming vibe. I could see why you would not choose anywhere else to stay in town.

Bishkek itself was also a far more interesting, not to mention modern city, than I'd ever imagined. With Kyrgyzstan once being a part of the former Soviet Union, its capital city had a very efficient feel to it, the streets all in grids, centres of administration built in a cluster, statues of Lenin in the background and a public square at the very heart of it. Here on an evening many hundreds of people would gather to have their photographs taken in front of fountains, the water dancing to the beat of music played over loud speakers. It seemed a wealthy city, with shopping malls, boutique clothes stores, expensive cars, and a night club where one evening a few of us from the hostel visited, fascinated to see local teenagers slow dancing to Metallica.

Finally, after a day or two of chilling out, it was time to begin the task of fixing Dorothy. In the gravel yard of Sabrybek's Guesthouse, I began by removing the front sprocket cover, immediately revealing the source of the leak. It was the gasket around the drive shaft to which the sprocket is attached that needed replacing, so nothing serious there. This did however lead me to a second problem.

The sprocket itself was worn to within an inch of its life. Instead of the teeth being thick and smooth, the teeth had been so badly worn it now looked like a ninja's throwing star. Were it not for the oil leak I wouldn't have noticed the sprocket in this state until the chain tore out all the teeth and there on the spot we would have sat, the engine spinning but the pair of us not moving very far.

There was also a third problem. At the bottom of the engine is the bolt you unscrew to drain out the oil when you're doing an oil change. That bolt had been in and out many times on the journey, at least every 1000 miles or so. It's what Joe had told me to do in order to make the engine last. On loosening the bolt this time I knew something wasn't right, and, when trying to tighten it again, I found it just wouldn't tighten properly. On closer examination I realised the thread was ruined, so the bolt wouldn't screw tightly into the hole. Since this was the bolt that held the oil in, that wasn't such a good thing.

Passing the blame, I thought back to the Indian mechanic in Delhi who I had paid to wash and service the bike. I'd noticed how ferociously he had swung on the spanner to tighten the bolt but had thought no more about it. I suspected that this was where the damage was done.

In total then there were three things the matter; the sprocket, the sprocket gasket and the sump plug. And I was in Kyrgyzstan, a former Soviet state with very few motorbikes on its streets, only German cars from the old Eastern bloc. Had this happened in Thailand or Indonesia there would be mechanics everywhere that would be able to help, but here, asking around, there was nobody who knew a thing about bikes or where I could get the parts.

Sabrybek himself took me to a local car market in the hope of finding the bits I needed, but to no avail. His cousin even offered to fix Dot for me, but I couldn't have allowed that. It felt like it was my job to fix my own bike, because if I didn't fix it properly and at a later date she stopped working, I would only have myself to blame and that would be alright, I could live with that. But if someone else wrecked it, I'd be crestfallen.

There was only one thing left for me to do; and that was to contact Joe and the gang at One Ten Motorcycles back in Caboolture, to see if they could somehow help.

All the way from Caboolture Joe had remained in touch, contacting me regularly to ask if everything was alright and if I needed anything for the bike. Back in the Indian Himalayas he had been a god-send when I needed help with the carburettor. Now I needed him more than ever, firing off an email explaining the various problems and asking what he suggested.

Joe responded almost immediately, instructing me not to worry as he'd boxed up a load of things he thought I might need and was ready to send them express delivery to the address I would give him. Joe explained that it might take two weeks for the parcel to show up, which was fine, as it would allow me the opportunity to figure out which route I would take from here.

My original intention was to try and drop back down into Turkey, resuming the route I would have taken had I passed through Iran. But that would be difficult. I would have to get visas for Uzbekistan and Turkmenistan, both of which required letters of introduction, which are expensive and time consuming to get. Not only that but I would then have to get a ferry across the Caspian Sea, arriving in Azerbaijan, then having to pass into Armenia, then down to Turkey.

There was a rumour of borders being closed because of the political tension there, so I might have had to detour through Georgia as well. As much as that was the preferred route, I just didn't have the fight for it, nor the patience, nor the money, nor the time. I needed a more direct route as by now all I wanted was to see if we could make it to England or not.

Looking at the map I saw that if I entered Kazakhstan to the north west I could ride above the Caspian Sea and eventually into Russia. West from there would bring me to Ukraine, then Poland, Germany, France, Belgium and England. I figured the distance to be around 7,000 kilometres, which to my mind didn't seem very far at all. I thought if I could ride as I had in Australia and Indonesia, covering 500 kilometres a day, then I could be in London in two or three weeks time.

After eight months trying to get there, that was a strange thought, as though all of a sudden, after so many borders and water crossings and hurdles to make it this far, we were now looking down the barrel of a gun aimed at England. People on email reminded me I wasn't there yet, that I still had a long way to go, and therefore to be careful. I couldn't argue. But in my mind I just had to hurry up and get there, before it moved on.

I was able to get the visa for Kazakhstan with no issues; a simple process at the embassy in Bishkek. The visa for Russia was much harder to get, having to take Sabrybek's daughter Anya to the embassy to have her translate, but even then it seemed I wouldn't be able to get a tourist visa, as to do this you have to provide a full itinerary of your time in the country, not to mention evidence of hotel bookings and transport arrangements. This I wouldn't be able to do as I was just passing through.

The only other option was a five day transit visa, which, looking at the map, would allow just enough time for me to get across that part of Russia and enter Ukraine. The problem there is that in applying for this visa you are forced to nominate the exact date you wish for it to start and therefore also to finish. That, of course, was a guessing game as I didn't know how long it would take to fix Dot or how long it would take to cross Kazakhstan. I just had to guess and hope I got it right. In the meantime all I could do was wait.

Also staying at the guesthouse were the Hülsmanns, a German couple in their forties — Andreas a freelance motorcycle journalist, Claudia working in a book shop — the pair of them riding Central Asia and Mongolia on a pair of BMWs.

Andreas's bike had electrical problems and also needed new parts sent from home. That meant we were stuck with each other, the three of us meeting most mornings for breakfast, Claudia becoming almost like a mother to me, cooking me eggs and showing me, after all this time, how to hand wash my clothes properly. We spent most of our days sat beneath the pagoda in the back garden, rescuing the kittens from Baby Denise, or wandering every now and again to the small shop next door, staffed by Nazgul, a young local girl who dreamed one day of studying in England.

Other visitors came and went. There was Hubert, a Frenchman who had been riding a Ural motorcycle and sidecar around the world for five years and had another five years left to go. He owned an opera house in Paris, had recovered from throat cancer and now wore a pair of wild red glasses. He was an interesting guy, his motto in life; 'Don't forget to take a risk today.' It was just a shame he only stayed a night at the hostel before heading off to see the gorgeous Song Kol lakes, about a three hours ride away.

A Polish couple arrived not longer after him. They were travelling in a battered old pale blue Russian motorcar, one they'd self-modified, chopping the roof off and covering the rest of the bodywork in bright motifs and painted flowers. They wore cowboy boots and bandanas and were hoping to travel just as far as their car, and their passports would take them. Finally, after a fortnight or more, the package from Joe showed up.

I opened it beneath the pagoda with everyone gathered around, slicing the tape with a large hunting knife I'd bought in China from the cattle market on the outskirts of Kashgar. The knife had a long blade and a jewelled handle, a replacement for the penknife Mandy had given me the day I'd departed, now lost somewhere on the road between there and here.

Now the spare parts for Dorothy toppled out across the table — almost enough to build a new bike, for Joe had not only sent everything I needed, but everything he thought I might need as well. More inner tubes, a chain, a rear sprocket, brake cables, brake shoes, all sorts of replacement washers and gaskets, not to mention a clutch of old rags and a new set of stickers advertising his bike shop.

With help from the Hülsmanns I went immediately to work, starting with a new front brake cable, the three of us thinking this would only take an hour to fit, but in fact it taking over half a day. We just couldn't get the tension right, it either binding on or not working at all. The new sprocket gasket followed, again with problems, it just not sitting right, moving around on the shaft, so it was back to Joe to check and yes, that was correct.

Joe had also sent a new carburettor needle, simple to fit but in doing so we messed up the adjustment in the throttle cable, which took an age to get right again. Then the biggest job of the lot: repairing the sump plug.

At first we tried rethreading it with the tool Joe had sent me. It was like a fat drill bit that clipped into a handle. You stuck the drill bit into the ruined hole and twisted the handle, the intention being to bore a new thread. I'd not done it before and neither had the Hülsmanns. With shards of metal being stripped from the bottom of the engine, it was clear the new thread just wasn't biting. Andreas was keen to keep trying, but my instinct told me to stop, and bodge it up instead.

I wrapped the old bolt in the plumber's tape Joe had sent me. This thickened it nicely, and then, with a smear of thread-lock, I tightened it in to a pinch. We smothered the whole lot in plastic-metal, a substance that turns solid once it sets, and then, as one final act to stop the bolt dropping out, we tie-wrapped an old toothbrush up against the base of the bolt, having drilled holes in the sump-guard to do so.

With that she was done, running perfectly once more. It had taken us almost four days to have her up and running again, but now the three of us could stand back to admire our handiwork. Andreas's bike was also fixed, the new ECU from Germany arriving and proving a big relief to everyone the way the bike fired up first time.

After all the three of us had been through we decided it only right that we leave together the next morning. I liked the idea of that: them on their

BMWs, me on Dorothy, all bikes fixed and ready for the road ahead, from here heading west, only west, first into Kazakhstan and then Russia. We wouldn't ride all that way together as they could travel much faster than me, but for a day we would share the road, a place I'd missed greatly the past three weeks of being stationary.

Things were also looking better all round. In recent days I'd received a phone call on Skype from Mandy, just calling to say, 'Hi, I hope you're fine, how's it going?' It had been almost four months since I'd last spoken to her, back at the end of Thailand when she'd asked me not to contact her.

It had been a tough time since then. Every day and every kilometre I'd missed her, I'd missed her so much. I'd thought so many things, considered so many options, but never found an answer, could never get the right words I wanted to say. So I'd obeyed and not said a thing. Now we chatted for an age, about what we'd been up to and what news each of us had missed. But it was much more than a phone call — it meant everything: redemption, atonement, the end of feeling so alone. It felt like I'd crawled out of the deep dark wood, and found the sun was shining again.

Now get on your bike and ride.

Chapter Twenty-One
Kazakhstan

We rode towards the Kazakhstan border in formation: Andreas at the front, me in the middle, Claudia bringing up the rear. At every red traffic light, Andreas's bike would stall and give everyone reason to worry, but always it would fire back into life and continue on to the next traffic lights before it would do it again.

Dot wasn't running perfectly either, just not quite as smooth as I remembered her, but the fact that these bikes were running at all was the only thing that mattered now. Seven thousand kilometres, that's all it was to England, the sense that this was the final push, the final furlong, especially now I could just ride, with no more visas to collect or water crossings to worry about until hopefully we reached the English Channel, needing one last boat to take us that final distance home.

The guard at the border into Kazakhstan wasn't a pleasant man; taking issue with my passport for the way the ink was smudged and the pages weathered. My passport the whole way had been kept in the cheap money belt I'd bought from the Chinese store back in Sydney, suffering not only the daily sweat from my belly but also the soaking it got in the New Year celebrations back in Thailand.

For some reason the guard also took issue with the Germans' passports, finally giving them all back in a huff and sending us to the Customs office, where one minute we needed an import form, the next we didn't, the next we did, the next we didn't. Then to the Immigration queue, where a pretty girl before us was pleading with the man at the counter to let her through. He refused point blank, before suddenly, after much persuasion, inviting her into his office, shutting the blinds and I suspect enjoying a good bit of head. She was allowed to pass through.

As were we, though not on our knees, but on our motorbikes, which now roared across the Kazakh steppe. This was a desolate place, a massive country, seemingly empty, and with endless horizons of gently rolling dry, grassy scrub. We passed through villages every thirty to fifty kilometres or so. It's hard to avoid the stereotype, but these were just like the places depicted in Borat: nests of weathered homes, built on the earth and made from whatever material they could get their hands on. Were it not for the occasional car parked outside you might well have been in a previous century.

Then there were the petrol pumps, sometimes guarded by a man with an old wooden rifle and always you would have to pay for your fuel in advance. This was troublesome as not only did you have to guess how many litres you might need, but also communicate this figure to the clerk, together with the type of fuel you wanted, which often dipped as low as 80 RON.

Bless the Hülsmanns for riding with me that day; it must have been unbearable given that their bikes could go much faster and that they just must have wanted to get home as well. For me, it was just nice to have some company for a change and not have to be totally alert as you always need to be when travelling alone.

Instead I sat in the shadows of the other bikes, thrumming along, my mind drifting off into its own little world, looking up at the sun and having that momentary realisation that it's not just me who can see that blazing ball of fire in the sky, but also a certain someone on the other side of the world. And when I thought of it like that the distance between us suddenly didn't feel so big any more. The possibility of seeing her again was my pull now.

We camped that night out in the wild; a simple case of pulling off the road and riding across the scrub for a kilometre until you were well out of sight. We put the tents up on a bed of flattened grass, my two-man tent from Kmart still holding up just fine. It was so simple to put up that I couldn't see why you'd have to spend any more. By now I also had a stove, having found a camping store back in Bishkek and buying a device that screwed on to the top of small gas canisters, of which I'd bought two.

Typically, with the way I'd been organised this whole way, I had no saucepan, no cup, no cutlery, so in a sense it was useless, but after eight months on the road it was a start. Thankfully the Hülsmanns were better equipped, their big metal panniers containing everything you'd ever need, meaning that soon we were sitting back in the scrub, drinking tea and dipping bread in bowls of instant noodles we'd bought from a local shop earlier in the day.

The Hülsmanns did this a lot; riding motorcycles a long way. Andreas had been editor of a motorcycle magazine in Germany and so once did it as a job, now for fun, Claudia joining him, the pair taking off every year or so, to Mongolia, Russia, Central Asia.

I sat back and admired them; finding something like this that two people can enjoy must be the best feeling in the world. I could see now how it might be true what they say, about how happiness isn't real unless shared, and so to be out here, with the person that you love must seriously take some beating.

The next morning we went our separate ways, me getting a good head start on the Hülsmanns and expecting them to go flying past a little later. The next time I would see them after that would be in Germany, where we had agreed I would call in at their house on my way through.

For now I needed to quickly cover the remaining 2,000 kilometres across Kazakhstan, because in six days my transit visa for Russia would commence — whether I was there or not — and once that clock started ticking I would have just five days to cross Russia and be out the other side in Ukraine. It was a big distance to cover, in not a lot of time, along roads not in great condition; rough and rutted, on Dot, who I was now a little nervous of given the bodge job we'd done on the sump plug.

In the past, this pressure to cover a great distance in a short amount of time might have worried me, but by this stage I'd developed a strange sense of confidence in the way that things have the habit of working out

— that you will get there, that the borders will open up, that things will always fall into place. Perhaps it's a confidence in your own ability, or possibly a new found faith in the world around. The best way to describe it is to imagine Neo's bullet time in the *Matrix*; an awareness of everything around you, the bullets flying past, the drop-kicks coming in; the sense that you can simply side-step them, and carry on your way. It was an incredible feeling in that sense, one I imagine I'll forever be trying to recapture.

I stopped in the small city of Shymkent, buildings rising like a mirage from the Kazakh steppe. I never failed to be amazed by just how wrong my preconceptions still were of a new place, just as they'd been of Bangkok, Pakistan and East Timor, and most other places I'd passed through on route. This city in the steppe was modern, clean and sophisticated.

In broken English a teenager at a bus stop directed me to an internet café down a side street, and there I sat, at a bank of computers, in the middle of Kazakhstan with a café across the road where I would later eat a decent beef burger. By now I was in regular email contact with Mandy, asking her if she wanted to come to England for my homecoming. I even offered to pay, though with what, I wasn't quite sure. But she'd got work and other things; a new life, new acquaintances, moving on. That was okay. It was just nice to be back in touch.

Whilst in town I also looked for a saucepan for my stove, but not being able to find one I bought a big tin of sweet corn instead, figuring that once I'd eaten the contents it would make a perfectly good saucepan. I also bought tea bags, bread and instant noodles — this would be my nourishment from now on.

Back on the road, I never did see the Hülsmanns come racing past that day. They must have overtook whilst I was in Shymkent and no doubt by now they would already be a couple of hundred kilometres ahead of me. That left me once more alone. Solitude or loneliness? I guess it was more of the latter. Though I knew my duty now; to just keep on riding. But you show me the open road. And I'll show you another bloody puncture.

It happened as I dashed through a lazy, dusty little town, fortunately right opposite a tyre shop that had a compressor and a yard for me to carry out the repair. It also had an eager attendant, quick to elbow me out of the way and show me how to do it, kneeling all over the spokes as he did so. I thought nothing of it at the time and was just glad to get back on the road, camping that night out in the wild, not even bothering with the tent.

I lay the sleeping bag in the dirt, the knife beside me, a full moon overhead, Dorothy in a ditch on her side so not to be spotted from the road. I always seemed to camp whenever there was a full moon, as this night was. Maybe it was coincidence, or possibly I wondered if my progress had somehow been in tune with the cycle of its rotation. It had been happening the whole way, ever since that first night camping wild in Indonesia, where it had shone brightly that night as well.

Perhaps the full moon was as an omen of my stupidity, for the next day I forgot to check the oil level until it was way too late. I'd ridden 300 kilometres in the morning, ploughing on as fast as I could, before suddenly realising that I'd not done an oil check that morning. I pulled over, unscrewed the dipstick, wiped it on my sock as I'd been doing the whole way, then dipped it back in, horrified to see barely a drop on it. Where it had all gone I wasn't certain, as the sump bolt was still held secure, the plumber's tape, plastic-metal and toothbrush all doing their job. I topped it up with the spare oil I carried, though it seemed the damage had already been done.

A few hours later I began to detect a slight unrest in the engine. It happened every time I went to pull away, a faint rattle, reminiscent perhaps of the one that finished off Doris, the first bike, 1,000 kilometres out of Sydney. I kicked myself for letting it happen, wondering if it had been a subconscious ploy to make life a little harder for myself. A form of self-punishment perhaps, which sometimes I wondered if all this trip was really about. A sufferance.

The next day the rattle grew louder, then, to make matters worse, the spokes in the rear wheel began to break. It was strange; everything was fine until I pulled over to take a photo of a burial monument in the middle of the Kazakh steppe.

Having taken a photo of the monument and of the wild camels

loitering nearby, I attempted to pull away, only to discover I was unable to do so; it was as though the rear brake was locked on. I climbed off and inspected the back wheel, stunned to find a spoke had somehow broken, bent out at ninety degrees and was now hooked under the swing-arm, preventing the wheel from going around. How that had happened while I'd been stationary I'll never know. All I could do was unscrew the broken spoke, tighten all the rest, cursing as I did so the mechanic who'd knelt on the spokes the previous day.

A little further along a second spoke broke, then a third. I was forty kilometres from a town. If only I could make it there. Then a strange sight travelling in the opposite direction: a cyclist, pedalling towards me. A mirage? No. He waved me down as I approached. He turned out to be a German cyclist on his way to China, covering a hundred kilometres a day. I don't remember his name, just him being there, with a little solar panel to charge his mobile phone and litres of water to charge his body. He told me a strange story. He said that two German motorcyclists were waiting at a café on the outskirts of the next town. They were waiting for an Englishman on a red Australian Post bike, but that this Englishman had best hurry, because they'd been waiting for four hours already and wouldn't wait forever. The Hülsmanns!

Broken spokes, grumbling engine, I hit Dot's throttle with all my might, riding smooth and hard in a desperate attempt to get there before they were gone. I didn't like being alone out here and certainly missed their company.

I needn't have worried, because as I approached the town of Aral I spotted two familiar faces sat outside a café on the left hand side of the road. I pulled up, jumped off the bike and hugged them like we'd just won the World Cup.

It'd only been two days since I saw them last, but it felt much longer, a lifetime ago. They said they were missing Dorothy too much and with no real urgency to be back in Germany they thought they'd wait and make sure I got across Kazakhstan okay. Thanks to them, I did.

My approach to fixing the spokes was to take three out of the front wheel and fit them in the back, my logic being that the front wheel takes less strain and therefore was more likely to cope with the missing spokes. After all, I was still on the original front tyre, but must have changed the rear more than half a dozen times already. By now I knew myself well enough to know I was simply after the quickest fix, the one that would have us stopped for the least amount of time.

The Hülsmanns were totally against this idea and wouldn't allow me to do it, insisting instead that we scour the town on the edge of the dried-up Aral Sea for a shop that might sell spokes for an Australia Post bike. Of course we had no luck. And as we searched, more spokes broke, meaning I had to push Dot through the dusty streets to prevent more from breaking. Fortunately, Claudia spoke a little Russian and was able to understand directions to the house of a man who might be able to help.

He lived down a dusty side street in a residential area. Kids taunted us as we pulled up outside his solid steel green gate and turned off our engines. They ticked in the blazing midday heat. We unsaddled, wearily, while one of the boys fetched his father, the man we were looking for, who welcomed us to his town and examined the broken spokes.

He said he would be able to help as he showed us inside his huge workshop, full of industrial machines, noisily in operation; such stark contrast with the quiet dusty town and the steppe around. Andreas handed the man six spare spokes from the handful he carried for his BMW and in half an hour the man had transformed them into ones that fitted my bike perfectly. I paid the man ten dollars, thanked him, and the Hülsmanns, for insisting I mend it this way, and back to the road we went, the spokes fixed properly and not another one breaking from that point on.

These were good days, riding as a trio again, going slowly; they didn't care, we all had company, memories to share. The road was shit for miles on end, just a big wide filthy dirt track with the occasional lonely café where we stopped for goulash and tea. A policeman in one village tried to take our passports and asked us for 'souvenir'. He meant bribe. Stupidly, I was going to give him my passport to inspect, until Andreas said don't do it, just ride, and so we all took off, leaving the policeman standing in the road, his form disappearing behind as that Kazakh steppe continued to roar — just as I did, in anger, at what I'd done to Dot's engine, which by now getting worse and worse. Andreas thought it would be fine, nothing to worry about. But I knew. I'd lived with Dot all this way; I knew when things weren't right.

After four more days together, now just a short distance from the Russian border, it came time to go our separate ways again. The Hülsmanns intended to take a different route to mine, one that arced north-west across Russia, whereas I was heading directly west into Ukraine. I thought about riding with them, given my concerns over Dot's engine; they'd even suggested it. But I felt that I'd come all this way on my own and it would be wrong to have them carry me the last stretch.

It might sound stupid, but whether I succeeded or failed in making it to England, I needed to be the one responsible, my two hands on the handlebars, and no one else's. I knew if I allowed them to carry me home I would have felt bitter, that I would somehow have avoided my fate. It wasn't just about doing the trip, it was about doing it in the *right* way.

I vividly remember that morning me and the Hülsmanns parting for the second time. We were a couple of kilometres off the road, our usual encampment in the steppe. This time they were heading off before me with the intention of crossing the Russian border that morning. I on the other hand had to wait until the next day, as the pace with which we'd crossed Kazakhstan meant my five-day Russian transit visa didn't activate until the following morning.

We had one last cup of tea before the three of us hugged, agreed, 'We'll see you soon.' Then they climbed aboard their massive bikes and fired them into life. I stood there, my tent still up, my gear still strewn across the ground, and waved as they pulled away, riding slowly across the steppe, down the trail and back onto the road. I watched them go until they were completely out of sight. I turned around and stood on the spot. Alone in this big empty land.

A wave threatened to wash over me and leave me stranded there forever. I could feel it coming. It was one of those moments where you feel utterly incapable of doing the thing you are most required to do. But you have to do it, there is no choice, no compromise; I had to make my way to England as the only other option was to stay out here forever, until I turned to rot.

I held my two feet firm, pushing back at the wave as it built and then slowly subsided. England was so close now. Focus on that. Focus on that single strip of road that will take me there. Ignore the engine problem, ignore Russia, Ukraine, Poland, Germany, France … focus on England. Shrink that distance, grip it in your hand. Though in some ways, this moment best sums up how I'd felt the entire adventure; alone in a wide open field, exposed, not a single thing to hide behind as the wind and rain blew fierce.

The next day I made haste to the border, riding for what seemed like an age before catching sight of it, a lonely outpost, like a fortress vending petrol in a *Mad Max* landscape. A group of wooden huts lined the approach, women standing in their doorways. I didn't know or care to ask what they were for. A barrier was ahead of me, with a queue of cars waiting, ready to pass into the compound beyond. I sat in line, anxious in the way all borders made me. You are at its mercy, powerless to the problems it might pose and only hopeful that you will be allowed quickly through. The riding is the easy part; it's the bureaucracy that really sucks.

Finally, the guard raised the barrier and we passed beneath it, pulling into the compound and coming to a stop, a port-a-cabin office to my left, a larger stone building to my right, all around a metal fence with an opening at the far end that hopefully very soon would lead me through to Russia.

I presented myself to the man at the window of the office to my left. 'You have import form?' He asked, referring to the document we were told we wouldn't need eight days ago, the day we entered Kazakhstan. I shook my head, I didn't have one. 'Problem,' he said.

I made my point about being told we didn't need one. He invited me into his office to solve the dispute, the door shutting behind me, the shutters on the hatch being closed. It would have been perfect darkness in there had it not been for the strip light flickering overhead. Three men joined us, all big strong Kazakh men, the four of them now standing over me, their arms crossed, looking down at the hairy pile of shit, wilting in the chair. I realised in that moment I'd just walked into a trap.

'You pay us 200 euros,' said one man, staring straight at me. I trembled inside but dared not show it. For a moment I hesitated, about to take out the $500 I had in my body belt; even starting to recalculate my budget accordingly having given most of what I had left to this bunch of thugs. I felt it inevitable, that I was going to give it to them. Then something triggered inside of me, a steely resolve, a limit of my own tepidness, and I thought, 'No, why should I give it to you, this is my money!' So I shook my head and tensed my whole body, because no way was I going to give up that money without a fight. The men didn't like this one bit, insisting I give them the money; I insisted I wouldn't. This went on for a long time, the men growing increasingly aggressive and determined to get me to give it to them. I held firm, shaking my head, until finally, the door opened and I was led to the building across the compound.

For two hours I was ignored by the officials sitting inside at their desks. I sat there, churning up inside. There was nothing I could do; getting irate wasn't an option either, because then I was at their mercy. I just sat, forcing a smile, eating bread and dropping crumbs on their floor, blocking the door, being under everyone's feet, doing what Andreas had told me to do in such circumstances: be as big a nuisance as I could possibly be.

Finally, I was summoned into an office where men with honest faces demanded one hundred dollars. Once more I refused, being sent back to the cabin across the yard where again I was asked for the two hundred euros. 'No,' I said, then back to the main office. One hundred dollars again. I shook my head again.

This went on for four hours. Still I ate my bread and made my crumbs. Still I smiled, still I waited patiently, until finally the man from the very beginning stamped my form and with a scowl told me I could go. I didn't know whether to believe him or not at first, startled and then determined to get out of there before he changed his mind. Never had I been so glad to leave a country behind as I was Kazakhstan. I hated those men. I hated the hassle they had given me. Now I was riding across no-man's land on the approach to the Russian checkpoint, confident I would receive similar treatment, given the reputation the country has for corruption. But I couldn't have been more wrong.

There was even a sign, written in English, explaining how you could report any extortion experienced at the border by ringing the number below. The soldier on the main gate was equally keen and helpful, the woman in the small glass kiosk was tough looking but accommodating, doing everything she could to make sure I had the right documentation, though stopping short at allowing me into the country without the mandatory third-party insurance I needed.

I was confused. I thought I would be able to get it here, in Russia, to which she replied, 'nyet,' meaning no, drawing a map of the compound I'd just escaped from, circling on it those damned wooden huts where the women were standing at the door. I should have bought it there, and now I couldn't enter Russia without it. There was only one thing I could do; ride back across no-man's land and get it.

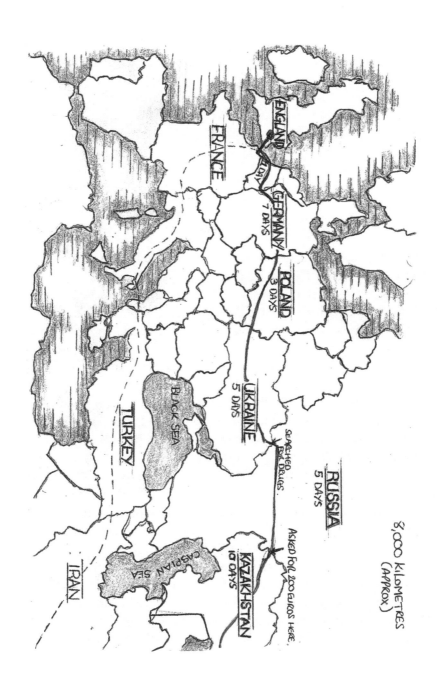

ENGLAND

FRANCE

1 DAY

GERMANY
7 DAYS

POLAND
3 DAYS

UKRAINE
5 DAYS

SEARCHED
FOR DRUGS.

RUSSIA
5 DAYS

ASKED FOR 200 EUROS HERE.

BLACK SEA

TURKEY

KAZAKHSTAN
10 DAYS

CASPIAN SEA

IRAN

8,000 KILOMETRES
(APPROX.)

Chapter Twenty-Two
Russia

From the moment I entered Russia — the insurance easier to retrieve than I'd anticipated — I would have just five days to ride across the country and be out the other side. That meant I had to take the most direct route: from the border first to Saratov, then Borisoglebsk, Voronezh, down to Belgorod then across into Ukraine, a distance of 1,320 kilometres.

At any other point in the journey I would not have worried about this — it was an easy distance in an easy time — yet at this moment I was concerned about the engine. The worry was that if she broke down in those five days it would likely mean that I would overstay my visa, and that, strangely, seemed like the end of the world. The pressure now was massive, just to finish this thing, to see it through, because anything less than England felt like it would be a failure.

Another puncture wasn't the best start to the journey. It happened in the pretty city of Saratov, just over the border and built on the banks of the River Volga. I'd stopped there to get some local currency, the puncture happening right beside a policeman booking people for speeding. He nodded at me and carried on. I used my last inner tube to repair it and so stopped at a tiny motorcycle spares shop on the hill out of town.

It was an odd place, selling tasselled leather clothing and staffed by a young woman in a very low-cut top with massive breasts. She had no inner tubes, so called her dad, a man named Alex, who came over in his car and drove me across the city to another shop that did sell them. Alex wouldn't allow me to pay for them, insisting it was his gift, and then, back at his shop, he handed me an embroidered patch of Che Guavara to stitch to the side of my panniers; the image of Che appropriate given the current state of my facial hair that by now was one big ball of mattered fuzz.

Outside the shop, two young men walking by stopped and introduced themselves, their accents giving them away as American. They turned out to be Mormons, in Russia for almost two years now, their mission to convert as many locals as possible to the Mormon faith. They did this by going door to door, one of them speaking fluent Russian, the other not speaking much Russian at all. They handed me a leaflet and we talked for a while.

I did have to admire them. To fly to such a faraway place, having to learn the language, not knowing the culture, but still determined to convince local people of their religion must take a great deal of faith in your cause, perhaps requiring blindness to the realities of it, something I found much empathy with given my blind pursuit of England.

Not far out of the city, cruising at a stable pace, something suddenly went wrong with the bike. Above fifty-five kilometres an hour she began to vibrate violently and struggled to push beyond that speed. It happened in an instant, like hitting a switch, and I just couldn't figure out what was wrong.

All I could think was that the episode with the oil had slowly began to cause its damage and this was the first sign of something serious about to go wrong. I was worried, though there was not much I could do but carry on, taking it steady, reducing the speed and trying not to panic, yet fretting endlessly, as if she broke down out here it would have been a case of trying to find someone with a truck who could carry us the rest of the way to the border with Ukraine.

I didn't ride much further that day, just far enough to leave around 900 kilometres to cover over the remaining three days. I turned off the road a few miles before a town I could see on the horizon. There was a forest with a small clearing that I rode into before turning off the engine and letting out a big sigh. It was getting dark and I began to wonder if I should worry about wolves or bears that might roam these parts.

I kept the hunting knife on me as I boiled the water in my sweet corn tin before adding a tea bag and two lumps of sugar. I was within earshot of the road, the lorries roaring past, though not quite able to see me. Behind thick bush I erected my tent and crawled inside, burying my head inside and shaking from the cold. The knife was inside the sleeping bag with me. I held on to the handle, the blade already outside the sheath.

I barely slept a wink; I just hoped, like you do at such times, that in the morning everything will have fixed itself and it will all seem like a bad dream. But of course it wasn't, it was real, Dot limping out of that forest campground just as badly as she'd limped in the night before, still sounding terrible, still unable to push beyond fifty-five without shaking violently. I decided the best thing to do, given that I only had three days to make my way across the county, was simply to carry on riding, maintaining the speed below that magic number and hope, hope to hell, that she hung in there for the rest of the way. I reasoned that if we could just make it Ukraine then we would be okay, with no need for a visa once there.

What didn't help were the Russian cities, such as Voronezh, which I had no choice but to pass straight through. The road would always lead me directly to the centre, not having anything to go by other than the name of the next city that I had written down in my diary or on my arm. The problem I had was that the names were written in English, and of course the names on the signposts around the city were written in Slavic. I had little option but to try and follow the path of the sun, staring up at it as I tried to navigate the city, looking to where it had risen and where it might set as a marker as to which way I should be heading. This wasn't as easy as it had been in Indonesia, with only one road across the islands. Here in Russia there were thousands of roads, most of which I rode down a dozen times.

I asked people by the roadside for directions, but my pronunciation of the places was completely wrong. 'Bel-go-rod, Bee-go-rod, Bel-gov...' I was met with blank faces and a shrug of the shoulders as people had no clue what I was on about. Dot was struggling equally, stalling at the traffic lights and not enjoying the slow moving, stop-start traffic of the cities.

She much preferred the pace of the open road, especially in her current condition.

I pulled into a petrol station, where two elderly pump attendants managed to grasp what it was I was spluttering, sending me off in the right direction, breathing a huge sigh of relief when finally we broke free from the city and followed signs to the next, where undoubtedly the chaos would happen again.

For accommodation across Russia I continued to sleep wild. There were hotels, but these were far too expensive, and besides, my mind was now on riding, with sleep just an inconvenience I didn't wish to pay for. Instead, I'd ride until sunset, at which point I'd begin to look for gaps in the hedge, or muddy lanes leading down into the corner of a farmer's field.

Sometimes it took a while to find one, growing anxious as the sun left the sky, then getting excited when finally I spotted one, waiting for the moment that no one was around to witness me dart through this gap or down the lane, riding until I was completely out of sight from the road. Only then, often under the complete cloak of darkness, I would unpack the tent and sleeping bag — kept in a plastic bag and strapped to the rack on the back — and make my bed for the night.

This being the beginning of September it was getting increasingly cold, often below freezing once the sun had gone. To keep warm I'd bury my head in my sleeping bag and sleep in all of my clothes. I even opened the survival blanket Claudia had given me and wrapped myself in it like a Christmas turkey beneath a gold tinsel blanket. With no roll mat (having long since thrown the one from Australia away) I could feel every rut and bump in the ground. Having lost all but two of my tent pegs, I used a screwdriver and a spanner to keep the other ends down. Sometimes I'd light the stove inside the tent just to keep warm. If my battery would allow it, I would open up the laptop around 9pm — bedtime wasn't long after — and play a few songs as I lay back and reflected on the day, thinking about the past and the future and the bits in between. Mandy was in that tent with me. At the handlebars as well. She haunted me in every way, perhaps running so fast in the hope of getting away from that.

Then the morning would come and I would rise with the sun, crawling out of the tent, colder than ever, firing up the stove and boiling some water for another cup of tea. I had no milk, but with tea bags and hot water I could at least get some heat into my tired bones. My leg was still sore at this point, though thankfully not yet broken. The ground around me would be covered in dew. I would survey the scenery, maybe do a crap in the hedge bottom, before rolling up the tent and sleeping bag, strapping it all to the back of Dot, who'd had the key left in her all night just so I didn't lose it. I would scour the ground to make sure I had everything, put my helmet and gloves on (now with socks over the ends for extra warmth) and then I would sit in the saddle, hoping that morning she was going to start.

This was always a tense moment, turning the key and watching the light go green, pulling out the kick start, taking a moment to inject some hope into the cylinder, before stroking downwards with my right leg. Of course she started. Of course she carried me out of that field and back onto the main road, which we now followed in a south westerly direction, still doing fifty-five, still counting every kilometre across Russia, which was much prettier than I'd ever imagined it to be.

The countryside was vast and green, the roads were always single carriageway and the few people I met were all incredibly helpful. More often than not it would be the people at petrol stations I would get chatting to. A man filling his car at the next petrol pump wished to talk motorbikes with me, while the Russian cougar behind the counter of another petrol station drew me a map, served me a coffee, and pointed me in the direction of the Ukraine border, a place I shall never forget, for all the wrong reasons.

The process began quite smoothly, arriving at the outpost of the Russia-Ukraine border on the very final day of my transit visa. There was no issue on the Russian side, simply having to complete a form and wait in line to leave. As I waited, a teenage football team in the line opposite began taunting me about something, though I couldn't understand what. They called out and heckled me. I fingered the knife, part of me wishing to show them my mood.

In no-man's land I stopped at the duty free shop to buy a large pack of cigarettes, as I'd been told this was the best form of defence against the corrupt Ukraine police I was likely to run into. Beyond that I reached the Ukraine border post, getting into a fracas with one of the Customs staff who insisted I wouldn't be able to enter his country on a Carnet. He wanted something else; an international registration card, whatever that was.

I tried to reason with him, showing him all of the other stamps in the book, before one of this senior colleagues stepped in, giving the other man a mouth full of abuse for preventing me from continuing on my way.

This was like a red rag to the bull, for when it came time to proceed through Customs, the man who'd just been on the receiving end of the grilling took this opportunity to deliver his retribution. Having queued in line with the rest of the traffic, I was instructed to pull to one side and dismount, the man enlisting the help of another colleague as they proceeded to have me remove and display every single item I carried. A sniffer dog was then brought around.

All the while the man sat beside me on a step, leaning in close and telling me how he wanted to see what was inside my wallet. I didn't like the idea of this as it carried the only money I had left and I was fearful that if I revealed it he would take it and leave me with nothing. I held it out at a distance, showing him there was nothing untoward inside while equally trying not to annoy him. Clearly, it was he who held absolute power here, and could have done anything he liked with me.

The man took a particular liking to my Chinese hunting knife, wanting to use it to loosen the screws on the back of my laptop to check for drugs or anything else he thought I might be hiding in there. I'd carried that laptop all the way from Sydney. Somehow it had survived the distance, being rattled about in the aluminium box, getting wet, being dropped in Bangkok and needing a new power socket. I treasured it as much as I treasured everything else I'd carried so far — even the clothes I'd abandoned along the way had had their sleeves torn off and tied around the handlebars as reminders of the part they had played. The worn-out sprocket was tied there as well. So no way was that laptop going to be ruined by this man, so I told him, 'No,' he couldn't do that, which to my amazement he obeyed and turned his attention to Dorothy instead.

I had to remove the seat so that they could check inside the petrol tank beneath (for drugs?), the headlight cover, and the side panels, and behind the battery. I shook like a leaf throughout, my hands trembling. The guard noticed this and smiled, trying my best to tame them so not to give him such satisfaction.

Mid way through the inspection a civilian passed through the checkpoint in his car, heading into Ukraine from Russia. Our eyes met and clearly he could read the trouble on my mind, for he stopped and asked the guard in Ukraine why I was being treated like this. The civilian translated that it was because I had been through Pakistan and therefore under suspicion of carrying drugs. The absurdity of this was not lost; riding all the way from Sydney to Pakistan, picking up drugs, then riding them the rest of the way to England. There must be easier ways of smuggling drugs.

Finally, after three hours the man said, 'Pack up,' and casually walked away. The ordeal was finally over.

Chapter Twenty-Three
Ukraine

That night I slept behind a hedge just over the border. I was tired, weary, and cold. An autumn chill was in the air and the falling leaves were starting to ruin my cover from the cars passing by on the road. It wasn't meant to be like this. I was supposed to be in Greece by now, or Italy, or the South of France where it would be warm and glamorous as me and Dorothy prepared for our final flurry through the badlands of Europe all the way to the English Channel, which we would cross by ferry. Instead, the detour around Iran had forced us north, through colder climates, where we now sat shivering in a Ukraine hedge.

It was a rough night. A missing tent pole meant the whole structure collapsed, leaving me to wrap myself in the fabric like a human fajita, burying myself deep within the undergrowth as the rain fell and dripped on my head. My matches were wet so I had no heat, no tea, no food other than bread. My trousers were falling apart, Dot's panniers were ripped, I'd not showered or changed my clothes for thirteen days, my eyes were red and we still had another 2,000 kilometres to go. England never seemed as far away as it did that night, buried like a Mexican dish in the Ukraine hedge.

I felt even worse the following morning. I didn't want to get out of 'bed'. I just lay there, shivering in my sleeping bag and all of my clothes. I could have stayed there forever. I didn't want to ride, I didn't want to do anything. I was just so worried about Dot and whether she would make it or not. We'd come through so much together, survived so many things. She'd been my friend, my companion, my everything for the past eight months. And now she was almost dead, my mood being one of not wanting to carry on without her. The sense of falling at the final hurdle was palpable.

Then came a startling realisation. I remember it vividly, it dragging me from my fajita tent and hitting me right between the eyes. Looking back it's all a bit stupid, yet at the time it really was my saviour that day. It was a voice inside my head that said, 'Nathan, you daft sod. Haven't you realised; me and Dot are two different things. She's a motorbike and I'm the voice inside your head. You've been talking to me all along. I am Dorothy; the spirit of adventure. And nothing can kill me.'

Again, as stupid as it sounds, I can't begin to explain how much pressure that took off of me, to realise that even if we had to put Dot on a trailer or on a train or even if I had to push her, then that would be alright. Everything would be alright. Because we'd make it home somehow, anyhow. And so the challenge of Sydney to London didn't matter anymore, not in the grand scheme of things in any case. If it all came to an end today then that's alright; we'd done alright, and with that all the worry and drama and stress suddenly lifted from my shoulders. And so I smiled and unrolled myself from the tent and stood up and stretched and looked out across the fields of Ukraine.

For now then we were just going to carry on riding and see how far we would get. One country, day, hour, kilometre at a time. I stopped at another McDonald's on the outskirts of Kiev to check my emails using their free Wi-Fi. I did this in the hope that Mandy might have changed her mind and wanted to come and meet me in Dover. But not today.

There was an email from my dad though. He'd read of my engine troubles and was on standby to drive all the way out from England, to Ukraine, with the engine out of the Honda C90 I'd bought to do the trip that first time around. It was still in the shed, Dad convinced the engine would bolt straight into Dot and so told me to just let him know and he would bring it out to wherever I was. I was so proud of him for suggesting this. In a way I hoped that it would happen, just so he could give his own

Dorothy a run out as well.

There was another email, this one from a man named *Round the World Doug*. He was an American, riding a Harley Davidson around the world. We'd exchanged a few emails in the past and now, on hearing that I was approaching Kiev, contacted me to say that he knew a couple who ran an orphanage out here and if I was in need of a place to stay or some tools to get Dot fixed up then all I had to do was call.

I scribbled their number down and found a payphone to dial it. A lady answered, Doug's friend, who was a bit confused by my phone call at first but soon understood, telling me it would be no problem at all to stay, except they were out of town that evening and wouldn't be back until the following day. I thanked her and said I would let her know what I'd decided, before hanging up the phone, turning to look at Dorothy, and concluding, 'What the heck, let's just keep on riding'. And that's what we did, well into the night.

Some would later say how this was being cruel to Dot, that I should have stopped and fixed her whilst I had the chance, but in my mind I genuinely believed she deserved the chance to finish what she started in her original form; to be the postie bike that with little more than an oil change had ridden across the world. To take her to a mechanic and have them pull her apart as a precaution at this stage didn't seem quite right to me. Let her fight on, with a gun her hand, blasting away, taking enemy territory while she can.

I'd heard the one about Trigger's axe, with five new handles and a dozen new blades and that wasn't going to be the case with my vehicular axe. If she blew up at the roadside, only then shall she be fixed. But not before.

Clearly, she must have heard me, because not far to go before the Polish border, she had another chronic seizure. This time it was as though someone had shot her dead, the speed cascading quickly down from fifty-five to twenty to ten. I thought this was it, her final resting place, surrounded by swamp, amongst the early morning mist, some seventy kilometres from the Polish border.

As we coasted to a standstill, I considered the distance to England from here and strange as it sounds reckoned it would take 100 days to push her there. I considered this a fitting end for this glorious machine, much grander, and more deserving than arriving on the back of a lorry. Besides, after the distance she had carried me, it seemed only fair that I should suffer too in the completion of her journey. From here it looked likely being my footprints in the sand.

It really had been a strange twist of fate the pair of us meeting that day back in Caboolture, her being prepared and ready in Joe's shop the day I dashed in there desperate for a reliable machine to take me to England. Joe has since said that there was just something about her, that she was a special bike.

That's the thing with postie bikes, because they all go through so much abuse in their early years they can soon develop a character based on who they were owned and ridden by. This one had been looked after better than any other, and under Colin's tenure had been treated well. I doubt any other of the bikes in the shop would have made it with such aplomb. And so yes, I certainly think it was fate that brought us together that day.

Perhaps it was the same fate that brought me and Mandy together in the first place. By that I don't just mean the speed-dating, as instrumental as that had been, but also the rest of the story and how we came to be in Sydney together at the beginning of this adventure.

I mentioned right at the very beginning how I'd flown back to Sydney after five months apart, surprising Mandy on the ferry she took to work that day. But that tells only half the story, because there's more to it than that. Not all of it I'm proud of, but it's the truth all the same and sometimes you just can't escape from that.

Odd as it sounds but after quitting my job in London (a dream job on a car magazine) and flying all that way to Sydney with the intention to surprise her, I suddenly lost faith in my conviction. I believe fear was the reason; fear of the commitment it would take to make things work out there. Moving to Australia, finding a job, turning my back on England and doing all that for a girl. It just seemed so massive, so intimidating.

I loved her, and I ached for her whenever we were apart. Yet at the same time I could see how she might be better off without me, my indecision and my doubt. This was something I never did like about myself, but as much as I wished for it I never could quite work it out, or cure it. And Mandy didn't deserve to be a part of that. She deserved better, she deserved better than me. And so I did a very strange and peculiar thing. I decided, having only been in Sydney a matter of hours, that I would turn around and go back to England, plead for my job back, Mandy never even knowing I'd ever been.

Before doing this I felt I needed to see her, even from afar, as she is beautiful and I wanted one final memory of that. I waited in the shadows down at Manly docks, hoping she would pass on her way home from work and from a distance I would watch her go by. Then go home to England, leaving her to get on with her life and do my best to get on with mine.

Sadly, after an hour or more of waiting there was no sign of her. I reasoned I must have missed her and so walked down to the ferry terminal myself, buying a ticket back to the city, hoping to change my flight and fly back to England the following day. I sat up on the top deck of the ferry, in a chair beside the window, land to my right, soon the Opera House would be in sight. I read a paper to distract me from the demons in my mind.

I must have been sat there for at least ten minutes when suddenly a figure stood above me, and from that figure a voice spoke out. 'Nathan, what the fuck are you doing here?' I looked up. It was Mandy, her face as white as a ghost. She thought I was in London, working on a magazine. Instead I was on her ferry, in Sydney, having lost the nerve to walk back into her life.

It turned out that she'd had been sat on the outside seats of the ferry as I boarded. She thought I'd looked strikingly familiar, thinking it can't be, he's on the other side of the world, then wandered around the decks to check if she was imagining things. It's then that she spotted me, in the chair beside the window, tears in my eye. She asked if I'd come here for work. To that all I could tell her was the truth, 'No, I've come here for you.' And that's how those nine months in Sydney, and this adventure, really began, with so much confusion and doubt.

With that, Dot spluttered back into life, her speed suddenly climbing, her health improving, the speedo needle rising to twenty-kilometres an hour, then thirty, then forty, until not long after we were back to fifty-five and doing just fine. I don't know how she had managed it. A mechanic might say she had simply seized, it taking a moment for her to cool down before she got going again. But I believed differently. I believed that this was her just giving it all she'd got, finding it hard towards the last hurdle but not being prepared to give up. After all that she'd been through; over the Himalayas two times, across the Outback on those killer fourteen hour days, along jungle paths and into the side of buses, dragged out of ditches and chained to a gate in an alleyway that stank of stale Indian piss. Now she was at the border with Poland, just three countries to go.

Chapter Twenty-Four
Poland

My intention was to carry on camping all the way through to England, but on the road just north of Pryzems'l – not many miles into Poland – I spotted a motel and decided to stop there. After all, I'd not had a wash or a change of clothes since Bishkek, now 5,000 kilometres and fifteen or so days ago. As a result, I must have looked a complete state checking in, the girl on the desk staring at me in bemusement. Who was I, where had I come from, where was I going?

I dumped all my gear in the room and stripped off my clothes, amazed to see skin and a body still there, though I was now slimmer, paler, and my eyes ached from the road they'd been tracing for so long. It was gorgeous to have a shower; to just stand there and let the water fall down, trying to untangle my hair and finding it impossible to do so for all the knots. My hair hadn't been combed since the man in Pakistan had just about ripped it out with his metal comb.

That night I ate pepperoni pizza and even had a beer. I was enjoying the moment. It was incomprehensible in a way. I just could not compute that in the last eight and a half months the road had brought me from Sydney to here, through East Timor, Indonesia, Malaysia, Thailand, Nepal, India, Pakistan, China, Kyrgyzstan, Kazakhstan, Russia, Ukraine and now Poland, with just Germany, France and maybe Belgium to go.

That distance felt tiny, just a speck on a map, something I finally bought for Europe and in doing so realised that Germany wasn't where

I thought it was; a little further up and to the left than I was expecting.

But first Poland, one of the prettiest places I'd been through. It was green and blue, the sky and endless rolling countryside all around. Yet it was modern, and perfect in the way it straddled the fence between the two extremes of east and western Europe.

There was that sense of unity, of brotherhood about it, such as in Indonesia, yet it was as modern as England; I could drink the water from the tap and pay for my petrol by debit card. I even came across an official Honda dealer for the first time since Pakistan, and despite Dot giving me no reason to believe she wouldn't make it now, I braked from fifty-five and steered her in, coming to a halt in the yard and asking the mechanics if they'd take a look.

A young mechanic named Bartek began the process of checking her over. By chance he had recently worked in the bacon factory not far from where my parents lived in Yorkshire. He said that he liked the old people of England, but thought the young ones were rude and violent. That was good. It sounded like nothing much had changed in the time that I'd been away. About Dot he said there wasn't too much wrong. The valve clearance was too tight, and he cleaned the carburettor and did a compression test, but other than that he could only attribute her current state to old age. She was simply worn out.

We changed the oil whilst we were there, having to suck the old fluid out with a syringe as she wasn't able to be drained the usual way, not with the sump bolt glued into place as it was.

Between here and Bishkek the only way I'd been able to change the oil, which I'd done on two occasions, was to remove the wing mirrors, lay the bike on its side, then lift her up into the inverted position, resting on the handlebars and seat, then removing the dipstick at the top of the engine (now the bottom) and letting the oil drain from there. Once drained, I would flip the bike back over and put fresh oil in. Not ideal, but it did the job.

Across the rest of Poland ran a motorway; three lanes wide, with vehicles travelling at an incredible pace. This wasn't the place for a bike going so slowly, but I wasn't taking the back roads now, I was just too desperate to get there. And I tried, through the night, dodging trucks as I tucked in tight to the hard shoulder until I realised if I went much further I wasn't going to survive the night. A truck driver would feel a little ripple, thinking it was of no significance, as an Englishman and his bike were squashed beneath his wheels.

Finally, I pulled into a layby around midnight; it was drizzling and there was nowhere for me to sleep. The ground was gravel and with the tent pole still missing it was no good even trying to put the tent up. Instead, I lay myself across Dot's seat in my sleeping bag, my feet over the handlebars, my head back on the rear brake light, with the fabric of the tent pulled over in order to keep the rain off.

Sadly I'd placed myself in the corner where all the truckers urinated. As I tried to drift off to sleep, all I could hear was the footsteps of another man crunching across the gravel, unzipping his trousers before proceeding to hose the ground only a yard or so from my ear.

I thought about getting up and moving, but I couldn't be bothered; I stayed where I was and drifted in and out of sleep, changing positions, trying not to tip over because inside my sleeping bag I still clutched the Chinese hunting knife, and if I toppled on that I probably wouldn't be getting back up very sharpish.

The next morning I couldn't wait for the sun to come up; for the darkness to pass, for the light to come because as soon as it did so I would be off, back on that motorway, making haste across Poland, a place I'd certainly like to revisit some day.

On the outskirts of Warsaw, the sky was angry and menacing, the black clouds suggesting my salmon pink overalls, the gift from the stranger in Nepal, were about to get wet. Then a moment I shall always remember; a hole in the clouds opening above me and a bright ray of sunlight shining through. It shone like a torch in the night. After a few seconds, the clouds moved on and the light was gone.

Had I been a religious person I would have seen that as a sign from God that I was almost home, but I still didn't believe in being carried across the sand by a divine force, so I just appreciated the beauty of the moment and rode on.

Actually, by this stage I'm not sure what I believed in any more. Maybe not in God, as a person, but in something. I had to, having made it all this way with no serious injury or incident. Fairies, angels, the Soul of the Universe as it's known in a book called the *Alchemist*; who knows? But I definitely believed in something, even if it was just that if you keep on going then everything will work out alright in the end.

At this point I wasn't sure how this journey would end; in England I hoped. But how would I feel and what and who would be there to greet me when I got there? It was a strange. In one sense I wanted to make it to England, but then at the same time I was nervous, because all of this would be coming to an end. This adventure, this journey, this challenge, and whilst I would have the book to write, and I was thankful for that distraction, I still feared the ending of all this, because I had been alive throughout all this. I'd been living. I'd been at my best. And a large part of me would miss that very much.

In Dresden, the first German city I came to, I wandered around in a complete daze, watching the tourists take pictures of the rebuilt cathedral that had been flattened by the RAF in the Second World War, Dot parked on the cobbled streets as the trams came past and the clock tower chimed on the hour.

I ate a hot dog, watched the punks and skaters in the park, then wandered into a camping shop and got excited about all the gear I could have bought to make my life easier. I even thought about getting a tattoo in one of the parlours, though I couldn't decide on the design. Rachel, a friend from home on Facebook, suggested I should get a single small black circle, a 'Dot.' I even enquired as to how much it might cost and it wasn't a lot. But I chickened out, too squeamish for needles.

Outside the busy shopping centre I was fixated by a woman pushing a pram. I assumed she was Muslim, wearing a heavy black veil covering everything but her eyes. I recognised her from Indonesia and from Pakistan. Now I felt a strange empathy towards her. I knew what it was like to be the odd one out, a stranger in a foreign land, people in the street pointing you out and not always being hospitable. To come from Pakistan (or wherever it was she was from) to here must have involved a terrible culture shock for her. Nervous and brave; that's how I imagined her beneath that heavy black veil.

It was still difficult to think that I'd been through all those countries, so hard to fathom, especially given the fear I had of them in advance. How perceptions can be so wrong and so misleading, to the point at which it'd be easy to let these things dissuade us from going anywhere at all.

At times I felt as though the world must have taken a deep breath and opened up just at the right time for me to carve a safe passage through. But then I thought of all the other travellers I'd met along the way, doing things even more random and dangerous than I was. And they'd all survived, as would the many more that followed.

Strange things also happen when you go out and see the world. It was at a petrol station on the outskirts of Dresden that a car pulled up behind me, the two occupants climbing out and walking towards me with intent. I didn't recognise them at first, not until the man spoke and asked if I remembered them from Thailand.

It turned out to be the couple I'd walked with at Khao Sok National Park, the day we'd all found ourselves covered in leeches. I couldn't believe it at first and neither could they. Five months before our paths had briefly crossed on the other side of the world, and now here we were, at a petrol station, in Germany.

They lived in Dresden and had been driving home when they spotted a familiar red motorbike flashing by, turning around to chase it. Now we chatted at the petrol pump for a good while, about the events of the past five months, until finally once more saying our goodbyes and going our separate ways again. It was surreal to see them again; like two worlds colliding.

From that point on I rode the autobahns across the rest of Germany. These have no upper speed limits, and cars would come roaring past at more than 200 kilometres per hour. But they do have lower speed restrictions — sixty kilometres per hour — which Dot wasn't quite able to reach.

The police pulled me over three times for being too slow. As the blue flashing lights came screaming up from behind I'd hit the throttle extra hard to try and nudge up the speed, and when they questioned me on such things I'd pretend we'd been doing well above sixty all along. It always took a while for them to believe where we'd come from, having to produce my Carnet and point out the countries the bike had been stamped in and out of. With that they would shake their head, allowing me on my way, insistent that I stay as far into the hard shoulder as I could.

After a night sleeping at the foot of a giant wind turbine by the side of the autobahn, I arrived at the home of Hülsmanns. It had been almost two weeks since they'd left me on the Kazakh steppe, them home three days already.

We hung out a few more days, great to have the gang back together again, driving to a town just outside Cologne for some sausage and curry, using their internet to book my ferry ticket from Calais to Dover for the coming weekend, then sitting to watch Ewan and Charley go the *Long Way Round*, and *Down* on their famous motorcycle adventures around the world.

It was fascinating to see how they had done it, obviously in a very different way to me, though I'd say with equal difficulty. To have gone through that with a camera in your face at times must have been tough. When you're at your lowest ebb, you just want to sit and think, listen and breathe, but instead they had to smile and perform for the camera.

I certainly wouldn't have wanted to have conducted my trip like that, even taking photographs and filming video diaries becomes a chore after a while. An obligation as well, to those who've come to expect it. I wondered though; had I watched Ewan and Charley properly, back in Sydney, would I still have set off? And I don't think that I would have. I think I would have considered it beyond me. That's why it was now so interesting to watch it in full, almost at the end of my adventure.

To see the equipment and the training and the planning they put into it, there was no way I could have managed that. Yet in some ways I had the only planning you really need for an adventure such as this — to be certain that it's something you have to do. Not want to do, because that's not enough. I think there's got to be the understanding that there is no other way out; that this is your only option, and therefore you must do this or forever wonder what if?

It was this fear of failing that had prevented me from ever quitting, or turning back, despite at times the incredible urge to do so. My advice therefore for anyone wanting to ride across the world on a motorbike, is to look around, see what you risk losing, then ask yourself if it's worth it. Because once you've gone, you've gone. Except for Sven on his push-bike of course, who had gone back for Caroline, for love.

I left the Hülsmanns two days before my ferry sailed from Calais to Dover, this now our third goodbye, the handshakes stiffer, the hugs longer. They had helped me across this last stretch of the world and for that I would be always grateful.

I now had forty-eight hours to cover just six hundred kilometres, and so instead of heading straight for the French coast took the opportunity to detour south in order to stop by the famous Nürburgring, a German racetrack over twenty miles in length that is open to the public for a small fee. I was going to take Dorothy around for a quick lap, if only so that she could say she'd been.

The track was in a beautiful part of Germany; thick forests and lakes, with pretty little villages burrowed into the landscape. I was excited about doing the lap, getting there mid-afternoon only to be told I was neither dressed appropriately or riding a sufficiently swift machine to be allowed to go around. The Porsches and other performance cars, clearly, were running scared.

Instead, I camped there that night, draping the fabric of the tent over the bike and using it as a make-shift shelter. I was hoping to make a cup of tea, but sadly had no matches. It was just one of those miserable nights, something I'd got used to and learned to live with since that fateful day of setting off from Sydney all that time ago. I'd learned a lot in that time. It felt like I'd been through so much, emotionally and physically. Now, after 263 days on the road, the next one would be our last.

To make it count I thought about detouring through Luxembourg and Holland, in order to bring my country tally up from eighteen to twenty. In the end I simply couldn't be bothered, taking the most direct route instead; into Belgium and along the main highway towards Brussels.

This proved much harder than I imagined, ending up on the motorway and fearing for my life, and sanity, as lorries squeezed us into the gutter. The map told of a smaller road running parallel, taking an age to locate, but once on it I was amazed to find it led me through towns and villages where, beside the butchers, the bakers and candle stick makers, shops with gorgeous girls sitting in the windows, wearing only their lingerie, would beckon you in whenever the traffic came to a standstill.

They were brothels, operating in the middle of the day, in the small towns and villages of Belgium. Of everything I'd seen on my journey across the world, this by far was the most unsuspecting sight of them all. I waved back and rode on.

I hit the French coast around midnight. It was freezing cold, the mist swirling and no one else on the road. I wore all my clothes, gloves and socks on my hands. This was it, not just the final day, but the final stretch. I traced the road, alongside a water ditch. I kept my eye out for illegal immigrants as there'd been reports of people being robbed by them.

I spotted one in the mirror. He had a bushy beard and tired eyes. I thought of the journey now, from Sydney to here. It wasn't regrets, just acceptance. Of everything: me, her, the way we were, the way things turn out, often without intention or conscious thought. But not by accident either. Nothing, really, can be put down to fate, or to chance. It's down to us. The good things and the bad. The buck stops here. And so does France.

***

It was 2am when I entered Calais, following signs to the ferry port. The town was empty — dark urban streets leading out to the sea. True to form, this couldn't all end without one last hitch. 'Your ferry sailed three days ago,' said the man at the check in desk. I'd only gone and booked the wrong date.

There wasn't much I could, only buy another ticket for the ferry leaving six hours later, the one I'd intended to be booked on. With that I walked out beneath the floodlights, picked my spot in the carpark and went to sleep on the ground. This would be the last time I wrapped myself in the tent, the last night I would sleep in the shadow of Dorothy, the last night I would wake up and have to ride the next day.

It was an odd sensation on the ferry that morning. I was neither happy nor sad; I was numb, overwhelmed and underwhelmed. An anti-climax in that sense. The fact that my friends and family would be waiting at the other end didn't seem real at all. How could they be there? I'd not seen them for eighteen months; surely they won't be in the same place as me, they couldn't possibly be?

Then over the loudspeaker came an announcement: that on-board was a chap who'd just ridden his 105cc Australia Post bike all the way from Sydney. And to that, some people applauded. I later found out that Paul Taylor, the friend who had lent me the money back in Malaysia, had alerted the ferry company. As a result I was offered a glass of champagne, asking if I could swap it for a hot cup of coffee instead.

A few people came over to congratulate me. How did they know it was me? Maybe it was the hair and the beard and the clothes that had survived nine months on the road. Maybe it was the BigZoner jacket I'd worn all the way from Indonesia; maybe it was the smell. I told them about my adventure as though I was talking about someone else, because I wasn't convinced I was the one who'd done it.

Nine months ago I was working in a café in Sydney making sandwiches for business people at lunchtime, trying to make a relationship work, trying to be the person I always wanted to be, and failing. From there to here, leaving after only two days, saying goodbye on the doorstep, nothing to do but run, take to the road and see how far I could follow it. It wasn't a sense of pride or excitement I now sat and nursed, just relief that it was all finally over. At least I thought it would be.

With that, the ferry docked. Me and Colin's old motorbike had made it to England.

Chapter Twenty-Five
Dover

Mum flung her arms around me and squeezed what life was left in me completely out. I could excuse her given what I must have put her through the last nine months. My dad approached in his usual loping manner and said, just as I'd imagined he would, 'So you made it then?'

Aunty Pat and Uncle John were there, so too cousin Jane, the one with a friend from Pakistan, and her husband Grant. Sadly my nan couldn't make it, not well enough. Then I noticed on the other side of the carpark, hidden by the pillars of the flyover bridge, another crowd, of at least twenty, maybe more, holding banners with, 'Welcome Home Big Teeth' in big painted red letters. It was friends from school, from uni, from various internet forums who'd caught wind of my arrival and come down to have their picture taken with the infamous motorcycle named Dorothy.

It was a baffling moment, faces and hands coming at me; where's my knife, do I fight them off? No, shake their hands, and give them a hug and thank them for coming and for their support along the way because I'd certainly needed it. I'd not been as alone as I'd thought on the road, as much as it sometimes felt, or wished to believe.

I felt a bit of a fraud in a way; they'd been privy only to one version of the truth, the one I'd presented in my group emails, which gave only one side of the story. There were others; this one, that one, Mandy's. All the same, but different. And no, she wasn't here, she was on the other side of the world, in Sydney all over again.

Finally, we made a break for the McDonald's at the top of Dover hill. It seemed like a fitting meeting place given how the fast-food chain had kept me in sustenance and free Wi-Fi at various stages of the journey. We didn't linger long as we still had to reach the unofficial finish line in London.

Paul led the way in a white Mercedes van that Dorothy sat behind, gradually taking advantage of the slipstream. With no fears over breaking down, I opened up the stops, blasted past the fifty-five limit I'd been sticking to for the last 6,000 kilometres or so and watched as the needle twitched past sixty, then sixty-five, then seventy, until she was stuck on seventy-five and didn't seem fussed by this at all. I thought if I'd about known this we could have been home the week before. Though it was probably because I'd treated Dot so gently that I could be rough with her now. And she seemed to like it, the dirty wench.

The countryside of England was a real pleasure to ride through, still so green and blooming despite it being late September. I liked the thick hedgerows and the church spires, the old pubs, and the signposts that for once I could understand. I liked the look of the people and the smell in the air. Suddenly England seemed unique. Home? I'm not sure. It was too early to tell. It was just so weird, looking in my mirror and seeing my mum and dad's faces in the front seats of the car behind me. What were they doing there, how had that happened?

It was a happy moment, to have made it, to have finally finished the journey, taking just under nine months, covering a total of 35,000 kilometres, riding through eighteen countries and costing… I haven't a clue. More than $8,000, that's for certain.

It was a beautiful afternoon in London as the convoy made its way through the outskirts. The sun was shining and the pavements were full of people enjoying the warm weather. I'd never really appreciated just what a great city it is, not until this moment when it all seemed so novel.

It was the architecture, and the pace of it; the red buses, the black cabs, even, dare I say it, the multiculturalism. Pretty much every place I'd passed through on my journey to this point had been populated by a certain race or ethnicity. Now, here in London, gathered everyone. The faces I'd seen in Indonesia, in Thailand, in India, Pakistan, Kazakhstan, Russia, were now all together, queuing at the bus stop, playing in the same park. Some might see that as a bad thing. I just saw it as evidence that we can all get along.

Our destination was the Ace Café, a famous biker hangout on the north-west of the city. People with Harley Davidsons and Ducatis tend to go there, proper bikes, though I doubt it had received anything more proper than a 105cc Australia Post bike that had ridden across the world with barely any issues, certainly in spite of my stewardship, not because of it.

Having been shown through the main glass doors, Dorothy took her place on the stage, most of the people in the bar wondering what such a crap little bike was doing there, but she looked impressive that day, caked in dirt and weighed down by all the saddle bags.

The toothbrush was still there holding the sump plug in, the shoelace still holding her headlight on, the old sprocket still tied around the handlebars, the BigZoner bell still chiming, the plaque still bolted to the back. Colin's old motorbike had not only carried him across the Outback but also me across the world and I was so proud of her for doing that.

With that I had a pint of beer and a plate of chips before taking one almighty sigh. The journey 'home' was over, finally ending just as abruptly as it had begun.

Had it achieved what I wanted it to achieve? Had I learned what I wanted to learn? Changed as much as I wanted to change? Found peace as much as I hoped to have found peace? What had I achieved in all of this and was it a sense of loss, or of gain? At this point, it was all far too early to say.

Chapter Twenty-Six
Notes from the Shed

I have been writing this in a shed at the bottom of my parents' garden on the laptop I carried all the way from Sydney, the one the border guard tried to take apart. The 'u' key on it is missing after a can of Russian tuna fell off the shelf and broke it clean off. The shed is not very big, only about two metres by three, with no windows but a draught from the door. It has light and electricity, and a desk and a chair, and photos from my trip all over the walls, just as a reminder, so that when I'm going stir-crazy I can look up and see that there is a world out there, even if I don't recognise the person in the picture. The first few weeks I even slept in the shed, with a mattress on the floor.

Gradually I have moved into the house and I actually quite like having a comfy bed and not having to pack it away the next morning. Dot's been parked in the garage next door. She's not moved much since we've been back, now six months ago. She can't, I think she's completely seized up, so for the time being she's wrapped beneath a blanket until I have the money and the knowledge to repair her. I would like to fix her; she deserves to be fixed.

In the meantime I've been riding around on the C90 I was going to do the trip on in the first place. It's not quite as sturdy as Dot, and no way do I think that would have made it across the world with such confidence, but it's been good to take a break from the book every now and again, riding through the Yorkshire Dales and up the coast, passing through the towns of Scarborough and Whitby.

At other times I have even equipped her with the panniers from Dot and ridden further afield, often visiting friends. It's been great to catch up with everyone. As anyone who's ever been away for any length of time will testify, it's surprising how quickly you can slip back into a social group as though you've never been away. Talk turns quickly to what they've been up to and who's been dating who and what the new hairdresser looks like and so on, until you forget you've even been away at all.

But it has been much harder this time. I suppose this journey has been my life, I have nothing else in it, I have nothing else much to contribute and that leaves me staring off into the distance thinking of the Outback or the Kazakh steppe, sometimes to the point that I wish I'd never seen them at all, as I might be more content with the current view if I hadn't.

I really miss those conversations I had in Pakistan, sitting around that table, or around the camp fire in Malaysia, or anywhere else there's been a nice group. I also miss that feeling of being on the brink, that taste of danger and that moment when you feel most alive. It's like taking a drug you can never have again, unless of course you're prepared to venture even further into danger in order to find some more. That might be why I don't end up listening to my mum, who still tells me to grow up and settle down. Though I know, now more than ever, that I perhaps ought to. Writing this book has made me confront that truth. It's perhaps why at times I wish I'd not had it to write, or even had the story to tell. Ignorance is bliss, as they say. I shall certainly not miss the keyboard. I shall not miss living in the past. And talk of change is stupid. I think we only adapt.

In other news, the Frenchman kidnapped in Pakistan has been released and so far, of everyone I met on my travels, all made it back in one piece. The two German cyclists in East Timor, Sven and Caroline, arrived home a good year after I'd met them, and the last I heard of Nat and Aki on the other postie bike they were in Japan.

Michel, Andrew and Amelia, from Pakistan finished their journeys, and even Daniel, entering Afghanistan in his 4x4, got through okay, posting some incredible pictures from that country on Facebook. He said it was completely safe in the north and fascinating to see a different reality from that portrayed in the media. I gather he's now in Georgia with no plans to come home yet. The Hülsmanns — Andreas and Claudia — they're doing fine. Nazgul, the girl in the Bishkek shop, made it to London and is studying English. Joe and the gang at One Ten Motorcycles have moved into new premises, and sadly Kevin Rudd is no longer Prime Minister of Australia having been forced out by Julia Gillard.

What's saddened me most since I got back is hearing of the terrible events happening in the places I passed through. First there was Bangkok with more of those riots, this time with so many more killed. Also Kyrgyzstan, where the death toll from a sudden wave of ethnic tension reached triple figures, and reduced the beautiful town of Osh to cinders. It seemed such a peaceful country, I can't understand it. Nazgul couldn't either; her family was affected by the troubles.

There's also been more trouble in Pakistan, more bombs and more blasts, and then the dreadful flooding that has swamped one-fifth of the land and left millions homeless. When I see the images on the news I feel for them. The people in those countries were good to me. Then to be at a local petrol station the other night and hear a moron shout, 'Rag head' from his car to a girl behind me wearing a veil had me wonder how a foreigner would fare travelling through our world on a motorbike. They certainly wouldn't be high-fived from the roadside, that's for certain.

As for me and Mandy, we're still in touch, still friends, on opposite sides of the world again. Of course I miss her dearly and often resent myself for being the type of person who might want to do a trip like this, because then I think maybe things would have worked out better between us. Though if I'd have been a more settled person then I wouldn't have been in Australia at speed-dating in the first place.

You can't help your nature, as my nan might say. And she's right, as she always is, and also a little better now. But I guess sometimes you have to — help your nature that is — otherwise you might spend your whole life searching for something that doesn't exist, and end up with nothing. So it's a balancing act. But who knows what's around the next corner or over the next horizon? Maybe the next challenge, a new horizon. Or just maybe, a full stop.

Three years passed

PART 2

RUNNING TOWARDS
THE LIGHT

NEW YORK TO SEATTLE

"If you're going through hell, keep going"
Winston Churchill

Chapter Twenty-Seven
England

I don't fear many things these days – except perhaps flying still, and writing books – but I do worry about where all this ends.

I mean, all my life I feel like I've been running. Running away from things, running towards things, but always, in every case, running. And I think finally I've realised that all I've actually been running from is myself.

It took my journey across the world by motorcycle to realise this. From Sydney to London I rode for a total of 264 days, covering 23,000 miles and passing through eighteen countries along the way, and yet despite all that, I never did quite manage to leave myself behind.

Certainly, there were times when I was running so fast that I got lost in the moment and allowed momentum to really make me sing and dance. But whenever I stopped, or was forced to stop, by hold-ups at borders and what not, I was always quickly surrounded by all those dark and destructive thoughts I'd been hoping to leave behind.

This was especially the case when I returned home and spent a year locked away in a room writing a book about this journey across the world. All of a sudden there was nowhere to run to and nowhere to hide. For the first time in my life I really had to turn and face myself and figure out who I was and who I wasn't. And I didn't enjoy this very much, mainly because I didn't always like the person that I found.

The publication of the book didn't help matters either, as the need to publicise it only served to chain me to the events of the past. Then when the Australian publisher decided not to publish it in England I began the long and difficult task of publishing it myself. This was hard and had I been less stubborn I would have walked away from it all and done something else with my life. But I stuck at it, and thus began a long and slow walk along the path of self-destruction, something I soon learnt can prove quite addictive at times.

I hit the bottom when severe burning sensations in all of my bones took me to the doctors, and the MRI scan said nothing was physically wrong, which made the doctor ask: 'how do you feel in yourself?' To which I cried and told her at times I just wanted to die.

'Do I need to worry?' she asked.

'No,' I said, 'I'm too indecisive for that.'

We both laughed. We laughed because what else can you do but laugh. Though I really did feel rotten that day and quite angry with myself. I say angry because at such times you can see yourself, and how you're acting, and how you're behaving, and all you want to do is shake yourself, or equally harm yourself, but you just can't. Instead you feel useless, and pathetic, and weak, and indecisive, and all of the other names you've been called by the people you love in the past. And they only hurt because you know that they had a point.

The doctor prescribed me antidepressants and a stint with a counsellor. I took the pills home and stared at them on my desk for a week before tipping them down the sink. As bad as things had become I felt that to take them would be cheating, and possibly make things worse. After all, I'd got myself into this mess, and it was up to me to get myself out of it. It had to be this way. That was just how I felt.

My fight back began with the rebuilding of the bike that had brought me all that way across the world. Dorothy – as goes her name – is a retired Australian Post bike, only 105cc, and a bike that had travelled all that distance needing nothing more than a few spare parts and a regular check-up and service along the way, only then to be abandoned in a shed at the bottom of the garden for the two years that followed.

For a while I hated the sight of her, reminding me most of the person I'd once been: riding through Pakistan, catching boats from Indonesia to

Malaysia, dodging traffic in India, climbing the second highest road in the world in the Himalayas, riding through the night across Kazakhstan, Russia and Ukraine. Fearless almost of everything. Two years later I was sat in the doctor's surgery, crying.

Despite covering all that distance, when me and my dad took her apart in the garage at the bottom of the garden we found she needed nothing more than new piston rings, clutch plates and a cam chain, which she didn't really need, but we put one in anyway, just to be sure. I had the mechanic in the local village repair the engine bolt that had been bodged up all the way from Kyrgyzstan. He couldn't believe the bike had come this far, and still looked fit enough to be turned around and ridden all the way back again.

She fired into life the very first kick. What a moment that was. The first step to getting back on the road.

The next step was to retrace my steps. I did this by flying back to Australia, spending a few weeks in Sydney, simply saying goodbye to the place and catching up with old friends. This might sound extreme – a flight all the way to Australia just to do this – but in so many ways Australia still felt like home to me. It felt like I'd left half of my life and half of my heart there and I needed to go back and retrieve them.

And no, Mandy didn't live there anymore; she'd long since moved back home to Canada.

While in Australia, I visited Joe and the rest of the gang at One Ten Motorcycles up in Caboolture. It was great to see them again. Joe, Katrina, Dan – they were like family in a way, the lot of us all going over to some big postie bike gathering down the coast in Coffs Harbour. After that it was just great to hang out back at the shop; Joe setting me up with all sorts of bits to make the bike run that little better, and hopefully faster.

It was actually Joe's mechanic, Mike, who said that sometimes in life you need to retrace your steps in order to make sense of things. It was this that helped me understand what it was that I was doing back in Australia, because up until that point I wasn't entirely sure.

After a week or so in Caboolture, I caught the bus back down to Sydney, spending a few more days there, wandering the streets, trying to make sense of it all, before finally flying home to England. Another step closer to getting back on the road.

In England I went to a few bike festivals, even took Dorothy for a run to the coast. But even with all that, I just couldn't seem to muster the conviction to get back on my feet again. I was lost, and at one point lit a fire and torched so many of my things.

I attacked the shed with a pitchfork, I punched myself in the face until it ached. I think I was trying to kill the past, and me in it. The worst moment was measuring up the rope hanging on the wall in the garage and staring at the beam and wondering if it would support it. But I'd be useless at suicide. I'd kick away the stool and immediately regret it. I can't begin to imagine the bravery such a thing must take.

In a way I don't think I would ever have got myself right again had it not been for two New Zealanders – Rob and Greg – who turned up completely out of the blue one day, arriving on the doorstep of my parents' house near Scarborough, the place I was living at the time.

It turned out that a few years prior they'd read in a magazine of an Englishman who'd ridden his Australian Post bike all the way home from Australia and, both on the cusp of forty, both with wives and children, decided they'd like to give it a try themselves; before they grew too old and developed too many excuses.

They bought a couple of postie bikes, and after a fair bit of planning, shipped them from New Zealand to Singapore, and then proceeded to ride them all the way to England, on a route a little more direct than the one I took, having been fortunate in acquiring visas for Iran.

Their journey took them three months (that's all the time they had due to work and family commitments), and having arrived in England they rode north, to Scarborough, to meet the guy they'd read about in the magazine all that time ago. Instead, they met me.

Rob and Greg stayed at our place for a few nights. Mum and dad put them up in the spare room and loved having a couple of guests to fuss over for a while. We sat and talked about our trips, comparing notes and stories from the road (I was curious to hear what Iran had been like). I think it was good for my parents to see that it wasn't just me that does stupid things; there are plenty of others out there as well.

Finally came time for Rob and Greg to ride back down to London, where they would be handing their bikes over to a shipping agent that was going to send them back to New Zealand, before flying home themselves. They asked if I wanted to join them on the 250-mile ride down to the capital, and with nothing else to do, and the bike now rebuilt, I said 'why not.' I loaded my old panniers with all my old gear, and enough equipment to last on the road for a few days, before following the convoy on its journey south.

We camped wild those few days it took us, sleeping in a bus shelter one night outside the town of Holmfirth, where they filmed *Last of the Summer Wine*. We passed through Mansfield, the town in which I was raised, as well as Oxford, a place they were both keen to see. It rained pretty much the whole way, but I was on the road again, after almost three years of not being able to find it. I remember feeling completely out of my depth, almost as though the journey from Sydney to London had counted for nothing and I had it all to learn again.

We arrived in London and handed over their bikes to the shipping agent. Rob and Greg caught their flight home whilst I rode back north a hundred miles or so, to stay at the home of Dave and Michelle, good friends who were on holiday and said I could use their place in Hinckley as a base to get back on my feet again. The plan was to settle down and get a job in the area; do the thing that people wanted and expected me to do. But I got to their house, and I sat on their couch, and I looked at myself, and I thought, 'This isn't you, this isn't what you want to do. You know what you need to do.'

I went online and booked a ticket to New York to fly the following week. I called the same shipping company that had sent Rob and Greg's bikes to New Zealand and asked Giles, a good friend and the man in charge there, if he could send my bike to New York by aeroplane, asking him how much as well. 'Bring her next week. Bring her on Tuesday, and she'll be there by Thursday,' he said.

It would cost £600, which I didn't think was so bad.

I spent the next few days processing what I was about to do: fly me and the old bike to America, with the intention of riding it all the way across to the Pacific Coast, and hopefully up to Alaska as well.

Why America? Because it was the nearest place west of England, and deep inside I always felt most comfortable when travelling west. Maybe it's something to do with the sun, and chasing it at the end of the day. I guess it's a simple case of *Running Towards the Light*, and the start of a brand new day.

I just knew that I needed to do something; something big, something desperate, to get myself out of the situation that I'd found myself in, because it couldn't go on for much longer, not like this. I felt so raw and angry; frustrated, desperate and lonely in the world. I suppose at such times some people turn to the bottle, whilst others turn to the road.

I didn't tell anyone of my plan, not even my parents. I couldn't, because I was struggling to convince myself that it was the right thing to do, let alone convince someone else. After all, I did fear getting back on the bike, and back on the road again. The first trip had in many ways been so destructive and taken me to such a dark place. Would going on another adventure improve or worsen that situation? I just didn't know. But as before I knew I had to try. And so once more, I cut the rope and fell.

That following week, completely in silence, I packed up my things, rolled the bike out of Dave and Michelle's shed, and at 5 in the morning began my descent to the shipping agent just outside of Heathrow. My heart was beating like a drum. I looked only forward, not back. I was excited. I was nervous. I was numb. Tell yourself: 'You're about to ship your 105cc motorbike to America and ride it across.' Now shit yourself, because today it's going to be done.

Looking back it was an act of complete madness. I had no plan, no money, no maps, no knowledge of where or how it might end up. It was just a case of taking an almighty leap into the unknown. Besides, by this stage I'd realised that if you happen to find yourself on the path of self-destruction then all you can do is see it through, and hope you come out the other side. There is no turning back.

The process of getting a bike ready for air transit was quite straight forward. I only had to take the front wheel off; the panniers I could leave on the bike complete with all my gear inside. The bike is then put on a wooden pallet, with a box built around it, and that's it, you walk away, or in this case, get a lift to the airport, catch your plane, and in two days' time you meet your bike in New York City.

And that's where this story begins.

Chapter Twenty-Eight
New York

I landed in America on the 12th August 2012. Dorothy landed a few days later on the 15th. In the time between landing in America and the bike showing up, I took a Greyhound bus up to a town just outside of Toronto, Canada, as this is where Mandy now lived. I hadn't seen her for two long years, not since I'd written that first book and jumped straight on a plane with the certainty that she was all I wanted out of life, only to learn I was too late; there'd been too much water pass beneath the bridge.

This had left me with a gaping hole in my heart, and I think that was half my problem.

This time – two years on – I was only going back to say hello, as the pair of us were still good friends and had kept in touch. For the day I was there we drank coffee, played tennis, went around the shops picking up the things I thought I'd need for my journey across America. I guess you could call it déjà vu, because we did the exact same thing in Australia as I prepared for that long ride home to England.

It was just great to see her again and if nothing else to be reminded of the reason behind all this. I had travelled a lot of miles in the last few years. I'd walked a lot as well. But seeing her again I had no regrets. I'd do it all again, tomorrow, in a heartbeat, though perhaps hoping for a different outcome next time round.

Then came the time for me to get back on the bus to New York and say goodbye again, which was harder now than ever; knowing that there's someone out there who you want to see every single day of your life, but knowing that it might be a few more years until you see them again, that's if you ever see them again at all.

I returned to New York on the Greyhound, checking into a hostel right at the end of the tracks in Brooklyn. It was run by a man named David, who had converted his two bed apartment into a place with ten bunk beds and a constant stream of travellers passing through. It was in a suburb deep in the heart of Brooklyn – the last stop on the subway – in a predominately black neighbourhood, which was unnerving at first, simply because I'd never stayed in such a place before. Yet no one even seemed to notice or care. We were invisible really, and I never felt unsafe. There was probably no reason to, much like the Aboriginals back in the Australian Outback, where I'd been scared to talk to them during the early days of that first trip, only to learn that it was only my own fears that was holding me back.

Now in New York, I caught the subway and paced the streets of Manhattan, walking through Central Park, past the Empire State Building, along Fifth Avenue, then sitting in Times Square on the steps, blown away by the scale and size of it all; the noise, the commotion, the traffic, the massive billboards and flashing neon lights. I'd been to New York before, but it felt different this time, like the start of something massive, which I guess it was; the second half of my journey across the world.

I walked along Broadway, picked up a slice of dollar pizza, then back to pacing the streets, still not feeling too good. I think it was just the reality setting in, that I was here now, and that I was going to have to somehow get to the other side of the country on the meagre resources that I had; around £500 by the time everything else had been paid for.

In the end, the shipping company had to contact me and ask if everything was alright, as I'd not been to the airport to pick up my bike yet, and if I didn't come for it soon then they would start charging me storage costs. The reality was that I was scared. I knew what picking up my bike would mean; that the journey would be underway and I'd have no choice but to hit the road and be alone again out there, this time knowing exactly what to expect.

The day I rode out of Sydney – after three short days of planning – I had the benefit of naivety and ignorance. I set off oblivious and discovered what a trip like this would entail as I went along. This time I knew exactly what to expect; those times of loneliness and worry, of breakdowns and struggling at night to find suitable places to sleep. I imagine it's a bit like getting married and then divorced, and wondering if you should get married again. Second time around you know what to expect and so you might be reluctant to give it another try. But what do you do; get on with life, or put your life on hold forever?

The difference this time was that I knew there was no happy ending to be found at the end of this trip, as I'd mistakenly thought there would be at the end of the first. Naively I'd seen that first trip as the solution to all my problems; the cure of all my faults. Instead I found nothing at the end of it. No sense of satisfaction or contentment. I just found England, and nothing in it to necessarily hold me there.

This seems to be one of the biggest deceits of life; that somehow you conquer it by achieving that one thing you dream of. Sadly it doesn't seem to work like that. Once you achieve that dream, you soon move on to the next one. Perhaps it's what makes us human; the endless desire for something better, or something else. That's why I sometimes think the concept of contentment is just an illusion; another dream to chase.

Finally, I went and collected the bike from JFK airport. It wasn't as difficult a process as I thought it might be. I simply caught the free shuttle bus to the Virgin Atlantic cargo department, paid a $40 documentation fee, had my documentation stamped, then took another free shuttle bus to the other side of the airport, to the customs office.

Here I had to explain that I was only bringing in the bike for a short length of time and how it was just for personal use and that I would be exporting it back to England at the end. The process of shipping a bike to America is actually easier than to most other countries, as you don't need an expensive Carnet de Passage, and the shared language definitely helps.

Back at the Virgin Atlantic cargo depot I was directed through to the main warehouse and told to sit and wait. A short while later, a forklift truck brought a large wooden box and placed it on the ground in front of me. It felt like Kathmandu all over again, only on this occasion, rather than a team of eager helpers to assist me crack open the crate, I was given a crowbar and left to get on with it myself.

As I ripped the crate apart, a man named Vince approached and asked if the bike emerging from the crate was Dorothy. I was puzzled for a moment until he explained that he had just read my first book on Kindle and recognised the bike from the pictures on the internet. He said he'd enjoyed the book, which was kind of him. It was surreal to meet someone who knows so much about you, yet you know absolutely nothing about them.

We stood and talked for a while, just about life and stuff. He was a long-distance truck driver, picking up his next load from the airport and taking it to a destination far away. Vince took some photos of me and the bike and emailed them to me a few months later. I looked happy that day, though it wasn't to last, as that fifteen mile ride from the airport to the centre of Manhattan was one of the most terrifying of this entire trip...

The front brake didn't work properly after I snapped the lever unloading the bike from the crate. The front wheel also had a slow puncture having snagged the tube changing the tyres over. It was drizzling with rain, making the road incredibly greasy, and with no maps or route planned for getting to downtown Manhattan all I could do was aim for the cluster of tall buildings in the distance.

Worst of all I had to take the interstate: six lanes of high-speed traffic, doing 40mph, head on the tank, flogging the bike and hoping that no one rear ended me in the process. That's when I realised I'd not tightened the back wheel nut, and so that sloppiness at the back end I was feeling was caused by the wheel wobbling around, and all I could do was hope it didn't fall out between the airport and downtown Manhattan. Thankfully it didn't and I spent the afternoon riding around Manhattan, waiting for it all to sink in.

To think I'd ridden that same bike around Darwin, Bangkok, Delhi, Islamabad, as well as London; it just didn't make any sense. Now I was here in New York and everything seemed so big and I felt so small. It was intimidating, especially the traffic, and I didn't want to think about which route I would take out of here. Instead I went back to David's apartment and spent a few days getting prepared for the journey ahead.

I bought a cheap compact camera, a couple of maps from a bookstore, and also spent an age trying to source a replacement brake lever as no where in New York seemed to have one for an Australian Post bike; with no surprise by that. A custom bike shop in Brooklyn was able to order me one, whilst from a nearby scooter shop – owned by a man originally from England – I was able to stock up on replacement inner tubes, as I always liked to travel with a few spare. It was all just a very strange and surreal time. It was almost like being on auto-pilot, just doing what I needed to do, one step at a time.

The day I came to finally leave New York I packed up my things, said goodbye to David and his temporary clan of travellers, and made my way through the streets of Brooklyn. As I rode beneath the subway on Broadway – the road that leads into Manhattan – I was pulled over by the police. I jumped off the bike and asked the policeman what the matter was. He said that I couldn't ride here with a foreign number plate.

I explained that many people do this – bring bikes from abroad to ride here – but he didn't believe me and said that I would have to go and speak to the DMV (the Department of Motor Vehicles), which had a big office on the other side of Brooklyn. He gave me directions to get there and sent me on my way.

I was tempted to just ignore him and carry on going. Get the hell out of the city and not look back. But I thought, 'if I'm going to get pulled over here, then where else am I going to get pulled over, and how often, and how long before someone impounds my bike?' So I followed his directions to the DMV, parking outside on the pavement with permission from the security guard patrolling the area, before heading upstairs to join a queue of people, waiting in line to see an attendant.

When finally called to the desk I explained my situation to a lady who consulted with her colleague and left me stood anxiously hoping for good news. But it wasn't good news. 'You're either going to have to ship the bike home to England, or ship it across to San Francisco if that's where you're heading, but there's no way you can ride it here.'

I didn't argue. There was no point, though I knew that this lady, and the policeman, were wrong. I walked outside and buried my head in my hands, wondering just what I was going to do. In truth, I didn't know what I was going to do.

In the end I rode up to a Starbucks on the corner as I knew I could get free Wi-Fi there and had with me a small laptop on which to do so. I began by sending an email to the company that had issued my liability insurance for the bike, as surely if you can get insurance cover for a foreign bike here in America, from an American company, then you can in fact ride it here. But the company was closed for the day as it was a public holiday.

I tried Googling for answers, before finally posting on ADVRider.com, an America-based adventure motorcycle site with members who've done this sort of thing before.

Several responded to say I should be okay; one of them contacting DMV directly and having head office in Washington confirm that as long as my bike was taxed and tested in my own country, and that I was the registered owner, then I was okay to ride it in America for the maximum period of a year. It was the confirmation I needed that the policeman and the DMV here in New York were both wrong, though I still remained incredibly nervous of being pulled over again in the future.

By this time it was too late to hit the road out of the city, deciding to check back into David's hostel and leave the following morning. Unfortunately the hostel was fully booked, as were most of the other hostels in New York that evening, what with it being a public holiday and all. Instead, I parked up in the centre of Manhattan, just off Fifth Avenue.

It was raining so I put a cover over the bike, as the panniers weren't waterproof, before going for a wander around the shops, just trying to get a grip of myself. It wasn't a good time. I was barely hanging on by a thread and felt quite vulnerable and alone.

I walked the streets of Manhattan, pacing myself out. I came to the conclusion while doing this that I really did need some help getting out of the city as I couldn't do it alone. I went into an electronics shop and bought a hundred dollar satellite navigation unit, as the bike now had a cigarette lighter that I'd be able to charge it from.

Sadly, when I returned back to the bike, I discovered that the charger was broken and that I wasn't able to make it work. The satnav only had a quarter of its battery life in it, I wouldn't be able to charge it, and I didn't know how long the charge would last.

I paced the streets some more. It wasn't long before it was midnight. I hurt right now. I hurt from the situation that I found myself in. Alone in this city, with an old motorbike, that couldn't go very fast, and the intention of riding it all the way across America. And still the rain would fall.

I wheeled the bike beneath the canopy of a loading bay. By this time there was hardly anyone else about. Between the wall of the loading bay and Dot's front tyre I squeezed myself, sitting in a nest of cigarette butts, trying to hide from the world.

A short while later a police car pulled up no more than five metres away. I hid behind the bike's front wheel, trying not to be seen. The lights of the police car were flashing red and blue. The occupants were getting out and looking around. There was commotion. I didn't know what to do. I sat there and didn't make a sound. They were there for almost an hour, and I still didn't know what to do. By now it was 2am. I was cold and wet. I didn't think they were looking for me.

At 4am I finally snapped, stood up, took the cover off the bike, put my waterproof jacket on, my helmet, and my gloves. I plugged in the new satnav system, keyed in a destination to the north west of the city, and set off. I couldn't sit there forever in that pile of cigarette butts; I had to move on.

The streets were full of puddles. There wasn't much other traffic about. I cruised through Times Square, half expecting to be pulled by another police car at any moment. I was scared.

With the rain falling heavier and my jeans getting wet, I hastily pulled into the driveway of an amusement park on the west shore of Manhattan, alongside the Hudson River. As I was putting on my waterproof trousers the security guard came out of his booth and asked if I was alright. I told him that I was, making small talk about the rain and about life in general. He had a whole family to feed and I felt for him, sat in his booth, alone through the night. I said 'Goodbye,' and this time properly hit the road.

The satellite navigation unit was nestled in the pouch of the tank bag that James and Nancy had given me all the way back in India, back when we rode over the Himalayas together. I followed the arrows of the flickering unit, holding so much hope in that little device and its quarter battery charge that it felt as though my whole life depended on it. I was certainly obedient to its directions as it took me from one dual lane highway to the next, hitting junctions I never would have made had I been on my own.

The battery ran out just as I hit New Jersey. I didn't have a clue where to go now. It was perhaps 6am, just light, raining heavily. I pulled into the car park of a bank that had a canopy under which I could shelter from the rain. I was cold, wet, and hungry; tired also from having had no sleep that night.

There was a supermarket on the other side of the road that had just opened for the day. I went in there and bought bananas, some bread rolls, a few other bits and pieces, and a coffee from the machine. Paying at the self-service checkout I knocked the coffee flying, spilling it all over the floor. As I did my best to mop it up, the woman using the machine beside me made some pleasant remark about the incident and from that we got chattering. She asked where I was going. 'I don't know, I'm lost,' I said.

This lady couldn't help me as she didn't know her way very well either. But she asked another man; a big stout man, with a kind face, who knew the area well, guiding me outside and beginning to point in all sorts of directions, instructing me how to get out into some clear open road.

'Take this road, take that road, left here, right there,' he said. I took little of it in, but was just grateful for the care that these two people showed me that day. Denise back in Mount Isa would have been proud; the fairies and angels of America were alive and well.

It wasn't long before I was completely lost again. I went round and around in circles. I ended up in an out of town shopping precinct which I just couldn't get out of. I could see the road I wanted, but I just couldn't figure out which slip road to take. Eventually I found it, and then I found myself on the busiest highway in the world, or that's what it felt like, waiting for the moment I got rammed from behind and pushed right through into the afterlife.

I pulled into a gas station to escape the heat, asking a woman filling her car with fuel if she knew exactly where we were. She didn't really know either, but she had a map in her car and together we studied it and tried to figure out where I should head. The conclusion was north-west, though which road, and to where, was anyone's guess. This really was quite stupid; riding across America with no real clue as to what I was doing, or how I was going to do it. I was just riding, because that's all at this time I knew how to do.

I returned to the highway of death, riding it for five minutes before realising I'm going to die if I don't get off it, taking a gamble on an exit, any exit, and following it around. And before I knew it, I was in peaceful suburbia; big old white-washed houses, perfectly manicured lawns, the American flag flapping on flag poles and the world suddenly appearing a whole lot quieter and calmer. It now about 2 o'clock on a warm Saturday afternoon, somewhere in New Jersey.

I passed a small car repair shop by the side of the road. A man stood outside sanding an old door on a workbench. I turned around and pulled into the yard in front of him. The man stopped sanding the door and asked if he could help. I told him about the power socket not working and wondered if he knew of a good auto electrician in town. The man said he was a good one himself, instructing me to unload all of my gear from the bike, while he went and got some tools from his workshop.

The man's name was John, in his sixties and a biker himself. He had a big Harley Davidson and planned on riding it across to San Francisco one day in the distant future. When I told him that was where I was heading, he just kind of scratched his head, looked at the bike and said 'Okay,' to suggest he didn't quite believe me, though I couldn't blame him for that.

John worked out that it was just a bad connection and that the wires had come loose from where the charger connects to the battery. He replaced the connectors, plugged it all back in and when we tried the satnav it was with great relief that it fired back into life and started charging again. I was so relieved, because now I had a vague idea of which direction I was going in. West; in the direction of the setting sun.

I reloaded all my gear, thanked John (who wouldn't take a dime), and returned to the road. For a destination I punched in Equinunk, the name of a small town in Pennsylvania where ten years previously I'd worked as a tennis instructor at a summer camp for kids from Manhattan as part of the Camp America programme. By chance, on that same ADVRider forum that had helped me with the DMV, I came across a man going by the name of Johnny Equinunk, and a few years back I'd emailed him and said: 'Is that the same place?' And he said: 'Yes, and if you're ever around this way then please drop by.' He knew I was in America. I'd emailed to tell him. So that's where I was heading now.

By this stage the road was single carriageway. The scenery to the side was quite pleasant. Green and rolling hills, home-made wooden white fences and huge red barns with tractors parked outside. This being a Saturday there were also a variety of local festivals taking place in the small villages I passed through. It was certainly a pleasant world out here, now in rural Pennsylvania.

There was however one moment that afternoon I'll never forget. I'd pulled over at a gas station that had a picnic table way off to the side of the forecourt, on which I sat and drank a coffee and ate a bag of crisps. The sun was hot and I was really tired, putting my head on the table and the next thing I knew waking up half an hour later with a jolt.

To suddenly find myself in this situation; to wake up in it – a random gas station somewhere in America, alone and scared and not really sure where I was heading – was a horrible moment. I thought: 'What the hell am I doing here, why am I doing this? I can't do this. I'm scared.'

The only answer I had to all of that was the harsh reality that I'd chosen to be there, because for whatever reason, for whatever purpose, I'd deemed this journey across America as the most important thing I had to do in my life, and I was doing it, whether I really wanted to or not. I know that sounds stupid. Surely you only do the things in life you want to do. But I don't really think it's as simple as that, otherwise we'd all be happy, and from my experience, many of us are not.

Finally, I peeled myself off that bench, slumped back into the saddle, kicked the old bitch into life and pounded her back on to the highway, adopting my regular spot riding right into the gutter, with one eye to the front, one eye on the mirror to see what was coming up behind.

You never relax travelling at these speeds on these kinds of roads. You're permanently alert, guarding yourself against the people that might not have seen you yet. I rode through the afternoon and into the evening, until I was perhaps five miles from Equinunk, when a motorbike shot past in the opposite direction.

It was a trail bike, a big KLR 650, which I thought was a bit odd as all I'd seen so far were Harley Davidsons. The next thing I knew the bike was right behind me, flashing me to pull over. I did so, putting the bike on the stand and going to enquire what the man might want. By chance it turned out to be Johnny Equinunk, on his way to fetch some food!

'Nate,' he said, 'I thought you might be heading this way. Come on, let's have dinner.'

And that's exactly what I did.

It was certainly good fortune that John had been travelling along the same road that evening, as while I knew he lived in Equinunk, I didn't know where exactly, as I'd forgotten to write down his address. I would have had to find somewhere to get online to retrieve it from the email conversation we'd had in the past. The reality, if our paths hadn't crossed that evening, would have been me sleeping in a tent somewhere out of sight by the side of the road, something I wouldn't have enjoyed very much at all, so to have met John that night was a godsend.

Chapter Twenty-Nine
Equinunk

John lived in a house in the woods. You took a long gravel drive from the main road to get there. In fact, it was a community of houses in the woods, all built haphazardly amongst the trees. To get to John's house we took a left off the main gravel road and then further along on the right it was there, built quite strangely in a basin in the earth as it rolled down and away from the road.

It would make a great Hobbit's house, the way you walked across a short wooden gangway to get to the main door, the first floor like a bungalow, with all the living quarters, then steps down into the basement which, because the house was built in a hole, had a door that opened out into the world, green and peaceful as it was.

John lived here alone after his mother passed away a few years before. He wasn't married, had no kids, and I imagined life out here could be quite lonely. He was a tall, stout man, with a thick bushy black moustache and a gentle demeanour. I believe he was in his fifties, working as a long-distance lorry driver and probably the kindest man you could ever hope to meet.

He said I could stay as long as I wanted, and so could Dorothy, who he doted on having read all about her on the internet. As well as the KLR he was riding when I met him that first night, John also had an old Yamaha sportsbike from the eighties, which he was slowly restoring in the basement, a handsome thing that John sat on and talked about with great fondness. He was going to ride it far some day. And I hoped that he would.

My bed was also in the basement, in the corner behind the stairs. I slept like a log that first night at John's, waking the next morning feeling a whole lot better than I did after the previous night, sat up amongst the cigarette butts of Manhattan. I was just relieved to have made it out of the city and out here to where there was a little more space to think and to breathe. After the chaos of getting from England to here it was just what I needed; a floating island of sanctuary to rest upon, in a sea of disarray.

The following morning we went for a ride on our motorbikes, taking a back road all the way into the main town of Hancock, some twenty miles away. It was gravel road for the most part, through this rural landscape of Pennsylvania; partly woodland, sometimes flat and agricultural, often with pretty lakes that you could ride right alongside, homes built on the shore, campsites nestled in the trees and wild deer darting amongst them. To say we were only perhaps 200 miles from New York, it felt like we were in another world entirely.

I followed John's shadow as he took it steady on his much bigger machine. My bike could only cruise at around 40mph, but on this terrain that was perhaps fast enough.

We stopped at a small festival taking place on the green outside an old wooden church. I bought a postcard from a man who took pictures of local wildlife and made them into cards. We were well away from the main road, passing through communities that felt as though they never wished to be found. It was a great way of spending a day, and John the perfect guide.

A little further along we swung off the road and into a clearing in the forest where we found a rifle range. When I say a rifle range, I simply mean a line of five targets built in a clearing at which anyone could turn up at their leisure and shoot. There were no marshals, no books to sign or fees to pay. If you have a gun you come here in the warm summer sun and shoot with it.

Practising were grandfather and grandson Frank and Thomas. Frank must have been in his eighties; Thomas was eleven or twelve, up from suburban New Jersey to visit his grandparents, who today were teaching him how to shoot. John and I introduced ourselves and stood around talking. Thomas couldn't believe it, he'd never met someone from England before. He wanted to take photos of me and text all of his friends to tell them about the weird hairy hobo he'd just met at the shooting range.

John told them all about my exploits on the old red bike parked across the way. I never talked about my trip unless I had to. It always made me feel a little uncomfortable, mainly because I knew the truth of it (the truth being how these adventures are never the heroic acts they are perceived and often presented to be, and that in fact they are often born out of a certain sense of despair), and I'd rather John not have said a word. But he was more proud of it than I was and so all I could do was stand there blushing, hoping that soon the story would end.

When Frank asked if I wanted a go with the rifle I told him I'd never fired a real gun before, but that I would give it a go. Carefully, I took a hold of the rifle; long, metal and wood, striding up to the shooting plate that had a plinth on which you could rest the barrel. Frank loaded five bullets, the most the gun would hold. He told me to look through here, and line it up with that, then squeeze the trigger, and watch it doesn't kick back and black your eye. I held the gun firm. I lined it up as best I could, then, 'whack.' I fired my first bullet. And cracked a massive smile. 'Whack, whack, whack, whack,' went four more bullets as I sent them down the range.

I half expected the man in the next village to drop down dead from my aim which had gone astray, yet when me and Thomas bounded over to the target and looked at where the paper had been penetrated we both stood there in silence, because I'd hit the bull, and the four other bullets were all within a two-centimetre range. Beginner's luck!

We loped back down to where John and Frank were stood and examined the target, to which they both said: 'Well I'll be darned!' I was a sharp shooter with a gun.

I have to admit to quite enjoying it; something I didn't think I would. I think it was the sense of power, or the release of power, almost as though the gunpowder is made up of grains of your stress and worry, and when you fire it down the range you let go of some of the stuff that's been on your mind. Perhaps that's the core of its appeal, and on this day I could well understand it

After a while we said our farewells to Frank and Thomas before carrying on our way into town. I needed some things from Kmart: a roll mat, some plastic storage containers and gas canisters for my stove. John explained how the superstore was the main employer in town now that main industry of mining had fallen by the wayside. He corrected me for taking my own trolley back to the rack, insisting it would do a man out of a job. This part of the world was certainly struggling just like so many others. Few jobs, dying industry, people struggling to earn a crust. John didn't earn much as a lorry driver, he just earned enough.

John had to go off driving the next day, planning on being out on the road for over a week. He told me to stay as long as I liked and gave me a key to his house. I shook his hand on the driveway and we gave each other a massive hug. I told him I'd see him again, though I wasn't sure when. He drove off in his truck, waving goodbye as he did so. I turned and walked back into the house, closed the door behind me, and spent the next three days getting my mind and gear together for the long journey ahead.

***

In the basement I lay everything out on the floor: clothes, tools, electronic equipment, camping gear; all the stuff I threw together before riding down to Heathrow with the two New Zealanders, Rob and Greg. I'd not packed for America, only for those few days riding down from Scarborough to London. As before, I would simply have to manage with what I had and pick up the things I was missing along the way.

That may sound scary, but what you soon realise is that as long as you have access to money, the internet, and a reliable motorbike, you can pretty much go anywhere and do anything. The limitation is largely mental. The trick is learning not to worry about such things, and letting go of the desire for routine and security which tends to characterise a life in the real world. There is none of that out here. There are no walls to hide behind. If it rains, you feel it. If it's cold, you get cold. If you're scared and feeling lonely. Then you are scared. And you are lonely.

In terms of clothing I had a pair of old blue jeans, bought from a shop on the high street and not worn for several years, but they would suffice as a pair of riding trousers. I had an assortment of t-shirts, a warm blue jumper and to keep me dry an authentic Royal Mail postal jacket, kindly donated by a stranger named Simon, who I met at a bike festival earlier in the year. He previously worked for the Royal Mail and said I could have his old jacket; fluorescent orange, with reflective silver strips and the Royal Mail insignia on the left breast.

For much of the journey I would also wear the body warmer given to me by the Indonesian bike gang I met back in Sumatra. They were called the BigZoners, their motto; 'Keep Brotherhood Til Die', embroidered on the back of the jacket. The jacket was something I'd treasured ever since meeting them in the early stages of that initial trip from Sydney to London, the lot of us all keeping in touch via Facebook ever since.

Beneath the jacket I wore a red-check flannel shirt, one that I'd picked up cheap in the sale and just felt comfortable in, rolling up the sleeves to the elbow and eventually wearing it until the fabric wore thin. In the hot midday sun I would roll the sleeves down to keep my arms from burning.

In terms of footwear, I'd brought a pair of old flip-flops, some white Converse high-tops and a pair of sturdy Australian work boots. The latter were brown leather, with an elasticated panel in the ankle and a toggle on the back to help you pull them on. They were one size too big and so required an extra pair of socks.

My helmet was an interesting thing. It was bought from a shop in the town of Matlock, an old bikers' haunt right in the heart of Derbyshire, England. I'd taken my Nan there for a coffee, the same grandmother who had given me advice at the beginning of that first book. She saw me pick up the helmet and try it on, and so kindly offered to buy it for me. It cost £40, and was white, with red and blue targets on each side. A lady in the Starbucks back in New York thought it was a nod to the famous cover art by The Who. Others thought it would make a good target for rednecks and gangbangers. But I liked it, I thought it was cool.

The rest of my riding attire consisted of a red and white neckerchief that I tied around my face to keep the sun off, while in the Kmart I'd been to with John I'd bought a four-dollar pair of sunglasses with a diamanté encrusted 'J' on the left pane. They were aviator style, and all in all, what with the flannel shirt, neckerchief and a new pair of beige gardening gloves, I looked like an extra from *Brokeback Mountain*.

In terms of camping gear, my tent this time had come from an automotive supplies shop back where Mandy lived in Canada. It had cost $18 and despite claiming to be a two man tent, when I put it up for the first time I soon discovered that my head pushed against the fabric at one end, and my feet pushed against the fabric at the other. It was however incredibly light, easy to put up and take down, and those are the two key areas when camping on a motorbike.

My sleeping bag was fairly new, picked up from a camping store back in England. My stove, however, was one I'd bought in Kyrgyzstan; the sort you screw on to the top of small gas bottles. I'd used it to cook instant noodles and tea as I passed through Kazakhstan, Russia and Eastern Europe. On that occasion I'd cooked everything in a reused sweetcorn tin. This time around I'd bought a set of collapsible pans, as well as a folding cutlery set with vivid blue handles.

I carried with me a ten-inch laptop, for ease of uploading photos and getting online, as many places you go now have free Wi-Fi. To take pictures I had the same Canon 1100D digital SLR that I bought back in Bangkok after the original camera had packed up there. After years of abuse, the auto-focus and built-in flash didn't work on this one either, but I would just have to make do as I couldn't afford a new one. I had a mobile phone but no local sim and didn't plan on getting one as who would I call if I broke down anyway?

For sentiment, and for protection, I carried the six-inch hunting knife that I'd bought from a market stall in the town of Kashgar, on the western fringe of China. I'd bartered hard for the knife, the seller agreeing a price, then changing his mind, paying around ten dollars for it in the end. The blade was useless really; made from cheap metal that would rust and bend at the tip. I liked the handle though. It was black, and encrusted with red and white stones, with a copper grasp joining the blade to the handle. The sheath was tan leather and decorated with metal eyelets and engravings.

I kept the knife in the black fake-leather tank bag James and Nancy had given me in India, it bought for their tour of the country by Royal Enfield. Whenever camping wild, I would sleep with the knife beside me, even inside the sleeping bag, just in case anything happened in the night. Thankfully it never did. Also in the tank bag I carried a small black diary, which I would update, all the way until Death Valley, at which point I would lose it, and so this book is written from memory, not from notes, for better or for worse…

As for tools, apart from being one, I had the original assortment I'd carried with me on that first trip. A motley crew of spanners, screwdrivers and wrenches. Hardly any of them served much purpose, but I daren't throw them out in case one day they did. For storage I slung them all in a blue tie-top bag previously used for tent pegs. I also carried a handful of spare spokes, a spare front sprocket, a couple of spark plugs, not to mention three or four spare inner-tubes in case we picked up more punctures.

Finally, to hold all these things I had with me the black canvas throw over panniers that I'd bought from a back-street bike merchant in Delhi, back when I was preparing to go into Pakistan and felt I needed something more subtle than the bright orange ones I'd originally set off with. They cost around twenty pounds and in a way were completely useless. That first day I used them on the ride up to Manali the bottom and rear panels began to tear, and so in Manali I paid three local Indian boys to cut up an old leather jacket and stitch it in place in order to reinforce the vulnerable areas.

This worked to some extent, but for the rest of the trip I had to carry with me a needle and thread and almost on a daily basis repair any new tears, often at the seams which just kept on splitting. I later decorated the panniers with stitched flags of some of the countries I passed through. As terrible as the panniers were, somehow I felt attached to them and saw them as being a part of this experience.

As for Dorothy, the bike that now sat in John's basement, it was quite surreal to think that this was the same bike I'd come across that day in Joe's shop, back in the Queensland town of Caboolture. From there to here, a distance of almost 25,000 miles, which, if you include the down-time in England, spans almost three and a half years of my life.

At times I could have pushed her off a cliff, if only to be rid of the obligation I felt to get her back on the road again. Strange to think your fate can become so entwined with that of a motorbike, but no way could I have left her in that shed and come across America on anything else. We had to get back on the road, just as much as I did.

Would she make it across America, and in what state? It's fair to say that a 105cc motorbike capable of cruising at around 40mph isn't the most sensible choice of vehicle for travelling so far on, but I'd come to realise that no vehicle is perfect for a trip like this; all make compromises somewhere, be it their weight or complexity or even something simple as it being difficult to get tyres for them. Dorothy's only weakness was her speed, but if she could do a hundred miles an hour that's how fast I'd have ridden her across America, not seeing anything along the way, so at least she slowed me down, and forced me to engage with the world through which I was passing. She was then the perfect complement to my mind.

All I had to do now was plan a route out of here. That was a daunting task in itself, as when you look at a map of America you see nothing but a tangle of roads and directions in which to go off in. And not wanting to use the interstates – because of the speed of the traffic – meant that I was going to have to pick a route cross country, along the back roads, and so suddenly America seemed a lot bigger than its three thousand mile width would suggest.

After all, it had been 3,000 miles across Australia, but the miles in that country involved one road up the coast, one road across the Outback, and one road up to Darwin. Two turns in that entire distance, which certainly wasn't going to be the case here in America. I would have to take lots of turns and no doubt cover more miles than I originally thought it might be.

My original plan had been to drop down from New York to

Philadelphia, on to Washington and then take Route 50 – the Lonely Highway – all the way across to the west coast. But with my fear of being pulled over again by the police I was keen to avoid the major cities, that decision pushing me much further north into Pennsylvania.

So from here to San Francisco I wasn't quite sure which way I would go; just head west I guess and figure it out as I went along. As for Alaska, I would give thought to that only once I'd made it across to the Pacific Coast, something I calculated would take around two to three weeks...

The reason for such haste was money. My budget to get myself across America was £500, that was simply all the money I had left after shipping the bike here, paying the £150 for mandatory third-party insurance and all the bits I'd needed to get myself back on the road. I didn't know if that was going to be enough money or not, especially as it had to cover food, fuel and accommodation. But sometimes, if you have the right time, and the right moment, you just have to go, and figure the rest out later.

Before leaving John's place I took a ride to Camp Equinunk, only a few miles down the road. I had worked there in the summer of 2001, for ten weeks between term times at college. For those ten weeks at camp I was a tennis instructor, though most of the kids were better than me, so my job really was to pick up balls after them. I also had a bunk of twelve kids to look after, my bed by the door to stop them from escaping and getting up to mischief at night.

They were around twelve years of age, all from privileged backgrounds in New York City, making them difficult to control. I really struggled and would often be woken in the night by sweets that had been thrown at my head. Or they would crawl under the bed and kick at the mattress, or set fire to aerosol cans and almost burn the place down. At the age of 21, with no experience of looking after children before, I didn't know how to keep on top of them, and so after a while I just stopped caring and let them get on with it.

Despite this, I had an amazing summer, mainly because of all the other international counsellors I was there with. At night we'd all sit outside the hobby centre or down by the lake, just talking and hanging out. Some nights we'd be taken in the yellow school bus to a town nearby for a drink in the Delaware Inn, a rough old place that I learnt has since been closed down. On the way back from the bar we'd all sing songs and put someone on 'deer watch,' as on these rural roads wild deer can and do jump out at any moment and cause real carnage.

Ten years on and I was now riding up the familiar driveway, past the nest of wooden huts to the left, up the hill, with the tennis courts to the right, and just before that the food hall where the kids would sing their songs and get up on tables and generally kid around. There were no kids here now; camp had just finished and they would all be back in New York, getting ready for the new school term, as by now it was midway through August.

At the top of the hill I parked outside the main office. Before taking a look around I thought I ought to ask the office staff if it would be okay, and having stepped inside I was stunned to see Caroline, the office clerk from the time when I was there, still there after all the time that had passed. I looked at her and said: 'Caroline?' And she said: 'yes,' and then I explained that I'd been there all those years ago and that I remembered her. She took a long look at me, before saying: 'Tennis, you taught tennis. Nathan isn't it?' It helped that I used to date her friend, Abi, who looked a bit like Isla Fisher. At least that's how I remember it.

Caroline was more than happy for me to have a walk around, leaving the bike at the top of the hill and taking a stroll down the bank to where the camp flattened out and the baseball pitch was found. Beyond that were the basketball courts, then the circle of benches with a camp fire often lit in the centre of them. I walked to the right, to where a new outdoor swimming pool had been built, then down into the square of bunk houses, almost thirty in total, with a giant lawn in the middle, and a lone tree planted in the centre of that.

The bunk houses had barely changed one bit, still red and white and made of wood. I had difficulty locating the one that I used to be in. Whether it was faded memory or that they'd remodelled the inside of them, I just couldn't fathom which of them it was. After wandering around a few and just reminiscing for a while, I walked down to the camp's lake, taking a wooden footbridge over the road to get there.

The lake itself is beautiful, surrounded by forest, with a jetty from which the kids would dive or just sit out in the summer sun. Despite the trouble they gave me, they were still great days and I would say that if you have the opportunity to do something like this you should do it, as the people you meet are what make it. I was just amazed to see that over a decade on and nothing much had changed, neither with me, nor the camp.

I found that interesting because in the time that had passed I'd been on all these journeys, I'd travelled so far and I'd chased internal change as much as the next man. But as I stood there and compared now and then I didn't really see that much difference. I'd certainly learnt a lot in that time, I'd grown and adapted, I was more aware of who I was and who I wasn't. Back then I still had all that to figure out. Yet fundamentally I was still the same person, with the same character traits, good and bad, which is why I still don't really believe in change, not in any conscious deliberate way in any case. Perhaps over time you just practice to be different. Which might mean all you do is learn how to act.

What I like about riding a motorcycle across the world, or on any big adventure for that matter, is that you can drop the act for a while and just be yourself.

Chapter Thirty
Pennsylvania

I woke in John's basement at 5am. I went upstairs and made a pot of coffee. The house was silent and dark. I took my coffee down into the basement and began to load the last bits and pieces on to the bike. I wasn't sure where to store the tent and the sleeping mat; on the tent rack above the headlight or strapped to the postal rack at the rear? Strange as it sounds, I was bothered about how the bike looked and whether it appeared aesthetically balanced or not. I just couldn't make up my mind and had to concede it was nothing more than a delay tactic, designed to halt my departure from this place of relative sanctuary, not necessarily wishing to return to those seas of disarray.

Finally, with everything loaded and a last sweep of the house complete, I opened the back door and wheeled Dot out into pre-dawn sky. It was colder than I thought, and a slight film of drizzle wasn't doing anything to help glamorise the day I had ahead. It was going to be a case of simply riding as far as I could, hopefully around 500 kilometres, in approximately twelve hours, then finding somewhere to stay at the end of it. But I had no markers, no place to really aim for. I had nothing booked, just a rough idea of the route and that satnav to help guide me along it.

The sad thing about the satnav was that it had revealed my true cruising speed. All the way from Australia I'd believed the speedo needle when it read that I was maintaining a steady 75km/h, or around 45mph. Yet when I bought the GPS and plugged it in I was faced with the grim reality that the speedo was over-reading, and that in fact I was doing less than forty, an average perhaps of 37mph. This made America seem even bigger than it already did!

Having made one last check of the oil, and of the tyre pressures, there wasn't much left to do but turn the key, no longer watch the neutral light glow green as the bulb had long since blown, flick out the kickstart, then proceed to give her a firm long stroke with the right foot, while maintaining a gentle twist of the throttle with the right hand, and generally she'd fire in to life.

I tied the neckerchief around my face so that it completely covered my nose, slipped on my helmet, fastened it beneath the chin and pulled on the pair of beige gardening gloves. I also carried with me a second set of welding gloves, which were too big, but this was good because it allowed me to pull them over the top of the gardening gloves to give extra warmth on a cold morning such as this one. And that was that. Too dark for my sunglasses, and with no visor, I would just have to put up with the drizzle in my eyes.

I crept up the bank, between the trees and up on to the gravel road that would take me down to the main one. No one else was around. It was just me and this pre-breakfast world. Cold and wet. Mid-August, two-hundred miles north of New York, at least three-thousand from San Francisco, and another three-thousand up from there to Alaska, and nothing in between but miles of uncertainty.

It would be unwise to pretend you are confident at this point. More accurately you're a bag of nerves and apprehension, almost like going to school for the very first time. That sense of having to go, but not necessarily wanting to go; it all feeling a bit better once you've passed beyond the perimeter gate.

Having turned right at the town of Hancock I joined Route 6 and from that moment on I was heading west through rural Pennsylvania. It was certainly exciting to be riding through America. Something as simple as the road signs really hit home that you're in another world, and when you stop for 'gas' (petrol), the gas stations are often big, with lots of pumps, you having to pay in advance, like in Kazakhstan, and in the middle of the shop they have a huge selection of filter coffee in glass pots. Many different blends and flavours, then a vast array of flavoured creams and milks; vanilla, nutmeg, liquor... It became routine to buy coffee with petrol, if only to keep the pair of us going.

Despite the tension of leaving New York, it did now feel good to be back on the road again. The appeal is its simplicity. You get up, and you ride, and do that day after day, making it up as you go along. But suddenly you feel in control of yourself again. It's your world. Your schedule. Your time-keeping skills. At no time do you have to be somewhere, on other people's orders. It's freedom, or as close to it as you can get.

I think this sense of 'travelling' can be achieved when doing anything that makes you feel like you're getting somewhere. Like working towards a degree, or setting up a new business, starting a family, or learning to how to drive a car. It's that same sense of moving forward, not standing still, and that to me is all that 'travelling' represents; the simple act of progress.

Of course, as I pushed west there had been temptation to go up through Canada, past Toronto, and back down into America by way of Detroit, but I think for personal reasons that would have been going over old ground, and so I decided on this less confrontational route instead, though yes, a part of me could quite easily have ridden back up to see Mandy again. That's what my heart would have preferred to have done. But sometimes you just have to stop yourself.

After a few hours on the road I pulled into a Burger King for some breakfast. I asked if there was Wi-Fi as I would have liked to have updated Facebook to let people know I was on my way, but this branch didn't have it yet, something that amused the counter clerk who called over to her boss, an older man, and informed him that I was another one, questioning the absence of Wi-Fi in this perpetually online world. It wasn't an annoyance, just a realisation that free Wi-Fi was my only connection to the outside world. At this stage, barely anyone knew I was out here. In fact, I'd only just told my parents where I was and what I was up to.

That sounds selfish, and perhaps it is. But my mum in particular had sniffed that something was wrong, and so it came as no surprise to hear one day out of the blue that I was in America, planning on riding across it. I'd not told her I was going to do it – not 'til I'd landed in New York – because I was afraid she'd try and talk me out of it and point out all the reasons I shouldn't be doing it (age, money, get a job), and that would have set in motion an avalanche of doubt, which I just didn't need right now. I figured it was safer to just set off and tell them after it was too late to change my mind.

I think deep down mum wished I'd just get a normal job, one where she didn't have to worry or have the difficult task of explaining to her peers just what it was her son was doing with his life. Though I think secretly she was proud. At least I'd hope so, as everyone would like to think that their parents approve of what they're doing with their lives.

Certainly, had it not been for the support of my parents and my friends, I don't know what would have happened during those dark days back in England.

That's what bothered me about this trip. I would be leaving that safety net behind and once again stepping out alone into the world. I worried what would happen if I started having those dark and horrible thoughts again with nobody around to catch me if I fell. It was all a bit of a gamble really, putting my faith in the road and hoping that I was doing the right thing, for the right reasons.

What didn't help, was that unlike the first trip, where I had the very solid destination of England to aim for, this time round the destination was vague. It was San Francisco, it was Alaska, but for no other reason than them being convenient markers on the map. There was no one I loved living there. Home wasn't there either, and I still maintain that an adventure needs a pull, as well as a push, if you're to avoid getting stuck in the middle. I certainly had the push – the desire to get on with life, and to get back on the road – but I hadn't quite worked out the pull yet. 'Give it time,' at least that's what I told myself.

Around midday, I passed through a town with a magnificent old wooden house that looked for all the world like one the Addams Family might have lived in. A passing girl explained that it used to be owned, or at least lived in, by a group of hippies who would sit up in the glass tower playing music as this sleepy town slept all around.

This mental image reminded me of Edward Scissorhands, and how he lived alone in that big old house at the top of the hill, until one day the townsfolk came with pitchforks and drove him out. I doubt it happened like that in this case, I just thought it sad that such a beautiful old building was left to rack and ruin.

But Pennsylvania in general was in that sort of state, teetering on the edge of financial survival, what with it being on the cusp of the Rust Belt; an area of north east America that has de-industrialised to such an extent that nothing much is left but the remains of a more confident era. Fortunately, in Pennsylvania's case, huge reserves of natural gas have recently been found beneath the ground, so much of it that a regeneration of the entire state might just take place.

This was explained to me by Richard and Lynne, a couple of retirees I met in the first instance at a lookout point, across a beautiful valley, and then later that day at a McDonald's, where both of us had by chance decided to stop for lunch. Outside in the car park they handed me $20 and told me to put it towards whatever I might need along the way. I thanked them enormously, buying a cheeseburger and coffee with it, before consigning the rest to petrol.

It was in that same McDonald's that I got chatting to a man who was inquisitive about my Indonesian jacket and the bike that was parked outside. Having broken the ice, this seemingly educated and well-dressed man asked, completely serious in his concern, if I thought the Iranian gas stations owners over the border in Canada would one day form a Muslim army and march on America.

I wasn't sure if he was serious at first, explaining that I'd been through several Muslim countries on my travels – Pakistan and Indonesia – and how I found the people there to be incredibly friendly and polite. I told him I thought they were little different to you and I, getting on with life and most of them not thinking about blowing people up at all. They might wish to come to America, but only for a better life. I could see in his eyes that he wasn't quite convinced by what I was saying, and that his mind had already been made up.

I felt sorry for the man if I'm honest. For whatever reason, from whatever source, he'd come across an idea, and a fear, that was just beyond belief, and yet he believed it, and considered it so possible that he thought to ask the stranger he'd just met in McDonald's if he too thought it was likely to happen. The media, politicians, his peers; where does a man get an idea such as that?

The irony of it was that as I'd been passing through this valleyed part of Pennsylvania I couldn't help but think how much like parts of Indonesia it was. Not necessarily the landscape or the foliage, just the way in which the road ran through the valley, houses and businesses built alongside it, communities stretched along its length, and while here they have churches, and there they have mosques, and here you get petrol from a petrol pump, and there you get petrol from a glass jar by the side of the road, the actual nature of life and the way it was structured around the road was completely similar, whether here in America or there in Indonesia. If only the man could have seen that.

I camped wild that night. This was as much a budget consideration as anything else; I simply couldn't afford to stop in hotels or motels. And while on that first trip it had taken me almost two months – right in the heart of Sumatra – to muster the courage to give wild camping a go, I felt it best, here in America, to just get that first night over and done with, because it is scary, the idea being to camp in a place where you're probably not allowed, with nobody seeing you, and you're there just long enough to get some sleep before getting straight back on the road the next morning.

I'd wild camped in Indonesia, Thailand, India, Pakistan, Kyrgyzstan, Kazakhstan, Russia, Ukraine, Poland, Germany and France. Sometimes I enjoyed it, sometimes I didn't. The best part about it is parking the bike right next to the tent, only unloading what you need and leaving the rest just sitting there, waiting until morning when all you need to do is pack away the tent and sleeping bag, strap it back on the bike and get going again. It all becomes quite routine after a while.

The area I was passing through now was mainly rural, with thick forest scattered along the length of the road, some of the trees covered in a strange kind of pink candyfloss that made me wonder what it was.

As I rode along I looked to dart up a fire road, or down a path leading into trees. But always traffic would be behind me or coming the other way, and I never saw the right moment or opportunity to make a dash for it. I carried on riding until I came upon a gas station on the right hand side of the road that looked to be the heart of a small hamlet.

I asked the clerk inside the gas station if he knew of anywhere that I might be allowed to camp that night. He had a think and I hoped he was going to say that I could pitch the tent on the grass out the back of the building. Sadly, he couldn't think of any place, but there was a customer in the store who reminded the clerk of Beaver Creek. 'Oh yes,' said the clerk, 'down by Beaver Creek.'

Having followed the man's directions along an increasingly quiet and remote single track road, I turned off at the sign for the creek. The road was now gravel and more forested than before, feeling like I was driving along a road you might see in a horror movie, the lead character in search of the missing girl, buried alive in the wood, the soundtrack creepy and you not wanting to look because you know something bad is about to happen.

After a few miles the road came to a dead end, circling on itself to form a small parking area right down by the edge of what was a huge man-made reservoir, surrounded by forest, and with an army of mosquitoes out in force. I sat on the bike at the edge of the water, swatting them off. I didn't get a good feeling about this place and just as I was about to drive off and look for somewhere else, a couple pulled up in an SUV, winding down their window and explaining they were looking for deer. We made small talk, before they said goodbye and turned around and drove off.

Once they were out of sight, and with the light almost gone, I kicked the bike into life and raced across the top of the reservoir to the far side of the water, figuring I'd just brave it down here for the night. Sure enough there was a small clearing, well out of sight; the plan being to put the tent up here. It was now dusk, with a mist spreading across the water, no sound but for my heavy breathing and the sigh of the trees as they creaked in the breeze.

Just as I was about to unload my gear I heard another vehicle crunching along the gravel and coming to a stop back on the other side of the water, over where the small car park was. I couldn't see the vehicle, or the two people that got out, but I could hear them as they began walking in my direction, their voices growing louder until they were well within earshot.

I reasoned that I couldn't have them come around the corner and suddenly find me cowering here, so I kicked the bike into neutral and pushed it out on to the path only ten yards in front of them, not quite sure who or what I was about to face.

It was a couple walking their dog, and despite a hairy, foreign-accented man in a bright orange jacket pushing a motorbike suddenly appearing from nowhere by the side of this remote reservoir, the pair didn't even flinch – just smiled and said hello as if this scenario were completely normal.

We talked for quite a while about the area and how the reservoir was once a thriving place, with a campsite just off into the woods where families from around the area would come and camp up for the summer months, the kids able to play in the water. The campsite has since been closed down due to budget cuts and barely anyone comes any more. It seemed like such a shame.

I asked the couple what the pink candyfloss was that I'd seen in the trees on the way here. They explained that it was moths that every seven years would show up in town, build nests in the trees and over the next few weeks strip the trees completely bare, killing many of the trees in the process.

'Nothing you can do about it,' said the man, and we all stood on the spot, staring at our feet, making small talk until they returned to their vehicle and drove off, leaving me finally alone in Beaver Creek.

In the end I put the tent up in that tiny oval car park, sitting it on the gravel beneath a sign that read 'no camping,' hoping to be gone by the time the ranger came the following morning.

Inside the tent I threw my sleeping bag and roll mat, plus my jacket to form a makeshift pillow. The rest I just left on the bike, even the key, which I would always leave in the ignition so that I never would misplace it. I cooked up a supper of instant noodles, making sure to tie up and hang in a distant tree anything with a scent that might attract the bears. I wasn't even sure if there were any bears in these woods or not.

With that I crawled into my tent, it now completely dark, the sound of the sleeping bag being zipped up, then the flap of the tent, feeling slightly safer now, even though it was only a sliver of fabric between me and the outside world. Strange how this makeshift set-up would make you feel so safe, almost a sense of being at 'home,' which in a way you are when on the road. Now I would lie back and try to get comfortable, which was never easy as the stones and the earth beneath you would push into your back, and your neck would get stiff and your hip would gradually become sore.

Then, to top it all off, just as you get comfy you would hear a noise outside and sit up with a jolt, grabbing the Chinese knife that is beside you and slowly pulling down the zip on the tent and peeking out to see if anyone was there. A monster, a bear? More likely an owl in a tree or a beaver doing more work on the creek. And then you would lay back down, fall back to sleep, and half an hour later go through the whole rigmarole again. You never slept well. You always woke tired and stiff. But your night's sleep was free, instead of fifty quid, and that was the whole point.

For breakfast that morning I stopped in the small village of Polk. It was just another name on the map the satnav was leading me through. I'm not sure how much I liked this, blindly following arrows blinking at me from the bag on the petrol tank; I had no real sense of knowing where I was going, a sense of being led instead. But perhaps that's what I needed for the time being. It allowed me to concentrate on the riding and everything else that goes with that, while leaving the navigating down to someone, or something else.

On this occasion the satnav brought me to the breakfast table of a man named Jim Miller, a convenience store owner who didn't know what to make of me at first; this stranger wandering through the door of his rural shop in Pennsylvania. But having parked up outside this barely signposted store – it made of wood, and nestled within a row of wooden houses, across from the wooden church – we greeted each other and I asked whether he had coffee. I bought a cup of that, a breakfast muffin from the hot counter from the back of the store and, as I paid – apprehension thawing – we got into a conversation about how our lives came to have crossed paths that day.

Jim had lived in this community all his life. It was his world, but he had a keen interest in what was happening beyond it. He asked me about England and whether it was true what he was hearing from American politicians and TV pundits about how bad the NHS was; this in connection with Obama's intention to introduce something similar to America. I told him that in my opinion it's not perfect, but it's alright. And that to be able to go and see a doctor or go to hospital without having to worry about how you were going to pay for it was a good thing.

Jim explained how he had to pay $400 a month for him and his wife to be covered by private health care. There was also a significant excess to pay – around two to three thousand dollars – with every chance the insurance company won't pay if they can find an excuse not to. I asked what about the people who can't afford the $400 a month and he talked through a scenario where the state might cover it, or that you might have to sell your house to pay the bill or not seek medical treatment at all, simply because you couldn't afford to.

By this time we'd taken a pair of coffees to the seating area – a separate part of the shop, like a knock-through to the house next door – where every Saturday night a band plays to entertain the locals. We talked about Mormons and how a community of them lived down the road, and that I might see them on my journey west.

It was also interesting to discuss the way in which the rural landscape of America was changing and how many people were moving to the city to find work. We talked about what that meant for rural Pennsylvania and how something similar was happening in the UK, where the old industries are dying and what with the cost of fuel and transport – not to mention the lack of jobs – there was an increasing number of people leaving their rural roots behind. And to what end?

We also talked about 9/11 and the impact that had on the psyche of the nation, that sense of living with the fear of another attack. My mind linked this back to the fears of the man I'd recently met in the McDonald's, with his fear of Canadian gas station owners. Jim explained that in the aftermath of 9/11, many Muslim-owned stores went out of business or came under attack, simply because they were Muslim.

There were other things we talked about, but having lost the diary in which I'd made note of it I don't now remember what they were. I just remember Jim to be a wise and open-minded person. I enjoyed talking with him that day. In fact we must have talked for almost two hours. And to think I rode straight past the shop, thinking I'd stop a little later for breakfast, but then experienced a massive urge to turn around and go and get something from that shop.

It made me wonder if there was something in that; and that somehow you can detect another soul you're meant to meet. Maybe there are a thousand shopkeepers in Pennsylvania who I could have conversed with that morning, or perhaps there was only one, and somehow, with the help of satnav, I managed to find him.

Chapter Thirty-One
Ohio and Detroit

Having left Polk behind I was now left aiming squarely for Detroit. I was heading there because I knew a man named Vermin, our paths crossing on a popular internet forum a few years before; the same forum I'd used to help me out with the DMV back in New York. Vermin lived just outside of Detroit and owned an old Honda PC800 named Cack, a bike he'd completely bastardised over the years. He'd sprayed it fluorescent orange and yellow, covered it with stickers and mounted a set of antlers above the headlight on the front fairing.

He'd also modified the exhaust pipe so you could insert a tin of beans when you were riding, meaning that they were warm by the time you arrived at your destination. The exhaust then bent upwards, rising vertically above the level of the seat, with a 'flapper' on the top, the sort you might find on a big old American truck. It was an awful machine, but Vermin had ridden this thing all over America and down into Mexico as well. He wrote up the most incredible stories and I admired, and was even jealous, of his carefree attitude to life.

I'd actually met him two years before, back when I'd gone to see Mandy in Toronto with the offer of commitment and found myself too late, and so instead of flying straight home I accepted Vermin's invitation to go and hang out with him for a while down in Detroit. Vermin even offered to lend me Cack, so I could go for a ride down to Florida or across to California if I liked. But another adventure just wasn't what I wanted back then. I certainly didn't want to be on the road. I wanted to be at home, hiding from the world for a while.

Now, two years later, I was back in America and heading in his direction again, this time on Dorothy, following signs for Cleveland but trying not to end up in the middle of the city. I was intending to trace a route to the south of its centre, in the hope of missing the worst of its traffic, something which only seemed to be getting thicker and thicker; the rural pleasantries of Pennsylvania replaced by the industrial sprawl of Rust Belt Ohio, the border between the two states being crossed not long after leaving Jim's convenience store in Polk.

The trouble I was having now was staying off the interstate. Despite programming the satnav to avoid them it kept wanting to send me on to roads of three-lane traffic, travelling way too fast for our speed. I resorted to intuition and road signs, the only physical map I had being one I'd picked up in a book store back in New York. It had a page for each state, which given the size of the average US state meant only the big roads were marked and so it didn't really serve any purpose at all.

But if I was having problems then so too was Gary, a man on a bicycle travelling in the same direction as me – along the shoreline road of Lake Erie – and so having blazed past in a haze of astonishment, I stopped a little way ahead to see if he needed any water.

Gary turned out to be the ripe old age of seventy-seven, and cycling all the way around the shoreline of Lake Erie, a distance of over 600 miles. Having introduced ourselves, Gary explained how his cycling adventures had begun back in his early sixties when he went on a guided tour of Alaska, travelling by 4x4. On the drive up there he met several cyclists, making the gruelling self-propelled slog to the top of the world. This inspired him, and not long after returning from the trip he bought his own bicycle and set about planning his own adventures.

In the years that followed, Gary cycled around Australia, through Central Asia, down along the Pan-American Highway to Argentina and up to Alaska himself. I think he'd even toured Europe and still had plenty of places he wanted to go to. I don't quite remember how long this trip had taken him, but like me he had camped wild in a tent and lived on the cheap. The day I met him was Gary's second to last on the road, him hoping to be back home in Ann Arbor the very next day.

I asked Gary why he did this, because to me he looked in pain and didn't always describe the experience as an enjoyable one, something I could well associate with. For him it was about the challenge and setting yourself the target and trying to get there, regardless of the suffering involved. For him it wasn't about what he saw or even where he went, just that he made it to his destination and could for a moment feel satisfied that he'd done it. Then, as he accepts, his mind turns to thoughts of, 'What next?' And straight away he's planning his next adventure.

Gary asked me about my bike and how much one similar might cost, as he conceded he was thinking of using an engine for the next trip. He was getting too old, or so he told me.

Before going our separate ways, Gary gave me his business card, his profession marked on it as 'Ski instructor, Boulder Colorado.' He was an inspirational man, and I think the sadness I felt when I rode away was of imagining that one day Gary will disappear from this mortal coil, and so too will his amazing tales of adventure. It just doesn't seem fair or right that a man can do so much with his life, and then for it almost to count for nothing. Perhaps it's a convincing argument for sitting on your arse all your life and not doing anything with it, and if you're happy with doing that, I guess why not, as it seems to count for nothing in the long run.

As for me, I'd didn't quite make it to Vermin's that day, camping instead on a site in the pleasant town of Sandusky, built on the banks of Lake Erie, and said to be home to one of the biggest roller-coaster rides in the world, though I never saw it. I just found a Subway sandwich shop and ate my sandwich before heading off to find the campsite, because for whatever reason I couldn't stomach the hassle of looking for somewhere to wild camp for the night.

Despite the price of $15, I much preferred this night to the one before it; the peace of mind of being on a proper site, with a proper tent pitch, with a shower block and toilets, and other people around. You certainly sleep a lot more soundly than when camped out in the wild.

The following morning I traced a wide arc around the city of Toledo in order to avoid getting caught in the traffic, finding myself on the long straight roads of the farming district, fields of corn off to either side, towering white grain silos shadowing isolated farms, then villages and hamlets built alongside the road where I'd stop for gas and end up chatting to people who would always enquire about the motorbike and where I was heading. It was a detour to see Vermin, forcing me north, for eighty miles, a distance I'd have to backtrack when I left, but I just felt the urge to go there, so I went.

Vermin didn't actually live in the area any more. He'd moved away a year or so before with his family to Colorado Springs, almost 1,500 miles to the west of here, but just happened to be in the area visiting his parents the same time as I was passing through.

There was no one home when I got there, so I sat on a chair in their garage, waiting an hour or so until they all finally arrived. His parents – Gil and Myrna – were a great couple, Gill himself a keen cyclist just like Gary, once riding from Tampa to Detroit (1,200 miles), and then another time from Seattle to Detroit (2,400 miles). The couple were about to downsize into a smaller place closer to the centre of Brighton.

I talked with Myrna about how strange that must feel, this being the family home in which the previous two generations of the Vermin family had been raised. Myrna was quite pragmatic about it all, seeing it just as a shell and a place not needed any more. There would soon be a new place to call 'home.' I admired the way in which she had rationalised this, her ability to let go of what was really just bricks and mortar.

Vermin himself hadn't changed one bit; a tall sinewy character with short cropped hair and glasses. His real name is Phil but Vermin was the name he often liked to go by. I think it was his alter ego, his riding name, and I could associate with this as I'd done the same with Dorothy and liked to think that I too had an alter ego whilst travelling these big trips. I was certainly more brave and decisive whilst travelling, and perhaps to be called Phil was a reminder that his life wasn't as exciting back in the 'real' world as it was when heading down to Mexico or wherever else he and his bike had been.

You could say Vermin was a complex character. But not really. He just hates the system, and the 'man,' and the 'cubicle,' and wishes the world was a little less keen to strap people to desks or routines and make them work like obedient dogs. He's an old hippy at heart, with his rants about the 'angry white man' – a nod to the white, right-voting old men of America – both amusing and ironic. Vermin has a friend named Gator-Jane, living in the swamps of Florida, who has dead alligators and snakes in his freezer. Vermin said I should go and visit him. I'm not even sure he exists.

The last time I met Phil I was in a bit of a mess and not much company. This time I was glad to be meeting him – his wife Linda was back home in Colorado Springs – under different circumstances, when I was leaning into the wind, with my sails at full mast and far more positive about life and its outcomes. That evening we all sat around the dining table, on the veranda, overlooking a small lake where wildlife would often be seen, not another house in sight. It was easy to see why Gil and Myrna would miss this place so much.

Myself, Vermin and his son Drew later headed into town for a beer in one of the sports bar, the kind of place you might drink Budweiser by the bottle and watch a game of American football on TV. This was a nice part of the world, not just the town itself but the surroundings and how there are so many lakes, houses built alongside them, the land much flatter here than it had been across Pennsylvania. This was now Michigan, the fourth state of my adventure. Next it would be Indiana, Illinois, and after that I really wasn't sure as the options from here would be endless.

I could either maintain this trajectory, spearing west across Iowa and Nebraska, possibly taking Route 30, the Lincoln Highway, all the way from here to San Francisco, the point at which it ends. I could also drop back down to try and rejoin Route 50, the Lonely Highway, which would also take me all the way to the Pacific Coast. Vermin thought it would be a nice idea to head west, riding until I hit the Mississippi River – a few hundred miles west of Chicago – at which point I could trace it south until I hit St. Louis, then head west along Route 50. I said I would just go west, in the direction of Chicago, and make the rest up from there.

Vermin kindly offered to ride with me all the way across to Colorado

Springs, him on another bike – not Cack – but still a proper one with a proper top speed. I've had people say this to me before and generally it doesn't last. They spend ten minutes at 37mph, get fed up and ride off, telling me they'll meet me when I get there. I told Vermin this but he was adamant he wanted to ride with me and I too liked the idea of it; a bit of company on the long stretch across the Midwest.

The following morning we loaded up our gear, said a fond farewell to Gil and Myrna, before hitting the road; a motorcycle gang of two. Five minutes later we pulled over and both agreed we couldn't ride like this, not for 1,500 miles, him hovering in my rear view mirror, struggling to go so slow. And I didn't like it either, feeling as though I was being pushed from behind. Besides, I find the mask starts to slip after a while and beneath it I can be short-tempered, moody and taciturn, which is not something I wish others to see. I think that's why I like travelling on my own so much.

It was at this moment – saying goodbye in a parking lot by the side of the main road – that I noticed three broken spokes in my rear wheel. I'd bent down to lube the chain, grabbing the spokes in order to spin the wheel and feeling one loose, then another, and another. It felt like Kazakhstan all over again, only this time I'd remembered to bring some spares.

Vermin told me that there was a Honda dealer just along the road and so I insisted he get going and that I'd hopefully see him in Colorado on my way through to the coast. The broken spokes were just one of the rigours of the road, a hiccup, and there was no point ruining his day as well as mine. I waved him off and turned to face my old bike and its sad broken spokes, in a town less than thirty miles west of Detroit.

The staff in the Honda dealer were sympathetic, though sadly couldn't replace individual spokes – for liability reasons – their only option being to replace the whole lot, at a cost of almost $200. I couldn't afford that, as it was almost a third of my total budget for getting across America.

I asked instead if they'd mind me using their car park at the front of the building to try and repair the wheel myself, using the spare spokes I carried with me. They were fine with this and told me to let them know if I needed any tools. You could see they wanted to help, but I think their manager had reminded them that this was a business, needing to make money, and not a charity to help out foreigners riding 105cc Hondas across the world.

The task of replacing spokes was much harder than I'd imagined. It took me three hours to figure out the way of doing it, realising how you had to remove neighbouring spokes to get the broken ones out, and then remember which went in where and which hole they should go back through. Despite the trials of the task in hand, it was a pleasant morning, one of those on an adventure that you could never foresee, and when it happens, you just get on and deal with it, and learn as you go along.

Midway through the repair I struck up conversation with a man who turned up on a gorgeous black Ducati sportsbike. He was friendly, quietly spoken and engaging to talk to. He'd been an accountant and done well for himself. He was now retired, and quite shy in the way that he conducted himself. We talked mainly about Detroit and what was happening there, and how it was hard to imagine that less than thirty miles down the road was one of the most violent cities in America. This after all was peaceful middle-class white suburbia.

Again, the issue of public health came up, and of course talk of Obamacare. For this man it was a simple case of providing for yourself, and the onus on you to work hard enough to afford to pay for medical insurance. It was not, in any uncertain terms, the duty of the state to provide care for you. When presented in such a way it was a very difficult position to argue against. People should take responsibility for themselves, but at the same time I knew myself how easy it is for people to fall and if there's nothing there to catch them then it's a long way to the bottom. And even harder to get back up again.

As far as this man was concerned, a move towards government healthcare – in the form of Obamacare – was a move towards communism, as though only two extremes existed; and so if you weren't all out capitalist, then you were all out communist. There was nothing in between. I tried to explain that in England we have a national health service, but we're far from living in a socialist state. But this man had drawn his line in the sand

and that's just what he thought.

It made me realise just how tough it can be in America. If you're succeeding, you're fine and possibly healthy. If you're failing, and having a tough time, then you really are in quite a lot of trouble. It certainly made me grateful to be born in Europe, though of course, they would say the same about where they were born.

With the spokes finally fixed, the day was half gone and I wasn't quite sure what to do with myself. I thought about riding back to Phil's parents' house, which was only fifteen minutes down the road, but I hate saying goodbye, then hello again, then goodbye again. It just gets messy. Instead I decided to head east to Detroit to have a look around, it being only an hour's ride away. Besides, having passed through it those few years before – back when I first met Phil – I was keen to see it again, as there is just something so fascinating about it.

The first time I visited the place I compared it to a circular doughnut (the type with the hole in the middle) and how the ground around the doughnut is relatively peaceful, white and prosperous. Then you enter the dough of the doughnut and suddenly the world changes. It becomes poor, destructive and unavoidably black. These suburbs go on for mile after mile, until you suddenly emerge at the centre of the doughnut – where the hole is – only to find the downtown district is relatively wealthy, white and prosperous again. The change between the two extremes is sudden, from one block to the next. And the contrast between the two is vivid.

Fortunately, there is an interstate connecting the outside of the doughnut with the middle of the doughnut, meaning that most people don't have to drive through the horrible outer circle, but not being allowed to ride on the interstates meant I had no choice but to ride straight through the batter, which I have to say was one of the most depressing and upsetting sights I'd seen from the saddle of this motorbike, and that includes the slums of Kathmandu and Delhi.

I think it's like that because you just don't expect it. This is America after all, the *greatest nation on earth*, and yet here is one of their major cities, and it looks like it's been in a war. There are houses burnt to the ground, others covered in graffiti, whilst the roads and pavements are full of craters and potholes. Everywhere you look is a desolate wasteland; boarded up shops and the general sense of despair, with street lights long since extinguished.

At least in the worst parts of India and Nepal you still got a sense of hope and determination. Even amongst the rubble of Kathmandu there are markets taking place, and the simple fountain of life bubbling away, despite the conditions being so harsh.

What was so upsetting about Detroit by comparison was that there seemed to be no hope, no optimism, no spirit in the air. It was a dead city, and this was a dead road (crossed by Eight Mile Road of Eminem fame), overgrown with large swathes of neighbourhoods abandoned. The only buildings that seemed to be prospering were the churches and the big corporate fast-food chains, which perhaps tells us something about what might have gone wrong here in the first place.

There is a huge debate as to what went wrong in Detroit. Those on the right (the Republicans) blame the blacks for burning down their own neighbourhoods back in the riots of 1967 and more specifically the black mayor Coleman Young – serving from 1974 to 1993 – who Republicans claim used Detroit as a socialist experiment that went catastrophically wrong, the city slipping from two million residents in its heyday, to little over half a million today.

Conversely, those on the left (the Democrats) blame the failure of the capitalist system to make the American car market a success. That people began buying superior Japanese cars, and that those in charge shipped jobs out to China is what some people see as the reason why Detroit's main industry – car manufacturing – went so badly wrong. They also cite the effect of 'white flight,' and how the relocation of the white Americans to the suburbs, just as industry was collapsing – while at the same time black immigrants from the south were flooding in – meant that there was a vacuum of jobs and opportunities which eventually broke out into the riots that destroyed half the city.

What I did learn was that the way in which the tax system works here – taxes paid by the local community stay in the local community – means that this situation is a long way from ever changing. Basically, the tax generated by the wealthy areas stays in the wealthy areas. So public amenities there get better and better. Whereas in the inner city slums there just isn't enough tax revenue generated to keep things fully functioning, hence why the roads in the suburbs go from being smooth and well maintained to being almost beyond repair the moment you enter the poorest areas of town. And then you reach the city centre – which is overly policed to keep it safe – and all feels and looks well maintained and civil again.

There are positive signs however. Detroit, apparently, is the number one city in the world for urban farming, while in recent years some of the worst neighbourhoods have been improved by the Arab and Middle-Eastern immigrants moving in and beginning to rebuild the place. Artists and musicians are also making the most of the abandoned buildings and factories, while the road I would take out of the city – Old Ford Road – seemed to be more prosperous than the road I took in earlier that day. I certainly had a soft spot for this place. I felt for it. I felt it deserved better and I hope one day it gets back on its feet and proves that regular people can perhaps succeed in a city where corporate America (or human nature, perhaps) seems to have failed.

Chapter Thirty-Two
To Chicago

I slept that night behind a mound of dirt in a lay-by just outside Ann Arbor (where Gary lived), before riding into town first thing in the morning for a coffee. I sat in a seat beside the window, keeping an eye on the bike outside. I wore my cap to hide my scraggly hair. I guess in a way I was homeless. That's what it feels like on these adventures. Your bike outside with literally everything on it. It's your lifeline. Without that bike I would be in a foreign town with no reason for being there, the trip would be over. I would have nothing else to do but come home and do something else with my life. This means that you do worry and fret about the bike, as if it were a child, and the thought of losing it catastrophic.

Later that morning I found another broken spoke, noticing it when I stopped to check if the ones I'd fitted the day before were holding up okay. Thankfully I still had plenty of spares, and now with practice I was able to repair it much quicker than the three from yesterday. A police car circled through the lay-by I was parked up in, making clear sight of my foreign numberplate. It was reassuring that he didn't stop or ask for any explanation. I think the policeman back in New York had just been over-zealous.

As for the spokes, it had been suggested on Facebook that if they kept on breaking then I was to try strapping tie-wraps around each of the points at which two spokes crossed. This would reinforce them, and prevent them from vibrating loose and snapping again. I was five tie-wraps short of doing them all, but a couple in a motor home, who had been watching me struggle with the repair, kindly offered me the rest.

I continued on that day through Michigan, travelling from Detroit to Chicago along Route 12. The world here was flat and featureless, pockmarked by small towns with little life. This wasn't a place I'd like to have lived. As mentioned, this entire region, from the Midwest to northeast, is known as the Rust Belt, with much of it suffering from the onset of de-industrialisation, much like some of the towns of Yorkshire and Derbyshire that myself, Greg and Rob passed through on our route down to Heathrow. Places such as Detroit are the focal point, but all outlying areas are affected (apart from places such as Ann Arbor, but that had the universities), with some people choosing to migrate to where the new jobs are (Texas and California), others staying put, riding out the storm, waiting for... Waiting for the world to change I guess.

Despite aiming for Chicago, I camped that night at the Indiana Dunes State Park, ninety miles shy of the city and on the shores of Lake Michigan, about to pay $15 for my own pitch before meeting Bojana and her boyfriend Adrian, a couple originally from Eastern Europe, now living in Chicago, who asked if I'd like to share their pitch, together with their friend Faisal, an Indian student here. The three of them were taking a weekend break from Chicago.

Having dropped off our things at the campsite we headed back to the beach for a swim, before driving in their car to get some food from a local gas station. I remember vividly the Foo Fighters playing on the radio; the acoustic version of *Times Like These*. As I relaxed in the back seat in a car full of new found friends, never had a song been more apt to sum up a moment such as this one.

During those times of despair back in England, I'd really begun to wonder who I was, and if I'd ever be myself again. At times I doubted I ever would, and it was a horrible feeling when the person you hate most in the world is staring back at you in the mirror every day, and all you really want to do is smash the mirror until your knuckles bleed.

I was just grateful that I had *this* to keep me going. As dark as the tunnel sometimes got I could always sense the desire to one day get back on the bike and start riding again. Without this, the tunnel would have been completely dark, and I imagine that for those in that situation, with no light to head towards, the decision to end it all must become a natural one.

I think generally you can see this in people's eyes, which is worth looking out for, because self-destruction, self-sabotage and the enemy within are not usually conducive to people asking for help themselves. Destruction is what you seek. Not help, and certainly not judgement. Sometimes just a cuddle will do. For now I was just grateful to be back on the road again.

On my way into Chicago the next morning I passed through Gary, Indiana. An ominous black car with blacked out windows pulled over to observe me as I took photographs of the city limit sign.

Gary is where Michael Jackson was born and all in all reminded me of the worst parts of Detroit, with its wasteland of abandoned buildings and general air of decay. A redneck in a pick-up truck pulled up beside me at a set of traffic lights, calling out from his cabin: 'Hey, you'd best be careful around here.' And so I might; nineteen people had been gunned down in drive-bys the night before in the Chicago area, with the city famous for its violence and crime.

I have to say, both here and in Detroit, I never felt any threat or danger. I guess in a way I was a sitting duck and an obvious target; a foreigner on a slow bike travelling through the worst parts of the city, with a target on the side of his helmet. But at such times I just kept on riding, minding my own business, and I think that's all you have to do, like going out to a nightclub and keeping your head down to avoid any trouble, though it's always there if you want it.

As for Chicago, I have to be honest in saying that once you've ridden through the hideous suburbs to get to the glorious centre it does kind of take the shine off things. You go from the run-down black part of town, to the run-down Hispanic part of town, then to the black again, then you turn a corner only to be greeted with a manicured golf course and white joggers pounding pavements beside a pristine waterfront park. I mean, are you really to believe that all those Starbucks coffee shops, museums and art installations are a true reflection of what's going on here? I certainly didn't think so at the time.

It didn't help that Chicago seemed to be full of so many homeless people. On every corner, outside most shops, people were begging. You could walk past them and pretend they weren't there, but they were there, and I saw each and every one of them, feeling as though I had more in common with them than I did with anyone else this day, much as I'd felt with the homeless of Darwin. I think that still remained my biggest fear in life; that I would end up like them one day, such was my ability to self-sabotage everything that was good, plus my inability to make things stick, and keep them stuck.

By now it was raining heavily so I parked the bike beneath the underpass and took a stroll around the main tourist area, centred around the Art Institute of Chicago.

I had another internet friend who lived in the city, Hollie, who had found me on Facebook having read about my adventures from Sydney to London, as she too had a CT110. Having spotted that I was now in America she contacted me to say that I was welcome to stay at her place any time. I let her know the night before that I would soon be in Chicago if her offer still stood. She said it certainly would, but that she wouldn't be in all day Saturday. And today was Saturday, which meant I was left with nothing much to do but take a walk around Chicago in the rain.

I took a stroll up the 'Bean,' an epic art installation that is simply a giant mirrored jellybean-shaped object, as big as a barn, the contours of which do weird and wonderful things with your face. You could walk beneath it and generally kid around. Families from all over the world were there. These are the times you feel alone, when you're in a city looking at a tourist attraction and everyone else is with their family or friend and you're there on your own, nothing to hold but your helmet.

There was also a water feature with a tall monolith in the middle of the water with a computer generated image of a smiling black child's face, that slowly changed expression, and then to another face completely. Behind it was an open-air arena on which concerts were regularly performed. Today, in the rain, came the sounds of Alaska, with dozens of artists scattered around the grassy arena making sounds with strange instruments, with no note sheets, just making whichever sound they thought would fit best. They were doing it to 'help' the native people of Alaska. I thought to myself they would be better off helping the people on their own doorstep, but that was just the cynic in me creeping out.

To escape the rain I finally headed to my second home, McDonald's; my sanctuary in the midst of all of this. I went there because the food was cheap, it was consistent, you didn't have to add tax on to the price and you didn't have to tip. More important was that in a McDonald's – as they all look and feel the same – I felt I could relax, because for a while I was in a place I recognised and was familiar with. On the road you're certain of nothing. In McDonald's you know you can get a burger and a coffee for $2.17. And that was important.

In this McDonald's I met a lady by the name of Lisette. Lisette had been homeless for two weeks and explained to me that she couldn't get a job because on her police record it showed she had a felony for marijuana possession. She looked a complete state; a middle-aged black woman, slightly glazed eyes and slurring. She had no teeth. I felt sorry for her and asked what she wanted to eat. She'd have two cheese burgers and a coffee. Done.

While we waited we just chatted about life; mine on the open road, hers in the gutter. What do you say to that? What can you do? At times like these I wished I had a magic wand that I could wave and suddenly Lisette would have a new set of teeth, and a decent home, and a stable life and whatever else it is people need to feel free. When her coffee came she added to it a total of eight sugars, so I don't think there's much that can be done about the teeth.

Later on, as I was trying to pass the time away, I got talking to the busker who was playing saxophone beside the spot I'd parked the bike beneath the flyover. On arrival I'd thrown a few dollars into his collection in the hope that he might act if someone tried to steal anything from it. But as I returned to the bike this time we got chatting.

Jacques was almost sixty years of age, a slight man, hardly any meat on him, sinewy in the extreme, wearing a yellow rain mac and hood. We made small talk about the downpour then, curious, I asked him about his life and how he busked out here for the money he needed to live on. He said it was the saxophone that had kept him out of trouble during his youth.

After that I asked him about Chicago. He said it was getting worse; the violence, the drugs, the guns, the shootings. He said for a black kid growing up in the rough neighbourhoods there's no real way out. For him it was his saxophone, that's what kept him on the straight and narrow. Now he says schools don't run music classes, or even gym classes. So you've got these kids with no purpose, no role models (except for rappers) and it almost becomes inevitable that they're going to get into drugs/gangs. And the gangs don't know how to deal with confrontation, except with a gun, hence nineteen shot dead last night.

Jacques said the police largely leave the worst areas unpatrolled. He believed that if they tried to intervene the violence would just spill into the richer neighbourhoods. Basically leave them to it, and let them kill themselves. I later learned how it was referred to by some as the principle of the 'self-cleaning oven;' effectively it being left alone to bake off its own mess. To me it was an epidemic of violence just waiting to spill over into the rest of the city streets, and surely the problem can't be ignored forever?

What bothered me most was that when I made mention of these people I was meeting on Facebook, some of the more affluent Americans who had 'friended' me over the years told me to ignore what I was seeing, and come to where they were, as it was a whole lot better in their version of America. They said that Lisette was undoubtedly on meths and how really it's just a simple case of trying harder in life.

This really pissed me off, because I thought how easy it is for them to say that; to tell someone in that position to try harder. I mean, if you're born in the positions most of us reading this are born in then we don't really need to try very much in life in order to maintain the status quo. Our parents give us a good education, they teach us to work hard and respect others. They send us to university. They plant seeds of expectation which most of us meet. To do relatively well in life is therefore almost a given.

But what if you're born at the bottom, surrounded by the very shittiest side of life. No one cares what you do or what you become. A good education is a distant dream and the most you can hope for is a job that most of those criticising would never wish to do, and if you do get that job, then those same people will still look down on you.

So no, I don't think it's as easy as telling someone to try harder; if it were, then those criticising would all be multi-millionaires, because they'd have climbed out of their middle-class suburbia instead of maintaining their own status quo.

I think it was at this point – and I was told as much – that I came to the conclusion that there really are two Americas within America. There's the one that we see on *Man vs Food*, the TV show where the presenter travels the nation's diners trying to eat their mammoth portions in a display of greed and gluttony – the vision of America it wants us to see. And then there's Detroit, and Gary Indiana, and downtown Chicago, where you meet people like Lisette and Jacques and the two are completely separate worlds; one where people can afford health care, and to live in the nice parts of the city, and have access to a decent job, and the other, in which nineteen people get shot in an evening, and nobody really gives a shit.

I had to concede however that maybe this adventure, born as it was from the darker recesses of my mind, was perhaps having an impact on the way I was seeing things. Maybe my mind only looked out for the bad things, and the people struggling in life. I think that's the thing with depression (I hate that word); not only do you see your own gloom, you see everyone else's as well, and just as you'd like to do something about your problems, you'd like to do something about theirs as well. And knowing that you can't do a damn thing about it only serves to make matters worse, until the point at which you really do feel lousy.

Equally, perhaps in being born and raised in a northern mining town with only one black family for miles around, I was conditioned to make the distinction between race and colour more than someone who grew up in a city for example. Future generations might not have the same attachments that people of even my generation have. It would be nice to think that would be the case. As it is, the elephant in the room for America, as far as I could see, was that there is a huge racial divide. Who causes that and why it continues I don't know. But to pretend that I couldn't see it from the seat of my Australian motorbike would be disingenuous.

***

Finally came word that Hollie was home and having said farewell to Jacques and handing him $20 for his accommodation that night, perhaps for no other reason than to assuage my own guilt, I hit the road in what can only be described as a torrential downpour. The gutters were overflowing, puddles were already as high as the foot pegs and to ride along it in was like continuously having buckets of water thrown across your face. But I danced along the road that night, glad to have a destination to head towards.

Hollie lived in a Mexican part of town, the buildings two storeys high, with colourful murals painted on many of them. I saw Mexican bars and Mexican cars. Hollie lived up a quiet alley, with so many telephone and power cables strung along it I think you could probably have swung from one end to the other without touching the ground.

I parked the bike in the alley, went up the steps and banged on this stranger's door. Hollie answered and thus was spoken the weirdness of virtual friends meeting in the real world for the very first time. But it was very good to see her; like the meeting of long lost friends.

Hollie shared her flat with a massive dog named Louie. He was so dopey looking and drooling from his chin, much like the one in *Turner and Hooch*. I'm not normally a big fan of dogs, but I liked this one, and sleeping as he did beside the sofa, he kept me good company that night.

Hollie told me how one day she wants to ride her CT all the way down to South America. She was certainly a cool chick, previously working in a custom bike shop and telling me I could stay as long as I liked. I told her that if I ever make it to Alaska then on the way back down we can perhaps meet up and head to Central America together on our bikes. I didn't stay that long, only a couple of nights, but it was long enough to get a taste for the place and make preparation for the journey ahead.

One of the evenings, after she had finished work, Hollie arranged for us to go for a ride through the city with a few friends of hers; the plan being to head towards the beaches on the north side. I also knew some other people in Chicago – more friends from the internet – so met up with them as well; Dave and his girlfriend Kara, both riding a gorgeous café racer that Dave had restored which was clearly his pride and joy. Our convoy of four bikes lit up the city streets; me and Hollie on our CTs, Dave and Kara on their café racer, and Hollie's friend Jonathan on his modern Ducati.

It was a warm night; no need for a jumper, the streets of Chicago so straight and grid-like. It felt different from New York, certainly different from Detroit. This northern side of the city is quite safe; it's to the south, the part that I'd passed through on my way in, that has all the problems. Having pulled up at traffic lights, Hollie pointed out that I had no back light and how it only illuminated when I hit the rear brake. The only solution to this, to avoid drawing the attention of the police, was to ride with my foot partially on the rear brake lever, just enough to keep the light activated, with intention of picking up a new bulb the following morning.

We rode on, through the thinning city streets, coming to a rest in a car park beside the beach, where we walked across the sand to the water's edge. The moon reflected across it. The water was relatively calm as this wasn't the ocean but a lake, Lake Michigan. I'd read that it was once heavily polluted, but in recent years efforts had been made to clean it up, with a tall lifeguard chair suggesting people now swam in it.

We rode a little bit further to another spot, one where we could look back along the shore to where the skyscrapers of Chicago rose from the ground and pierced the dark blue night. A police car circled past making a loudspeaker announcement about everyone needing to be out of there because soon they were going to close the park, the time getting on for midnight.

We hadn't left by the time the patrol car circled back around, it pulling to a stop right behind us. 'Who's bike is that?' shouted the policeman from his open driver's side window, pointing to the red CT with UK numberplate.

297

I walked towards the police car, fearful of what was to come.

'That's an old Trail 90, what year is it?'

'It's a 2004,' I replied.

'They didn't make them in 2004,' he continued.

'They did in Australia.'

'Is this from Australia then?'

'Yes,' I said.

'How did you get it here?'

'I rode it.'

The policeman was so amused by this that he told us not to worry and that we could take as long as we liked. He explained that they cleared everyone out of the park to prevent homeless bums and other such people (it could have been me wild camping) from sleeping there over night. I wished him goodnight and watched as he drove off, police lights still twirling a bright red and blue. I returned to the group and carried on taking snaps of the Chicago skyline, twinkling in the late night sky.

We arrived back at Hollie's house way past midnight. We parked the two CTs up in the street and hit the sack, but not like that. What a good few days it had been. I'd made some good friends, learnt a lot about Chicago and the people that lived here. More than that I'd had a good opportunity to take a breather before pushing west, as from here on in I would be crossing the prairies of the Midwest, through the Bible Belt and on towards the looming shadows of the Rocky Mountains.

Regardless of what happened from here, it was nice finally to be back doing something that I could just get on with and chop away at. I didn't have to think too much or question what I was doing. I just had to ride. And it did feel like I was leaving some of my troubles behind. I was just grateful this time – unlike the first time – that I understood the dynamic of it a little better. I didn't see this as my solution, or my answer to life. I held no hope in it fixing me, or curing me. I was doing it because it's just what I felt I needed to do.

This trip was certainly an important part of moving on. I still found that hard. I still had an inclination to just turn right and head back up to Canada and knock on Mandy's door, whether she wanted me there or not. But I couldn't be so selfish. Passing that vertical alignment with her house up in Canada had certainly been a difficult but necessary step. It represented me leaving that period of my life behind and moving on. Who am I kidding? We never move on. We just try and paper over the past. And in the meantime, all that's left is the road.

Chapter Thirty-Three
Route 66

I decided to take old Route 66 out of Chicago. This is the famous highway heading all the way to Los Angeles. I had thought (like Vermin suggested) about heading due west until the road hit the banks of the Mississippi, and then I could trace it south until St. Louis, and then west towards the Rockies. But for so many people Route 66 is such an iconic road that the opportunity to ride it for myself was too powerful to resist.

I'd heard much about the road; about how it no longer exists in its entirety and how you have to hop on and hop off it as you trace its path all the way from Chicago to Los Angeles, a total distance of almost 2,700 miles. Of course, the road hasn't always been broken up like that. Back when it first opened in 1926 it was a solid ribbon of road – later becoming known as the 'Mother Road' – transporting entire families and communities from the hardship of the industrial north-east of America, to the more optimistic climates of the Pacific Coast.

Sadly, just like most things, progress came along and made the road redundant almost overnight. It was decommissioned as a federal highway on June 27th 1985, the day the interstate was completed. From receiving a steady flow of traffic, the towns along the route one day fell almost silent, bypassed completely, with many of them struggling to remain in existence ever since.

Scottish comedian Billy Connolly filmed a TV series about the road not so long ago. It painted quite a sad picture of people hanging on by the skin of their teeth, doing their best to preserve a way of life that to many is now considered outdated. It's just fortunate that in recent years efforts have been made to promote the old road and increase the numbers of tourists and travellers along the route.

More important than the road was that ahead of me now sprawled the vast expanse of the American Midwest. If you look at it on the map you can see that from Chicago all the way across to the Rockies there is nothing much but prairie. Of course, I'd tackled such vast places before; the Australian Outback one example, the main roads of Kazakhstan being another, but somehow the vastness of the American continent just felt a lot more intimidating.

Maybe it was the thought of twisters, or memories of *The Texas Chainsaw Massacre*; that sense that you're about to let go of the handrail and take a step into the unknown. It doesn't help that there are so many routes across it. As well as Route 66 you could take the Lincoln Highway, running through Iowa and Nebraska. Or Route 50 – the Lonely Highway – passing through Missouri and Kansas. Or you could take any number of other main and back roads and get lost out there forever.

Thankfully, despite the broken spokes and the signs of old age from the engine, the bike was still doing just fine. I'd changed the oil twice already, and fitted a new rear tyre back near Detroit, during one of those spoke fixing occasions. It was the highways that were proving to be hard work, just trying to keep up with the flow of traffic and get out of the way of the big trucks that squeezed us into the gutter.

The question still remained as to where this adventure might end; in San Francisco or in Alaska? I thought about this a lot while riding. The concern was that I'd left it too late in the season to go up to Alaska. I'd read that the end of September is the absolute latest to be heading up that way and it was the end of August already. I still had to get to San Francisco, and Alaska was another 3,500 miles north from there.

I could if I'd have wanted gone straight up from Chicago to Alaska – shortened the distance by a great deal – and perhaps made it with plenty of time to spare, but I'd always had my heart set on getting to San Francisco, and to miss it out would have felt like cheating. Besides, this route across the Midwest was going to take me through the state of Kansas, and as I was riding a bike called Dorothy, named after the previous owner's favourite character from *The Wizard of Oz*, my childish side couldn't help but get excited by the prospect of that.

And so it was, Route 66, heading out of Chicago, the road beginning almost exactly outside the McDonald's where a few days prior I'd met Lisette and heard her story. From there it heads west along Roosevelt Road, before turning on to Ogden Avenue and following that in a south westerly direction, all the way out of the city, following the brown historic route signs as you do so.

On the way out I stopped at the bike shop where Hollie used to work – where Jonathan still does work – picking up a couple of bulbs for the rear light to get that working again. By choice, I think Jonathan would have grabbed a bike from the shop and come along with me.

I suppose that is the impression people get; of being on a fabulous adventure full of excitement and joy. I think they would be less keen to sleep in hedge bottoms or be caught out in the rain or have spokes break on them in the middle of Detroit. For what it's worth, I look at other people's lives and wish mine was like that: when they seem to have everything sorted out; a place to call home; someone to love, and someone who loves them; a good routine; friends and family close; interesting hobbies and a job they like. Though I don't think it pays to wish for a different life, not unless you know all of the facts.

Once clear of Chicago the world really opens up and flattens out. There's a lot of space out here. Everywhere you look you either see fields or roads, or roads through fields. At times the old road would run parallel with the new interstate, just a wire fence between them, leaving me to look across at the massive trucks travelling at more than twice my speed. Had I been on a faster bike I would probably have joined them on the interstate, but that was beauty of this bike, it forced me to take the road less travelled, directing me through the places that most visitors – and locals – would consciously avoid.

The road would then hit a town, such as Wilmington, where at the side of the road a giant green man stands, almost as a guardian of the past.

His name was Gemini Man and he symbolised everything about Route 66; the nostalgia, the kitsch, the remnants of what was perhaps back then a more optimistic future, where giant green men were cool and good for business and people would pull over to have their picture taken with it, as I was doing now.

I met an Irish couple here, travelling Route 66 in a rental car, hoping to reach LA in just two weeks' time. They had a route mapped out, a plan, an itinerary, and were the first foreign tourists I'd met since leaving New York. They weren't ever so friendly at first (or just nervous). I got the impression that they were a bit upset to have met someone else travelling the route, as they gave off the sense of wanting to be pioneers of the road that day, and they couldn't do that if they found themselves part of a procession. We took each other's photos and carried on.

I wrestled with the road to stay on it. There are just so many twists and turns, endlessly having to keep your wits about you so you don't end up on the wrong road. At one point I followed what I thought was a signpost for Route 66, only to find myself heading up a farmer's field, having to ask the farmer which way the old road went from here. I found it all quite frustrating. I don't know why. I think it's because I had a mission to try and reach St. Louis that evening and just wanted to get it done, not faff around chasing nostalgia.

Ninety-eight miles out of Chicago I found myself in the town of Pontiac. By Route 66 standards it's quite a big town, with a museum in honour of the iconic road. I parked outside it, but didn't go in, as I'm not that big a fan of museums. I'm probably not a good tourist full stop. I mean, the Taj Mahal as I passed through India was alright, but it wasn't the highlight of my Indian adventure. I preferred instead the dark alleyways, where you sit on a step drinking a five-rupee shot of chai tea, served in a porcelain cup that you smash on the ground when you've finished. It's things like this that are worth going to India for, not an old building, as nice as it was.

Here in Pontiac it was now lunch time and while I never did have a big appetite whilst travelling it was simply time, after all morning on the road, to have a break from it and recoup. I found a small bakery, serving fresh pots of coffee in polystyrene cups with a cabinet of doughnuts, all covered in a brightly coloured glaze.

'Been a lot of drought,' said one of the old timers I got chatting to in the queue. 'You'll see a lot of that on your journey west,' he continued. Indeed I would, reading later how back in 1930s this entire area was known as the Dust Bowl; the combination of drought and new farming methods sending huge clouds of dust into the air, transforming into storms that blew as far east as New York.

Visibility was cut down to a few feet, forcing many people to flee their homes and head for the Californian coast. With the Great Depression still raging it was a difficult time for everyone, with it not until post World War II that the industrial machine of America got into full swing and made it the superpower that it is today.

I'd never had much interest in American history before; in the past it had no relevance to me. But out here you can't help but think about how this was all formed: the voyage of Christopher Columbus in 1492; then over the coming years the European colonisation of a land already inhabited by indigenous people, with the first British colony formed way back in 1607.

This exodus from Great Britain, I learned, came largely as a response to the religious persecution of groups such as the Quakers and the Puritans, sailing to America in search of a place to worship free of persecution, not to mention the opportunity to own their own land for the very first time. And from that a new nation was born.

By 1770, twelve more colonies were established, with a total population of around two and a half million. Tensions between the new colonies and the British Empire from which they came continued to grow. In 1775 the War of Independence began, the new colony refusing to pay tax on imported tea and throwing it all over board in a mark of defiance known as The Boston Tea Party, which set in motion the war that was eventually won in 1783; America allegedly the first colony to successfully revolt against colonial rule.

From that point on, western expansion of this new nation began, with Thomas Jefferson purchasing land from the French west of the Mississippi, effectively doubling the size of the American territory overnight. The year 1861 brought the American Civil War; which in a way could be construed as the agricultural south trying to do to the industrial north what the north had previously done to the British; beat them, and go it alone. An estimated 750,000 people died, the war lasting four long bloody years.

In the twentieth century, America was initially reluctant to enter World War I. There was Prohibition, the building of the first mass-produced motorised car by Henry Ford, and Mickey Mouse was born. Then came the Great Depression, the roaring forties, the involvement in World War II, Pearl Harbour, the Cold War, the first man on the moon, Vietnam, the assassination of JFK. Then later, the First Gulf War and, in this century, Iraq, Afghanistan, and the sabre-rattling over Syria and Iran.

It felt then that I was passing through a nation built on the actions of defiance and western expansion, and I have to concede that not at all times did I like this place. I felt that it had a high opinion of itself, 'the Greatest Nation in the World,' which is an easy thing to claim if you've never left your own shore. A man in New York argued with me that it was also the freest nation on earth, though he'd never set foot outside of America, so how could he say whether it was or not, only regurgitate what he had been conditioned to believe.

I felt there was a lot of fear here as well, more than I'd encountered in any of the other countries I'd passed through so far. I wondered if it was because, having fought to claim their own freedom and land, the American psyche is one that believes that someday, someone else will come along and try and do the same thing to them.

To my eyes, this had resulted in a fear of communists, of black people, of Muslims, of the State, of God, of paying for someone else's health bill. To extend this line of enquiry makes you question if it is this latent fear that gives rise and sustenance to the American propensity for gun ownership. Guns as a means of defending themselves and their country; a weapon against their own fears perhaps.

I certainly struggled with it at times during these early few weeks. I don't know if it was my own mood, still low at times, or the route that I'd taken, with my passage through such places as Detroit and Chicago revealing a side of America that rarely gets talked about, standing at odds with the image the nation generally projects of itself.

What I'd seen was confronting, and at times upsetting, but it was what it was, and all you can do is sit and look at it all, and try to take as much of it in as possible as you slowly drift on through. The people though, even if I didn't agree with them, had all been warm and kind, just as they had been across the rest of the world. I wonder if that's because they're humans first and foremost, and Americans second.

Despite best intentions, I never did make it as far as St. Louis that evening. Somehow, despite the satnav, and the route signs, I managed to get lost, riding the back lanes of rural Missouri, tracing the edge of corn fields, having to go back on myself and generally becoming a little flustered until I finally landed in Carlinville, a small country town some seventy miles to the north of St. Louis.

I found myself in the town's main square, around which all the shops were built. There were four main exits from it. I wasn't sure which one to take. I turned left, only to find myself at a dead end, overlooking the old Country Hall, a grand old building that looked a bit like the one struck by lightning in *Back to the Future*. I photographed it, before spinning around and heading back up to the main square in the centre of town, determined to try again.

I stopped to ask directions from two men sat on a doorstep smoking cigarettes. They turned out to be recent arrivals from Vietnam and whilst friendly, didn't know their way around either. As I chatted with them I tried to imagine what their journey must have entailed: growing up, a sense of discontent, hopes of one day living in the western world, saving money, booking tickets, landing, arriving here and getting work in a local restaurant, in a town in the middle of nowhere. It reminded me of something;

Sonder; 'the realisation that each random passer-by is living a life as vivid and complex as your own – populated with their own ambitions, friends, routines, worries and inherited craziness – an epic story that continues invisibly around you like an anthill sprawling deep underground, with elaborate passageways to thousands of other lives that you'll never know existed, in which you might appear only once, as an extra sipping coffee in the background, as a blur of traffic passing on the highway, as a lighted window at dusk...'

Taken from the online Urban Dictionary.

One of the men thought he knew of a campsite on the edge of town and sent me off in a direction where all I found was another McDonald's, resigning myself to another coffee and cheeseburger, just to stay on budget, which by this stage was just about hanging on in there. By chance, I parked beside a car with an open window. A girl was sat inside the car reading a book. We exchanged pleasantries, before I headed inside and took a break from the road for a while.

On the way out – it now dark – the girl was still there, still reading her book with the interior light illuminating the words. I was curious to know why she was still there, so asked her. It transpired that her friend worked in McDonald's but couldn't drive. And so this girl – Nikki – would drive her the forty miles from home, and instead of going backwards and forwards to pick her up at the end of her shift, would bring a few books and, for the eight-hour shift her friend was on, sit in the car and read them.

Nikki was a great girl: a big smile, easy to talk to and it was just one of those moments where you're stood in a fast food carpark, talking to a stranger in the car next door, and it's dark, and you don't know each other, but it feels like you know each other, and it's completely surreal because at the end of it all you ask if she knows of any campsites around and she says, 'yeah, down by Beaver Dam.'

And that's where I camped that evening, in a clearing in the forest, the entire place to myself.

In St. Louis the following morning I decided that I should go and visit the Gateway Arch. This is an easy building to find as it stands 192 metres tall (630 feet) and rises like a steel rainbow from an area of parkland right beside the Mississippi River. It was built in 1965 as a monument to Westward Expansion of the United States and 'typifies pioneer spirit of the men and women who won the West and those of a latter day to strive on other frontiers.' A monument to imperialism I guess.

It was actually in 1804 that two explorers – William Clark and Captain Meriwether Lewis – set out from St. Louis on what was called the Corps of Discovery, an expedition commissioned by then President Thomas Jefferson in order to map and explore that land he'd just purchased from the French. A total of 33 men left on the expedition, it taking them over a year to reach the Pacific Coast (the place I was heading to). At which point they turned around and came back again.

For the expedition, the US Mint prepared special coins inscribed with a message of friendship and peace, called Indian Peace Medals, which soldiers distributed to native people they came across on their expedition, the coins symbolising US sovereignty over indigenous inhabitants. I think it's fair to say that the indigenous people of the land suffered in all this: the western expanse of the Europeans; the taking of the land; being forced on to reserves, well away from the places they would have chosen to inhabit.

You'd like to think that if the same scenario played out today, and we discovered new territory, maybe even on the moon, but the moon already had tribes of moon-men, then we would work together and strive to get along. Or would we once again take what we wanted and not really care about the men who already live on the moon? Maybe it's a simple case of survival of the fittest, a reminder that men are tribal, and conflict is inherent. Conflict seems inherent in relationships and families, let alone nations. So perhaps it'd be unrealistic to expect anything other than bloodshed.

To get a better picture of the arch I decided to push the bike between the security barriers and up on to the mound of grass in front of it. Having done this I took quite a few photographs, from various angles, moving the bike around and repositioning it for ten minutes or more. It was then that a security patrol car approached, the two officers (wearing shorts, with fat calves, dark glasses and pistols in holsters) getting out and walking in my direction. I knew I was in trouble; I knew I shouldn't have been on here with the bike and certainly didn't imagine this was going to end so well.

One of the officers demanded my passport, which I handed to him. He then proceeded to ask a series of questions about what I was doing in St.

Louis, how long I'd been in America and what the purpose of my visit was. I explained what I was doing – riding the old bike across – apologising for bringing the bike up here and explaining that it was just for a souvenir snapshot. The officer radioed my details to what I assumed was a central command centre, waiting for them to be processed and come back with a verdict as to whether I was who I said I was or not.

It all reminded me of something John had told me back in Equinunk, about the security in Times Square, Manhattan. John's belief was that the reason I was able to push the bike up on to the pavement and position it right in the middle of the pedestrian part of Times Square for a photograph was because facial recognition cameras would have detected me – along with everyone else – the moment I entered the area, cross-referenced the image of my face with that taken by border control when I entered the country and verified whether I was a known threat or not.

I questioned the plausibility of this, before remembering how Facebook is already doing this whenever you upload a photo, detecting who is who. And that's only the technology we know of.

As it was, the two security guards here in St. Louis were happy that I posed no threat, insisting I go back out through the security gate and park the bike in a proper location next time. I rode down and parked it alongside the Mississippi River, a wide brown vein of water passing right through the heart of St. Louis. There was a steamboat moored nearby, old rusting factories on the other side of the bank, and high above it all towered that huge silver rainbow.

It was only $10 to take the tiny four-man lift to the top of it, which I did, hearing how the lift was very clever in the way it was able to move up and across, crab-like, as it climbed the leg of the arc. At the top you emerge in a slender viewing capsule, windows on either side and room for some forty people.

For a while I was too nervous to look out the window. It was that sense of being so high up, with nothing really beneath your feet, except for a long drop to the ground. After a while I pushed my nose right up to the glass and looked out, first to the east, back in the direction of New York, perhaps now a thousand miles away, and then to the west, across that land that Lewis and Clark, only two hundred years before, had first explored, planning to follow in their tracks on my old Australian Post bike, the one I'd ridden some 25,000 miles to get here.

It was a shame that Dorothy had lost some of her allure and mystique of that first trip, where she really had become her own character. Though in truth, I'd probably been guilty of giving too much life to an inanimate object, possibly in the belief that if I gave life to Dorothy then I wouldn't feel quite so alone on that nine-month journey from Sydney to London.

The obvious truth is that I was alone, and I think that's what had scared me about doing this second trip; being on my own again. I wondered if this is something that bothers all of us at times; that sense of living and dying alone. Hoping we won't, but knowing that we probably will, as grim as that might sound.

Having returned to the bike I decided from here that I wasn't going to continue along old Route 66 as it just wasn't for me; I neither had the time, the money or the pace to explore it properly, and to be totally honest, it was quite disappointing in comparison to what I'd been expecting. The other route – along Route 50, the Lonely Highway – which passed through St. Louis, was not only more direct, but also a lot less complicated and hard to follow. It would also take me straight through the heart of Kansas, and Dorothy was excited by the prospect of this.

***

Heading out of St. Louis I passed through some more run-down neighbourhoods, not realising at the time that this was the third most violent city in America. Flint, in Michigan, was first; Detroit was second; meaning I'd passed through two of the top three. Once again, it's hard to avoid the visual evidence that the worst bits are always the black bits, and as I rode out through another ghetto I couldn't help but wonder why it is like this. I mean, is the trouble in these neighbourhoods because the residents are black, or is the trouble in these neighbourhoods because the residents are poor, and just so happen to be black? Later I read a little about it, to try and make sense of it for myself.

I read that the first African slaves arrived in Virginia in 1619. Slavery was made illegal in Northwest Territories one hundred and sixty years later in 1787, but with demand for cotton increasing, so too did demand for slave labour, giving rise to the Underground Railroad; a chain of sympathisers helping to traffic Africans out of the south, to the sanctuary of the north.

Laws were in place to stop the slaves from escaping, with people punished, and hanged, for trying to do so. Finally, in 1808, there was a ban on the importation of slaves from Africa. In 1820 it was banned completely in the north, but not in the south. However, the famous Dred Scott case of 1857 cited that congress did not have the right to ban slavery in states, and furthermore, that slaves are not to be classed as citizens.

Even Abraham Lincoln – often credited for abolishing slavery – was once quoted as saying: "I will say then that I am not, nor ever have been, in favour of bringing about in any way the social and political equality of the white and black races; I am not nor ever have been in favour of making voters or jurors of negroes, nor of qualifying them to hold office, nor to intermarry with white people…

"I will say in addition to this that there is a physical difference between the white and black races which I believe will forever forbid the two races living together on terms of social and political equality. And in as much as they cannot so live, while they do remain together there must be the position of superior and inferior, and I, as much as any other man, am in favour of having the superior position assigned to the white race."

(Debate at Charleston, Illinois, September 18, 1858)

Then came the American Civil War, slavery used as a justification for that, though it was a war that had been brewing between the industrial North and agricultural South for quite some time. The true aim of the war was to preserve the Union; to preserve the United States, rather than have it split into two opposing parts. Of course, the North won, the Union survived, with the Emancipation Proclamation of 1863 deeming that a person held as slave shall be free, except those in border states where slavery was still allowed.

It was only in 1869 that blacks were classed as American citizens for the first time. A year later they were given the right to vote, but with legalised segregation continuing under Jim Crow laws for another 100 years, this gave rise to separate schools, hospitals, streetcars, public waiting rooms, restaurants, boarding houses, theatres and parks. It was in 1964 that President Johnson finally signed the Civil Rights Act, prohibiting discrimination with regard to race, colour, religion or national origin, this all taking place just a lifetime ago.

The succeeding years brought the race riots of Detroit and Newark in the eighties, and later Los Angeles in the nineties. Malcolm X was assassinated, so too Martin Luther King. Now you have Barack Obama in the White House, but is it really plausible to think that after the events of the last four hundred years or more, that black America can pretend everything's forgotten and move forward, united?

It would be nice to think so, but I just know with myself that once too much water has passed beneath the bridge, no amount of back-pedalling can change things. It takes time, patience and forgiveness, on both sides. Trust is important too, and I would say, from my brief experience so far, that it is trust that seems to be so lacking between these two colours of America. And it does no one any favours for one party to tell the other that it's a simple case of trying harder, not after the events of the past.

As a counterpoint to all this, as I made my way out of the city in the direction of the Lonely Highway, a man pulled up alongside me at a set of traffic lights. He was a black man, wearing a suit and tie and driving a top-of-the-range Cadillac Escalade, an expensive SUV.

'Where are you off to?' enquired the man from his driver's seat. 'San Francisco,' I replied with mild embarrassment. The man laughed in a kind hearted manner, wishing me the best of luck on my journey ahead. In return I complimented him on his car. 'Thank you,' said the man. 'I've had to work long and hard for this.'

A simple act of *trying*? Perhaps it is. Though surely the same must apply to all of us.

Chapter Thirty-Four
Across the Midwest

This night on the road was possibly the worst of any I'd encountered in the last 25,000 miles. From St. Louis I'd ridden all afternoon, along this Lonely Highway, which wasn't lonely at all. It was full of trucks and traffic and endless little towns, down on their luck; dead fields of corn after the drought had struck; and one gas station, where I sat drinking my coffee and eating my sandwich in the canteen section while having to listen to some guy talking about Obama and how he's a 'moslem' and not even American and how no way should he be President.

I just kept my head down. Clearly they weren't keen on outsiders around here and if any of them spotted my Indonesian biker jacket, and knew it to be the most populated Muslim country in the world, I might well have been chased out of town. You'd like to say something, try and reason with the man, perhaps try and convince him that not all people of that religion are evil, but that would have done me no good, and so I kept quiet and ate my sandwich.

As for this night on the road, I'd passed through a few towns along the Lonely Highway, asking at several gas stations if there were any campsites or creeks where I could camp. I think when doing this you secretly hope they'll say, 'Sure, come and camp on my land.' But not this night, and by now it was getting dark and even outside of the towns there just didn't seem to be anywhere to pull off the road and pitch a tent out of sight. Everywhere was either farms or fields, with private land ownership meaning every inch of it was fenced off or too exposed for wild camping.

In a way this was no different to riding across Indonesia, or other places where there just seems to be no space beside the road left vacant or accessible to rough campers such as me. Indonesia thankfully had a network of locally owned guesthouses, some of them brothels, which were cheap, quite grim, but they did the job of providing you somewhere to sleep. Here in America, where land ownership is absolute, and hotels too expensive, the biggest problem I was having was finding a place to sleep at night.

In the town of Tipton – it now almost dark – I stopped at an ice-cream kiosk having spotted a biker sitting on one of the benches. He rode a Harley Davidson and was with a woman who had a set of comically enhanced breasts. I asked them (the couple, not the breasts) if they knew of anywhere nearby I could camp for the night. They were quite dismissive and unhelpful, mentioning something about a park just down one of the side streets. I thanked them and headed in that direction, finding the park to be surrounded by houses, and people walking their dogs. This wasn't a good place to sleep, it was too exposed. I imagined I'd soon be woken by the police and moved on.

I rode back towards the main road. As I stopped at the junction I looked to the left along the rural road that meandered off into countryside. Just beyond the last house was a trail leading off into forest land. The last house overlooked this path and I thought that if they saw me go down there they'd no doubt call the police, but it was dark now, and that was the best chance I had of finding a place to sleep.

I turned left out of the entrance to the park, rode the few hundred yards until I was almost at the turn for the dirt trail to my right. I scanned around, making sure there was no traffic, then darted down the lane.

As the headlight on the bike is permanently illuminated whenever the engine is running, I cut the engine, knocked her down into neutral, leapt off and pushed like crazy down the trail – hoping that the people in the last house hadn't seen me – until I hit the cusp of the bushes and the forest. I kept pushing, right through the branches and along the remnants of an old trail, long since overgrown, just pushing and pushing, as hard as I might, the bike and me galloping over the ruts and dead branches, wading through the trees until all of a sudden the trail came to a halt at a dried-up riverbed.

I put Dot on her stand and looked around. I looked behind to see or hear if anyone had followed me. I looked over the other side of the dried-up riverbed to where there was a tall fence with a farm installation on the other side, perhaps a good stone's throw away. I could see the light on top of the barn above the fence, but no one could have seen me over the fence, though I did hear voices in the yard.

By now my heart was beating like a drum. It was made worse by the fact that every time a car drove along the road I'd just turned from, it would shine a faint beam of light through the trees and on to the small clearing on which I was stood, which made me think it was the torchlight of the person looking for me. I stood like this for ten minutes or more, perhaps even twenty. I was in an eerie dark forest; all the light had gone. I shouldn't be here, but I had nowhere else to be. I would have to sleep here, and hope that no one would come.

To make matters worse, in my panic, I thought it was time I did an oil change, because with a knocking noise beginning to be heard from the engine I thought for some strange reason it might help. So right there, in the middle of the forest, I dug a small ditch beneath the engine and, not proud of this, undid the engine bolt until the oil started flowing out and into the hole I'd dug in the ground. Returning it to nature, I justified to myself, knowing I shouldn't have done it. I was just desperate to do anything to keep this bike running as it was my lifeline.

While doing this I dropped the engine oil bolt in the dirt and couldn't find it anywhere because it was pitch black now. I didn't have a torch, and I couldn't have shone one anyway because it might have given my position away. My mind was telling me that any minute someone was going to wade through the bushes and scream at me for being there, or point a gun at my head, and I would have a bike without an engine bolt, draining oil into the earth.

I could have hit myself. And did. It was a horrible evening, one where you could tear yourself limb from limb. I don't think I was thinking rationally. I don't think I was sane. I was alone in America, deep in the Midwest, at night time, camping in the dirt.

Finally I found the bolt, wiping off the soil and debris, before screwing it back into the sump, replenishing the oil and putting up my tent. I threw in my sleeping bag, got in that, gripped the knife, lay on the hard dry ground, and slept until 4.30am, when the alarm clock on my sim-less mobile phone woke me from my slumber. I quickly packed up my things, and under the cloak of darkness, pushed the bike back out along the path, fighting with the trees and branches, hiding amongst them until I could check the lights of the last house were still out and there was no one out on the road.

Coast clear, I pushed like crazy, back along the dirt trail to the road. At the end I fired Dot into life and, having already put my helmet and gloves on, raced straight off, back up to where the ice-cream kiosk was, as a gas station was located on the opposite side of the road and was already open for the day. I bought a coffee and sat on the step outside, looked upon suspiciously by the people around me. I checked the bike's valve clearance with the feeler gauge, before thinking I'd got nothing better to do than hit the road and hope this day was a better one. Thankfully it was.

***

Instead of staying on Route 50, which by this time would have been dual carriageway all the way into Kansas City, I took Route 5 running due south for around 70 miles until it hit Route 54, running almost parallel east to west to Route 50, but hopefully a little bit quieter, with less heavy traffic. By taking this route I would bypass Kansas City completely, which in a way was a shame, as I'd heard the town was famous for its BBQ food and I think to be doing this trip on a 'proper' bike, on a 'proper' budget, being able to find a decent hotel and spend my nights meandering around the city, would have been quite pleasant.

Sometimes I did resent the way I travelled; with haste, on a low budget, often desperate to be at the next destination. Though equally, I chose to avoid the cities as they just made me sad. I rarely saw anything that I liked in them. They were difficult to navigate, dense in traffic and largely all looked the same. Too many people in too small a place. And on a bike like this it just felt like an unnecessary chore, hence the reason for avoiding Kansas City this day.

Fortunately, Route 5 was the quietest road I'd been on for a while and with it being so early in the morning there wasn't so much traffic around. As per usual I stopped at my favourite fast-food diner for breakfast – talking to the counter staff about local sights that might be worth seeing (a lake, I skipped) – before taking something of a shortcut, finding myself riding amidst a world of water, where perfectly still lakes cut across the land and long flat bridges carried you from one bank to the other. Combined with the thick forest surrounding it, it seemed a nice change from Missouri's flat agricultural land, which is mainly all I'd seen of it so far.

Route 5 finally dropped me down to Route 54, which, for whatever reason – it's hard to pinpoint exactly why – just seemed a more pleasant place to be than Route 50. It was quieter for a start, and felt like a road that served communities, rather than one designed simply to get you somewhere. Odd to think of a road as having a soul, but that's what Route 54 seemed to have; a simple liveliness about it as it rolled gently across the landscape, meandering left and right, through small dilapidated villages, past fields of burnt-out crops, the air so hot and still.

I didn't stop much out here (only to take a photo of Dorothy beside the Kansas state sign). I didn't have reason to, and there didn't seem much worth stopping for either. This was short-sighted really, as I bet all of these down-on-their-luck towns would have a story to tell, about their rise and their fall, the shops that have closed down and the people that have moved away, or still live here, scratching out an existence for the simple reason that this is their home and that's where they belong.

I passed through these places, wondering what it must be like to live out here, so far from the coast, landlocked for thousands of miles. No wonder some of them were a little bit insular. The world to them was small out here.

It was out here in the middle of Kansas that I ran into Klara and Flo, two young German cyclists riding across America on a pair of push bikes. I saw them at first as two dots on the horizon, travelling in the same direction as I was, gradually catching up with them until I pulled alongside and slowed to ask if they were okay for water. They were fine and so I carried on, stopping in the next town, a few miles away, to wait for them. I reasoned it would be good to share the joys of the road for a moment.

The two cyclists finally came to a halt in the Dollar Store carpark where I waited for them in the shade. It was midday and stinking hot. They wore dark lycra, helmets and were covered in sweat. Their skin was red from where it was exposed to the sun. I was always fascinated by cyclists doing this kind of long distance touring. It seemed like a sufferance, averaging around 100 miles a day, having to pack and plan for the limitations of what could be carried by bicycle, not being able to rush through the bad areas like even I was able to do, having to pedal through them, so vulnerable in so many ways.

The pair told me how they had started in or around Washington, riding the Appalachian Trail, passing through West Virginia and Kentucky, their intention to make it all the way to the coast and possibly drop down into Mexico after that. I asked them how they had found it so far and they said many of the areas they had passed through had been incredibly poor. They said that a lot of time they found it hard to explain to people where Germany was. Some of the locals thought you could ride there, not realising that it was on the other side of the Atlantic. But like me they'd only met good people, who had helped them, or people of the other persuasion, who had baffled them. But they were enjoying it, and it was a pleasure to have met them this day.

The rest of the day was simply spent riding along Route 54, before later drifting into the centre of Wichita just as evening approached. To me Wichita was one of those towns that you've probably heard of, either from a movie or a song or some other piece of pop culture, but you have no clue what is there or even where it is in relation to the rest of America. All I knew was that when I saw it on the map I was excited that my route would take me there.

It's certainly not a big place. Instead of the vast expanse of Detroit and Chicago, there was instead a moderately long entry road, lined with cheap motels and liquor stores. It was downbeat and downtrodden, Chinese and Mexican restaurants inhabiting the tired single-storey brick buildings, serviced by parking lots cracked by weeds and guarded by broken wire fences. I considered the prospect of stopping in one of the motels (budget notwithstanding), but would have preferred another dried-up riverbed any day of the week.

The centre of town was an improvement, though strangely charmless. Everything was built on a grid, office buildings no more than three or four storeys high. It felt like a place of bureaucracy, and I learnt later that it was in Wichita that the aviation industry grew. Boeing, Airbus and Learjet all still had operations there, with Wichita also home to the very first Pizza Hut. The city now has a population of around 400,000, making it the biggest city in Kansas, bigger than Kansas City in fact. In a way it reminded me of the Australian capital of Canberra, and how you had to know where the pockets of life were or else you'd never find them.

I stopped at a McDonald's just off the town centre. I thought that if I'm going to camp that night then I'm best eating now and so got in line to order a 99 cent cheeseburger and a $1.17 cup of coffee, which was my usual order on this journey across America. As I stood there, lost in my own world as I so often was, I was interrupted by the Asian man ahead of me who enquired as to whether that was my motorcycle parked outside. I told him that it was and he asked where I'd been and where I was going. I wasn't particularly interested in talking about it. It was just life, my life, I didn't think it was at all worth talking about, certainly not at that moment.

The man asked where I would sleep this night, and I said wherever I could find to put up my tent. He couldn't believe it. He couldn't believe that I would just ride along until I found somewhere out of sight, park up, put up the tent and go to sleep. He was quite stunned by this, but obviously, to me, it was just a part of my life out here.

The man was with his son, the pair of them driving to Colorado for the start of the son's new university term. He said they were doing the drive over two days and that the father would drive straight back having dropped his son off. They invited me to sit with them. I waited for my coffee and cheeseburger, and then did so.

The pair were from Taiwan; the father (Kol) I gathered was a relatively successful businessman. He spoke good English, asked direct questions and genuinely seemed interested in what I was doing. I asked what his impressions of America were and he said the country had been good to him, commenting that it was a relatively new country, only a teenager compared to the countries we'd come from, and so still had room to grow and to learn.

He also reasoned that if a man was walking outside and got attacked by another man or a group of men then people – strangers – would rush over to intervene. He said that in our own countries (Taiwan and England) that just wouldn't happen; we'd turn a blind eye and keep on walking. I think he was right, we would. We'd convince ourselves it was none of our business and look the other way. This is what I did like about America, how people are strong as individuals and not afraid to be heard and act when they feel a need to. We in England are often too concerned about what others think to be like this. Perhaps we are cowardly. Perhaps we have less to protect.

The man told me he wanted to help me out. I asked what he meant by this and he said that he was going to pay for me to have a room in the hotel that he and his son were staying in over the road. I told him I couldn't possibly let him do that. But I think as a father, speaking to someone's son, he wouldn't take no for an answer, and was adamant that he was going to book me a room, whether I liked it or not.

I followed the man outside, being told to wait whilst he got the car and then I would follow him to the hotel that was just around the corner. Shortly after a top of the range Mercedes E55 AMG pulled up, the son driving, who was only around 17 years of age. I followed the car to the Best Western that was in sight of the McDonald's we'd just left. Kol told me to wait outside while he went in and took care of the room.

He came outside five minutes later and handed me the key. He told me that I'd never see him again, that he didn't want anything in return, reassuring me that the room was paid for and that I was to have a safe trip.

I shook his hand and thanked him dearly, almost to the point of stunned silence, before beginning the task of carrying all my gear up through the lobby of this grand hotel – explaining to the confused receptionist what events had just transpired (a stranger, buying a room for another stranger, who he had met just moments before in McDonald's) – before using the key card to access a beautiful room with twin king-sized beds, a bathroom, a kettle, a TV, clean towels and not a single dried-up riverbed in sight. There was also safe parking for Dot, in the multi-storey next door, chained to the railings with a lock I'd been carrying, with no use for it until now.

I unpacked all of my things, re-organised them, took a shower, then had a long hot bath, followed by some time on the internet uploading photos and sharing my excitement with friends back home. After that I lay back to watch a few hours of TV, before falling asleep.

The next morning, before heading down for complimentary breakfast, the invoice was slid beneath the door. I thought for a moment I would have to pay it, before realising it was just a receipt for the almost $160 room the stranger from Taiwan had paid for last night. One night in a dried-up riverbed, the next in a king-sized bed in a fancy hotel; the surreal encounters of the road.

Chapter Thirty-Five
Kansas

I didn't ride far that day. I just didn't feel like it. Instead, I spent most of the morning trying to figure out which way to go, because not far from Wichita, up near Dodge City, there would be a fork in the road and I had to decide which way to turn. I could either carry on along Route 54 until it rejoined Route 50, and from there follow it all the way to Colorado Springs, the town in which Vermin and his family lived. Or I could take the fork to the left, and follow the old Santa Fe Trail, a nineteenth century trading route (now part of the highway system), that was once used to transport arms down to the front line during Mexican-American war of 1846 to 1848.

It was one of those decisions where there isn't really a right or wrong answer; all roads lead to the same place, so it was a question of what I would prefer to see along the way. I really wanted to go to Santa Fe as I knew it to be a quaint rustic town, with a strong Mexican influence and a town centre of buildings that could have come straight out of a *Flintstones* cartoon. I knew this because I'd been there before, ten years prior, when after that summer teaching tennis back in Equinunk I'd taken a three-week organised trip all the way from the east coast of America to the west.

A total of fourteen of us were crammed into the back of a mini-van, with a guide named Abi, a prescribed route to follow, and nothing much to think about because everything was done for you. The route was also different to the one I was taking now. From New York it went down through Washington, then into Alabama and Louisiana, reaching New Orleans where we stopped for a few nights. From there it meandered west, to Carlsbad Caverns, Roswell, then up to Santa Fe and west from there, all the way to the coast.

By chance, we landed in LA on the 10th September 2001, the night before the planes crashed into the twin towers. I'll always remember that morning, waking up on a campsite and being told to go and look at the television in the communal lounge as something bad had just happened.

The rest of the day we all sat pretty much in silence, unable to believe what we were seeing; no doubt the same emotions as everyone else who watched their televisions that day. I remember being in a lift a few days later with an American man, raging and insistent that we just go and bomb the lot of them in retaliation. Sadly, that's pretty much what we did, and I don't think the world's been quite the same ever since.

To think that now, because of those attacks on New York (or those attacks on New York being used to justify what followed), American drones are being flown over areas in Pakistan not far from those I rode through on that first trip (I'd passed through Abbottabad, the town where Osama Bin Laden was found) killing people – some innocent – in a bid to win this War on Terror.

I can't help but question the irony of that. I think that's why at times I struggled to like this place, because I didn't always like its politics, and as you travel through the guts of America you can begin to sense how as a nation it chose to respond in the way that it did; lashing out, as a victim might, thinking it had the right not to be attacked, a sense of righteousness perhaps, a Manifest Destiny, aligned with that presence of fear of people and cultures they don't always understand. To fight force with force, to wield the biggest gun, in the way that the West was won.

It was perhaps ironic then that the town I passed through next was Dodge City, home of Wyatt Earp, one time sheriff of the town. The town isn't so dangerous now. In fact it seemed to have more churches than any other town I'd passed through. In the centre of town was a museum, featuring a full size recreation of an old 19th century street, complete with wooden shops. Historical re-enactments took place here, whilst out in the parking lot an old black steam train overlooked a gift shop, where you could buy all sorts of trinkets from the past. Across the road was a McDonald's, meaning the trappings of the 21st century were never that far away.

I didn't plan on staying long, I was simply passing through, only my feet seemed to get stuck in the mud, and as much as I tried to plod on I just couldn't seem to muster the conviction to push myself over the inertia. Some days you get like that, when the call of the road just isn't strong enough, and I think by now I'd begun to relax a little more and accept that you get there when you get there, and not a second before.

I hung around Dodge City instead, chatting to some other bikers riding huge and beautifully painted Honda Goldwings, towing matching trailers on the back. It was the antithesis of my approach to travel, with no right or wrong. Just different spokes for different folks.

By evening, I'd conceded my riding day was done and having enjoyed my time in Dodge City – more pleasant than I'd ever expected – I headed out to a campsite where I pitched the tent beside a dried-up lake and watched as the full moon shone into view.

To say the tent only cost $18, it was doing okay, as were the rest of my things. I'd even become quite attached to my J-Lo sunglasses and had refined the packing of my equipment to such a point that I knew where most things were. The saddle bags had kept on ripping. I now fixed them with tie-wraps holding opposing panels together. I was making do, as by this stage I was halfway through my £500 budget, and still with so many miles left to go.

Times like these didn't help – paying $20 for a tent pitch – but sometimes the last thing you need on an evening is not to feel safe at night. And to be truthful, I wasn't quite as destitute as I could have been, mainly thanks to a man named Malcolm, who I probably should have mentioned before.

I'd met Malcolm at a bike event one weekend in England, a few months before embarking on this adventure. Malcolm had asked me for a copy of my first book and told me that if I were ever to do America then he'd sponsor me £200. I didn't think anything of it until he emailed me out of the blue just two days before I shipped myself and the bike over to the States.

'Good news Malcom,' I responded, 'we're on our way.' 'Great,' he said. 'Now give me your bank details and I'll wire you that money'. I told him not to be so daft, but he was adamant.

Reluctantly I'd sent him the details and a little later checked my account only to find he'd deposited £500! Then, when I told him my budget for the entire trip was not much more than that and how grateful I was, and how silly he was, he sent me another £150, to make it up to £650, which was incredibly kind, and meant that I was doing the trip almost in the black, rather than even further into the red, as I otherwise would have been. It was this money that had paid for the satnav.

Apparently, it was upon reading in that first book of my trials and tribulations and recognising those feeling of frustration in not being able to make it work with the person that you love that compelled him to lend a hand. He'd been there, as most of us have – Malcolm was of an age where he had a pair of grown-up sons, and his hope for them was that they never fall properly in love, because to him it only proved to be ruinous.

I found it difficult to disagree with this; the eternal hole in your soul caused by the feeling – real or otherwise – of letting someone go, or letting someone slip through your fingers, really can have a detrimental impact on your mood, and your mind, from that point on. But then again, the pain of that, as crap as it is of times, makes us who we are. It makes us do the things we do. And so I see it perhaps as a double-edged sword. Were it not for the way I had been feeling, I would never have done this, or found need to do this. I would not be here on an Australian motorbike, in the middle of America. Heading west in search of an unknown future. And by now, I was glad that I was.

I had however decided not to rely on satellite navigation quite so much from here on in, packing it away and relying once again on my own intuition. I often think in modern life how there's too much reliance on the things that have the capacity to guide us (removing our own input from the equation), and at times I wondered if there was a correlation between those anti-depressants the doctor prescribed me, this satnav unit that guided me, and even the organised religion the lady in our local post office wished for me to join during my darkest of days.

After all, such things give us a hand rail to hold on to, which seems necessary when we need them most. But later, for me at least, I felt it necessary to let go of that rail, and stand on my own two feet again, as terrifying as that can sometimes be. Which is why I said no to the anti-depressants, the organised religion, and finally packed the satnav away in the panniers, and went in whichever direction felt right. Which of course was west, in the direction of Colorado Springs.

**

The following morning I got the hell out of Dodge, ploughing out across the prairie, my tail feathers on fire and racing hard and fast away from the rising sun. It really is a strange place out here, highlighted by the road signs campaigning against abortion. 'I regret my abortion,' read one roadside placard, accompanied by a picture of an empty armed woman looking forlorn. 'One in four murders are caused by abortion,' read another.

The villages through which I passed felt guarded and mindful of outsiders. They felt like closed communities, and even the traffic from behind felt cold and unfriendly, overtaking too fast and too close, often forcing me into the gutter. Fields of rotating wind turbines sat on the horizon line, almost a surreal sight given the volume of them. The road through all this ran arrow straight across a dusty prairie, passing through small gas station towns as it did so. At one gas station I was made nervous by a group of men in a pick-up truck, eyeing me and the bike up in such a way that made me look over my shoulder for the next twenty miles or so.

The American frontier must have been a wild place back in the day – no certainty about it, gradually encroaching on the land as the new world of the United States advanced west, bridging the gap between St. Louis and California.

The term Manifest Destiny is, to a large extent, the ethos and tone behind that western expansion of the nineteenth century; the presumption that this New World, this United States, had divine right to the land. Basically, with God's blessing, they took it, which is an awkward theory to get your head around and accept, especially when you apply it to what is happening in the Middle East right now and the wars that are being fought there. A new Manifest Destiny; or again just human nature?

It is though perhaps unfair to single America out for acting in such a way. The British Empire has no doubt been guilty of it in the past. So too China, which I saw for myself as I passed through it on the way back from Australia. In the city of Kashgar in the western province of Xinjiang, the rapid migration west of the Han people has eroded and displaced the people and the culture of the Uighurs; a Central Asian tribe, once with its own country, East Turkestan, which in the fifties was annexed by China, their way of life now threatened by the 'pioneers' that surge from the east.

I met Emmett out here, a man in his sixties, also on a bicycle, cycling almost all the way across America, though not all in one go. In fact, he began his journey way back in the seventies, getting as far as Colorado Springs before his life in the army took over and he had to abort his cross-country trip and go through the rigmarole of living and earning and raising kids. Now retired, he explained how once more the world was his, and he had resumed his cross-country journey almost thirty years later, now heading for Cincinnati, and then on to the East Coast, perhaps as part of a third instalment of the trip.

Not far behind him I came across another cyclist, this one Japanese, studying in San Francisco and spending the summer vacation riding as far east as he could before term resumed. I told him he would catch a man named Emmett soon, though I felt sorry for the pair of them, as in the town I'd just ridden through, the temperature was stated as being some 103 degrees Fahrenheit. It certainly was baking hot out here.

To keep the sun off I had all my skin covered: the long-sleeved flannel shirt, BigZoner waistcoat, sunglasses across my eyes and the red and white neckerchief tied across face so that my nose, cheeks and neck were completely sheltered from the throbbing midday sun. This still wasn't enough to prevent a hornet, or a wasp, or whatever it was, from stinging me clean in the throat.

I saw the black dot looming as I rode forward, flying object meeting throat with incredible force. The sting was sharp and painful, providing one of those moments of irrational thought, when you imagine a sting can turn into an allergic reaction which can turn into your throat swelling up, which can mean a loss of breathing, and the onset of sudden death.

I pulled over beside one of those tubular mail boxes with the little wooden flag that pops up to let the owner know they have mail. It was just there by the roadside, the house it belonged to way off in to the prairies, not even visible from the road. There was no one around. Not even any passing cars or windmills. Just nothing. Only me, sat on Dot, with my helmet off, trying to get a look at the fast-swelling lump emerging on the front of my throat. I think nature was trying to tell me something: go easy on Kansas (and America), or else...

It wasn't long after this that I crossed the border from Kansas into Colorado. I'm not sure why but this caused a huge sigh of relief, the sign a good indicator that the Midwest had been crossed and from here the next challenge would be riding up and over the Rockies, a challenge that didn't seem too daunting given that me and the old bike had already ridden the second highest road in the world during our crossing of the Himalayas back in India and then Pakistan.

Meanwhile, in the first town of Lamar I stopped for a respite from the road and to stock up on maps and advice at the tourist information centre in the centre of town.

One of the volunteers, Elizabeth, was a lady well into her seventies, perhaps even her eighties, who had lost her husband four years prior, yet still maintained a cattle ranch, with over one hundred cows. She was an incredible woman, full of life and curiosity, reminding me of Gary (the seventy-seven year old cycling ski instructor I met at Lake Erie) and how at similar ages they're both out there, still doing their thing.

Elizabeth was working with a lady called Judy, the three of us chatting extensively about life and the journeys ahead, all the while a straggle of other travellers dropping by for bits of information on where best to go.

These tourist information centres really do offer a great service to anyone heading across the country in the way that I was.

Strangely, as I sat there that day, I thought about the concept of legacy, and how life is often centred around the desire to leave one behind, as no one would like to think they were here, and they were gone, and no one really remembers them. I wondered if that's what I was trying to do with these trips, and maybe even these books; trying to leave my own indelible mark on the world, as small a mark as that may be.

Maybe it's because I didn't have any desire to have children or start a family – not yet in any case – and I couldn't help but wonder if that's a large incentive for having children; so that in that one single moment of procreation you have left a mark that will outlive you and ensure that your name lives on. I don't know which is easiest; to have children, or to ride a motorbike across the world? Perhaps both have their complications, though I imagine having children leaves you with fewer questions, whereas riding across the world only seems to provide you with ever more. Or perhaps I am completely wrong on that, as I might one day find out for myself.

***

That afternoon I rode towards the thin line of the Rockies, across the wilderness of Colorado, being able to just make out the mountains in the distance. It was like riding towards the gates of Mordor, that formation of rocks resembling an impassable fort, in place to impede my progress to the Pacific Coast and San Francisco beyond.

Sadly, the road didn't lead directly to Colorado Springs, but instead to the town of Pueblo, seventy miles or so to the south. That wouldn't have been a problem had the road connecting the two not been an interstate, meaning that I would have to detour west, then back east, adding around sixty miles to the distance. I didn't like the idea of that. Sixty miles is almost two hours of riding at my pace, and already the sun was beginning to sag low in the sky. I checked Google Earth at another McDonald's, realising that a dirt trail known as Overton Road ran parallel the entire length of the interstate.

I took that option, riding it now, the thick and towering line of the Rockies to my left, and the never-ending expanse of the prairies to my right. It was a beautiful evening; the perfect road, the perfect bike, the simple act of riding through a lonely landscape, kicking up dust trails and staring out at the sky; a mellowing redness about the clouds, mirrored in the red tinge of the ground below. It was a dream world, feeling the warm breeze on my face, the loose ends of the neckerchief flapping rhythmically against my sun-tinged neck. An hour's ride to Phil's house. Then a beer. Perfect.

It wasn't to last. As darkness fell I realised the front headlight wasn't working properly and I was still a good thirty miles from Colorado Springs, leaving no choice but to ride without a headlight in the dark. Not only that, but the engine didn't seem to be pulling very well either, struggling to maintain speed and gradually feeling more and more sluggish. From euphoria to panic in the space of five miles or less.

Finally, the dirt trail joined the road network, and through the outskirts of Colorado Springs I did my best to tuck in behind the cars, following their tail lights, hoping that the fluorescent postal jacket would have me seen by other road users that night. The last twelve miles to Phil's house felt like a thousand.

Phil wasn't home when I finally made it there. It was perhaps just before nine in the evening, after almost seventeen hours on the road. I wasn't even sure I'd got the right house as I'd picked up an email back in Pueblo from him saying that he was going to be home. I asked the lady next door if my friend lived here and she didn't know, she'd only just moved in.

I took my passport from the bike, my laptop and camera, most of my paperwork, and left Dorothy parked at the end of the drive. I walked away, feeling for the first time in all these years a strong desire just to abandon it, to do something else with my life and never have to see or ride the bike ever again. After all, I was in a foreign town, in a foreign country, with barely any money, and a friend who I couldn't contact by telephone because I didn't have a sim card, and who wasn't in, and I didn't even know if this was his house.

I walked away from that. I had everything I needed to start afresh. My credit card, driving licence, camera, passport, laptop. I walked through the suburbs and back to a country fair that I'd seen taking place on the way through. It was perhaps a twenty minute walk away, with people who'd been to the fair coming in the opposite direction. They looked so happy with life, and I felt so lousy. Like I had this massive obligation to do this trip, and I just didn't want to do it any more. How quickly your mood can change out here.

Now I walked to pass the time. I walked to avoid answering questions of what I was doing here and why. Dark thoughts that night. Back in the hole. Falling down a well, trying to stop yourself from falling, finger nails grating against the walls, still falling. 'Pull yourself together man. Come on, come on. Come on.' It felt like that time I was trying to find a boat out of Sumatra, riding back to the port, bracing my arms and letting out a primal scream, forcing out the fear and the anger. Roaring until your brain explodes.

I marched back to what I thought was Phil's place. When I got there he still wasn't home. 'Sod it,' I thought, flinging open the side gate that led to the backyard and going for a look around to see if I could make any sense of all this, to see if I'd got the right house.

I saw the garage and the back of the house, and that the lights were on, but no one was at home. There was another gate to another part of the backyard. I pushed through it, not expecting to find much, and yet there it was: the piece of shit that Vermin rode; Cack, the bastardised Honda PC800 with the antlers on the front and the chimney on the back to warm your can of baked beans. I was so relieved at the sight of that bike. My body oozed its tension all over the floor.

I wheeled Dot around and through the gate. I was hungry, so took out my gas burner and heated up a tin of ravioli. Dinner by moonlight, eating it with the folding cutlery set I'd bought from Kmart, back in Equinunk, the day I'd gone riding with John. I sat on the step and filled my stomach with this shit tin of food. Until all of a sudden the family came home, Phil and his wife Linda and his two kids, Dana and Drew, who'd all been out for ice cream. Was I glad to see them!

'How was your ride across the Midwest?' asked Vermin, over a bottle of cold beer as we bummed out on his sofa that night.

And there, from the beginning, I told him.

Chapter Thirty-Six
Colorado Springs

The journey from here changes. The start and the middle are done. As I entered this stage of the journey across America, I felt calmer about things and in a better place to slow down and enjoy the world through which I was passing. I was excited about this stage, as it contained all the places I most looked forward to visiting, such as Monument Valley, the Grand Canyon, Las Vegas, Death Valley, then on to San Francisco. I was certainly making good time, with it taking me just under three weeks to get from New York to here. It might seem quick (or slow) to some people, but it was the perfect pace for me, as it was all about maintaining momentum.

I didn't realise at the time but Colorado Springs was founded in 1871 as a place through which the railroad could pass. It later became known as 'Little London,' thanks to its relative luxuriousness that proved popular with visitors from England. And in fact the town's founder, William Jackson Palmer, had close connections with England as it was from that country that much of the railroad's funding had come.

The town also has a long established military history, with Peterson Air Force Base on the outskirts, Camp Carson serving the army and the North American Aerospace Defence Command – or NORAD – built into the mountains overlooking the town. This is where all of America's air defence command is based, and if you've watched the film *Independence Day*, with Will Smith, you'll know it as one of the first places the aliens destroyed in order to give themselves free passage through the American airspace. It's this weird blurring of fiction, sat upon the framework of reality, that makes travel though America so involving, especially given the interaction most of us have had with Hollywood over the years.

I spent two days in Colorado Springs with Phil and his family, the break from the road I needed before pushing west. Crossing America had been a lot tougher than I'd ever imagined. I'd perhaps been guilty of underestimating it, and not entered it with the right frame of mind in the first place. Those first thousand miles or so had really been a battle, those across the Midwest weren't always easy either. But we'd made it to Colorado Springs, still in one piece, everything just ticking along like the internals of a relentless clock.

I did still think about Alaska and whether I would make it there or not. I was optimistic that I might, but realistic enough to know that it was starting to reach the end of the season and that if I wasn't heading up that way soon then it would be too late, and that I would have missed the window for this year. I don't think it mattered really. There would be achievement enough in reaching San Francisco, which was still around 2,000 miles away. The shame in not reaching Alaska on this occasion would be that in September – the month I would arrive there – the Northern Lights shine at their brightest. Thus the title, *Running Towards the Light*, had never seemed so apt.

Such concerns for now could wait, because for those two days I rolled the bike into the garage and closed the door, happy not to have to look at it or ride it for a while. Instead, I was taken sightseeing by the Vermin family – Phil, Linda and their son Dewy who was soon to be joining the military.

Having grabbed an early morning coffee we went for a drive up into the Garden of the Gods. This is an area just beyond the city limits – one of the reasons they chose to build the city here in the first place – like a giant naturally forming rock garden with a road running through the heart of it and a massive boulder perched on a ledge that people stop to photograph. There are also many hiking trails, and rock faces to climb. We didn't really do any of those things, just cruised through in the car, parking up a few times to take in the beauty of it all.

After that we drove up to look at where only a few months prior a savage bush fire had torched almost 300 homes, killing one person and turning the entire mountainside black and charred. It was unbelievable to see; the way in which the fire had rampaged down the mountain, destroying most of the houses, yet somehow leaving some completely untouched, almost as though it bore a grudge against some, but not against others. On one street the fire had even jumped the road and only burnt two or three homes on the opposite side, which for those residents must have been perplexing, wondering what they'd done to deserve it, whilst their neighbours still had an unscathed home.

We ate lunch in a great cafe, before pulling up at the gates of a private complex for wealthy Christian residents, with security cameras and an enclave of homes set well out of sight, at the foot of the mountains. Phil hinted at how there might be more of this to come – the wealthy living in private communities – especially with talk of privatising the police force in various parts of America and the implications that come with that.

Even back in New Jersey I'd read of a city district that had just sacked its entire police force as it simply couldn't afford to pay them, and this was a city – Camden – with one of the highest homicide rates in America. Equally in Detroit, the head of the Police Union had just declared that you enter Detroit at your own risk, with him citing his officers as being overworked and grossly understaffed to cope with the troubles there. A sense then of those with money being able to pay to privately protect themselves, and the rest no longer able to rely on the state to provide such fundamental things.

Then when you hear how the Government wishes to fly armed drones over the nation and possibly inject microchips into each citizen – containing their medical information – you do begin to wonder if George Orwell's vision of 1984 may one day turn true.

One of the most troubling whispers I heard was about the privatisation of the prison service, and how there was profit to be made in putting people in jail, some even going as far as to suggest that the war on drugs is nothing more than a ploy to populate the prisons. To combine that with talk of privatising the police force really does make you stop and wonder just what the future holds for America if that's the game that is increasingly being played.

I always remember meeting a traveller back in India – at a coffee shop in Manali – who genuinely believed in the concept of the New World Order, and the power of the few, to rule and dominate the rest of us; the intention being to create a single world government. At the time I didn't agree with him, nor believe it to be possible, and in a way I still don't (I just don't believe in such passiveness of man to allow it to happen). But crossing America, you do get a sense of the murkiness that lies beneath the apparent order of the world, and how things are changing, and how this plateau of peace and civilisation we currently enjoy might not be as permanent as one would wish for.

Perhaps once more it may just have been down to me and my own mind. I mean, once you've been to a dark place, combined with the way that a trip such as this allows you to stand back and observe the 'traffic' rushing past, then possibly I was riddled with nihilism, and so looked out for signs of decline, rather than success. I really don't know. I just remember coming across America that first time – on that organised trip – and seeing or thinking none of these things. I was just on holiday, blown away by the brilliance of it all.

This time I was looking at things from a different angle, wondering what direction the world takes from here; worried as we all are at times about its future, yet equally being resigned to whatever does become of it, because to worry about things beyond your own control is to send yourself senseless. But with so many hours in the saddle to pass, you have to have something to think about. And these were the things I thought about.

***

As much as I was enjoying my time in Colorado Springs I knew that I had to keep moving, because to stay any longer I would have needed a real big push to get back on the road again. When you're on the road momentum keeps you going, but the moment you stop and start to feel comfortable in your environment the labours of the road suddenly don't seem so appealing. Why sit on the bike for fourteen hours a day and sleep in an undersized tent by night when you can stay here lounging on the sofa, drinking beer and watching TV? That's why I knew I needed to get going again.

To fix the faulty light we picked up a new battery from an auto parts store, it not making a blind bit of difference because in the end it turned out to be the bulb. As for the drop in performance, I'd not realised it at the time but all the way from St. Louis the road had been climbing, imperceptibly, for almost 1,000 miles, all the way from the Mississippi River, meaning that by the time I'd reached Colorado Springs I was at almost 7,000 feet. This is enough to mess up the air mixture and make a small carburettor-fed bike like this one really begin to struggle.

It was for this reason that I decided that rather than take the main tarmac roads up and over the mountains, I would take the dirt roads over the Rockies instead. Not only would this make for more enjoyment, but it would also keep me away from the traffic, which by now I was simply tired of; the traffic across Kansas particularly ferocious. It was the trucks squeezing me into the gutter that did it, making me wish at times for just a little bit more speed and engine power. I dreaded to think how the cyclists coped with it all.

Before leaving Colorado Springs I went through all of my luggage to dispose of any surplus weight. I threw out some T-shirts, pants, a few tools, reorganised my chargers and electrical equipment – this takes up much more space than you'd think – before facing a dilemma about which pair of shoes to ditch as I couldn't be bothered to carry two pairs any longer.

I'd barely worn the Converse high-tops, instead riding in the Australian workman boots almost the entire way. Sounds odd, but the boots made me feel quite manly and strong. It's what real men wear (at least that's what I told myself), whereas Converse is what the youth of today wears. And so perhaps I had to accept that this mindset didn't fit me any more. I'd grown up, moved on. And I never thought that moment would be so symbolically represented by a single pair of shoes. But whether I liked it or not, I didn't feel comfortable in Converse any more, leaving them – and my youth – beside the bin in Vermin's backyard. Perhaps in thirty years' time I'll come back for them so that I can dance the funky chicken.

Once again Phil said he was again going to ride with me, for half a day at least, but with little surprise, after no more than a few miles, just as the road started to steepen, he changed his mind and we pulled over on to a patch of gravel to say goodbye again. I didn't blame him, as travelling this slow can be quite miserable at times, especially if you're on a bike capable of going much faster. Regardless of this, he and his family had helped me no end on this journey across America. Without them I would have been lost out here and struggled to find a safe base at which to gather my breath. I hope to repay the favour some day.

***

Once more I was back alone, leaving Colorado Springs behind as the dirt trail made its way up the mountain, the Midwest fading beneath me and this new challenge ahead, of climbing mountains and finding my way down the other side.

This was a recreational road, nobody using it but those wishing to get off the beaten track in their 4x4s or off-road motorcycles. As the altitude climbed so did the fullness of the forests, currently on the cusp of switching to their autumn colours. It was all silver birch and an atmosphere of discovery, along what was known as Old Stage Road, not far from where the famous Pikes Peak hill-climb race takes place.

At various times the trail took the path of the old railway line, built up on the top of banks and bridging shallow valleys and ravines. These expanses proved a perfect place to stop and take a photo of the scenery. I barely saw another soul, only the occasional 4x4 travelling in the opposite direction; the rest of the time it was just me and a sea of a thousand trees.

Having circled around Sugarloaf Mountain and Knights Peak, the road spits you out an hour or so later at the old mining town of Victor. Victor was founded in 1891, back when this entire region was the biggest gold-mining district of the United States. The industry declined during the early years of the twentieth century, before closing completely by 1961. In recent years there have been efforts to kick-start gold mining in the area once again, with the Cripple Creek & Victor Gold Mining Company opening the Cresson mine in 1994, with its mine head visible from the town.

Victor wasn't a big place, just 440 residents, a couple of streets, a museum, a pizza diner and a police car that slowed to take a look at my number plate as I parked up in the street. If the town and the region reminded me of anything, it was the setting for the original *Rambo*, a small town with a local sheriff, and a place up in the mountains in which to hide.

Coincidently, in the pizza parlour on the main street, the toilet walls were scrawled with messages of support to, and from, American soldiers dating back as far as the Vietnam War. The owner was a tough female in the mould of Linda Hamilton from *The Terminator* movie, looking as though she might have served in the forces herself. Rambo would certainly have been welcome here.

I stayed for a pizza, before taking a quick look around the town's museum. I discovered that in 1903, Victor was home of the Colorado Labor Wars, between the Unions and the mine companies, with bullet holes still visible in the town's union hall as that's just how they seemed to settle their disputes back then. Meanwhile, in a shop window on the main street of town, two old skeletons with animal skulls for heads sat at a table in their dungarees about to eat dinner. In a way this image summed up the town perfectly; a place with plenty of character, out of kilter with the modern world perhaps, but all the better for it.

Beyond Victor lay the bigger town of Cripple Creek, which was built at 9,554 feet, and alongside Victor became a prominent hub for gold mining back in the late nineteenth century. By the 1970s and 80s the town was nearly deserted, with only a few hundred residents remaining; some running cafés and restaurants for the steady flow of tourists passing through these parts.

Then, in 1991, gambling was legalised and from that moment on everything changed. The town prospered, with casinos, diners and restaurants all opening their doors. It wasn't quite Las Vegas – not in the visual sense – but the spirit was there. It was odd and somewhat bewildering to discover this casino town in the middle of the Colorado Rockies, many of the buildings the same timber style as they would have been back when the town was established. I didn't stay long, simply riding up and down the main strip in order to take stock of it all, before making haste towards the setting sun.

At the gas station at the top end of town I chatted with three late-teens filling their truck at the pump next to mine. They were Republicans and worried about what Obama was doing to their country: robbing it of jobs, killing the economy, infringing on personal freedoms. Politically, it seems this place is explosive; a chasm between the two parties, yet both leaning further – at least to my mind – to the right than Labour or the Conservatives here in England. I would say the Democrats in America sit more atop the Conservatives than they do Labour, with the Republicans even further to the right than that.

What that means in practice is that most people are more conservative than they would be in Europe. The divide in recent years has been between those that are financially conservative, and those that are religiously conservative. Those anti-abortion banners back in Kansas, for example, were a sign of the latter. There seems to be a growing faction in the right whereby God and Christian values are increasingly overlapping with politics (despite secularism at heart of the constitution) and perhaps linking back to what was said about Manifest Destiny and the backing of God.

From what I gather this is different from how it was in the eighties, when it was more about fiscal conservatism: balancing the books, running a good business. I wondered if such religious dogma entering politics to such an extent is due once more to that concept of fear; fear that the American Dream hasn't quite materialised, resorting back to religion (a form of anti-depressant or satnav perhaps?) for some kind of comfort blanket. Perhaps it's to do with racial tension and the fear of the dilution of the racial pallet. Fear of a new hegemony. Fear that things are changing. Fear that nothing stays the same and people aren't quite ready to move on just yet.

In a strange way, I couldn't help but feel a certain empathy with America as I journeyed across it. To me it seemed to be in the same place I was after that first trip from Sydney to London. It's been on a massive journey, trying to conquer something, in a way sort of succeeding (America becoming *the* global superpower), and now not quite sure what to make of it all, with the question of what happens now, what happens next? How do we sustain this, how do we move forward? The fear of losing all momentum and sliding all the way back down to the bottom, where the black dogs roam; it now a case of picking itself up and finding a new direction and horizon to aim towards. It will perhaps just take time, and lots of self-analysis.

As for me, I just carried on riding this day. I was back on tarmac now, but this wasn't highway or those busy roads of Kansas; this was two-lane, meandering across the plains of Colorado, the biggest climbs behind me for the day. The yellow road markings down the centre of the road bringing extra colour to a world that was already vivid; mute green of the trees and the parched brown of the sunburnt grass. Then clouds, angry and vast. The sense of a storm ahead, creating an eerie mood as I rode beneath an ocean of tumultuous sky.

Then the clouds would scatter and blue sky would shine through. The world would light up. I'd sing, I'd think to myself, reflect on the past, ponder the future, still with my own questions of why am I doing this; where am I heading to; where will it end; what will it lead to?

A times, I imagined a crowd of thoughts chasing me, like monsters beneath the bed, and at the front I'm fleeing from them, like that reoccurring dream where no matter how fast you run you can't get away. Time to face, time to run. This time I felt like I was running towards something (even if I didn't necessarily know what it was), not running away from something as it had often felt on that first trip. I much preferred it this way. I certainly spent a lot less time looking over my shoulder to what I was leaving behind, focusing more instead on what lay ahead.

This night I was aiming for the town of Salida, but constant with most other best laid plans I didn't quite make it, arriving at a junction where the road I'd been travelling on rejoined Route 50, the Lonely Highway. This was the road I'd detoured from back in Pueblo, in order to go and visit Phil in Colorado Springs. To turn right now (to face west) would take me the seventy miles down into Salida, whereas turning left revealed that just along from the junction was a campsite which, for whatever reason, just seemed more appealing than another two hours on the road, especially as it would soon be nightfall.

My issue with stopping too early is knowing what to do with myself until it gets dark and I have to go to sleep. I have nothing to entertain or amuse myself whilst camping and the simple fact is that I generally find more amusement in riding, than I do in standing still. This is why I'd rather be riding until the cusp of darkness, at which point there isn't much left to do but put the tent up and go to bed. Stopping now was a touch too early, but it had been a long day, and the driveway down to the Royal View Campsite just seemed so appealing.

A sign gave instructions as to what you should do if you arrive after hours, which clearly it must have been as no one was around to check me in or take my money. The sign instructed that you take an available pitch from the slots on a board, go off and find it, then pay in the morning. The price of the pitch was $35, something I baulked at and was reluctant to pay, but I simply didn't have the heart to ride any further. It just seemed an awful lot of money to pitch a six-by-four tent for the night.

It was a decent site though, with its own picnic bench and firepit, surrounded by bushes and the branches of low lying trees. I could hear and faintly see the family on the pitch across the other side of the path. They were laughing and playing, the only sound in this still, silent valley, the air starting to cool and the orange glow of the sun slowly fading to nothing. I cooked up some instant noodles on the stove. I had some bread to dip in the juice, whilst to drink I had with me a litre of water.

Making the most of the last rays of sunlight I wrote some notes in my diary, even taking out my laptop and playing some quiet music through that. I was glad that I'd come to this early rest, sitting up well into darkness, slowly getting my things ready for bed and finally closing the zip on my tent.

The next morning I considered doing a runner to avoid the extortionate amount of money for the site. I figured that if I packed up and left early enough then no one would even know I'd been. I could get away with it and save myself some money. Annoyingly, my conscience got the better of me and wouldn't allow me to do this; it would have deemed it bad karma, and sometimes karma is all that counts on journeys such as these. I concluded instead that I would just have to pay the fee and grumble about it later.

Strangely, even at 7am there was still no one around to pay, which was frustrating as I needed to pay by card as I only had ten dollars in my wallet and, equally, I just wanted to get on the road and keep on trucking. The compromise I came to was to write a note, explaining my predicament, and putting it in an envelope, along with the last ten dollars I had (promising to send the rest by post at a later date), and sliding it under the door of reception. This, I felt, would appease my conscience and help retain some hard-fought karma. Annoyingly; five miles down the road, in the direction of Salida, I rode past a state-run campsite that I could have camped at for free. Karma.

Chapter Thirty-Seven
The Rockies

I rode down the valley towards Salida early this cold morning. The valley was cold as it hadn't received any direct sunlight yet. There was also vapour rising from the churning water of the Arkansas River as it flowed down the barrel of the valley, making this the coldest I'd been for quite some time. As a result I had everything on, even the fluorescent jacket and two pairs of gloves. The last time I was this cold on a bike was when riding into China over the Himalayas, through a wind-whipped valley, being chased by that blasted tourist bus.

Here in Colorado – some 8,000 miles of riding to the west of that border between China and Pakistan – I passed a little restaurant that had just opened for the morning. I ordered a coffee and some toast. The girl who served me was stunning; I was quite smitten, until a regular asked how she was doing at school and I felt quite repulsed with myself. This was just the state of my mind out here. Not really sure of anything any more, only that if I carried on riding west I would hit the coast eventually and hope that I was somewhere in the vicinity of San Francisco.

Beyond Salida that morning (a nice town, once prosperous through ranching, now through tourism) I turned left onto Route 285, then a little way along turned right off the tarmac and found myself at the start of another dirt trail. I had decided to take this route along the back road trails, as to take the tarmac would mean circling around many of the mountains, whereas these routes would take me right over the top of them.

At the start of this first trail was a notice board warning of bears in the area. It also said to inform someone of your intention to take this dirt trail in case anything happened to you. Good advice, but without a sim in my UK phone or anyone to call even if I had one, I skipped that part and set off into the wilderness alone.

The path was rocky and made its way through forest as it climbed over Mount Ouray, along County Road Xx32. I was nervous of this trail. It looked lonely, spearing right through the heart of the Colorado wilderness and far more isolated than the trail I took out of Colorado Springs.

I worried about bears and what to do if one suddenly jumped out of the forest. I was doubtful of being able to outrun it. After all, I only beat the wild dogs of Kyrgyzstan by the momentum of a downhill road. This trail however ran uphill, and so if it's true that bears can run at up to 40mph then I was done for. It was reassuring then to soon come across a lone cyclist heading in the same direction. He cast a lonely shadow out here, and I thought that if the bears are hungry this day then surely he will be first for dinner. I slowed to see if he was okay and ask if he needed any water. He was fine, so I carried on.

The question of what happens if you break down out here does occasionally fill your mind. If it was as simple as a puncture then I would fix it. If those spokes broke again – and I feared they might, given how rough the terrain was – I would try and fix them, as long as I had plenty of spares. If something serious happened with the engine or anything structural broke, like the frame snapped, then I suppose it would be a case of pushing out, or walking out and coming back with the cavalry. As for falling off and injuring yourself, at times like these you just make damn sure that you don't. 'Ride hard, but ride safe,' that was my motto.

The trail climbed through the sea of silver birch trees for a good hour or more. It was slow going but enjoyable, stopping every once in a while to stare out at the view; one of green carpeted hills that appeared to go on for ever and ever. To compare the empty vastness of here to the dense population of somewhere like New York or Chicago felt like going from an ant in a big nest to being the last man on earth. One country, and yet so much variety and change. This is what I did love about America; the land and the landscape. It was simply phenomenal, and the best views were still to come.

At the top of this summit I met five other motorcyclists admiring the view of the valley beyond. I was glad to see them, pulling to a frantic halt, climbing off and cheering 'hello,' to which they waved back. The men rode proper enduro bikes, with big wheels and knobbly tyres. They also wore heavy-duty motocross clothing, meaning big boots, body armour, elbow pads, full face helmets, goggles and colourful tops and trousers that belied their age, as most of them must have been in their fifties, some of them older.

They told me they were out riding for a few days, taking in the trails and generally spending a boy's weekend out on bikes. They asked about my bike, slightly puzzled as to what a foreigner on a small bike might be doing up here. I explained, them looking not quite convinced by my story, though I assured them it was true.

But would you believe it? You're at the top of the mountain in the middle of Colorado. A weird looking guy on a weird looking bike, with a weird foreign numberplate pulls up next to you, climbs off and explains that his journey began almost four years ago in Australia. That since then he'd covered almost 30,000 miles on a 105cc machine – smaller than most lawn-mowers – riding through such random places as Indonesia, East Timor, India, Nepal, Pakistan, China, Russia, Kazakhstan, and he's just ridden that same bike across America as well. I wouldn't believe him either.

Having chatted a while we agreed it was time to take the trail down the mountain. I invited them to go first as undoubtedly they would be faster than me and I would just get in the way. That was a big mistake, because as soon as they set off I took off a few minutes later in hot pursuit, determined for no real reason other than pride to try and catch them and keep up with them, despite them being on 400cc bikes and wearing all the proper protective gear. I was still in jeans and my flannel shirt, down on power, but with gravity now on my side.

I rode like an idiot that day. Flat out, both wheels skipping and drifting across the dust and gravel surface, minimal grip from my cheap road tyres, little suspension travel, all the weight of the saddle bags kicking around at the back, and my brakes not that great either. But I had venom in my eyes and it couldn't be stopped. I chased and chased, down the mountainside, the road snaking back on itself, tree lined and precarious in places, heavily stoned in others, opening out into a fast section at other times, my eyes behind those J-Lo glasses shining like emeralds. 'Slow down,' I said to myself. 'Get lost,' said the other me, intent on catching these old timers on their proper machines.

I almost did, blazing out from the end of the trail that just so happened to end right beside the gas station where the men were just about to start filling their fuel tanks. They couldn't believe it. They thought I'd be miles behind. But I was there. Dot was ticking from the flogging she'd just received and I was grateful to have made it down in one piece. It was stupid to have gotten carried away like that. But I was enjoying myself.

I ate lunch at the gas station diner with Pat and John, two other trail bike riders up on a trip from their homes in Texas. They were just deciding whether to ride the bikes back or rent a van and drive them back in that.

Good times these, I felt part of something, a real sense of camaraderie with the off-road riders of Colorado. It was certainly a beautiful place to be riding a motorcycle, with some of the riders doing what was called the Trans-America Trail. This is a completely off-road route, starting all the way back in the Appalachian Mountains and finishing 2,700 miles to the west, somewhere along the Pacific Coast. I had thought about taking this route across America myself, but figured I'd miss too much of the country's intrigue had I done so.

Obviously, there were many places I'd have to miss and skip completely. I would have loved to have gone down and seen New Orleans, having visited it before on that organised trip and enjoying the spookiness of the place. Roswell too, and Nashville, and Memphis, and it would have been good to see Santa Fe again as well. But across America you can't see everything. It would take a lifetime to do so, meaning that the line you take across it is only one representation. It does not represent the whole.

A series of off-road trails continued this day, some as many as 70 miles long, right through the heart of nothingness. It was mind-blowing really, to find yourself on a dirt trail, the satnav no good out here, the paper map (picked up from Liz back at the start of Colorado) no good either as it had long since blown away in the wind, leaving me little choice but to take a guess on a direction and hope it brought me out in the right place, based on a vague visualisation I had of the map, moments before it blew away in the wind.

Fear washed over me as I found myself on a dirt trail, no one or nothing around for miles. Then quite by chance I met a friendly lady on horseback tending the cattle on her ranch, who assured me I was travelling in the right direction.

Occasionally the dirt trail would turf me out on to tarmac for a brief while, before another back road would present itself for me to take. On one stretch of tarmac I met a man named Doug, a larger than life Brian Blessed like character on a huge intergalactic BMW who pulled over to chat as I stopped to take a photograph.

He was a businessman, philanthropist and all-round good guy, who had even heard of Dorothy having read about our adventures on the internet. I never stopped being surprised by this. For this man, a strange man, to know of me, an Englishman, here in the middle of the Colorado hills. How completely random life can sometimes be.

Doug had a seat on Dorothy and I took a photograph of the pair. He told me to drop by his place just outside of San Francisco if I was ever passing through and gave me his business card. We shook hands, his massive engine roaring into life like a giant animated thruster, and away, Brian Blessed was gone.

For the rest of the day I found myself on narrow trails running through forests and across open dusty plains. At times the trail would open up and give plenty of space in which to breathe. Other times it would negotiate around trees and drop down gullies. I stopped at one point completely perplexed by a sign at a three way junction, not sure of which avenue to take. I took a moment, relying on instinct and intuition, letting go of conscious thought and just going with it. The trail turned more beautiful from here, passing remote cattle ranches with cows penned in by rustic log fences, and then a river, along the banks of which the trail roamed.

It wasn't long before finally, after what must have been three hours of riding almost completely alone along those dirt trails, I emerged on to bitumen, coming to a halt at a junction at which I could turn left or right.

The signpost told me that to the left was Creede, while to the right I'd find the town of Lake City. By this time I'd covered a lot of ground that day and just needed somewhere to fill the gas tanks and rest my head for the night. A car came up behind me (probably one of the campers I'd spotted down by the river), turning on to the road and taking off before I'd even had time to flag it down for directions.

The next car I wasn't letting pass so easily, frantically bringing it to a halt and having it stop at the point at which dirt road joined tarmac. The occupants – an elderly couple – seemed reluctant to help at first, or even wind their window down. I was after all a scruffy-looking stranger, flagging them down in the middle of nowhere, and if that were me, I would be apprehensive as well. But I was that high from the vapours of the road that day that they soon let go of their tension and we talked for a while. Their names were Jeanie and Gerald, a couple in retirement with a little yapping dog on Jeanie's lap.

'Where do you want to go?' they asked.

'I'm not sure. Should I go left or right?'

'Well, left takes you to Creede, right takes you to Lake City.'

'I just need somewhere to sleep for the night. Which is the best place to pitch a tent?'

'There are a few spots just outside Lake City, but there's a hostel in town. Why don't you stay there?'

I thought about it.

'We know the owners, Lucky and Amy-Jo. I'm sure they'll do you a good price.'

With that I was sold on the idea, Jeanie and Gerald giving me directions to the hostel, before taking off in that direction themselves.

The road from there was downhill, beautifully surfaced with fresh tarmac, running like a serpent through a density of trees. It was like a road you might expect to find in the Alps. After around ten miles it reached the bottom of the valley, where the river ran, and there, on the brink of evening, I rode into Lake City, which wasn't a city at all, just a great little town, all made from wood, nestled deep in the mountains of Colorado.

Jeanie and Gerald were waiting for me at the old-fashioned petrol pumps on the entrance into town.

'We thought we'd treat you to dinner tonight. Go and dump your stuff at the hostel and we'll meet you back here in ten minutes time...'

And later that evening, that's what the three of us did. Another surreal encounter of the road.

Chapter Thirty-Eight
Lake City

Jeanie and Gerald lived in Florida, but every year, to escape the ferocious summer sun, they would drive up to Lake City to spend three months in a caravan beside the river. Both were retired teachers, with Jeanie liking to make a fuss and be the life and soul of the party, while Gerald preferred to take a back seat, being the quiet one, perhaps learning over the years it was the easiest route to happiness. I couldn't have met a nicer couple that evening. Outside their caravan we had pre-meal drinks of red wine, served in plastic wine glasses that were battery operated and so changed colour, from red to blue to green to yellow, and then back again.

The caravan was on a site down by the river, along with around twenty other vans, all positioned in a circle, as though they were about to ward off an Indian attack. A bridge over the river took you into the main hub of the town; a quiet, sleepy little place, popular with nature-loving tourists, the shadowy mountain peaks – skiable in winter – looming all around. It was certainly calm and peaceful, and I could see how you could spend three months of the year here and not feel restless.

We ate in a pizza parlour called Poker Alice, a wooden cabin opposite the old gas station on the way into town. The staff were predominantly from Poland, working here for the summer before travelling around for a while and then flying home, much like I'd done with Camp America. A few of Gerald and Jeanie's friends joined us, and it was a night of sharing stories, elbows resting on the red and white plastic chequered tablecloth, plastic flowers in a vase in the centre, and great pizzas all around.

I could see one of the group – an elderly married man – was quiet but curious about my travels. It made me wonder if there's a part of every man and woman that has the simple desire to take off for a while, to escape the world, to leave it all behind and be free.

The man was curious to know what that feels like. I told him that it feels good, but that you have to accept that you can never leave it all behind, not completely. You can only take a break from it, with the problems you were escaping still there when you get back, only now more stubborn than ever. The solution perhaps is to deal with them first, and then go. Though if you did that you might never go at all.

We talked about the road ahead and how I would be taking the nearby Cinnamon Pass. They laughed at this, having seen the size of my bike, and explained that it's a tough, steep route, over the top of the mountain. While I thought I could do it in a morning they thought it would take me all day, if I made it at all. I get protective of the bike at such times, insisting she can do it, will do it, even if I have to push her we're going over that pass, because to not do so would involve a long detour, and that just sounded so tedious. But still they looked dubious at my mountainous proposition.

I planned on leaving the next morning, this being 12th September and I still had some faint hope of reaching Alaska by the end of the month. But I just didn't feel like leaving. I liked it here in Lake City, so stayed another night. The hostel was simply superb. Lucky, the owner, was an Irishman, early thirties I would have said, who seven years before had been hiking the Colorado Trail when he stopped off in Lake City to find a place to sleep for the night. By chance he met resident Amy-Jo, and the rest as they say is history. Lucky quit his walking trip, moved here permanently, and now they have kids and a trio of dogs.

Lucky built the hostel himself; a simple single-storey wooden structure in the back yard of their simple single-storey wooden house. The Raven's Rest, as it was called, was such a beautiful place, with double doors leading into the kitchen and living room area. The kitchen had a huge wooden table made from reclaimed wood; the lounge had comfy sofas; and beyond that were two doors into sleeping rooms with bunk beds to sleep four in each room. It had been done with such amazing attention to detail, out of local timbers, so rustic and charming. It was perhaps the best hostel I'd ever stayed in, and I'd stayed in a quite a few.

Despite being the only guest that first night, I was joined the next night by a motley crew of individuals. The first to arrive was Snow Cat, a lady who must have been in her sixties and walking the 500-mile Colorado Trail – from Denver to Durango – all on her own.

Snow Cat was her trail name, a tradition maintained by trail walkers, and not so different to why Phil goes by the name of Vermin whenever the bike is involved. I never did catch Snow Cat's real name, just sat bewildered by how it all works: walking for three days or more through the wilderness like the one I'd passed through, having to carry all your water, food and supplies to last for that time. Then, when you arrive at the next town, you collect a parcel that you posted ahead from the last town. In that parcel might be spare food, a sewing kit, shampoo, spare shoes, anything that couldn't be carried on a day-to-day basis, but with the right amount of forward planning could be continuously posted on to your next destination.

It was an astounding system, and Snow Cat an astounding woman. A tough lady, skin like leather from the sun, a peaceful soul behind all that, and still a fiery determination to explore the world and see it from the ground up. I sat and had a coffee with her in the rustic cafe next door to the hostel, listening to the stories of her travelling and living in Europe and Australia. She had a husband who just had to wait patiently while she went off on these adventures, such as this one, through bear territory, with no weapon of defence, no nothing.

The next arrival to the hostel was the Old Minister, another walker, this one even older, in her seventies at least, walking with poles to keep her going. The Old Minister was walking even further than Snow Cat!

I couldn't fathom these women. They were unstoppable and without fear, with terrific planning and forethought put into their routes. But then also with such a faith in the world, like Snow Cat who had arrived at the end of the same trail as I had (where I met Jeanie and Gerald), before hitch-hiking the ten miles down into town with a random man that pulled over and even offered to pick her up and take her back to the start of the trail once she was done in Lake City. What a story to be told. What a legacy to be leaving.

The last arrival of my stay was a man named Craig, travelling in a Jeep with his dog, and I think just coming out here to get away from it all. He had a brother in the Marines who'd served in Iraq, and around the solid wooden table we all talked one night. Conversation grew quite heated at times, Craig defensive about America's role in the Middle East and how it was there to do good, and he wasn't having any of it when we tried to argue otherwise. Jingoism, perhaps, but I don't think he was fooling himself. He genuinely believed that America was out to do good in the world and I accepted it wasn't my place or anybody else's to try and convince him otherwise. In fact, I admired his resolute defence, because that's genuinely what he believed.

On my final evening in Lake City I was given a blue rubber wristband to wear by Jeanie and Gerald, inscribed with the motif, 'God is big enough.' The words were a representation of their faith, Jeanie telling me that even right-wing Alaskan politician Sarah Palin wears one!

The wristband wasn't really to my taste, but it was sweet in a way and I promised to wear it on the rest of my journey across America (and did wear it, though I turned the words to face my wrist). I wore it because irrespective of my lack of belief in their faith, deep down I did believe in something, something bigger than this. That's not to say I believed in organised religion as such, but I certainly believed in faith, even if it's only faith in yourself, your fellow man, and in the world around you.

During my darkest days back in England I went and sat in the church in the centre of our local town of Malton. I don't know why I felt compelled to do this. Maybe it was simply to feel the power of being in a place born out of faith. I certainly didn't go to pray, or give my life to Jesus, I just found this quiet, peaceful church, at the heart of the town's commotion, a necessary place to retreat to, and be at peace for a moment, well away from the world and the screaming nature of my mind. I didn't feel the need to go back after that, one visit was enough. I just think it's hard pretending to be strong when you're actually weak, and when I think back, that was the moment I finally started to climb, having first had to admit defeat.

***

The day of riding Cinnamon Pass was signalled by a blue sky morning. Once more I left my temporary sanctuary behind, taking with me memories of a happy time there in Lake City. Jeanie and Gerald, Lucky and Amy-Jo, Snow Cat, the Old Reverend, and Craig who I had a coffee with before both of us hit the road. We bought it from a baker's that had suffered a spate of bear attacks, bears breaking in and stealing the food. That was a daunting thought for the journey ahead, as the road was only going to get wilder from here.

It was a cold morning so I wore most of my clothing. I wore those sturdy Australian boots, blue jeans (even some thermal leggings), a good few layers of tops and a jumper, not to mention the BigZoners jacket, then over all of that the fluorescent orange Royal Mail jacket, the beige gardening gloves which by now were well bedded in, the helmet, the neckerchief around my face – the bump from the wasp sting still there – and the J-Lo glasses, now covered with scratches and the frames a little bent.

The bike was also beginning to resemble a travelling gypsy. The bulbous sleeping bag in a grey sack was strapped fiercely to the tent rack on the front. The green tent and blue roll mat were strapped to the rack on the back, while a spare tyre – purchased from a helpful bike shop on the outskirts of St. Louis (Flying Tiger) – was wedged over the top of the left pannier. The yellow bell given to me by the BigZoners back in Indonesia was still on the handlebars, while on the opposite side of the bars I had tied with a piece of string a blue plastic cup bought from a cheap Chinese store in Toronto, back at the start of the trip when I went to visit Mandy. The cup had never been used and was just there as a strange, clattering inconvenience tied around my handlebars.

What surprised me most about the trail up to Cinnamon Pass was just how precarious it was, with huge drops by the side of the track and no guard rails or warning signs. It felt like being back in India on the road through the Himalayas, where there really is nothing to stop you just going over the edge. Thankfully, in being up so early in the morning I was the only one out here, for the time being at least, with a wave of 4x4s hunting me from behind as the day progressed.

The trail soon turned to switchbacks, the severity of the turns being just enough to sap all momentum, meaning that on the approach to the corner, just as my speed was slowing, I would have to leap off the bike, push like crazy up and around the corner, then, after momentum had been regained, hop back on and gas it all the way to the next corner, where I would do it again, and again, all the way up this mountain, at least fifteen turns in total, pushing through each and every one. I was completely shattered by the time I reached the top of Cinnamon Pass, but at least we'd made it.

I stood and shared the moment with a pair of fellow motorcyclists, plus a convoy of Jeeps, the passengers of which had all climbed out to take photos of the breathtaking mountain scenery all around. One lady was originally from England and we chatted a while about her time there in the seventies, before she moved permanently to America. The lady said she barely ever went back to her English homeland, which I always found strange, or admirable, the way some people are able to abandon the past like that, and start afresh. Unless the past was really unpleasant of course, in which case I could well understand it.

I followed their Jeep down the mountainside; a brutal, slippery descent, with curling corners and oné or two buckaroo moments when the bike would try and shoot off in all manner of directions. At one point – due to my own carelessness and greed for speed – I ended up pointing back up the mountain, having completed a full 180-degree rotation, doing well not to fall off in the process. 'Slow down Nathan, slow down,' I said to myself insistently.

At the foot of this devil's tail of mountain trails were the ruins of what was once the town of Animas Forks, an old gold mining community, founded in 1877 and built at 11,600 feet. It boasted several general stores, a hotel and a saloon, but was prone to avalanches and was abandoned at the end of the nineteenth century. Since then the town has slowly been lost to nature, the timber buildings in slow decay, some of them crumbling and falling down, others almost completely intact and you able to go inside and look around, as though you are stepping right back in to the carcasses of the past.

What it must have been like to live up here. How bitterly cold in winter, how gorgeous in summer. And then when the gold was gone the community moved on, no time for sentiment or despair. I found that quite common in America; this ability to let go of the past and migrate to (hopefully) better times. Perhaps in a hundred years time people will do the same with Detroit; nothing but an abandonment along the prairie, for tourists to stop and take photographs of.

Beyond the remains of Animas Forks came the toughest task of them all. It was a steep valley, the dusty trail running right up the heart of it, culminating in what appeared at a distance to be an impenetrable slope, though I was guaranteed the trail did go up there.

After a mile or so of winding trail, it soon arced to the right before turning a sharp left on itself, the incline increasing with every metre of travel. Even down in first gear it was too much for the bike which threatened to stall at any moment; just not enough power in that little engine to sustain sufficient forward thrust, not at this altitude, with the lack of air robbing the carburettor and therefore the engine of all its power.

I dismounted and ran alongside the bike, pushing it with all my might. I made it to a corner, a tight right one, which led on to a part of the trail I knew for certain I couldn't ride up, and would even struggle to push up, especially now at over 12,000 feet. At that moment I spotted an off-road super-powered golf buggy that seemed popular in these parts. It was travelling in the same direction as me and I thought if I could ask the driver to carry my panniers and thus lighten the load, I might just be able to shove the old bike to the summit.

I watched as the vehicle came closer and closer. Perhaps it was my mistake, but I assumed it would just stop or at least acknowledge the breathless traveller at the bottom of this steep climb, alone in this wilderness, with the day fast losing light. Instead, the two occupants didn't even acknowledge me. They just drove past, and I could have killed them both right there and then had I been given the chance, such was my rage.

As it was, I filled my lungs as best I could, dug my heels into the dirt, eyed up the long steep slope leading to a corner, before another long steep slope, gunned the throttle, flat out in first, the bike barely able to haul its own weight, me leaning into the handlebars, no helmet on, every muscle straining, the mountain fighting against us, and in that moment I let out the loudest, fiercest primal scream I could muster. I was pushing that bike to the top of that mountain even if it killed me, and it almost did.

I screamed, and I screamed, and I shoved, and I shoved. My legs burnt like flames as my heels pushed against the dirt, those sturdy Australian boots being squeezed into the earth, step after step after step. It was a brutal rush to the summit, thinking that I was never going to get there.

I made it to the top and collapsed, taking an age to catch my breath. A little later I came across a couple in a 4x4 who said they'd heard screaming from over the other side of the mountain and I had to confess to it being me, and how I'd almost shouted the mountain down in my determination to get over it. As tired as I was, I wasn't going to be beaten that day, I'd come too far to allow it.

From that point on, it looked as though I was going to have to push up and over yet another mountain. Thankfully, just as I did finally hit my brick wall and concede that I might need to camp out here on the mountain overnight, a local guide on a quad bike, leading a group of two others, came down the hill towards me, telling me that if I turned around and took a right turn back at the 'junction' I'd just passed, the trail would lead me all the way down into Silverton, the town I'd planned on reaching that evening.

I followed the guide's instructions, turning around, putting my whole world into neutral and gliding down the hill into Silverton, camping that night beside the railway line on the outskirts of town, where the next morning I was told about the bear.

Chapter Thirty-Nine
Silverton

The bear had been spotted wandering the town that night, no doubt looking for an Englishman to eat. I was told about this by the staff in the Avalanche Cafe, one of them a beautiful girl named Stacey who spent the summer months living in a tent on the outskirts of town, sleeping with a gun beneath her pillow. A couple of other bikers in the cafe that morning, Bill and Graeme, suggested I try and sleep in Stacey's tent for protection next time. It would take a braver man than me to attempt such a thing.

It was certainly a nice atmosphere in the cafe that morning; Silverton itself a very friendly and inviting town, built on what was probably the only flat piece of land for miles around, the mountains rising high on either side of it. The main street was wide and lined with old-fashioned wooden buildings. You could almost imagine a time when the road was made of dirt, not tarmac, horses tethered up outside rowdy bars, and men with long moustaches and ten gallon hats. Colorado in fact still had many men with long silvery moustaches; it's what seemed to set the men apart from those found in the rest of America.

I had thought about staying at the town's hostel, arriving in the evening, and enquiring about the cost, which at around $25 wasn't so bad. For whatever reason though I just didn't feel in the mood, heading instead to the Avalanche Cafe for some supper and use of their free Wi-Fi.

As it was about to close for the evening I rode briefly out of town, beyond the fringe of the residential streets, finding the abandoned railway line and setting up the tent in the dark, careful not to draw any attention to myself. It was only the next morning, when I went back into the Avalanche Cafe for a hot cup of coffee, that Stacey told me about the bear, though around these parts it would have been a black bear rather than the more dangerous grizzly.

From Silverton it was a case of taking the road down to Durango, perhaps only forty miles from here. The road's nickname; the Million Dollar Highway, was said to have been given for one of two reasons. The first, as some claim, is because it cost a million dollars to build. The other explanation is because the views it offers whilst driving along it are said to be worth a million dollars. I preferred the latter, although it's a shame that in joining it on the outskirts of Silverton, I'd already missed the best part of it, that being the stretch of road running north, from here to the town of Ouray.

This was still a beautiful section though, and it was actually a relief to have tarmac beneath the tyres instead of more rock and dirt. That passage over the Rockies had been one hell of an adventure. I'd enjoyed it immensely and in a way was quite sad that this road down into Durango, and then west from there, would effectively signal the end of the Rockies, and the end of Colorado, as it had been my favourite part of the journey to this point. I was glad to have come this way rather dipping down beneath the Rockies, which is where that route through Sante Fe would have taken me.

Durango was also worth visiting, the town named after Durango in Mexico, which itself is named after Durango in Spain, the word Durango originating from the Basque word 'urango,' meaning 'water town.' The Million Dollar Highway indeed runs downhill in the direction of Durango, shedding almost three-thousand feet of altitude in the space of just those forty short miles.

While in town I called in at a Honda dealer to pick up a new headlight bulb and to change the oil as Dorothy had taken a battering coming over the Rockies. She was now fast approaching 90,000 kilometres, still running original engine, and generally that's unheard of for a bike of this size, especially one put through such rigorous testing. Far from being paranoid about her longevity though, as I was on that first trip, I was more of the opinion that we'll simply ride as far as we can, and if she packs up, then we'll fix her, and then ride some more. It really was that straight-forward.

West from here was now a case of following the Navajo Trail, a name that perhaps makes it sound more glamorous and triumphant than it actually is. It was just a road, running down from the remnants of the Rockies and out across the sandy floor of the encroaching desert. Ahead lay Utah and Nevada; Las Vegas not much more than 500 miles away, the Grand Canyon a few hundred less than that. I'd been to some of those places before on that organised trip I took after summer camp. I remembered them well and was really looking forward to seeing them again.

I also realised that by taking this route I would soon pass right by Mesa Verde National Park, a place that Elizabeth, back in the tourist information centre in Colorado, had told me about, insisting that I go and see it if I got the chance. These are a series of cave dwellings built into thin lips of rock and said to have been abandoned by the Ancestral Puebloan Indians that lived there way back in 1300AD.

Having been discovered, photographed and explored in the late nineteenth century, the cave dwellings were slowly vandalised and stripped bare of much that made them fascinating – walls being torn down to let in more light, beams of roofing timber burnt as fire wood, floors dug and graves disturbed. It was only in 1906, when Theodore Roosevelt declared Mesa Verde a US National Park, that it was finally preserved in its current state.

Some assume that the Ancient Pueblo Indians were primitive, but even back then they were building homes out of rock, using a form of cement. The homes were built to a blueprint, as much as they could be, given that they had to embrace the contours of the cliff walls. It's been suggested that the indigenous people of America, before the Europeans arrived, were quite advanced, culturally, socially and mechanically, but that a great plague decreased their numbers to such an extent that the arrival and subsequent expansion west of the early European settlers was met with such modest resistance. We'll never know.

Having left the main road and entered the park via a steep twisting road, I took a walk around the ruins of Mesa Verde, climbing a ladder down into a circular pit, once used as a larder with the air much cooler than it was up above. From the cliff top I then made a photograph of the eagle that hovered overhead. It was such a hot day, the eagle easy to spot against the cloudless blue sky. I didn't linger long however, soon running out of excuses for not being on the road, returning to the bike and riding away from the cliff tops of Mesa Verde.

I didn't get very far however, as I simply couldn't be bothered. I was hot, sweaty, tired and content to instead simply pull into the campsite at the base of the National Park and pay too much to pitch the tent for the night. It was expensive but I'm glad I paid it, as the following morning I woke to find my tent surrounded by wild deer, tame enough to allow me to take their photograph as they meandered past and into the trees beyond. The simple joy of nature passing.

Later, in the next town of Cortez (the last in Colorado), I met a bus load of Australian tourists on a guided tour of the region, a few from the group spotting the Aussie post bike and coming over to have a chat.

I liked other tourists. It created a sense of community and camaraderie. After all, we were all out of our comfort zones, even if they got to sit on air-conditioned buses, while I sat on a well worn saddle. We chatted a while before they marched inside to stock up on maps and leaflets about all the things they intended to see whilst they were here, leaving me to push west alone.

***

From Cortez I travelling briefly along Route 441, in the direction of the town's airport, before taking a turn on to County Road G. This was a back road, and a route that sadly would bypass Four Corners (the point at which the states of New Mexico, Colorado, Utah and Arizona meet), something I wasn't aware of at the time, realising only once it was too late and I'd ridden well past it. Again, on a journey across America, you can't possibly see everything.

What I saw instead was a very strange road. It ran at times through isolated countryside, road signs along it shot through with bullets, the verge littered with the endless remains of beer bottles – some smashed, some intact – shards of glass twinkling in the sunlight. So too were there empty cardboard boxes of beer, cans of lager, bottles of rum and whiskey. It seemed like someone had been having a party the entire length of the road, for mile after mile, leaving a trail of destruction, as well as an air of intimidation for people such as me who wondered what vermin lived around these parts. I wouldn't want to have ridden this road at night, when the bottles are being tossed, and the signposts being shot at.

I later learned that the road was used by local native Americans who aren't permitted to drink alcohol on their reservations, and so drive into Cortez to pick up beer, and drink it on the way back, tossing the bottles into the scrub so as not to incriminate themselves when they return to their reservation. I wish I'd have known this at time, as that explanation didn't intimidate me as much as others might have done, because they had vague justification, or you could at least trace back the mental process, whereas if it had just been hillbillies, with no real reason, then that would have been more intimidating.

More attractive were the wild horses that roamed these parts. I came across a gathering of them on the road, half a dozen in total; some black, some grey, some white, some brown. They didn't shift as I approached, simply staying put in the road, staring at me as I passed, chewing on grass. I'm sure they said 'hello,' and I said 'hello' back. Because it was just me and the horses out here, and the broken beer bottles, twinkling in the grass.

Beyond this lay the small town of Bluff, just over the border in Utah. The town was overlooked by a fabulous rock formation; layers of sandy rock, almost like a flaky pastry, with huge chunks of beef – or rocks – sat on top. I parked up and stared at it for a while. It was so beautiful and elegant, carved over how many millions of years by the hands of nature, and now with a cafe built at the foot of it, popular it seemed with those on Harley Davidsons who roamed these parts, like two-wheeled flocks of those wild horses.

This makes them sound like a band of outlaws, when in fact, most were German and French tourists on rented bikes out of Vegas or LA. It was always amusing to park next to them, and watch them as they looked down on me, and in return, if that was the case, I would look down on them.

Some of them were alright though. They were doing nothing more harmful than living their dreams, most of them in their forties and fifties, having bought all the Harley Davidson attire, riding recklessly without helmets and in just shirt sleeves. They'd perhaps seen it in the movies and longed for a similar experience all their lives, and now here they were, doing their thing, on these massive motorcycles that were twice the size of mine. Maybe I was jealous and secretly hoped one was going to ask me if I wanted to swap, and deep down I probably would have done so, had I not felt so indebted to my little red machine.

I sat and drank a coffee and ate some deep fried doughnut bread on the veranda of the cafe, watching the bikers and the motorhome drivers come and go, those big lumps of rock towering above us, casting shadows on us like ants scurrying about below. I think finally I felt sure-footed of my position, and of my intention. I drank my coffee as cool as I could, before paying the bill, returning to my bike, and roaring off at a GPS-verified 37mph with the target helmet and my gardening gloves on. What a seriously weird guy I must have looked that day.

Beyond Bluff I turned off the main highway and into the Valley of the Gods, a circular loop of dirt road, approximately seventeen miles in length, taking you right through the heart of the Utah landscape. Regular cars can drive along it, but it's sandy, and in places the trail dips down into dried-up riverbeds requiring a careful bit of acceleration to climb out the other side. There were a few cars on the trail this day, but for the rest of the time, I was completely alone in this blazing-saddle landscape, the desert floor before me dotted with plants and scrub, rock towers rising from the earth, and beyond that a wall of vast stone formations, having you wonder just where the road is going to take you.

The Valley of the Gods finally spits you out at the foot of the Moki Dugway; a series of switchbacks cut into what looks to be an almost vertical wall of rock, the road climbing 1,100 feet in less than three miles. It was built in 1958 by Texas Zinc, a mining company, to transport uranium ore from the 'Happy Jack' mine in Fry Canyon, Utah, to the processing mill in Mexican Hat, just south of here. It was certainly a stunning piece of road, the pictures not doing justice to how fierce the battle must have been between the mountainside and the workmen that built it.

When you stop at the top and look back out across the flat plain beneath you, it gives the impression of riding a massive rock wave, about to tear across the landscape and swamp it like a giant tsunami.

I imagined everyone I met on my travels standing up here with me; Joe from the bike shop, Denise and her fairies from Mount Isa, Rita from East Timor, the cyclists from Germany, BigZoners from Indonesia, Tobias and Manus, the backpackers I hung out with in Bangkok, the people of India I met, those travellers in the Internet Guesthouse in Lahore, Daniel Sprague, Michel on his BMW, Andrew and Amelia in their Land Rover Discovery. Abdul the Chinese guide, Claudia and Andreas who I rode with across Kazakhstan, Bartek the Polish mechanic who tuned the engine on the last stretch. Then everyone so far from America: John, Vermin, his family, Jeanie and Gerald, Stacey from Silverton with her gun under her pillow. All of us stood at the top of Moki Dugway this day, all staring out; a journey of so many different faces, very few of which I'll ever see again (Sonder).

For now, I was riding along the road on which Forrest Gump famously stops running, uttering the words as he does so; 'You've got to put the past behind you before you can move on.' If I'm honest, the landscape in real life doesn't quite match the drama as it appears on the screen, but the feeling of being here, at another one of those iconic Hollywood sights, is electrifying and utterly surreal, as though you can't possibly be there. I'm dreaming it.

It was here, having stopped to take a photograph, that I met a motorcycle tour guide from England who explained the mystery of the broken bottles by the roadside back near Cortez. He was on a Harley Davidson, leading a tour group of fellow Brits with his wife. Not a bad place to call your office.

For me, the excitement came in knowing that Monument Valley lay just beyond the horizon. For whatever reason this location had represented something of a milestone on this journey, the one place I needed to reach, and see again, having visited it on that first trip across America and fallen in love with the place.

You might recognise it from a thousand western movies, the towering pillars of rock rising from the earth, as a cowboy rides past on his horse, in pursuit, or being pursued, by Indians.

It had changed little when I finally landed there. The road to the visitor centre was now tarmac, not dirt. The car park was much bigger, and the viewing area now a tarmac floor. The building housing the cafe and gift store had been rebuilt and redesigned, removing some of the rustic charm of the place. But the view was still the same; the famous Three Mittens, like giant rock hands pointing upwards from the ground.

I sat there for a while, enjoying the view and the sudden moment of calm that had flooded over me; Dorothy parked behind, on the kerbside, caked in the dirt of almost four thousand miles of riding, still with all my gear dangling off the back like she was the transport of an old rag-and-bone man. I spoke with several people who came asking about the bike and the UK plate. This gave me two emotions. The first was one of gratitude, that I was seeing this on my own schedule, riding my own bike, no one telling me what to do or where to be (the people I spoke to on the other hand all had jobs to get back to, or rental cars to return, or hotel reservations that night that meant they had to move on).

The second emotion was envy; that they had other people with them to share this moment with. To look across to the wife and point and say, 'Look at that.' Whereas Dorothy just wasn't interested, and so I sat on my own and stared out at the scenery for what seemed like an eternity, a mind of racing thoughts and distant dreaming.

With no particular place to stay this night I sauntered back down the five-mile access road, realising there to be a holiday resort named Goulding's, with a hotel, campsite, shop and swimming pool, just over the other side of the main road. I inquired about the price to pitch a tent and paid the $25 begrudgingly.

I was glad I made that decision, as the campsite was pleasant, surrounded as it was by red cliffs, the site full of travellers, those next to me on an organised walking tour for French people, run by French people.

Having put my tent up and unloaded my things I spoke with the French lady left behind after all the others had suddenly disappeared.

'Where have they gone?' I asked.

'They've gone to watch the sunset over Monument Valley, aren't you going?'

'When is it?'

'In about fifteen minutes' time.'

I looked at Dorothy, now lightened of her load. I considered the five or so miles it was back down to the visitor centre and the plateau looking out across the Three Mittens. And in that moment my eyes lit with flames at the thought of a race against the sun. I jumped on the bike, just my jeans, T-shirt, like Maverick in *Top Gun*, chasing after Kelly McGillis, but with a helmet on, blasting out of the campsite and roaring off along the road towards the sunset splendour.

Forty-five miles per hour (flat out) never felt so fast, the remnants of the sun glaring over my shoulder, stabbing me with its final shards of light, threatening to dip beneath the horizon before I made it there in time. The lady on the toll booth recognised me from earlier and let me through, roaring away and screeching to a halt in the car park, racing to the edge and looking out just in time to see the final shafts of natural daylight slither down the Mittens and creep along the ground, until all that was left was dusk.

I rode down the tourist trail to take a picture, before returning to the top and making the most of this evening, sat on a rock, still at peace with the world, then finally riding back to the campsite, crawling into my tent, and going to sleep, beneath a blanket of warm content.

I woke the next morning to see the sun rise above the red scorched land. This was what travelling was all about. These moments. These memories. You have to fight hard for them. They don't come easy. They don't last long. But when they happen, everything you've gone through suddenly all seems worthwhile. I treasured this day, and just wish you could have been there.

Chapter Forty
Zion

That morning I passed through Kayenta, the largest Navajo town in the area. It looked and felt just like any other town; it even had a McDonald's at which I stopped for breakfast. A cheerful Indian man named George approached me as I parked. He was wearing a wide-brimmed cowboy hat and clothes he'd probably slept in the night before. We chatted a while before he asked if I had any spare change so that he could buy himself a coffee. I handed him all the coins in my pocket, which must have totalled $5 or more. George thanked me, walked straight past the entrance of McDonald's and off into the distance, possibly to buy bottles that would soon end up smashed by the side of the road.

On journeys such as these you do get used to being approached by beggars and homeless people, especially in India and Nepal where in the cities there can be so many. I'll always remember from the streets of Delhi one young boy who approached me whilst clutching his head, stemming the flow of blood from a nasty open wound right on his scalp. He was crying violently, tears running down his filthy face, all the while holding out the other hand motioning for money. You hear stories of how a boy like this might cut themselves deliberately, in order to elicit more sympathy, but this was just horrific, and you stand there not knowing what to do, because half of you wants to help the kid, and the other half is just repulsed and wants to tell them to go away and bother someone else. It's a horrible internal contradiction.

The Navajo have also encountered bloodshed over the years. In the nineteenth century this entire western flank of America was home to a wide variety of tribes all in competition for supremacy. Along with the Navajo, there were the Comanche, the Apache, the Mexicans, the Spanish and after 1846, the new white tribe of settlers joining the melee as well. A power struggle took place. Groups would go on raids, steal horses and take prisoners as slaves. Power rose to the top.

The Navajo were said to have been without strong leadership and a united government and so lost out to other tribes. They also caused trouble for themselves, rustling cattle and not obeying the laws of the land. The dominant white settlers grew tired of this disobedience, and so at gunpoint in 1864 forced between 8,000 to 9,000 Navajo to walk 450 miles from their homeland in Arizona to Fort Sumner in the Bosque Redondo area of New Mexico, two hundred of them dying along the way. They were forced to live in camps, with the ordeal later described as the Long Walk of the Navajo.

Two years later, with a change of heart, or recognition of failure, the US government disbanded the camp and relocated the Navajo back to their homeland here in Arizona, a vast area, much bigger than I'd imagined, spanning around 27,000 square miles, covering parts of Colorado, Utah, Mexico and Arizona. The Navajo Nation now has its own laws, its own courts, police departments, hospitals, schools and, unlike the rest of America, free health care for all. The rate of tax is also very low; there is no property tax, and while voting for their own government, they also get to vote in the national elections as well. Almost like a country within a country.

For a long time the Navajo Nation – unlike other tribes – rejected a vote to allow gambling, which would have led to casinos being built. There were concerns over the effect it would have had on the Navajo people who, for a long time, had been against the principles of gambling. But power, money, and the need for financial survival finally changed their minds, with the decision being revoked in recent years and the casinos being built. From tribal Indians to members of a modern economy, new-found followers of the American Dream.

Compare and contrast with the native Aboriginals of Australia, who seem to have no purpose or place in Australian society at all. They are completely on the fringe, isolated and treated with indignation by so many they now share their country with. They exist almost as ghosts in a society that doesn't really want them there. They have no casinos, no forward thrust or seemingly any purpose in life. Instead they are static, arguably decaying, memories of the Stolen Generations still lingering above them (when babies were removed from Aboriginal parents and relocated to white families in the city).

And then the Indonesian BigZoners I met on my first trip in Sumatra, seemingly desperate to have the same trappings as the western nations, keen for their own country to emulate ours, at least in terms of economic success. I'm not sure what all this means; perhaps just that there are those who have and those who have not, and those who want and those who are able to get. Ultimately it would seem however that all people are the same the world over; they just want to be prosperous; whichever way they choose to personally measure that prosperity. But always, it seems, such things must start with a clearly defined purpose and direction. Without it, all of us seemingly are lost.

The path now lead in the direction of Zion, a national park some 216 miles to the north-west of Kayenta. Zion wasn't on my way to San Francisco – it would take a long detour of at least two days to get there – but I felt I had to go because, on that previous occasion crossing America on the organised tour, we came to Zion to climb a trail called Angels Landing and, at the time, due to my fear of heights, I dared not even attempt it. I wouldn't say it haunted me, but it was just one of those moments in life when you're disappointed with yourself, and wish you could do things better. I felt that now, with the wind in my sails, it was time to try and rectify that.

Twenty miles out of Kayenta I turned right on to Route 98, heading in the direction of Page. It was a world of clouds out here. It's amazing just how fascinated you can be by nothingness. I never grew tired of it, or wished for more attractions to stop and see, the sensation perhaps born out of that desire we all have at times to feel like we've disappeared off the face of the planet for a while. After all, no one knew I was here, only the occasional blur of traffic as it passed me by, but they wouldn't have cared. They would have been too lost in their own worlds to notice.

What I like most about such occasions, lost out here as I was, is that you can just explode, with no containment or walls to hold you back, especially across America where there are no borders to slow you down. Ride as hard as you want. Ride as long as you want. Ride until that fire in your heart has simmered for a while. Back in the real world there are so many parameters preventing us from unleashing all this anger and energy, making us bottle things up until they fester. But out here there is the space and opportunity to release it all. To scream as loud as you want. To be who you really are.

In the distance you begin to notice the chimney stacks of the Navajo Generating Station, a coal-fired plant, supplying power to California, Arizona and Nevada. It's an ugly thing; three chimney stacks puffing clouds of smoke, or steam, high into the sky. It sits incongruous with the surroundings of vast desert expanse; a carbuncle on the land. Lake Powell sits behind it; a man-made reservoir created by the flooding of Glen Canyon and the building of the Glen Canyon Dam, the work beginning in 1956, completed seven years later having claimed 18 lives in the process.

The man who commissioned the dam, Floyd Dominy, said at the time: 'Now I admit that nature can't improve upon man. We're probably the supreme being.' And you could forgive Floyd his arrogance when you stand up on that bridge and look out across this endless sprawl of water, 560 feet deep in places, 186 miles in length, 5,370,000 cubic yards of water when full, and all of that held back by a sixty-year-old concrete wall built by the fallible mind of man. It was certainly an amazing spectacle, and Lake Powell an amazing sight, serving as a vast oasis in the desert.

In Page – the town built on its shores – I noticed a bolt was missing from the bike's cam-chain tensioner screw, having adjusted it a few days earlier and forgotten to re-tighten the locking nut. It wasn't a disaster, just hinting at the general abuse and wear and tear she was receiving. The red dust and dirt of Colorado was still caked upon her. Her chain was dry and stiff after I lost the can of chain lube coming over Cinnamon Pass. I needed to buy some replacement, dabbing the chain with engine oil in the meantime to keep it moist. The spokes in the rear wheel also required regular attention, at least three times a day, feeling for the loose ones and tightening them up with an adjustable spanner I kept in the tank bag. I still changed the oil as often as I needed to, but the engine wasn't running that great; she was just beginning to feel her age.

I was battered as well: tired, dirty, a little sunburnt and not so well nourished, not from my diet of coffee and 99 cent burgers from McDonald's. If anything I'd lost weight, not gained it. Eating, or sleeping for that matter, just doesn't seem so important when you're on the road, not until you look in the mirror and see the state of yourself.

For the rest of the day I simply meandered along the road between Page and Zion, passing through the town of Kanab, where a man I met outside a gas station gave me a decent map of the area, as he worked for the land agency and had a box full of them. On the way through to Kanab I crossed the state border line from Nevada into Utah, pulling over to take a picture of the sign; brightly coloured – orange and blue – with an illustration of Lake Powell in the background and the words 'Life Elevated' written at the front.

If you ever get the chance to travel this part of America, be it in a rental car, a motorhome, a motorbike, or even on a pushbike, then you really must come and see it. If there's a group of you it's not even that expensive, especially in a motorhome, staying on campsites and cooking in the van. A manageable road trip for anybody, and you'll never stop being enchanted by the desert.

I arrived on the outskirts of Zion National Park just as daylight began leaving the sky, finding a campsite half an hour's ride from the centre of the park, before you begin the descent into it. Across from the campsite was a souvenir shop and cafe, where I bought a few slices of cheap left over pizza and talked to a young girl in the shop about her dreams of taking off and travelling; to London, to Australia, to anywhere but her home of Zion National Park. You could see she'd got that bug, that desire to go, even if she didn't at the moment have the time or the money to do so. But she would find it someday, and no doubt finally come back to Zion, with many stories to tell.

I also met a group of Christian tourists, of senior age and travelling by minibus, keen to hear where I'd come from and pose for a group photograph. I showed them my Sarah Palin bracelet, which they applauded, before wishing me well and heading off in the direction of their hotel somewhere, while I bunked down in my $18 tent that was still doing me proud; a real life home from home.

The following morning I made my descent into Zion, entering via a long winding road cut through the heart of soft-red sandstone. It was a different world to any I'd passed through until this point. The colours were mute and pastel, the rock faces smooth and less violent than anywhere else. Tufts of grass and shoots of trees grew out from the rock in haphazard style. The road was a burgundy red, swooping along the shallow valley, a yellow centre line dividing the lines of traffic passing through the park on that busy day, throngs of tourists in rental cars heading in the same direction. I met a German couple just married in Vegas, and honeymooning in Zion. We were all in the midst of new adventures that day.

The road passed through a long black tunnel, too dark for my headlight, forcing me to hang off the bumper of the car in front, using its headlights to see the road ahead. Then suddenly, from darkness into bright light, the tunnel spits you out into the Zion Canyon. You appear to be halfway from the bottom (and halfway from the top), riding along a ridge, looking out over a paradise that is beneath, above and all around you. It is a startling realisation of scale, as you feel so tiny. Zion Canyon is fifteen miles long and half a mile deep. And I am just a speck.

The first human settlements here date back 8,000 years, to a small family group of semi-nomadic Native Americans known as Basketmaker Anasazi. The Parowan Fremont followed, then the Parrusits, and finally, in 1858, came the Mormons. The park was originally named Mukuntuweap National Monument in 1909, then renamed in 1918 as Zion, as it was thought a more appealing name to those who may wish to visit; Zion often used as a synonym for Jerusalem.

Down at the bottom of the valley, right in the heart of Zion, lies the small town of Springdale, not to mention the visitor centre and state-operated campsite, where a pitch cost $16, regardless of whether you're on a 105cc motorbike or in an eight-berth motorhome. A warden patrols in a golf buggy, making sure people have paid, and that they obey the one way system that wraps itself around this cluster of trees.

Like all the other National Parks that I would visit, Zion is incredibly well organised and preserved. Vehicles are only allowed along the main route. To get to the start of trails you must use the scheduled shuttle bus service, running at regular intervals, each bus at this time of year loaded with eager hikers and walkers, keen to get out and meander through the valley, which is like no other valley I've seen before. To have stumbled upon it, back when this land was first being discovered, must have taken breaths away, and left those people speechless, just as it continues to do to this day.

I set up camp, and unloaded most of my gear into the tent, including the panniers and everything else strapped to the bike. I never worry about things being stolen. It doesn't pay to. I put on a pair of shorts, T-shirt, and those sturdy boots I'd now been wearing all the way from New York. I filled one of the red water bottles that had been holstered in racks on Dot's frame, and secured it to my belt buckle. To cover my head from the sun I wore the One Ten Motorcycles cap given to me by Joe, back when I saw him in Australia last.

After catching the shuttle bus and hiking a mile or so up the valley, I reached a section called Walter's Wiggles, a series of man-made switchbacks stacked right on top of one another, elevating you a good ten floors or so in the space of only a few minutes. With every step taken I could almost hear the beat of a ceremonial drum, like the one in old movies when colonialists are about to be burned alive over a wild tribe's fire. I was nervous and scared; I didn't really want to do it, but knew that I couldn't chicken out either. It was simply the altitude I was scared of, having never been very good with heights. Then, with a few more steps, you emerge, on a ridge overlooking the canyon of Zion.

The canyon trails off to the left and to the right, but strutting out across the canyon floor right in front of you is the towering rocky ridge that is Angels Landing. A half mile trail, running across the top of this razor's edge, leads to a point at which all you can do is turn around and walk back again, because to take another step would lead you off the end. It is then like a pier into the sea, but one that runs out into a valley rather than a sea; the challenge being to walk to the far end of it, before turning around and coming back again.

The ridge is 1,488 feet high, with chain rails to hold on to. A warning signs states the number of people to have died on the ridge, with six in the last eight years. I doubt this route would be allowed in England. It would be fenced off completely or regulated by the State. I like how in America responsibility is still left in the hands of the individual. It is your life, to do with as you wish (which perhaps explains why so many are against universal healthcare, as self-determinism is valued highly here in America). The only advice is that you wear appropriate footwear and don't tackle it in bad weather. But if you slip, fall and die, then that's your choice to walk out on the ledge that day; don't blame anyone else.

The last time I was here I didn't get much further than this. While most of the others in the group went off and tackled Angels Landing, I waited for them at the bottom. Now I was here to attempt it again, twelve extra years of knowledge, wisdom and experience with which to propel myself. In a weird way, I perhaps saw this as an opportunity to quantify just how far I'd come in life. A measure of my advance. In reality, I was petrified.

Stepping out, I grabbed hold of the chain and began to scramble. I leaned into the rock, almost embracing it, as over my shoulder the ground gradually gave way to a very long drop, with an even steeper drop on the other side, almost as though you're walking along the blade of a knife, or as it looks in the pictures afterwards, the trunk of an elephant. It was no use though. I'm not brave enough for this, coming to a frozen halt at the point at which the first set of hand-chain ends and there's a small ledge to rest upon.

Other hikers passed me by. Some were completely unfazed by the trail ahead; they walked it as though it was the pavement on the way to the shops. Others battled their demons; one man equally as terrified as I was, resting at the same spot and gently coaxing himself to go on. He didn't want to, but needed to, if only for himself. And I can well understand the awkwardness of that.

A girl by the name of Lisa passed by with her friend. She too was nervous. We chatted for a while. Lisa lived in Seattle, but for the last ten days had been travelling across America on her own, living in the back of her pickup truck with a canopy on the back, the simple task of getting away from the world for a while. She was slim and pretty, with dark brown hair and a smile that made you smile. Her friend Sam had flown down to Las Vegas and for the next few days they were exploring Zion together. I admired Lisa's spirit; she had plenty of it, and having composed herself, she took off up the trail, leaving me to watch in awe.

The man I'd talked to on his way up now came back down. He looked pale and troubled. 'Not today,' he said on the way past, explaining briefly how he'd reached the middle plateau – a third of the way along the trail – but couldn't go any further, as the path gets much narrower from there to the end. He was disappointed with himself, though he shouldn't have been as he'd done all right. I on the other hand couldn't go any further. It was that hypnotic urge to leap off the edge that was doing it for me.

I think when you've had death on your mind, as I had done for a while, you can't help but see that cliff as a shortcut to the end. And from that comes the fear that part of you is still in desire of it. To have that part of you that just wants to throw your whole body off feels like a relentless internal battle to stop yourself from doing such a thing. I wondered if it's perhaps because it represents an opportunity to skip all that fear of failure and endless worry that you hope won't dominate the rest of your life.

A shortcut to your own final solution perhaps, which sounds macabre, but I think when you find yourself with no meaning or purpose in life – and you don't know how to do anything about that – then what is the point? To prolong it? To endure it some more? Or to just be done with it, because your fear is that things are never going to change, because you are not going to change, so why would you want to live a life of that? Thankfully I wasn't at that point anymore, though I still don't think I would have had the bravery to take that final step. A coward caught in the middle, trying to take a step back from the edge.

I scaled the chains back down to safety, disappointed with myself. I'd only made it a few more paces than the first time. I sat on a rock and fed the chipmunks with the scraps of food that I carried. Time passed by in the shade. I listened to my thoughts and to my feelings. They didn't betray me this day; they weren't defeated just yet. If they had been then I'd be back down that trail already, heading back to camp. Instead I just sat there on the shaded rock, churning, letting the water slowly simmer until it reached boiling point, causing me to force my legs into the ground and stand up; bracing my arms against the bars and taking steps back in the direction of the start of Angels Landing.

I scrambled back up the chains to the point at which I was previously at. I looked once more at the reality of my situation – a long way from the earth – then down at my feet, and for once I put faith in them, staring at my boots, grabbing hold of the chain, and ignoring the sliver of rock and the vertical slope on either side. I took strong short steps, staring at my feet, clinging to the chain, trying to shut everything down but my feet. Trust them. 'Believe in your feet.'

I don't think I've ever walked with such fire burning through my legs; strong and firm, clinging on with my left hand as I traversed the slope, the ground rolling away to my right. 'Don't look down, don't look down. It doesn't exist. It's just a path. There is no drop. Trust your feet, they won't let you fall.'

I arrived at a point around halfway up the elephant's trunk; the ground now flat and stable here. I assumed this was the same place the other man had reached. I looked up at the trail as it continued along and above the precipice, perhaps another quarter of a mile to go before the end point. For whatever reason – perhaps the fear of carrying on, or the satisfaction of getting this far – I felt contentment in how far I'd come and didn't feel any urge to go any further. I'd beaten my demon that day. Perhaps I'd beaten myself, and if anything it just reminded me that when faced with hurdles you don't think you can tackle, sometimes it's just a case of taking that first step. And from there, come the rest.

Chapter Forty-One
Grand Canyon

The next morning I headed out of Zion in the rain. I was aiming for Las Vegas, detouring via the Grand Canyon and hoping to be in the Sin City the following evening, just in time to hit the strip and gamble everything I owned on red, which I suppose I already had. For a short distance this day I would have to retrace my steps, back to the town of Kanab; then on from there, past the entrance to the north rim of the Grand Canyon, then all the way around its eastern edge until I was able to turn back west in order to stop off at the southern rim of the park.

The north rim is said to be much quieter than the south, but for me, in leaving Zion that morning, the southern rim represented the perfect riding distance that day of around 250 miles. In fact, this turned out to be one of my favourite days on the road. There was one stretch, between Kanab and Jacob Lake, where the road meandered through a vast open valley, a river running along the bottom of it, strong iron bridges built across it, and Navajo people selling their wares on the other side.

At times such as these I would just cruise on through, my hand lightly on the throttle, maintaining that constant speed of 37mph, doing my best to take it all in, feeling the warm breeze on my face, looking up at the sun and across at the other vehicles that trickled past me throughout the day. I passed isolated farms, stopped at lonely outposts for gas, and met other travellers, most of whom had hired motorhomes and were doing it as a couple, or with their kids.

Later that day my mood changed and I started to feel quite lonely. This can happen at times and there isn't that much you can do about it, only hope that it will soon pass. I think it's the realisation that you're out here on your own, the mind suddenly skipping from seeing that as a good thing, to seeing it as a bad thing, because what if something goes wrong or you suddenly lost the ability to live like this? What happens then? How do you find your way out? Just keep on riding; that seems to be the only answer, much like life itself.

Finally, I turned off the main highway and along the fifty-mile access road that would lead me to the edge of the Grand Canyon. The first time you see the canyon you can't believe it's real, because it's on a scale that can't possibly be real. Not only is it deep, but it's also massively wide, and your expectation is of vertical walls, with a flat bottom. But it's not like that at all; instead there are fingers of outcrops dancing out into the canyon with the chaos of lightening strikes. Ridges of rock and dirt zigzag towards you, the other side of the canyon ten miles away, with that space in between filled with crevices and cracks, long plateaus and the Colorado River raging at the bottom. It is impossible to take in the complexities of what you're looking at.

We'd passed through this way on that organised trip, doing a day-long hike down to the mid-way point, arriving at the end of the Plateau Point Trail; an outcrop of earth that seems to have you hovering right in the heart of the canyon, it still another day's hike all the way down to the bottom. I wouldn't be doing any hiking this time, just passing through, with the plan being to spend the night at the Grand Canyon campsite and continue on the next morning. Money and momentum were both urging me along.

I stopped at several more lookout points along the roadside; parking up and wandering over to the railings, to lean against and look out at this big scar in the earth, bathed in tranquil fading light as it now was. I tried to photograph the spectacle but didn't get very good results. I think even my camera was overwhelmed by it all.

From there, the road leads to the main visitor centre. A short distance from this visitor centre I came across a lone female rider standing beside her motorcycle in a pull-in on the left hand side of the road. She looked out of place, there on her own, and so I stopped to see if she was all right and needed any help.

It turned out that Naomi was waiting for a friend; the two of them from Los Angeles and soon to make their way back there having spent the past ten weeks covering 12,000 miles on a tour of the southern states of America. She rode a Moto Guzzi, an unusual choice in a way, being a slightly temperamental brand of Italian motorcycle. It may or may not be relevant, but she was of African American descent, and female, unique amongst the other riders I'd met so far.

Naomi explained how the previous night she and her friend had ridden into the Grand Canyon National Park in the midst of a rain storm, her friend reaching the gate house at the entrance and deciding she'd just had enough, parking up her bike and sleeping in the gutter, beneath the canopy of the gate house, much to the annoyance of the gate house staff. Naomi rode on the extra twenty miles or so until she was at the hotel she'd pre-booked for the night. Having chatted a while, Naomi said that if I was ever to make it to LA then I was to give her a call and I could hang out with her for a while, her apartment overlooking the Hollywood sign.

At this stage I wasn't sure if I was going to pass through LA or not. I had thought about it, but hadn't yet decided. I was waiting for an email from a man who lived near LA, who was storing a motorcycle that I was keen to go and see, and if I was able to go and see it, then I was going to detour that way. It's a strange story really, one that captures the bittersweet nature of life perhaps more than any other;

Some eight months prior, when I was dealing with my own demons back in England, I received an email out of the blue from a gentleman in America who had a friend with terminal cancer. His friend's name was Mike. One of Mike's wishes before he died was to ride from his home in Louisiana – not far from New Orleans – down to Florida, and also across to California to visit his dad.

At the time, Mike didn't own a motorbike to do the trip on, and couldn't afford one either because of his illness. To rectify this, Mike's friend – the one who had emailed me – posted on ADVRider.com (the same site that had helped me many times already), wondering if people would be willing to have a whip around to raise enough money to buy Mike a bike for him to do his final journey on. The donations came flooding in.

With the money raised a bike was bought; a second-hand Honda cruiser, styled like a Harley Davidson. Mike was still weak from the chemotherapy and so was only able to muster ten minutes a day on it, hoping to build up his strength in order to embark on these trips he had planned. Sadly, Mike died before he ever got to go on them, and so this bike, bought for Mike's adventure, had no one to ride it.

The email I received was an invitation to come and do just that; take Mike's bike on an adventure, something I felt incredibly privileged to be offered. Sadly, at the time, I was still in the midst of my own battle, and didn't feel I could do it justice, so had to let them down, though it was a very hard decision to make. The bike had since been sent to another friend's house in LA and kept in storage there. I thought now, if I was passing through, then I would like to go and see Mike's bike and pay my respects to it. I was just waiting to hear if it was going to be convenient for me to stop by on my way through or not.

***

I camped that night on the official Grand Canyon campsite, beneath a sea of stars, and besides a friendly German couple who fed and watered me from the massive motorhome they'd rented for the fortnight. The next morning I rode in the direction of Williams, seventy miles to the south of the canyon. Here I intended to turn right, to point west, and from there carry on in the direction of Las Vegas, which I hoped to reach by that evening.

Having reached Williams I hit a snag, as the only road west from there was the I-40 interstate (the one that had replaced Route 66), and whether legal or otherwise on such a small bike, the thought of doing battle with all those massive trucks just didn't seem so appealing. I had done such things before, on the German Autobahn and the busy motorways of Poland and Belgium, but on those occasions I was so desperate to reach

England that I would have gone through any danger to make it. Now, in America, with far less desperation in reaching San Francisco, I accepted that I would just have to find another way around.

Fortunately, the owner of a motorcycle shop in Williams was able to give me directions along a dirt trail running parallel to the interstate for some forty miles, at which point the interstate would have ended and I would be able to rejoin the tarmac road, rejoining old Route 66 in fact.

Having found the start of the trail beyond the town's golf course, it was then a case of following it through the forest and alongside the railway tracks. At times I would encounter campers tucked away in the forest, families enjoying their weekends closer to nature. I waved at them as I passed, and in return, they would wave back.

The trail finally spat me out in the small town of Ash Fork, a dilapidated little place, broken and ruined, right by the side of old Route 66. Had I stayed on Mother Road, rather than leave it in St. Louis, I would have come down through Oklahoma and Albuquerque, missing out the Rockies, Monument Valley and Zion, something I didn't regret.

As for Ash Fork, I read later how the town was originally built as a siding of the Atlantic and Pacific Railroad in 1882, back when the first settlers were flooding west in search of unclaimed land. Fire gutted the entire town a decade later, with it rebuilt on the opposite side of the tracks.

The town's prosperity improved in the 1950s, thanks to the increased traffic along Route 66, though it wasn't to last; the Santa Fe railroad deciding in the 1960s to move its main line north and away from the town, resulting in half the town's population moving out overnight.

Another fire destroyed most of downtown in 1977, before completion of the I-40 meant that trans-continental traffic – the only thing keeping the place alive – now bypassed the town completely. Finally, a third fire gutted almost everything that remained in 1987, and from the looks of things, not much work had been done since.

I couldn't help but feel sorry for the place; it had fought, lost, and been battered severely by the winds of change. It now looked to have accepted its fate, even being used as a backdrop for the 1992 movie *Universal Soldier* as the land was cheap and the misery of the town just what the director needed.

It was then with some surprise that in the museum on the outskirts of town I should meet a girl who claimed to have finished fifth in a recent series of *America's Next Top Model*. I could well believe it: a face like Denise Richards from *Starship Troopers*, legs all the way to the ceiling, short skirt and cowboy boots. *Yeehaa!*

Her name was Hannah, from Texas, driving across the country with her mum and all her gear, hoping to find fame and fortune in Los Angeles. They didn't seem rich and were completely down to earth. I admired that Hannah had this dream. Her mum was behind her all the way, they were going to LA, and she was going to make it as a movie star or model or whatever she chose. She was on a mission; running towards her own light, you could sense that.

Hannah said that if I was passing through LA, I should stop by and visit her. I must admit, the idea of spending the weekend hanging out with one of America's next top models in LA did sound a little surreal. After all, what would I do with Dorothy, and what would I wear? I've been wearing the same red flannel shirt all the way across America. I couldn't hang out in LA dressed like that. I'd have to buy new shoes, and a shirt, and cut my hair and use deodorant, and I was too old and sour for her. But maybe I could go to a photo shoot and watch. I don't know. Her mum was hot though; a real MILF.

We exchanged details in the car park, before I strapped on my crap helmet, pulled on those daft gardening gloves, fired the old bike into life and, as cool as I possibly could, rode off at my usual miles per hour, making sure they went ahead of me, so I didn't have that embarrassing moment where they would come streaming past, tooting their horn, and I would turn bright crimson, and return their signal with a half-cocked wave. Girls; the things they make you do.

I continued on along old Route 66, it now just a threadbare road across the prairie, the interstate over in the distance, and a train line in-between, on which a long blue freight train chugged along, causing me and Dorothy to try and race it. Naturally, we lost that one, and after a while the road brought me to the next town of Seligman, a place that served as inspiration for Radiator Springs, the fictional town in which the

Pixar movie *Cars* was set.

Seligman is one of the few towns along old Route 66 that has managed to survive out here, becoming a tourist attraction in its own right. There isn't that much to see; a single strip of old burger joints, novelty gift shops and all manner of kitsch, bringing bus-loads of day trippers from Las Vegas and beyond, when in truth, they'd perhaps be better off carrying on to Ash Fork; arguably offering, as it does, a more accurate representation of the state of modern day Route 66.

I hung around for a while, taking some pictures and observing the way hordes of coach-trippers would disembark from their vehicles, race around with cameras and buy souvenirs, before being scooped back up and returned to Las Vegas. When one coach left another seemed to arrive. It was smash and grab tourism, but as long as it keeps the town afloat I suppose there's nothing wrong with that, and not everyone can afford the time and opportunity that I was enjoying on this trip.

Wandering to the end of the short little strip I came to the last souvenir shop of the row. It looked to be an old converted home, seeming quite lonely on the end. In the front garden was a collection of motorcycles, four of which were bikes just like mine, or at least the American version, and a few decades older so of slightly different design. I was intrigued by this and felt that I had to meet the owner.

I was told by his wife that he was out doing some shopping all the way back in Williams and wouldn't be back for an hour or more. I decided to sit and wait.

Two hours later a grumpy old man showed up. He had a wooden leg, from the knee down, but still rode bikes. I never did catch his name. He explained that he just loved the old Honda bikes, and that was that, no more explanation or small talk. I asked if he had a socket that would fit Dot's engine oil bolt as I'd left mine at Vermin's by mistake. The man had just the thing, suggesting I keep it for the oil changes ahead. He was a kind-hearted man really, just didn't know much how to show it.

By this time it was falling dark (it always seemed to be falling dark), making the final 175 miles to Las Vegas seem less than appealing, despite having a reservation in a hostel there that apparently had a scene from

The Hangover filmed in it.

Instead, two precocious boys on pushbikes – who both dreamed of leaving Seligman behind – told me about a campsite on the outskirts of town, and I considered heading there, before looking longingly at the motels across the street, their neon signs twinkling in the early evening sky.

I'd not yet stayed in a proper American motel, and regardless of budget, which was now very much thin on the ground, I decided to bite the bullet and go and inquire about the cost of a room for the night. The two boys told me to try the Romney Inn, as that was alright, although they did tell me it often smells a little funny.

I wondered what they meant by this, but in passing through the front door of reception could immediately understand. The motel was owned by an Indian couple, and the fabulous smell was that of authentic Indian cuisine. All of a sudden I found myself back in Delhi again.

I was offered a room for $45 in the old style motel, built in the shape of a horseshoe, with parking outside each room. Having paid, we chatted a while about the various paths we'd taken to be in that same reception room that night. The couple told me how they'd previously lived in LA, buying the motel in recent years and completely refurbishing it.

I asked them how they'd been received by the locals, and the customers for that matter. They'd said they'd had no troubles, certainly not from the customers, just the usual hassle you get from some members of a small community when 'outsiders' – of whichever race or religion – move in. They were enjoying it, which was certainly good to hear, although it did look a difficult business to sustain. In winter barely anyone passes through Seligman, at which point they move back to LA to earn a crust.

Helping the Indian couple to run the motel was a man named John, who also owned a ramshackle grocery store across the road. John was originally from Macedonia and had travelled the world through various means and for various different reasons.

John talked about retirement having previously lived in Las Vegas, buying the grocery store and moving out here for a quieter life. It was a wish he looked to have been granted, spending his evenings hanging out with the Indian couple, and the waifs and strays that passed on through this sleepy little town, which, when all the tourist buses had departed, was actually quite pleasant and charming; certainly the best time to see it.

John explained how he hoped to move back to Macedonia in the next few years and use his American pension to live on. He told me that he missed home; the dark rings beneath his eyes hinting at a hard and difficult life. But a nicer man you couldn't wish to meet.

Having chatted for a while in reception, John offered to make me a sandwich over at his shop. I joined him there, chatting for ages as he sliced a mound of ham and cheese, salad and pickle, handing me the biggest sandwich I'd ever seen, along with bags of crisps and chocolate bars to go with it. In return he wouldn't accept a dollar, so I forced ten of them into his collection jar that he had on his counter, money going towards people in need in the community.

John was definitely one of those people you meet that make it all worthwhile. It's almost as though you are meant to meet them, because they might say something, or explain something, that makes you stop and think, and reflect on how you're living your own life. John was a religious man, believing in God and in faith. I think most of all he believed in kindness and in the goodness of people. He had a warm heart, and his sandwiches were simply divine.

I often felt guilty meeting people such as John. They seemed to give so much to me, and I felt like I often gave so little in return. It would make me feel embarrassed and extremely humble. There are so many good people in this world. They are literally everywhere, and I think it would do us some good to remind ourselves of this from time to time, rather than believing all the doom and gloom on the news.

Before hitting the road the next morning John loaded me up with more sandwiches and all sorts of cakes, crisps and biscuits. In return I wished him well on his future adventures in Macedonia. I hope he's found himself there by now, or at least is on his way.

***

It took me a long time to reach Las Vegas that day, simply because I didn't feel like I was in any hurry to get there. I stopped in the big town of Kingman for a McDonald's and some time spent on the Wi-Fi, uploading photos and confirming to my parents that I was still alive. I also passed Hoover Dam and stopped for a look around. To my eyes it wasn't half as impressive as the dam at Lake Powell, though I did meet a lady named Mia, a glamorous black lady, originally from Gary, Indiana – the place I'd passed through on my way into Chicago – who was interested to hear my experiences, as she ran a youth education programme for kids from the poor areas I'd been witness to.

This all meant that I didn't get to Las Vegas until dusk, the casino towers rising from the desert earth amidst a haze of dust and fading light. It really is just plonked here in the middle of nowhere, a city on the fringe of the Mojave Desert.

I had been before, as part of that organised trip, staying in a motel just off the strip for two nights, the big group of us taken on a tour of the city in a white limousine, drinking cheap champagne as a treat, then gambling what little money we had in the casinos. For some reason I agreed to do a sky dive, something I soon regretted the second the wheels of the plane left the ground, and then certainly regretted when, at 12,000 feet, I was forced to the open exit of the aeroplane, strapped to a burly bloke, and then pushed out into nothingness whether I wanted to or not. At least the views, once I'd stopped screaming, were terrific.

Las Vegas first sprang up in 1905, starting out as a place where steam locomotives stopped to fill their water tanks. The building of the Hoover Dam between 1929 and 1935 brought thousands of well paid employees to the area, and in 1931 gambling was legalised, when across the rest of America it was still considered a crime and a sin. The gambling in Las Vegas was said to have grown off the back of mob money, formalised casino gambling being a type of 'grifting', something that the mob excelled at. The new interstate and the invention of air-conditioning made the city popular with outsiders, while laws banning publicly held companies from owning casinos were eventually scrapped, giving rise to the corporate gambling mecca that rises from the desert today.

In recent years Las Vegas has been hit hard by the economic downturn, it dependent totally on the tourists coming to town, and if the tourist has no money, then neither does the town. I'd read before of homeless people living in the sewers beneath the city and it has one of the highest unemployment rates in America.

In a way I wish I'd been one of the millions of tourists flying into the airport, taking a taxi to one of the massive casino-hotel complexes, spending the week getting drunk and dining on all you can eat buffet, not caring what was happening out the window, because to see Vegas like that must be paradise. A real fun loving town.

But riding through the scruffy downbeat suburbs on a tiny motorbike, booked in to a cheap hostel on the wrong end of the strip, having no money with which to enjoy myself or dull my senses with booze, I was always bound to see a different side of things, and to be honest, Vegas this time was probably my least favourite place in America. Instead of the grand casinos I saw the discomfort of the promo girl outside the bar, with the surgically enhanced breasts, having to smile for the lecherous bastard who wished to have his photo taken with her.

Or I saw how seething the street performers, dressed up in various costumes as they were, became when tourists would take their photo and not offer the obligatory tip in exchange. Beneath the crass veneer was a place of utter shit, people doing the things they despise, simply to stay alive, in order to … I was going to say, in order to live the American Dream, but I think the word is survive. They do this to survive.

It was then just not a place for me, though I appreciate others thrive in this town, and find their amusement. I on the other hand, was much happier two days later, as I passed through the wonderful Death Valley.

Chapter Forty-Two
Death Valley

It was around this point – between Las Vegas and Death Valley – that I lost the diary I'd been writing my notes in, assuming it must have fallen from my tank bag during the 121 mile ride between the two places.

I considered turning back and tracing my steps, but in a way, I was quite relieved. A diary (much like a book) can chain you to the past, and while it would have been handy for remembering the names of more people when writing this book, I learnt from the first book that sometimes it's easier to start with a blank page and write down the things that you remember, in the way that you remember them, rather than attempting to stitch together old sentences and thoughts written in various moods of the past.

What I remember most about this relatively short journey between Las Vegas and Death Valley was the colour of the sky. I'd not taken to the road until late in the day, so as I passed through the desert the sky ahead of me was a sea of crimson red and deep burnt orange. It was one of those irreplaceable moments, a warm breeze on your face, the familiar sound of the engine ticking along beneath you, still hanging in there, mile after mile, hour after hour, even chuckling at the roadside billboards encouraging people to vote in the next local elections for a lady with the unfortunate name of 'Judge Kim Wanker.' How many people would stop to take a photo of that? I know I did.

I happened upon the town of Pahrump, trying desperately to find somewhere to park up and sleep for the night. The onset of darkness didn't help, with it not looking like there was a campsite for tents, only for motorhomes and statics. There didn't seem to be any lanes or paths to dive down either. It was just one of those miserable evenings where you find yourself frantic, trying desperately to get off the road and shut down for a while.

Finally I found a building site at the top end of town, taking the access road and parking up behind a mound of dirt, laying the bike on its side and folding down the wing mirrors so no reflections could be seen by anyone on the road. I put up the tent in the dirt, drank some water from a bottle I'd been carrying, using the rest of it to brush my teeth, getting into bed, completely clothed, with the knife beside me, and then nervously trying to get some sleep. It was one of the worst night's sleep of the trip; the occasional passing car casting beams of light from the road, which made me think I was going to be detected at any time.

I rose early, packed away the tent under the cover of darkness and made my way down to the town's McDonald's for a routine cup of hot coffee. I must have stopped in most McDonald's between here and New York. I stopped at quite a few between Sydney and London as well. It would have been nice to have used more local cafés and diners, but it would have cost far more, and meant that at each stop I would have had to engage in conversation, whereas in McDonald's I can find a quiet corner and keep myself to myself, as I did this morning, using my laptop to check online while I drank my coffee and ate my muffin.

Around 6.30am, as I was back outside in the carpark prepping the bike for the journey into Death Valley, I met a mysterious man returning from the Californian mountains, after a futile search for gold.

The man was a tramp, or at least had the appearance of one (we both did). His clothes were tattered and his hair was long. He was perhaps sixty years of age, possibly more, and travelling on a beaten up old bicycle with a chain that slipped, which he told me he was trying to fix. Scattered on and around this battered old bike were all of the man's belongings, stored in white cylindrical plastic buckets hanging from the handlebars. Other bags and containers were strapped to a rack on the back and, best of all, he had a dog with him, tethered to the bike by a bedraggled piece of string.

The man told me that he lived down in Texas, sharing a caravan with his long suffering wife, but having heard whisper of this gold up in the Californian mountains, had set off on his bicycle, his dog trotting alongside on what must have been a 1,500-mile odyssey in either direction. Sadly, the man told me how he never did strike gold, despite panning the entire hill side for the summer, and was now on his way back to Texas, empty-handed, in need of appeasing his wife, and still with so many miles left to go.

The man told me how he would push the bike some of the way, simply because of all the weight, and the difficulty he had in pedalling it. Other times he'd take lifts, or the police would pick him up and drop him off at the next town. He lived on nothing. I don't know how he lived. I don't know how he survived. He was a man completely at odds with the modern world; far more off grid than I ever was.

As inspired as I was by this, deep down I remained hopeful that it wasn't a premonition of my future; a life on the road, searching far and wide for this piece of 'gold,' and still not being able to find it. Perhaps this man will return home and realise it was there all along, right under his nose. Or just maybe he was having me on, and instead of returning empty-handed he had actually struck upon a massive bounty, and in one of those buckets, or in one of those plastic bags on the back of the bike, was a bar of gold so vast it would set him up for the rest of his life. His wife could have a new caravan. He could have a new bike. And his dog could have had a new lead. No one deserved to find gold more than that man, whose name I never could quite remember. I probably had it written down in the pages of that blasted diary.

From Pahrump I took the old Charles Brown Highway, crossing the border into California not far out of town. San Francisco was still some 500 miles away, but it felt much closer now, being in the same state and all. It looked unlikely that I was going to divert down to LA to check out Mike's bike, or see Hannah, or Naomi, as the current keepers of Mike's bike hadn't got back to me yet. Also, the desire to see Death Valley would take me a little too far north to drop back down to LA. Some other time, that's what I reasoned to myself.

For now, the road dropped me down to the small community of Shoshone, the name of an Indian tribe that still live in these parts; their main reservation down at Furnace Creek, deep in the heart of Death Valley. In Shoshone there is nothing more than a gas station, convenience store, campsite, small museum and a few other bits and bobs, the town surviving as a jumping-off point for people heading into Death Valley.

The price of petrol reflected this, proving more expensive than anywhere else at $5.60 per gallon. Across the rest of America it had cost me around $4 a gallon, and in needing roughly three gallons to fill the bike, I could travel approximately 250 miles on twelve dollars (about £8). That's really how I'd managed to afford all this.

The lady inside the gas station told me that it was approximately ninety miles to the next pump at the visitor centre at Furnace Creek, which was well within range. The only time I'd had to carry extra fuel was when riding over the Himalayas in India, from Manali to Leh, where the biggest distance without anywhere to get gas was over 400 kilometres, though there's always someone with fuel if you get stuck.

Water was more of an issue out here, feeling the need to buy a four-litre drum from the gas station, along with a bunch of bananas, biscuits and a few other snacks that I strapped haphazardly to the back of the bike. I had spare inner tubes, my pump, necessary tools, still no mobile phone, but that was okay because I figured if I broke down in the middle of nowhere I'd just walk at night and take shelter by day.

The hottest temperature in the world was recorded in Death Valley, reaching 134 degrees Fahrenheit on the 10th July 1913 (about 56 degrees Celsius); though this being mid-September it was unlikely to get that hot. To prepare the bike for the heat I was already running a thicker grade of oil in the engine, hoping to counteract the way oil thins and loses effectiveness during really hot temperatures. Anything to keep this bike in good health, though she was certainly starting to feel her age.

Pretty much since St. Louis she'd not been running or sounding in great health. This hadn't really effected the speed, as it wasn't too great to begin with, but being so in-tune with the bike as I was I couldn't help but hear the rumbles and the slight ticking from the engine within, and when you're alone out here, the smallest of noises becomes an avalanche of fear that it will lead to something catastrophic. The heat of the impending desert certainly wasn't going to help from here.

Beyond Shoshone I turned left on to Jubilee Pass Road, stopping to take a photograph of the brightly coloured sign marking the entrance to Death Valley National Park. From here the road begins its long and winding descent towards the valley floor, seemingly getting hotter and hotter with every step.

Death Valley got its name from a time in 1849 when a group of pioneers got lost out here, one of the men apparently dying (though some accounts claim that not to be true), and, as the others eventually climbed out to salvation, one turned around and was reported to have said, 'Goodbye, death valley.' And from there stuck the name.

At the bottom of this long descent the road turns to the right, and there before you stretches the vast expanse of the valley floor. It is completely flat at the bottom, and wide, with steep rock slopes on either side, like being at the bottom of a bath tub with a road running through it. The colour of the rock is the most amazing sight. It is so fiery and red, like the colours you see when volcanoes erupt. Second to that is the absence of anything on the valley floor. It is flat and featureless. Scant plant life exists out here, just shoots of bushes and grasses. The rest is salt flats, white and hazy, the road hugging the safest part, where the salt flats meet the red rock walls of the valley.

This being early morning I was the only one out here, which perhaps led me to experience so much enchantment. Had there been a steady procession of rental cars, as there was during my passage through Zion, then my passion for it would have been less strong. As it was, I was alone and free, in the valley of the heat, sauntering along with all my skin covered, as patterns of sand and dust skipped across the worn tarmac ahead of me. When I stopped to take a photograph I removed my helmet, surprised not to hear a single sound. The whole world was at peace. Until a Ford Mustang V8 shot by with its roof down, and I remembered where

I was again.

Around the next corner lay Badwater Basin, officially the lowest point in America at 282 feet below sea level, something made possible by the sheer heat of the valley, plus the impenetrability of its walls, preventing fresh water from entering. The salt plains are a remnant of the sea, back when this part of the world was under water.

The appeal of Badwater Basin is that you can park your car beneath the shadow of the rock, use the recently built toilets if need be, then proceed to walk out across salt flats on to what resembles a large white catwalk, stretching out for a couple of hundred metres or more into the heart of Death Valley. The ground underfoot is solid salt, while either side is a bubbling cauldron of salt-contaminated water, the taste of which lends the place its name, 'Badwater'.

What I enjoyed most about Death Valley was that you were completely immersed in it. You weren't looking at it from a distance, as you are at the Grand Canyon, parked up on the rim. Here you were actually in the heart of it, riding through it, and for me, travelling by motorcycle, and being able to ride that same motorcycle through here just made it that perfect experience. By far it was my favourite place in the whole of America.

Morning turned to afternoon, and in the full heat of the day I stopped to take in the Devil's Golf Course. This is an area at the heart of the flat of the valley resembling a carpet of tremendous white golf balls, each as big as washing machine drums and closely packed together. They're made from crystalised salt, and you can hop from one to another, the carpet of them stretching out for almost as far as the ground you can see. They took their name from when one of the first European settles came upon them and declared, 'only the devil would play golf on these.'

Not far from the Devil's Golf Course I took a ride along what's known as Artist's Drive. This is a narrow, one way road, running through a shallow side valley of beautifully coloured rocks, made that way by the metal in them that had oxidised over the years, turning them various shades of blue, red and green.

I leap-frogged a couple of travellers in a rental car throughout all this. It turned out that they were on a fortnight break from their home in

Philadelphia; the guy originally from Germany, the girl from Chile, the couple now living in America together. We agreed to camp together that evening on a campsite at the far end of the valley, carrying on at our own pace until then.

I stopped at the Furnace Creek visitor centre to take on fluid and shade, finding it an enclave of activity in this vast empty valley. Coach loads of day-trippers, again from Vegas, were unloading and re-loading, having spent their dollars in the canteen or in the souvenir shop. Many posed with the thermometer, which at its peak this day hit almost 120 degrees Fahrenheit, or 48 degrees Celsius. This was as hot as it had been when coming across India, but in that country, with all its commotion, traffic, dust, noise and trickery, the heat just feels that little bit more intense, though it certainly took your breath here in Death Valley as well.

Beyond Furnace Creek I met another cyclist. I passed him by, heading in the opposite direction, before turning round and going back to check if he needed any water. He was a handsome man, tall and strong, wearing Lycra, and cycling with no luggage or bags, and barely any water, just a litre bottle in a pocket stitched to the back of his shirt. His destination was Las Vegas, riding there for a cycle-expo he was attending as he owned a bike shop and had a stall selling cycling equipment that he'd sent there in a container.

Rather than fly or drive, he'd decided instead to cycle the three-hundred miles from his home on the far west side of Death Valley to Las Vegas. He hoped to cover the distance in less than two days, and judging by the size of his thighs I wouldn't bet against it. He told me he had a wife and kids, but lived for adventure, keen whenever he could to get out and do something strenuous.

We talked for a long time, finding equal fascination in one another's adventures. Richard (I believe that was his name) hoped to take in Asia at some time, and possibly Australia as well. He was fascinated to hear about Pakistan, thinking it would be too dangerous to travel through at the moment, but I told him about the Austrian girl I'd met in Gilgit, only in her twenties and cycling the length of the country all by herself. Richard looked quite amazed by this, and I think, quite faintly, you could see his eyes light up, as the scope for his adventures had just doubled, tripled perhaps, because previously he'd imagined them extending no further than North America. Now he saw the world, and it was my pleasure to have given him that.

***

That evening, rather than push any further, I found a lonely little campsite just on the rise out the other side of Death Valley. There was only space for half a dozen vehicles, wooden log dividers between the pitches, and each pitch with a pebble floor, picnic table and firepit. It was the only sign of civilisation for miles around, with the view back across Death Valley a simple brilliance of nothingness, with a wispy pink sky and stars that would start to dazzle brighter the darker it became.

I only intended to rest there for an hour or so, before pushing on to where the couple from Philadelphia were camped, but there was just something about this campsite, as low key as it was, that made me stay there for far longer, laying back on the wooden picnic bench and drifting off to sleep from around 5pm to 7pm, waking just as evening was beginning to set, and the last wave of tourists and travellers were making haste out of Death Valley for the night, leaving me alone on this little stone pitch, an ocean of dry sand and rock all around.

Other campers eventually joined me for the night. The first were a couple of old Czech men travelling by people carrier, out here to do some climbing, one of them bragging that he was on incapacity benefit but still able to climb. A lone woman sleeping on the seats of her rental car followed, somehow managing to unbolt and position them on the ground beside her vehicle. Lastly came a two-car convoy of young campers, arriving in darkness, cooking their food and heading straight to bed.

I lay on my back and looked up at the stars overhead. I thought about so many things, finding it hard to believe that it was only just over a month ago that I'd been in England, putting this bike on a plane, not sure what I was to encounter, wondering how things would turn out.

From there to here, lying back on a bench in the midst of Death Valley, made me realise just how far I'd travelled in that time. I was glad I'd put my faith in the road and not those tablets, or anything else prescribed by others, who I realise were only trying to help. But I'd always known deep down what it was that I needed to do, it just took me longer than expected to muster the courage and conviction - and clarity - to go ahead and do it.

One person told me that at such times you just have to make a decision, jump in with both feet, and stick with it, but I'm not so sure. To me, if you're stood in the middle of a cross-roads, not knowing which way to turn, then sometimes it's better to sit it out, to feel the emotions and feelings seep through you, standing firm on the spot and pushing back against the wind until the moment at which everything becomes clear, and you can now take that path, simply because you know with all your heart it's the right one to take. Patience, not haste; that seems to be the remedy to such periods of despair.

I got up the next morning, packed away the tent and left before any of the other campers had even woken. The sun was just beginning to rise, casting long warm shadows across the dusty earth, the road climbing to the top of the valley and dropping back down the other side. I pulled over by a side road, on a patch of gravel with a view of red-hot valley beyond. I killed the engine, took off my helmet and just sat there for a while, enjoying the silence that had enveloped me.

For so many years – pretty much for as long as I can remember – I've always had a mind of competing voices. Some wanting me to go one way, other voices wanting me to go another, feeling as though I'm being pulled in every direction and leaving me stranded on the spot, as I've just explained. But on this morning, finally, I didn't hear a single thing. The competing voices had been silenced, or perhaps had learnt to get along, because every single one of us wished to be nowhere but here, on a plateau overlooking the magnificence of Death Valley. The sensation was overwhelming and I hoped my mind would remain this way forever. Of course it wouldn't, but for this brief moment it did so. Nirvana.

Chapter Forty-Three
California

A mission now lay ahead of me; aiming to be paddling in the waves of the Pacific Ocean by the end of the day, signalling that my journey across America would be over. It had been just over five weeks from landing in New York to here. In that time I had covered almost 5,000 miles, my funds were sorely depleted and the bike was beginning to fight against the onslaught of old age, the tripometer now ticking ever closer to 100,000 kilometres. Thirty thousand kilometres as a postal bike, ten thousand in the hands of Colin – the man who gave her the name – and almost 50,000 kilometres in my wicked hands.

No way would I make it to Alaska now, and besides, I no longer wanted to. I'd seen and ridden enough coming across America and I think I'd got out of it what I needed to get out of it: a cleansing of the soul, to leave something behind and have a new story to tell. I didn't need to ride up to Alaska to gain any more of that, San Francisco would be just far enough, my plan being to be there in two days, just in time to give a talk at a bike club in the neighbouring city of Oakland. I'd been invited there by a lady who had followed my travels on Facebook and happened to be a member of the Oakland Motorcycle Club. It was good to have this presentation booked in place, as it would provide the necessary pull to get me over the finishing line.

For now I was leaving Death Valley behind, making my way out on to Route 395, a long straight boring road, the opposite of what I'd just passed through. The trucks and lorries had returned, so I was once more riding with one eye on the rear view mirror and tucked well into the gutter. These are the times when you wish for just that little bit more power, when 37mph just feels so painfully slow, but you know that's all you've got, so that's just what you have to stick to.

We turned right on to Isabella-Walker Pass Road, shortly beyond the town of Indian Wells. This began a stretch of road that didn't have a very good aura around it. There was something just not right about this one. It felt like riding through a scene out of a scary movie, though I'm not sure why. For whatever reason it felt creepy, with random houses and ranches out here. The rest of the time the road ran through shallow valleys and alongside riverbanks, and then through towns and villages that seemed okay, but again, I didn't feel like stopping, imagining a pickup truck full of hillbillies to start trailing me at any time. Strange how the mind works like that, it all quite irrational really.

I was thankful then when the road turned into a canyon, the tarmac becoming like a set of rapids that you might ride down on a rubber tube, gushing from left to right, such was the way in which the road rolled with the contours of the valley floor. It was beautiful riding, perfect on this bike, because the corners were at times tight, the road narrow, allowing me to scoot on through like a child along a helter-skelter, about to pop out at the end, into a large splash pool.

Instead I splashed down in Bakersfield, a large town I'd much rather have avoided had I known what was coming. Traffic, lots of traffic, with that infernal satnav system (retrieved from the bag) not able to decipher interstates and jam-packed three-lane highways, which is where I ended up.

At such times I would gun the throttle, perhaps seeing a GPS-verified reading of 45mph, little more than that. It wasn't good for me or the engine, but when you have a wave of traffic ploughing up behind, you have little choice but to do all you can to get out of its way.

I braced myself for impact as I felt the 'whoosh' of a car careering from behind, swinging right across the tail light and being so close as to almost graze the right pannier rack, then careering across the crud at the side of the road and swinging back in front of me. I don't know what the guy was thinking, but I could have killed him that day, as he hadn't been that far from killing me.

These final stages of an adventure do seem to be the most perilous. It is during this time that you seem inclined to take more risks, to carry on riding where normally you would stop and think things through. I suspect it's because when you have the finishing line in sight you are so desperate to get there that all sense and sensibility goes out the window. You just want to get there, before it slips away.

Upon sight of an exit road I took it, breathing a sigh of relief as I was finally able to shut off the throttle and return to normal cruising pace. From here I headed west, not entirely sure where I was (much like that first day through New Jersey), finding myself in a world of farmed orchards, the road flanked either side by fields of planted trees, and with the onset of evening I wondered if I should try to find a spot to camp among them. But there were so many farm workers driving along in pickup trucks, heading home for the evening, that the mood just didn't feel right to be trying to find a wild camping spot right now.

I turned on to the Paso Robles Highway, the plantations now gone, the land flat and lifeless, shadows in the dark, a sky turned heavy and bleak. The road crossed over the West Side Freeway. The encroaching darkness was broken by a field of gas stations, motels and fast food diners. It looked to be the place where truckers would stop for the night, and so the roads around this little grid were riddled with heavy traffic. I found it to be an awkward moment; the thought of stopping and finding a cheap motel amongst the madness, or riding on into the darkness that lay west?

I pulled into several motel yards, only to be dissuaded by the sight of burly truckers leaning against the railings, smoking cigarettes outside their rooms. I didn't think I quite fitted in around these parts, deciding instead to ride on.

The road led me through a landscape of nodding oil pumpjacks, their silhouettes picked out by the faint orange glow lingering at the pit of the sky. It was an incredibly moody, apocalyptic sight; this field of nodding donkeys extracting oil from the earth as though it were a scene from a *Terminator* movie, after the machines had taken over the world. It reminded me of parts of Kansas, which at times had been an endless horizon of wind turbines, spinning hypnotically for as far as the eye could see. The road now was long, dark and straight. I was glad to be wearing the fluorescent postal jacket, as the rear light on the bike was still terrible, and the traffic from behind still dense. It was foolish to keep on riding, but clearly, I was a fool.

I reached Paso Robles at around 10pm. It is a town roughly forty miles inland from the Pacific Coast. I pulled into the town's McDonald's, deciding I was in serious need of respite from the road, as I was tired now, and on edge from not finding a place to sleep. I sat in a seat by the window, a life-sized Ronald McDonald on a bench beside me. I waved and said hello. The clown said nothing back, he just carried on smiling with his thick red lips and stripy tights.

The young man mopping the floor chatted with me. We talked about the area and how the town seemed to be growing at an alarming rate, thanks to migrant South and Central Americans arriving to work in the agricultural industry. He also told me that crystal meth use was becoming a large and persistent problem (meth on the west coast, crack cocaine on the east). This surprised me, as it seemed to be a nice town, immune to that sort of thing. I later learnt that Fresno, a city one hundred miles to the north of here, has the highest meth addiction rate in the country.

Hearing such things was very sad, and also hard to understand being someone who has never had any interest in drugs. Yet at the same time I had to concede that we all have different vices. My vices were these adventures, running across the world on a motorbike, and that wasn't always healthy for me either. People around me told me that I should quit, get clean, lead a normal life. But what did they know? How could they say if it was good for me or not? I knew that I needed it in order to try and cure my own unhappiness.

Maybe it was the source of my unhappiness and I just couldn't see that. But I knew deep down I needed to keep on doing it, for now at least, because that's just what I felt I needed to stay alive. It was my drug, my fix. So who was I to judge the people who shoot up their arms to enjoy similar respite from a world they can't deal with? Who are any of us to judge?

Around midnight I walked back out into the sodium light. The city was dead, just me and the McDonald's parking lot, even the clown was sleeping. I strapped on the old helmet, threw a leg over the battered old bitch, slipped my hands into the well-worn gardening gloves, making sure the trusty sunglasses were safe in the tank bag as I wouldn't be needing them at this moment in time but couldn't bear the thought of losing them, not now, not having carried them all this way.

I rode to the gas station on the other side of the junction as it was still open, the forecourt empty, just a lone man in the cashier's desk, who darted out at the sight of the bike. He was excited to hear about my trip, and keen to hear just how this old bike had managed to bring me this far.

Enquiring about a place to sleep, the man told me how beneath the bridge, just across the way, was a shallow valley where homeless people slept. A woman walking past with a pushchair vouched for this (it was far too late to be out with a baby), saying she'd slept there a few nights in the past, but just to be careful as the police regularly go down there to move people on. I told them that I would go and take a look for myself, riding off in that direction, but instead of heeding their advice, I took the road out of town instead, as being just forty miles shy of the coast, all I wanted to do was see it, no matter how late it was when I made it there.

Unsurprisingly, I was the only person on the road this late night, winding out the throttle as the air continued to turn colder and damper the closer to the ocean I got. It was an exciting feeling; everything finally coming to a head. Less than two months before being in a world of confusion and self-inflicted pain; hurting myself, hurting others as an unfortunate consequence of that – which is by far the worst part of it all – to being out here, in California, the journey across America almost over.

And then there it was, the Pacific Ocean, our arrival point being the seaside town of Cambria, one hundred miles north of Los Angeles, 225 miles south of San Francisco. I didn't dance, nor cheer, just exhaled, a long exhale, and perhaps my shoulders sagged as well; the heat would certainly have come off the throttle and I would have said something profound, such as, 'Well Dorothy, we've made it. We've made it across

America. I think we did okay.' And then I would have patted her on the tank and carried on riding.

***

Cambria didn't seem a big place, but a pretty place, a nice spot to vacation for those travelling up from LA. The plan now was to find somewhere to rest for the few remaining hours of night, then hightail it up the coast at sunrise, to make it to San Francisco and Oakland in time to give that talk I'd been booked to do that very evening.

I considered a campsite, even sitting by the entrance at 2am, wondering if I should sneak in, and then out the following morning without having to pay; that age-old dilemma of karma. I sat there trying to decide what to do for almost half an hour, taking a pee in the bushes and generally coming to terms with the reality of being able to hear the Pacific Ocean in the background. A long boat ride west from here and we'd be back in Australia, having gone all the way around the world.

I certainly would not have anticipated any of this that day I rode out of Sydney. I didn't even know if I'd make it to the end of that first day, or even out of Australia. And yet here I was, nineteen countries later, on the other side of the planet.

In the end I slept in a lay-by, little more than a stone's throw from the beach, beneath a sign that read 'No Camping'. I didn't put the tent up, but simply lay the sleeping bag on the ground, tucked myself and the bike away in a bush as best I could, so to be out of sight, and attempted to sleep this cold moist night, waking up to find my sleeping bag soaking from the moisture that had been whipped up from the sea. But what a sensation to wake to the sound of the waves, pounding against the rocks, just over the other side of the fence.

The journey now would take me all the way up the Pacific Coast Highway, or Route 1 as it's also known, a legendary road built not that many decades ago. Previously to access these remote corners of the coastline you would have had to have taken a boat. Then the road came, connecting Los Angeles with San Francisco, the tarmac clinging on to the sides of the cliffs, snaking in and out of coves, running across bridges and along the edge of thick lush forests.

I passed through Big Sur this morning; a well-known surfing community found on Route 1, famous for the artists and writers it has attracted over the years. Jack Kerouac, Hunter S Thompson and Henry Miller all had retreats out here. They'd come to write in cabins in the wood, a small community forming over the years, the place with no real centre to it. Instead, a scattering of businesses can be seen dotted along the road side, with signs for isolated guesthouses and hidden-away campsites. I stopped at a rustic cafe for coffee and a pain au chocolat. The atmosphere out here was just serene.

Beyond that the wind really began to pick up. As the bike had so little power it almost literally brought me to a standstill, making the queue of traffic behind grow longer with every mile, which in turn made me rage and scream at the wind with such venom that I felt like my head was going to explode.

It would have been different had it been a tail-wind. That would have been joyous, like a helping hand pushing you from the rear, increasing our speed and having our kite fly right up into the sky. Instead, I was down to twenty miles per hour, frothing wildly at the mouth, worried any moment that my head might blow off and be cast out to sea. It felt like I was in a battle with nature; and at her I would scream.

The afternoon that followed was equally miserable. Not just the wind, but after a while (somewhere around Monterey) the single lane nirvana of Route 1 was replaced by the hell of a three-lane highway, and no matter how hard I looked for alternatives, there didn't seem to be any escape from that.

It was made more complicated by the fact that I wasn't heading to San Francisco itself, but the neighbouring city of Oakland, as that's where the bike club was based. There is a bridge connecting the two cities, but as the bridge is almost three miles long and classed as an interstate, I wouldn't be able to take the quieter coastal road to San Francisco before crossing the bridge to Oakland. Instead I would have to ride up through the heavily populated cities of Salinas, Gilroy, Morgan Hill and San Hose.

Heading slightly inland, the landscape now was one of agriculture and crops, with fields of strawberries and greenhouses being picked and tendered by what looked to be a roaring influx of South and Central American workers. The roads would run alongside these fields of activity, before dipping in and out of towns and villages. I didn't really know where I was, and the satnav proved strangely useless. Instead I just followed my nose, guided by the position of the sun once more, finding myself on a narrow, winding road that I wouldn't be able to find again, even if my life depended on it.

Soon I was back in the throng of the agricultural industry, featuring a roaring flow of heavy traffic and trucks. Once more I was a sitting duck, and the bike, unsurprisingly by this point, was beginning to feel a little out of sorts. I believe it was the heat of Death Valley that had done it. She made noises, and the power just wasn't there. It led to a sense of fear, as I just didn't want to break down out here. Fear turned to panic. Panic turned to dread. Then came another one of those surreal encounters of the road. Another one of Denise's fairies perhaps.

Riding along the edge of these strawberry plantations, approaching a right hand corner on a quiet country road, somewhere south of San Jose, I noticed two bikes parked up in the shade. As I drew closer it revealed itself to be the oddest juxtaposition of mismatched worlds I'd encountered for quite some time. In this world of South American strawberry pickers, I'd stumbled upon a pair of white middle-aged men, on brand-new BMW motorbikes, by the side of the road, in the oddest of locations – on the outside of a corner, standing in the grass – drinking cans of Coca Cola. I flew right by them, before turning around and coming to a stop.

At first they thought I was an alien crash landing from space, such was my tale of recklessness. They were somehow bowled over and in disbelief at the distance Dorothy had travelled. It took a while to convince them that I wasn't having them on.

The two men worked locally, owned their own businesses, rode brand-new bikes, wore top quality clothing and, perhaps, were out here trying to snatch a little bit of peace and quiet from their wives. They asked where I was heading. I told them Oakland, and to that they sucked their teeth and shuffled their feet. 'That place is bad,' they said. I said that was alright, it couldn't be as bad as Detroit and Chicago. They told me of the best way to get there without going on major roads, but it was one of those convoluted sets of directions that go in one ear and out the other.

I told them about the problems I was having with the bike, and how at tick-over she was beginning to sound like an old diesel tractor. I fired her into life. They said she sounded alright. This puzzled me – were my ears and my mind deceiving me? I didn't think so. And the gradual power loss was real. I could feel that. Yet to now have two random men I'd just met by the roadside tell me she sounded okay and that I should just keep on riding (though not necessarily to Oakland!), took my nerves out of the day and allowed me to carry on my way a little more relaxed than I had been up until meeting these men, whose names I can't for the life of me remember.

Shortly after I began my passage through San Jose. It was traffic light after traffic light, picking a way through this endless sprawl of suburbia. I would have given anything to have been back in Death Valley right now. Instead, I was sat at red traffic lights, surrounded by big SUVs and pickup trucks, feeling conspicuous, especially in some of the rougher neighbourhoods I passed through. At times like these I really wish I'd been on a regular motorcycle, looking like a regular chap, without a target on the side of my helmet and a pair of gardening gloves on my hands.

At least in America I think you can get away with putting your head down and minding your own business. Try looking like this in downtown Nottingham, Manchester, Birmingham or London and perhaps you'll receive more negative attention, yet thinking about it, me and the two New Zealanders, Rob and Greg, had been just fine riding through London, even around Buckingham Palace and through Leicester Square. Maybe half the problem is wondering too much what other people are thinking, instead of sitting there at the lights, minding your own business.

Finally, on the eve of that long, long, 16-hour riding day, I made my final approach to Oakland. Granted, it did seem a little rougher than some of the other parts I'd passed through that day, but certainly nowhere near as bad as the parts of Detroit or Chicago I'd been witness to. In fact, it seemed like quite a decent place, and I certainly saw plenty of it, mistaking the street I was supposed to have arrived on with one on the opposite side of the city, meaning that I had to cross it at breakneck speed in order to make the presentation in time.

A fellow biker helped me find my way; a black guy who complained how the police kept pulling him over and giving him a hard time, though admitted he had no insurance and his licence had been revoked, so I guess he brought that bad luck on himself.

It did still feel weird though to be in one of these big American cities. They do have an atmosphere about them; intense, moody, dramatic. You feel like you're in a movie. You feel that none of this is real. This is Hollywood, especially when you see one of the police cars or fire trucks, because you've seen them on the silver screen, and now you're here, sat beside them at the traffic lights. At times it was all so very surreal.

Finally I found myself beneath the underpass, near a railroad, on the dark side of the city. It was a place of dim street lights, tyre depots and high mesh fences topped with razor wire. There was a roadblock, forcing me to take a detour around the block, following the line on the map on the satnav as it lead me to a point which just didn't seem plausible. It was fixated with a spot in the midst of a square of industrial buildings, finally finding the entrance to a shadowy run-down estate, the scene, surely, of a potential homicide.

It was now completely dark, crawling up this alley, not certain what we were going to encounter: henchman, our own brutal murder? But no, it was the sight of a dozen or so high-end motorbikes, all lined up outside the Oakland clubhouse door, which was just an old wooden building. 'This must be it,' I thought, parking up at the end of the row, taking off my helmet and walking through the door. Little did I know the day was only just beginning.

Chapter Forty-Four
San Francisco

I'd walked into a room of older men, all wearing orange duffel coats with Oakland Motorcycle Club embroidered on the back. I was nervous at the sight of them; a room full of angry white men, as Vermin might have called them. Fortunately Suzanne was there, the lady who'd invited me to give the presentation in the first place. While the chairman went through the club's formalities, Suzanne led me to the back of what was effectively a big scouts' hut, with a bar and a kitchen at the rear, where a plate of food they'd been saving me was heated up, and a fresh cup of coffee made. I wolfed it down, feeling quite nervous, knowing I would soon have to speak in front of all those duffel-coated men, when really, I just wanted to go to bed.

Finally came the time to introduce me to the fifty or so people sat in a square of chairs, many of the men with their arms folded, my stage right in the middle of them. But first impressions can be deceiving, because they were a great bunch, immediately voting to allow Dorothy to be the first bike allowed into the clubhouse, so that I could have her taking centre stage for my talk. We wheeled her in, placing a cloth beneath the engine to catch any dripping oil.

I began telling my story of how I came to be there, in their clubhouse that evening. How, starting in Australia, one day I decided that rather than fly home to England, I would ride home instead. And so began a 23,000-mile journey across the world, leaving after only two days of planning, in only the clothes that I had, not sure if I had enough money, not even sure which way I was going to go. But knowing full well that I was going to give it a damn good go.

I talked to them about Indonesia and what that was like. I explained the process of putting the bike on a plane to get it over Burma, and then the carnage and chaos of India, the surprising delight of Pakistan, and then what a rush it had been coming across Kazakhstan, Russia, Ukraine and Poland with the engine oil bolt held in by a toothbrush, and a real panic as to whether we were going to make it or not.

I skipped briefly over the three years that followed before explaining how finally one day I snapped, riding the same bike down to Heathrow airport, putting her on a plane to New York and landing with no real plan other than to get back on the horse and start riding again. I told them about Chicago and Detroit, how slightly disappointed I'd been by Route 66 and how Kansas had been a weird old place, which they laughed at, because everyone says that about Kansas. Poor Kansas.

I shared my joy of Colorado and the Rockies, telling them how I'd had to push the old bike up and over the mountains, then down through Utah and Nevada to see the Grand Canyon and Monument Valley. I told them of my failed attempt at climbing Zion, mentioned Las Vegas briefly, before Death Valley – my favourite place – and how the last two days, from there to here, had been moronic and destitute in trying to get here in time. I made apology for my lateness, talking for a good hour or more until finally they decided it time to shut me up, at which point I received a warm round of applause, which was nice.

Kindly they said they'd have a whip around for me, to thank me for coming, and having collected over $300 in dollar notes, the club chairman said they'd double it, and so I got handed what amounted to around $650! I told them I didn't think they realised this, but that amount was almost equal to my entire budget for coming across the States, and so it meant a great deal to me. After that I was almost lost for words, because these were just strangers, and they didn't have to have given me a dime.

Stranger still, in the audience that night was a member of the San Francisco Motorcycle Club, who invited me to give a talk the next night at their clubhouse, which I did, and because there's a friendly rivalry between the two clubs, they too handed around a collection bucket at the end, being instructed that they had to beat the $650 I got from Oakland. And they did beat it, by about twenty dollars. This meant that having crossed America on bits of fluff and cheap McDonald's burgers, I now had over $1,300 in cash in my pockets, much of it one dollar bills, fives and tens, so my pockets were practically bulging with folded money. I felt like a pimp.

The cash injection was certainly handy, as I'd just missed my return flight out of New York (I'd booked it as a return rather than as a single), and had no other means of getting home. This money would pay for a ticket to get me there. How things have a strange way of working out in the end.

**

During this time in San Francisco I was staying at the house of a man named Pete, the nicest of guys who had attended the first presentation in Oakland, who had himself ridden around the world on a motorbike a few years prior. Pete had invited me to stay well before I arrived in San Francisco, with it comforting to know that I had his place as a base. Pete lived not far from the Oakland clubhouse, in a wooden house on a pleasant street, with a garage in which he kept his collection of motorcycles. He owned as many as six in total, most of them of a vintage age, with bags of character and stories to tell.

In Pete's garage I changed the oil on my bike and fitted a new back tyre. I still wasn't sure what I was doing, or where I was going to go from here. I'd arrived in San Francisco, not giving any thought to what would happen next, and so took a few days to think about it. Alaska by now was well out of the question. Too late in the season to even think about it. Though I knew that already.

I had thought about leaving the bike in Pete's garage, or at another address in San Francisco, flying home and maybe coming back next year to do some more. But for whatever reason that just didn't feel right. It didn't quite feel that my journey was over, or that I'd reached a suitable conclusion to this leg of it. I felt restless and anxious. Try as I might I just couldn't stand still. The road still beckoned. And from the north it called.

Lisa, the girl I'd met at the top of Angels Landing in Zion, told me that if I was ever passing through Seattle then I was to stop and say hello. We'd got on well, keeping in touch via email whenever I could get online. I liked her. And I did want to see her again, perhaps part of the process of moving on.

I looked at the map and calculated that it was over 900 miles to her door; straight up the west coast, ride out of the city and just keep going, don't stop until you get there. I buzzed at the thought of this; the sense of excitement that swells at the beginning of any new adventure. And once again, I had nowhere to be, no house, no job, no home; just a tired old motorbike, and enough cash in my pocket to take me to Lisa's door. I just needed to get Dorothy patched up first.

With the help of the satnav I found a decent mechanic right in the heart of San Francisco, deciding to take my chances on the interstate bridge connecting it with Oakland, the distance between getting on and getting off some four miles, which were a little hairy to say the least, but it saved me a massive detour around the bay, and certainly got the adrenaline going; four lanes of heavy traffic, with no breakdown lane or hard shoulder to ride in.

Having taken a ride around San Francisco – stopping off at Pier 39, riding down the twisting Lombard Street and staring out at Alcatraz – I eventually found the bike shop down a narrow side street, where I parked up and headed inside.

'Sounds like piston slap,' said one of the mechanics as they all gathered outside to figure out what was wrong with the bike.

I asked what that was.

'It's when the piston's not firing straight in the barrel and so you're getting this rocking motion, a vibration, which will only get worse.'

I asked what the solution would be and they said a new piston and rebore.

I asked how long she might go on the one she'd got.

'Not sure,' they said. 'Could go for a long while yet, or it could go

411

tomorrow.'

They asked where I was heading.

'Seattle,' I said.

They scratched their heads; 'Yeah, she should make it.'

And that was good enough for me.

Outside the bike shop I struck up conversation with a lady by the name of Patricia, who was riding a bicycle as her motorbike was broken and the garage was trying to fix it. She was there to see how they were getting on.

Patricia was an interesting sort, a little kooky, but very interesting to talk to. Not long after saying goodbye our paths crossed once more at a set of traffic lights in the centre of San Francisco. Given the fate of such a thing, we decided to grab a coffee together, parking up our bikes and heading into a trendy cafe that happened to be around the corner from where lines of homeless people were waiting to check in to a homeless shelter for the night.

I'd read somewhere how back in the sixties and seventies the mayor of San Francisco had promoted the city as a safe haven for those wishing to escape their current predicaments in other parts of America, and so flooded in the people who couldn't necessarily take care of themselves. This legacy is thought to be what makes San Francisco a magnet for homeless people to this day, with far more here in this city than anywhere else I'd ever seen. It was quite shocking, and a situation impossible to ignore. But if anything I'd begun to understand it now. America is the freest nation on earth; the freedom to completely succeed, or equally, the freedom to absolutely fail. It's where you fall between those two extremes that matters, though I still didn't fully understand it.

It was over coffee Patricia told me an unusual story, one that made a great deal of sense to me. It was about how one day she had found a massive block of grey polystyrene down on the beach, describing it as something you could barely hold it was so large.

Despite this, Patricia decided to take it home with her, and for the next two years carried it around with her wherever she went. She took it to work, to restaurants, to the theatre; she literally took this giant piece of grey polystyrene everywhere, even strapping it to the back of her bicycle and carting it around the city.

She called it an art experiment, hoping to gauge the reaction of the people who saw her with it. She wondered what questions people would ask, and what they would say. This went on for two years, with Patricia telling me how she was unable to leave the house without it, eventually reaching a point where the lump of grey polystyrene had become such a burden to carry yet something she just couldn't dispose of, as much as she hated having that burden.

As I sat and listened I couldn't help but identify with this, and how one single inanimate object and your devotion/commitment to it can start to dominate your life and demand a certain obligation to it, at the expense of almost everything else. I'd certainly been the same with my motorbike, feeling a strange obligation to not leave it in the shed to fester any longer, as though I had to bring her here and do this, for her sake, as much as for mine.

For Patricia, her freedom came one night in a bar when, with her back turned, a girl ran inside, grabbed the polystyrene block and ran outside with it, jumping on the back of a motorbike and speeding off, never to be seen again. After the initial shock, Patricia described a moment of massive relief, almost as though she could get on with her life again, because while she could never have given up the polystyrene voluntarily, to have it stolen, with that decision made for her, meant that she was finally free of her obligation.

Perhaps this is no different from relationships, friendships or jobs that have run their cause, but you just can't bear to be the one to end it all, because then it will be you who gets haunted by the possibility of regret. And so we might stick them out and put up with them, in the deep-down hope of being sacked, or dumped, or cut adrift. Weak and indecisive? Perhaps. Or maybe a simple case of not really knowing what you want in life, and letting time slip through your fingers while trying to figure things out.

In my case, whether I liked it or not, I was still chased by the regret of how this journey had all panned out. I was on this adventure, but I still missed the woman I loved. And no number of miles would ever

413

compensate for that; just that sense of needing to drag yourself forward, drag yourself out of it, with her shadow behind you at all times, pursuing you like clouds across a desert. But damn it Nathan, move on.

***

Having stayed a few more days in San Francisco, in a hostel overlooking the Golden Gate Bridge – paying for it with my new-found money – I was finally ready to hit the road again, those 900 miles ahead of me with someone I wanted to see at the end of them. It's amazing how focused and determined you are when you have a mission such as this ahead of you, with a clear goal and purpose. The simple task of sitting in the saddle and doing what you do best: riding a motorbike a bloody long way.

Having crossed the gorgeous San Francisco Bay and ridden up the hillside to take a picture overlooking it, the first day was spent gripped to the coastline, circling in and out of the coves and through the pretty fishing villages north of the city. Progress was slow; the road so tight and twisty. I remember it cold and windy as well, though that didn't dampen the enthusiasm of the tourists taking to the beaches of these northern shores. You could say it was utopia out here. The waves, the beach, the white wooden houses, the coffee shops and the cafés; a real surfer's paradise.

I met other bikers, some surprised by my ability to keep up with them. They were on proper bikes, and could travel much faster than me, but they would stop far more often, for cigarettes and coffee, and in that time I would catch them up and dawdle by, either stopping to chat or beeping and waving as I went. The tortoise overtaking the hare.

What I noticed as I pushed on the next day was how the towns changed the further north you went. Out of San Francisco, the communities were scenic and pleasant. Gradually they became more run-down and grubby. More people would be wandering aimlessly, either out of work or just fooling around.

I was told how cannabis is legal up here, and it did seem as though people who liked to indulge in that had migrated north, to the small towns on the coast, where perhaps they could be left to their own devices. I read

414

how the biggest town up here, Eureka, has serious problems with meth users, resulting in a serious number of crimes and burglaries (perhaps all vices aren't equal after all).

It was in Eureka, during that second day on the road, that I met another man by the name of John. This one was parked beside me at the local McDonald's and stepped out of his truck to ask about the bike I was riding on. He unnerved me at first, looking as unwell as he did. He was lent on a stick, his hair falling out in patches, and his eyes wearing a strange dull sheen. He looked in a very bad way.

His story was one of sadness, telling me how he'd served in the Vietnam War, becoming a truck driver when it was all over, having a terrible accident in his truck, shattering his back and being on medication that he believed had made his teeth fall out and his appearance look like it did now.

He told me how he lived up in the hills with a friend, trying to get his life straight. He said he'd come to live up here as weed was the best and most natural remedy for the pain; anything to get off the medication. His issue was with the pharmaceutical companies and the drugs he'd taken and how addicted to them he'd become. He saw America as now being slave to the corporation, it ruining the country, and the people within it. He had a passion for what was happening in Iraq and Afghanistan; the shame he felt, the future he saw for his country.

Before departing, John said something that really resonated with me, about the power of the subconscious, and how it dictates everything we do in life. He said that there is no point in fighting it, that it is happening and making decisions at a level that we can't even comprehend, and that perhaps our internal anguish is most felt when we try to fight it and impose our conscious thought upon it. Deep down we always know what's best, and we should trust it more.

I often wondered how I ended up riding out of Sydney on a motorbike that day, and I suppose this made sense of it; deep down I must have wanted it to happen, over and above anything else (such as finding a way to stay), and so conspired to make the motorbike trip happen, whether I was consciously aware of this at the time or not. I say this because at times

I felt guilty about riding out of Sydney that day and was perhaps looking for a little peace in what John was saying. I found some (or at least found some salvation), with it good to have met him this day.

I rode well into darkness those first and second nights, not the wisest thing to have done, but I was on a mission and had so much energy to dispel. It was perhaps 9pm when I finally decided to pull off the road at the end of this second day of riding up to Seattle, turning into the carpark of the La Kris motel in the small and pleasant coastal town of Bandon, eighty miles or so over the border into Oregon.

It wasn't a big motel, perhaps only ten rooms, with me able to park my bike right outside. Having unloaded all my gear and taking a shower, I watched *Batman Returns* on DVD, before falling to sleep in a king-sized bed, waking the next morning and continuing to push north, in the direction of Seattle, along that stunning Oregon coastline.

The atmosphere reminded me most of Colorado. California had seemed a little pretentious and trendy, whereas Oregon had an honest and earthy feel about it, the people more calm and relaxed, serving great clam chowder from their restaurants, with the stretches of road between the towns dominated by breathtaking views of the ocean, and meandering through giant redwood trees.

It was a shame that I was in such a hurry to get to Seattle, doing these great distances of some 400 miles a day, as to have taken my time and enjoyed this coastline would have been sublime. But my soul said ride so that's what I was doing.

One thing that struck me was how many cyclists there were coming down from the north. Some alone, others in groups, the road relatively quiet, though steep in places, with plenty of campsites dotted along it, making the route ideal for cycle tourists of all abilities. I also spotted a few hitchhikers out here as well, something I'd not seen on my entire trip across the States, suggesting how outdated it is; but here in Oregon it still went on.

Midway through the third day I arrived in the town of Astoria, at the mouth of a bay, with a huge and impressive bridge built across the estuary. The town was where the iconic eighties movie *The Goonies* was filmed. I double checked this with the attendant in the gas station, who confirmed that it was indeed the town, and asked if I was going to go up and see the Goonies house. I asked if he was serious and if you could genuinely go up and see it. He told me to go inside and ask the lady on the counter for directions.

The lady drew me a map – a treasure map – with the house only a few miles down the road, through the main town, then up on the hill, overlooking the bay and the buildings. The town looked as though it still belonged in the eighties as I rode through it, with antique shops and rustic cafés, a million miles away from the big cities I'd passed through on this adventure. Five minutes after being given directions in the gas station, I was stood on the very same spot that Chunk was seen doing his Truffle Shuffle.

The current owner was outside sanding wood, and more than happy to have me come up and take some photographs, his only plea for visitors to park at the bottom of the drive and walk up, as he shares the drive with three or four other houses and from what I gathered their owners had kicked up a bit of a fuss.

The man told me that as many as 10,000 people a year come to see the house, which by the way is now known as 'Goon Docks' (as I'd ridden up the coast, I had tried to spot the rock formation that One-Eyed Willy's pirate ship breaks free of at the end, but had been unable to pinpoint it. Apparently I'd passed it somewhere along the way).

By this time it was late in the afternoon. Seattle was still 270 kilometres, 170 miles, or over five hours of riding away. I wouldn't get there until at least ten in the evening, maybe even later, as the route I was taking into the city – to avoid the interstates – would involve catching a ferry across Puget Sound, the ferries only sailing every hour and a half. The last one was beyond midnight. In hindsight I should have just stopped in Astoria for the night and had a look around, but inside my body was churning, it just wanted to keep on moving, and so to have found a place to stay would only have left me restless.

Mist descended. The road appeared to skirt around swamps and the marshland of the tidal waters. At one point the road directed me on to

417

the main highway that I had to ride for twenty miles before I could get off and continue along more of the back roads. Dusk faded to darkness as I rode along it. I had my high-vis postal jacket on, and I was glad I did, as when I finally pulled off the highway, stopping in the first town to check my rear spokes were still tight, an angry driver in a pickup truck shouted at me for not having a rear light.

He said he'd seen me on the highway, but only at the last minute, having to swerve around me in order to avoid rear-ending me. He couldn't believe someone would be riding without any lights on. Neither could I. Clearly at some point the rear bulb had blown again, Lord knows when. I could have been riding the last few nights without a light, lucky not to have been flattened.

The man's name was Lewis and after his initial agitation he calmed down, helping me to find a replacement bulb in the supermarket over the road. He was a big walrus of a man, with a thick grey moustache and broad shoulders. Lewis was a biker too, the owner of a Harley Davidson and a boat he took his children and grandchildren sailing on. He seemed to lead a happy life, and asked if I could take a picture of him sat on Dorothy, using the camera on his phone, to show to his kids when he got home.

Lewis paid for the replacement bulbs and wouldn't take any money for them. He was just glad to have helped me on my way, though it did make me wonder why no one had flashed or signalled to me that I had no rear light before that point. It would have been nice if they had.

These were dark roads I was riding now, and with the fear of the bulb blowing again I would turn around every few minutes to check the rear light was still illuminated. When traffic came up behind I would pull over and let it pass. I shouldn't have been on the road at all. But there was no stopping me now. I was closing in on Seattle and just wanted to see Lisa again.

Finally, I reached the port in Bremerton, hoping to catch one of those ferries that would take me the last short distance across the Puget Sound. This is a vast inlet of water, with Seattle on the other side, the distance way too big to build a bridge. Sadly I'd just missed a ferry and had over an hour to wait for the next one, getting me into Seattle at around 2am. This wasn't ideal, but just one of those things.

The port had a Subway sandwich shop that was still open, so I ate a late-night dinner and used the Wi-Fi to check in with the world and let people back home know I was still alive, surprising them with news that I was not far from Seattle, not San Francisco, where I'd last checked in. In two and a half days I'd ridden over 900 miles.

Finally the ferry arrived and I rode aboard, part of a stream of traffic all desperate to get home that night. The ferry was a decent size with a large passenger lounge upstairs. I sat on a seat with my head and elbows leaning on the table, almost asleep, tired and weary. Very tired, and very weary. What an adventure it had been. From New York to here, with it feeling like it was almost over, just that final distance – once the ferry had crossed the Puget Sound – across Seattle and on to Lisa's door. Not much else to say. Just thank you, to so many things, and people, for helping me make it this far.

The boat docked and off I rode, emerging on the bright streets of Seattle. They were quiet; the occasional car and a zombie-like invasion of homeless people, just there in the gutters (I never did stop seeing and feeling an empathy with them). I relied once more on the satnav, following the arrows as they flashed up on the tank, just as I had done that first night back in New York, some six long weeks ago.

It was around eight miles to the house of the girl that I had met back in Zion, both of us dealing with demons up on Angels Landing that day. From there to here; that sense of excitement of seeing someone again, a person who got under your skin the first time and made you think that just maybe there is life after all this, and love, and everything that comes from that. Maybe it was the start of a new adventure. It was certainly the end of an old one.

PART 3

POSTCARDS FROM ALASKA
SEATTLE TO ALASKA

Chapter Forty-Five
Seattle

I stayed in Seattle with Lisa for two weeks. We went camping to Puget Sound, a peaceful island network to the north of Seattle. It was great to spend some time with her as we had a lot in common and connected in the way that at times two souls do connect. I enjoyed being shown around Seattle, going out for dinner, for walks around the neighbourhood and down by the old market, where the famous 'fish flingers' of Seattle do their trade. I liked Seattle, it was one of the nicest American cities I'd experienced. I left the bike parked out on the street during this time, perhaps a part of me finally wishing she'd be gone when I woke the next morning.

Eventually, I used some of the money donated to me by the San Francisco and Oakland motorcycle clubs to fly myself home to England. I couldn't hide out here in Seattle forever, as much as I might have wanted to. The flight that I finally booked was a return flight, returning to Seattle in six months' time, after winter had passed. In the meantime, I would leave the bike in America, go home to England, see what I found there, then return in the spring to make the final push north to Alaska.

I knew myself well enough now to realise that having set my sights on Alaska, I would have to do it at some point, as I knew the desire wouldn't just go away or expire, and as the bike was already out here it made sense to leave it, go home, then return once the weather was better and my mind was better prepared for it. Besides, I couldn't stay in America as I wouldn't have been allowed to work legally, or stay for longer than three months (and I'd been there almost two months already), due to the nature of the visa I was on.

Lisa took me to the airport. It was perhaps a case of right people, wrong time and I'd learnt not to fight such things as that. I would miss her though, not really wanting to go back to England, as part of me was worried that I would be returning to the darkness that I was in before I left for America. But I knew that I had to go back, as I'd left things in a bit of a mess the day I suddenly took off, and felt I needed to go back and clear that mess up. I just hoped I could make a better job of things than I had done in the past.

The difference this time would be that I was taking with me all the strength and clarity I'd just won on the ride across America. Those times of sleeping rough in dried-up river beds, of arriving at Vermin's house in Colorado Springs and wanting to be done with it all. These were big tests and I'd passed them. I'd survived, and in a way, I'd already won the battle I'd been fighting with myself.

During my time back in England I would leave Dorothy with Jon and Natalie, a couple I'd met on the internet a few years earlier. They'd followed my first trip on Facebook, even buying themselves a Honda CT and naming it Dash, in Dot's honour (Dot and Dash, Morse code, as Natalie worked as a computer technician). Having spotted that I was on my way up to Seattle they'd invited me to drop by and say hi. It was then that I'd asked if there was any chance of leaving my bike in their garage over winter, to which they said it would be no problem at all.

I met Jon and Natalie at a local bar and diner called Cafe Racer, a place where just four short months prior, a gunman – thought to be a disgruntled customer – had entered the premises and shot four people dead, wounding a fifth, and then shooting and killing another person as he car-jacked a vehicle, trying to escape from the police.

It was hard to imagine it happening in such a place. It was an ordinary cafe-come-diner, next door to a music shop, up from a traffic light junction in a pleasant part of Seattle. There is live music and the walls are decorated with the art of local residents, intentionally 'bad' art, just to give the place some character.

It's popular with motorcyclists, as the food is good. For someone to burst in and shoot four random people didn't make any sense, especially as Ian Stawicki, the man responsible, shot and killed himself at the end of it. What a senseless and pointless thing to have done. Why did he just not start, and finish, with himself?

You could join the dots between many things mentioned to this point: the sense of discontent, the prevalence of drugs (prescription or otherwise), the propensity for firearm ownership, the sense of despair you can so easily find in yourself, the rage this can invoke, the desire to unleash that rage, mated to a success-driven society that punishes those at the bottom for not 'trying' harder in life. Add to that a perceived future with no hope, not to mention this human instinct to leave a legacy behind, even if it's a brutal one. Run and jump, or shoot the world to hell? That's not to make excuses, simply suggesting that banning things doesn't necessarily help, not if the problem is more deeply rooted in the minds of those and the societies involved. I'm not even certain that a gun free society would be good for the sense of American liberty. Too many agents there that I'd distrust. Perhaps a new war is looming.

In the recently reopened Cafe Racer, Jon, Natalie and I drank coffee and ate delicious pulled pork sandwiches. We talked for a few hours, about bikes and big trips. They were about to embark on their own big adventure, something they'd never done before; riding a couple of bikes down to Mexico and back. They were nervous and apprehensive, though excited nonetheless. They had two weeks holiday, and they intended to make the most of it. If I'd had any advice it would just have been to enjoy it, and take from it what you need.

After a while we headed over to their house, where they had cleared a space in their garage, beside their own collection of bikes, including a British-made Triumph Bonneville, the bike Natalie was going to use on that journey south in to Mexico. They were certainly a sweet couple, giving me no reservations about leaving with them the bike that had carried me all this way. I was certain it would be as safe here as anywhere else, and the time apart would do both of us some good.

Later that week I landed in England and took the long coach ride home to Yorkshire, back to the house with the shed in the garden where the first book was written, it still bearing the scars of the attack by pitchfork. It was strange to be back there, especially after the events of the past two months. Such a long distance travelled with so much having taken place. So many people met. So many thoughts and experiences had. And now I was standing on exactly the same spot as when Rob and Greg had turned up that day, with their postie bikes all the way from New Zealand, their dose of reverse inspiration clearly working.

I definitely felt better in myself now, as though I no longer had that mind of screaming voices, all competing for my attention, all wishing to pull me in different directions, threatening to tear me apart. I also had more direction and purpose in life, combined with an appetite to get my life back on track.

Of all the paths I could have chosen, I was glad that I had chosen the one that I was on. Had I gone with the prescription drugs I imagine I'd still be here, attacking the shed, though probably with less conviction.

A national motorcycle newspaper offered to print some copies of my first book and sell it through their shop, taking a huge weight off my mind as it would bring some much needed money in. I was then invited to sell books on a stand at the big bike festival at the National Exhibition Centre near Birmingham.

I also finally found the focus and decisiveness to move out of the family home (I'd ended up back there when writing that first book), moving to the town of Leamington Spa, in the heart of the Midlands, the nearest town to the university I once studied at. I didn't really know anyone who lived there any more, only a friend named Aide. I moved to Leamington because it gave me clear space, away from family and the majority of my friends. It meant I could concentrate, I could breathe.

I moved into a cheap shared house with rooms for sixteen other people, more like a hostel really, though it didn't require a big deposit and the minimum term was just three months, a commitment even I could deal with. It was cheap, furnished, and had Wi-Fi included. The bathrooms were shared, so too the kitchen and the lounge, but it was close to town, and for the first time in almost four years I finally had my own place, my own set of keys, my own bed, my own desk, and even a little stray black cat that would come and howl outside my window. And because in a strange way it reminded me of myself, I would let it in and feed it, especially during the cold winter months when snow was on the ground.

I found work in a local cardboard box factory, working on the production line, counting the unassembled boxes into bundles of ten or twenty, binding them with strong nylon cord, then stacking them on pallets and sending them down the line. It paid a minimum wage of some £6.50 an hour, with a loud whistle to let you know when your shift started, when you could have a break, and when you could stop for lunch.

It was the antithesis of my life on the road. While I was there, I was completely controlled, and in a way I quite enjoyed it. It took some of the pressure off. I would get up at the same time every day, roll out of bed, put on my scruffy clothes, quick breakfast, rush to work, work hard, get stuff done, then come home and feel that something had been achieved that day. It was the routine that I needed, and the people I worked alongside were a real mix of ages, races and backgrounds. It was racial integration in action; Sikhs working with Poles, working with Brits, working with Muslims. And everyone got on and did their job. It was great.

Some of them, such as Donna, had been there twenty years, working the same machines for all that time. At first I thought it crazy that they could do that. Did they not get bored, did they not wish to move on and see more of the world? But the more I got to know them, the more I realised that they were, for the most part, far more content and happy than I'd ever been. They came to work, did their job, went home, and lived. About my adventures I said little. They made me feel very humble and grateful for what I had seen and done.

I also worked at a supermarket the few days up to and over the 2012 Christmas period. I gathered trolleys in the carpark, collecting them together and pushing them back to their bays after they had been left lying around by lazy customers. Again it was minimum wage, but I loved darting around the carpark on Christmas Eve, everyone in high spirits, wishing each other a Merry Christmas, before loading up their cars and driving home to feed their families over the festive period.

I joined a gym and attempted to get fit; going to boxercise, pilates, even step aerobics, for fitness of course, not to perv on hot girls. But it was good, providing more of that routine I so desperately needed and had been without for so long.

During this time in England I spent as much time as I could with my Nan, visiting on a Sunday and taking her for a ride to the local pub where we'd have a carvery, and then to the garden centre for a coffee. Sometimes we'd load the car up with other old ladies from the warden-controlled flats and head out down memory lane. One lady, Cath, was in her nineties, requesting that we took a particular road one day as it was somewhere along it, 75 years earlier, that she'd done most of her courting. She was almost speechless at the sight of it, as though she'd seen herself again, like a ghost in the rear view mirror.

I find it necessary to spend time with older people. They are great motivators, reminding you of what we all become, and the situation we will all find ourselves in; when we don't have the health to do those things we always wanted to do, and so all that's left is to sit and stew on them, as the long minutes tick by. Far too much time to sit and to think.

I know this is what frustrated my Nan. She'd always been so active, so keen to go and to see things (perhaps it's where I got it from), and now she had to accept that she couldn't do it any more. Only she couldn't accept it. She wanted to fight it, and did fight it, but ultimately it's a battle you can never win. What I take from this is the emphasis to do things now; do things while you still can; even if it's just: 'hello, I'm sorry, I love you.' And we all have someone in our lives we need to say that to every now and again.

The months went by and before long I was facing the prospect of returning to America, and to Dorothy, who'd been waiting patiently in Jon and Natalie's garage for all that time. I'd not bothered to check on her very often. I knew that with them she would be fine and in a way it was a case of out of sight, out of mind. I enjoyed this time apart. Like Patricia and her grey block of polystyrene, these things can be such a burden, and when they're there right in front of you they can taunt you with their fixed stare that is impossible to escape or to avoid. They make you feel guilty for not riding them more.

A month or so before my flight back to America I left the job at the box factory, to begin the task of writing this second book, aiming to have it done before I returned to America, at least the bit from New York to San Francisco. I didn't even get close.

I lay down a rough first draft, sat at my desk with the window ahead offering views over rooftops that I'd drift off and stare at. The hardest thing about writing a book is determining the tone; the way you say things, the mood you evoke. Maybe it's me, and the way my mood fluctuates so wildly at times, making it hard to be consistent, because some days you're up, and some days you're down. But this was nothing compared to what it was like before. I didn't look at ropes or beams. I didn't punch myself in the face. I just got on with it, sat down and wrote.

Finally time came for me to return to America, and complete the push north from Seattle to Alaska. My flight was on the 23rd April 2013. Originally I'd planned on being away forever, or at least with no fixed plan (finances permitting, and they weren't great), but in the weeks preceding the flight I'd been offered a job working on a magazine that specialised in long-distance motorcycle riding, working in their editorial department, finding other people on big trips and making their stories heard in a bi-monthly magazine.

It wasn't the job per se that attracted me, more the sense of security and sustained routine that it would afford me. In summary, it would provide me with the perfect excuse to sit still and stop travelling for a while. And so this trip back to America, to complete the ride up to Alaska, was simply an obligation I felt I needed to fulfil so that I could stop for a while without it being on my mind.

With the job due to start at the beginning of June I would have just over six weeks to complete the journey north. This wasn't very long at all, but having consulted with my dad, it was agreed that for most people wishing for these kind of adventures, there usually is a time frame to work around (like Rob and Greg) – be it family or work commitments – and so

429

it wouldn't do me any harm to have one either. It would just mean I would need to be more focused and hit the ground running when I landed back in Seattle.

From Seattle to Alaska was a distance of only two to three thousand miles – depending on where in Alaska you are heading to – with me having covered six thousand miles, in six weeks, on that original trip across America. So time, really, wouldn't be too much of a problem (or so I hoped). The only issue would be getting me and the bike home at the end of it, though that would be something to worry about at a later date. Let's get there first…

I do wish to state that living like this does take it out of you. This calamitous nature, this life of having no plan, simply feeling the way the wind is blowing and going along with that. I suppose in a way I was in a state of perpetual panic, circling on the spot, surrounded by a wall of flames, waiting for the right avenue to open up and darting down it before the gap was gone again.

I didn't plan on checking out of my rented room while I was away. Instead I locked the door, put the keys in my pocket, boarded a bus to the airport and got on the plane, relieved to know that in six weeks' time, on my return, I would have a place, and a job, to go back to. And I can't begin to tell you just how much I liked the dynamic of this.

I'd even told my parents this time, with no dramatic mad dash to be on the road, but a bit of time to organise and get together all of the things I thought I might need on this journey to the top of the world.

I watched movies on the flight out there, sitting looking out of the window at the world below, not so scared any more as I knew there was nothing left for me to do but this. And I think I was free of almost all regrets.

I fidgeted in my seat, read the in-flight magazine, listened to the in-flight radio. I was flying via Iceland as this had been the cheapest option. In the hold I had packed my familiar open-faced helmet with the target on the side. So too the orange postal jacket, the welding gloves, the manly Australian boots, the laptop, the camera (a new one for the trip), as well as a host of new things, such as a warm biker's jacket, thick trousers, proper winter gloves and some thermal underwear as it was only just breaking out of winter and into spring.

Seattle was scorching when I landed, in the midst of a heatwave. Lisa picked me up from the airport. It was almost six months since I'd seen her last. By now we were friends, nothing more than that. It was just great to see her again. She was a strong girl, fighting her own fight, and with a heart as big as a bucket. I was glad our paths crossed that day up on Angels Landing. She had been just what I needed. Someone to think about and ride towards, with it now just great to see her again and spend some time in her company.

The following day I caught the bus to Jon and Natalie's house on the northern side of the city. It was good to be back in America. I felt as though I was approaching it with a new set of eyes this time, ones not as critical as they'd been first time around, which is more a reflection of me than it was of America.

***

The bike was just where I left her, in Jon and Natalie's garage, though shuffled around a little, as in the past few days they'd attempted to get her going again. To manage this they'd had to drain the fuel and change the spark plug. She always was a little stubborn after being stationary for such a long period of time. But it was good to see her again, like finding a big part of yourself buried in the back of the garage, or old heirlooms up in the loft. On this occasion I sat in that familiar seat, grabbed those familiar handlebars and took her for a quick spin around the block. She felt small, slow and old. To think I'd ridden all that way on this. To think I was going to ride her some more.

There were two things I wanted to fix before pushing north. Those two things were the spokes in the back wheel, which had relentlessly needed tightening ever since that handful had snapped on the way into Detroit. The second issue to be fixed was the engine and that piston 'slap', diagnosed back in San Francisco. Neither of them were major jobs, but it did scupper the initial plan of going back, getting on the bike and setting off for Alaska.

I pitched my tent on Natalie and Jon's back yard while we went to work fixing up the bike. The house was on the north side of the city, in a quiet suburb, well away from any traffic. Jon fortunately had some time off work – he fixed boats for a living – and so offered to drive me around the bike shops, doing our best to find someone who could help us with the parts we needed. Jon had a fixation for bikini latte, a strange phenomenon, native to Seattle (thankfully), where drive-by coffee huts, located at the side of main roads, feature young female baristas wearing bikinis or skimpy lingerie, and making a lousy over-priced coffee, in exchange for a glimpse of their bust and gusset. I felt dirty and cheated, both at the same time. Jon lapped it up (thankfully not literally).

As for the spokes in that back wheel, having asked around the local bike shops, we were told about a man going by the name of the Wheel Wizard, his premises some forty-five minutes' drive away, on the south side of the city. Jon called the guy and asked him about the wheel, which he said he could fix. We also asked him about the engine, which he agreed would need re-boring and a new piston fitted. He said he could do that as well. Perfect.

We disassembled the bike in Jon's garage and drove down with the engine in a box and the wheel in a plastic bag on the back seat. We passed through the heart of Seattle, a place I was really beginning to grow fond of. The outlying suburbs were for the most part pleasant and leafy. Downtown was full of cool bars and restaurants, the Space Needle overlooking it all, then the famous markets where on a Sunday morning the world really came to life. I liked this north-western part of America in general; people just seemed more relaxed and more open-minded up here.

We found the Wheel Wizard's house out in the southern suburbs; a simple bungalow with a huge workshop built in the yard. The Wizard's real name was Murray, a man in his seventies, if not approaching his eighties. Murray told us how he had served his apprenticeship at Boeing, which is based in Seattle, his job to make the aeroplanes work by operating machines with such accuracy that everything fit just right.

Murray took great pride in his work, caring much about the job in hand and gracing us with cans of Coke as he gave an almost two-hour explanation into various parts of the machining process. He talked us through the milling machine and the drill that would re-bore the cylinder, explaining it in meticulous detail. We'd certainly found the right man for the job. Murray was also a religious man. On the back of his car a bumper sticker read: 'My boss is a Jewish carpenter.' I was more than prepared to put my trust in him getting the bike ready for the journey to Alaska.

Of the wheel he said he'd cut new spokes and laced the wheel in such a way that would make it stronger than it had originally been. He said he would re-bore the barrel to accommodate the one oversize piston and leave it to me to put it back together again, which I felt comfortable doing after the practice I'd had in recent years, rebuilding the bike in the garage with my dad. With that, we left the parts with Murray, returned to the city and hung around for a few days, drinking more bikini latte, waiting for the work to be done.

Murray had done an amazing job when we returned to pick them up. The back wheel looked magnificent and appeared solid enough to take twice the weight of what it previously would; perfect then for the long slog through the wilderness of Canada and Alaska. The re-bore on the barrel looked perfect as well, the measurements being checked twice and Murray giving us instructions on how best to put everything back together, which we managed with no real problems.

Jon predicted she'd start at third kick, and she did, firing into life once more. Sadly the noise that had plagued her all the way from Death Valley was still there, meaning that it probably wasn't the piston after all. It was more likely to be much deeper inside the engine, the bottom end perhaps, which was far beyond my knowledge and budget to investigate. This made me ponder the journey ahead, riding into Alaska on an engine that wasn't running quite right. I suppose it was an increasing lack of confidence I had in her, and I'd never had reason to say that before.

I put some thought into it over the next few days, running the engine in gently on a ride out with Jon and Natalie and the rest of their scooter gang, at least fifty of us in total, tearing through the city, some of the bikers blocking the junctions to allow everyone through, red light or no red light. It made me sweat and feel uneasy. I tried to enjoy myself but this sort of thing wasn't for me. It made me realise that I'm a bit of a lone wolf. I like my own company too much.

Finally, I loaded up the bike and still didn't really know what to do. That engine really bothered me. I thought I'd play it safe and ride down to Las Vegas instead, attend an overland bike show that was happening this coming weekend and then fly myself and the bike home to England straight from there. It would be the easiest and safest option.

But as I rode out of town heading south, getting about seventy miles out of the city, I decided that it just didn't feel right (if Sascha had been here, the fearless guy I met riding the Himalayas, he would undoubtedly have called me 'gay'). So I turned the bike around, rode back to Seattle, camped in Jon and Natalie's garden one last night and made haste towards the border with Canada the following morning. It was just a hundred miles or so to get there, riding through the suburbs, then into rural landscape, before arriving at the border.

I recorded a video diary having just crossed it, completely perplexed at being in Canada. I was confused, and bemused. I was in the twentieth country of my trip, the sun was blazing hot, and the guy at the customs booth had been inquisitive about who I was and where I was going.

'To Alaska,' I told him.

'On that?'

'Yes sir.'

(Shrugs) 'Okay, have a good day.'

The plan now was simple. There wasn't one. Just ride north, and figure it out along the way. It would be a case of riding up through Vancouver, taking the back roads that would lead me through the ski resort of Whistler, then continuing north, towards Dawson Creek, picking up the Alaska Highway from there and then following it all the way through British Columbia, then the Yukon, before crossing the border into Alaska and getting as far north as I could get before needing to go back for the new job, starting now in just four weeks' time.

I didn't know how I would get me or the bike back to England in time. All I knew was that I was now riding to reach the end of the road, because I was tired now, and I think I was just tired of running.

Chapter Forty-Six
Canada

I rode first into Vancouver, very much liking the look and feel of the city. The streets were full of life and activity, with it hard to believe just how warm it was; this coastal side of North America was enjoying record temperatures during these early days of May.

My intention wasn't to stay in Vancouver very long, aiming instead for Whistler that night, as the distance from Jon and Natalie's house was just perfect to get me clear out of the gate and a safe distance from the 'turning back' zone. It's a trick of the mind perhaps, something you need to do in order to get yourself clear of your starting point. This being my third big trip on Dorothy, I was quite used to the psychology of it by now.

Having crawled through the city streets, I stopped for a quick look around Stanley Park, a 1,001-acre public site on the far western edge of Vancouver. Before British Columbia was colonised by the British in 1858, the area on which the park was built was used by indigenous people for thousands of years. Now it was completely manicured, peaceful, and being cycled around by tourists and locals on push bikes. I circled the perimeter road myself, before taking Lions Gate Bridge across Vancouver Harbour, landing on the north side of the bay.

From here I traced the Trans-Canada Highway as it ran west along the coast. As I wasn't permitted to take it, due to the engine, and the speed, I took the suburban roads running parallel instead, passing beautiful sea-view houses that reminded me of those in Sydney, the way they'd sit up high, looking down on the water, with perfect views.

From there the road, and the land, turns ninety degrees, almost like riding around the outside curve of a bent elbow, the road now pointing north, following the edge of an inlet known as Howe Sound, named after Admiral of the Fleet, Earl Howe. Just after the curve the interstate becomes a quieter two-lane highway and I rejoined it, leaving the last traces of suburban Vancouver behind.

I was now riding the Sea-to-Sky Highway, a road infamous for the number of people that have died driving along it. The cause was often the bad weather, the unguarded cliff-top drops, the poor visibility or in some cases, the alcohol consumed. It was only in 2010 as part of the bid for the Winter Games to be held at Whistler that the road was finally improved, and so now, high above the water, snakes a smooth and for the most part dual carriageway road, that on this evening was almost entirely free of traffic.

Some forty miles north of Vancouver I stopped in the town of Squamish. There was a Tim Hortons here which, as anyone who has been to Canada will know, is a native chain of coffee shops, selling a variety of doughnuts, bagels, sandwiches and soups. Think of it as a more rustic version of McDonald's, and from this point on it would serve as my resting place when seeking sanctuary from the road. Once more, I would need to travel on the cheap, with the intention again to camp as much as I could.

Beyond Squamish I spotted my first black bear. It was sitting on the top of a bank beside the road, staring at me as I rode by. I was nervous, my fear stemming from a book I'd read in anticipation of my journey to Alaska. The book was called *Bear Attacks*, and written by a man who had studied bears and their attack patterns for many years. The book gave graphic account of the incidents that have happened, and what became of the people involved in them.

The stories were terrifying, with some victims stumbling across a bear and its cub whilst walking a trail and the mother attacking out of defence for her kin. Not everyone managed to get away. There were other stories of grizzly bears actively hunting people while they've been out camping, dragging them from their tents and tearing out eyeballs and chewing off legs. The advice was not to run, but to stand still, not looking the bear directly in the eye and, if attacked, play dead, which sometimes worked and the bear would eventually wander off, but it didn't always work, and then it would be time to fight back; the advice being to go for the eyes.

What surprised me most was the speed at which bears can run. Apparently, a bear at full speed can reach forty miles per hour (so about as fast as my bike), with their acceleration said to be phenomenal.

In a way I wish I'd never read that book, as all it did was instil a fear in me, and so on passing the bear that evening I was quite concerned about what it might do. I watched it intently as I passed on by, its eyes following me as I did so.

Later that evening, when I arrived in Whistler, I was asked if I'd pulled over to take a photograph of the bear, to which I questioned if they were serious or not, and it seemed as though they were. In reality, the chances of being involved in a bear attack are quite rare, with other vehicles and traffic remaining, as it always does, the biggest danger on the road.

Whistler though was lovely; a purpose-built ski resort and village founded in the 1960s, the hotels and shopping district all clustered at the foot of the slopes, the snow well clear of the streets, but up on the mountainside there was still enough for a few more weeks of skiing. In fact, the resort didn't close until the end of May, such was the snow cover up on the mountain. I had a friend working in Whistler, Milene, who I'd met on previous travels. She was now a manager at a hotel here in the resort and was able to get me a luxury room in a central location for a heavily discounted $40.

It was nice to treat myself, the bike parked below in the underground carpark, whilst I took the time to gather my thoughts before the journey north. I was nervous, as once again it felt as though I was taking a giant leap into the unknown, and while I was better prepared and more experienced now, I still felt uneasy knowing that so much uncertainty lay ahead of me. But nerves I think are good for you. They focus the mind, and must mean that you're doing something that will take you forward in life. They are a good indication of a worthy challenge ahead.

I spent two nights in Whistler, even thinking about heading up on the slopes to do some skiing. Instead, I hung around the town centre, sitting in the sun, meeting Milene and her friends for drinks in the evening. It looked to be a great way of spending a winter for those from Europe and Australia wishing to explore a different part of the world; earning some money and making good friends as they did so. When you look around, there are so many opportunities to work overseas and to travel; to Australia, to Canada. It really isn't so difficult if you're interested in doing it, and who knows to where it might lead.

From Whistler I headed north. It felt strange to be heading north, possibly because I'd spent so many miles of this adventure heading west (all the way from Australia), and now I was pushing towards the summit, along a different trajectory, the sun passing overhead, from right to left, not from behind and to the front. It felt like the temporary scrambling of my internal compass.

Just outside Whistler I stopped to look back at the town, and take a photo of the red bike in front of the crisp blue lake, the snow-topped ski mountains behind it. It was around 7am and still quite chilly. I was wearing all of the clothes I had with me, but knew that soon the day would thaw, and once more the temperatures would soar.

From the shores of the lake, the road began to climb and climb, circling Cayoosh Pass, before reaching a peak of 1,275 metres. Compared to what I'd ridden in India, Pakistan and Colorado, this was of no real altitude, but with the freshly rebuilt engine, and the steepness of the incline, I couldn't help but feel nervous, with little choice but to leave the engine in first gear as this poor old bike – Dorothy – weighed down with all my gear, chugged her way up the mountain, the road running between a towering chasm of pine trees.

Until the 1970s there wasn't even a road running through these parts. Prior to that, the terrain was deemed too steep for the building of such a thing, although when James Duffy, a Royal Engineer, mapped these parts back in 1859, his intention had always been to clear a route through. More than a century later, the road was finally laid.

A lake was named after him, Duffy Lake, the road eventually leading me along its shoreline, my impulse being to stop and savour another early morning moment. I parked the bike down by the water's edge, and what grabbed me most was the way in which the land, the trees and the snow-capped mountains were all reflected in the water, creating a perfect mirror image.

The world too was very quiet out here. There was an occasional passing of a pickup truck or a timber lorry, but nothing else of much distinction. Perhaps it was the scale of the place, as all of a sudden you realise you've entered a grand wilderness, with a road just so happening to be running right through the heart of it. This leads to a tendency towards paranoia, thinking of breakdowns, accidents and bears, and what you would do if any of them happened. Generally, you're best trying not to think of such things.

In the town of Lillooet, some eighty miles to the north-east of Whistler, a man I met at a gas station was kind enough to give me a can of bear spray, something not always easy to buy as there are questions over its legality. The man worked on the land and so carried a few spare cans in his truck. The can he gave me was a few months out of date, though we figured it would still do the job.

Bear spray is like regular Mace, though with greater distance, designed to deter the bear should it look to attack, or come too close for comfort. The book I'd read advised carrying a can of the spray, though you need to be careful when spraying it, especially if the bear is upwind, as the Mace will just blow back at you. Even so, I was grateful to the man for offering it me, tucking it within easy reach inside that same Indian tank bag given to me by Nancy and James all the way back in Manali, now four years and some eighteen thousand miles ago.

I heard from them both sporadically, understanding that after their trip through India on a Royal Enfield together, James had gone to New Zealand on a working holiday visa and enjoyed it so much he'd stayed, becoming a resident having been granted his own New Zealand passport. Nancy, meanwhile, moved back to Germany, writing screenplays for TV shows and generally trying to figure out the meaning of life, and how she best contends with it. There is certainly something about the traveller that leaves them looking for answers, or conversely, using travel as a means of going in search of answers.

As for Lillooet, I read later how it was once one of the main population centres of the St'at'imc, an indigenous tribe also known as the Lillooet Nation. Lillooet was also at the heart of the Fraser Canyon Gold Rush from 1858 to 1859, when it reckoned to be the largest town west of Chicago and north of San Francisco. Situated on an open plain, enjoying scorching hot days in the summer and bitter cold days in winter, the town was now much quieter. It was difficult to imagine it as a thriving gold rush town. From that to this. It made me think of Detroit and how such places expand and contract, just as Lillooet did, almost a century and a half ago. The rise and fall of towns, and empires, I suppose.

From Lillooet, Highway 99 continues along the valley until it meets the junction with the Cariboo Highway, the main artery road heading north. The road I had taken through Whistler to this point was the scenic route and I was fascinated how the landscape changed so quickly, from the frosty alpine mountains of Whistler and the area around, to this stretch north of Lillooet, which was much more open and barren. It was almost as though I was back in the prairies of Kansas; even the temperature was nice and warm.

The Cariboo Highway led me all the way to Williams Lake, the biggest town in the region. It was founded in 1860 and acted as the meeting point of two roads on the gold rush trail. I did nothing but pass through Williams Lake, stopping only for gas and refreshments.

I talked with two local men at the gas station, one of them warning me about the bears. It seemed that everyone I met wished to warn me about the bears. It was the same script as I'd had back in Australia, though there it was the snakes, the spiders, the crocodiles and the Aboriginals I was to be mindful of. Here it was the bears.

***

I covered a total of 321 miles this day, taking me all the way from Whistler to the town of Quesnel, a place that once claimed to have the largest gold pan in the world, and which now survives on tourism and logging. The town appears from nowhere, you suddenly come upon it as it is camouflaged so successfully by the landscape.

I had a friend living in Quesnel, a lady by the name of Danielle, who had read of my first trip and kept abreast of my movements ever since via Facebook. She taught at the local college and, having seen that I would be passing through her town, had invited me to camp down for the night, which I was grateful for, as it served as another beacon on the horizon to which I could head towards.

Sadly I was a little agitated that night, and the following morning, not proving to be the best of company. I have to concede that the mask does slip at times, and the impatient, tetchy and sometimes morose character comes out. I don't like it when it does that, but I find it increasingly hard to hide and so just have to go with it, and do my best to be pleasant and gracious in the meantime.

I believe this is why I avoided many invitations of accommodation from people online, especially on that initial trip across America, as I just didn't fancy wearing the mask on an evening, even if it meant sleeping in dried-up river beds instead. Perhaps it's a fear of not living up to the expectations people have of us, so avoiding those situations all together. What I mean by that is people probably expect a happy-go-lucky adventurer, and I'm just not always like that and I didn't wish to disappoint them, or spend all evening acting. That trip across America would certainly have been a lot easier had I accepted these invitations.

Danielle rode a bike herself, a much bigger model than mine. She planned on riding it up to Alaska one day. She just needed that final push to get her over that first hurdle. It was then heart-warming to hear a little later that she had in fact done that very thing, not many months after my flying visit. She'd ridden her bike up to Alaska.

It would be unfair to take any credit for that; Danielle was obviously on the cusp of doing it herself. It was just nice to think that the passing through of Dorothy had given her that final nudge, to have seen this tiny little bike and know where it had come from, and know where it was heading to, and to think, 'well, if that can do it, then so can I.'

From here I followed the Cariboo Highway in the direction of Prince

George, a town at which I would have a decision to make. To continue north would take me to Dawson Creek and the start of the Alaska Highway. Or I could turn left, taking a slightly longer and more remote route along the Cassiar Highway. That route would involve fewer towns, gas stations and services, but ultimately leads to the same place, rejoining the Alaska Highway up in the Yukon Territory, some 1,000 miles north of here.

At any other time I might have considered the more remote option, but I think now, with the bike as old as she was, and not running as well as she could (though thankfully still running), I considered it more sensible to take the more populated route, in case things went wrong and I needed some help along the way. Besides, to ride the Alaska Highway had a certain appeal about it, and just felt instinctively that it was the right path to take.

That day riding out from Quesnel I vividly remember going through everything that had brought me to this point, almost as though my past was laid out in front of me as I rode along. From travelling to Australia on a working holiday visa all those years ago, meeting a girl at speed dating, coming home, going back, bottling it, crossing paths on the ferry, trying to make it work for nine months, failing, getting on my bike and riding home, realising what I'd lost, missing it dearly, writing that first book, becoming chained to the past, finding myself on a downward spiral, not knowing how to get back up, crying, punching, wrecking, until Rob and Greg turned up; back on the bike, to New York City, across the guts of America, to San Francisco, Seattle, back on my feet, home to England, job, stability, time to breathe, then back to Seattle, to complete this, to complete this six-year episode of my life. And now I was here; slowly working my way up to Alaska.

Chapter Forty-Seven
The Alaska Highway

Having stayed the night in a dingy cabin behind the gas station at Mackenzie Junction, travelling north-east along the John Hart Highway, I finally landed in Dawson Creek, a frontier town sadly not the same place as the TV show of the same name. It still felt like an important place to be arriving at, the town marking the official start of the Alaska Highway; the main artery that runs through the rest of Canada and up into Alaska.

In its early days the town was nothing more than a small farming community in the centre of these windy northern plains. It grew in 1932 when the Northern Alberta Railway was extended, then exploded in 1942 when it was suddenly decided that a road connecting Alaska with the rest of the United States was needed to counteract a potential strike on the state by the Japanese in the midst of the Second World War.

Without a road, America wouldn't be able to send supplies and equipment up to Alaska, and so, in just nine short months and using a workforce of around 11,000 military troops (a third of which were African American), a road from here in Dawson Creek to Fairbanks in Alaska was built, work commencing on the 8th March 1942.

The road eventually totalled a distance of 1,700 miles, built at an average of six miles per day, and cut through the savage wilderness of Canada and Alaska. The men had to fight against the frost, the terrain and the wildlife, with the road completed on the 20th November 1942. It was a staggering achievement of engineering and manpower, with

Dawson Creek the supply town into which everything was initially sent: men, machinery and equipment, with some of the men deciding to stay there once the road was completed.

The main industries now are tourism, oil and gas, agriculture and retail. At the height of the summer season it is the place where convoys of motorhomes gather, before making the long slog north. This being so early in the season I would thankfully be missing the stampede, much preferring that the roads would be quiet, and lonely, and that I would have them largely to myself. It all added to the sense of adventure.

One of the reasons so many gather here in Dawson Creek and head north together is for a greater sense of safety. I'd even heard that some Americans won't travel to Alaska as they aren't permitted to carry their guns through Canada, and don't wish to travel through this wilderness unarmed. To think that Gary, the 77-year-old cyclist I met back on the shores of Lake Erie, came though here on a pushbike and lived to tell the tale.

In Dawson Creek I stayed at Mile 0 Campsite, a site on the edge of the town, the zero representing our position at the start of the Alaska Highway. There weren't many others camped here. In fact, I'd heard that many of the tourist facilities north weren't even open yet, due to the late breaking of spring and it being so early in the season. There were mixed reports on this, though I was sure it was going to be okay.

Two of the few other travellers on the campsite were Jack and Renee, a retired couple (though they didn't look so old) from Wisconsin, travelling up to Alaska to work on a campsite just outside of Anchorage. They had sold their house and bought a huge motorhome, which they were now travelling and living in. It was a fabulous thing, with enough space in the rear for Jack's Harley Davidson, with a ramp so that he could ride the bike right up into the back of the motorhome.

The bike was a classically styled Harley Davidson, with a huge white fairing and a custom paint job; the panels painted white with the image of a bear sprayed on the front fender, and a barbed wire motif wrapping around the rest of the panel work. It was a nod to Jack's past as an unsavoury character: part of biker gangs, involved in violence and other unpleasant things, then finding religion and becoming a different man; a better man as he saw it.

He was certainly imposing; tall and stocky, with a thick moustache and beard, as well as a pair of fists you wouldn't wish to be on the end of. Yet at the same time he was such a gentle soul, who I think had finally found some peace in life. We talked in great depth about many things, the pair of us almost welling up at times, such was the connection.

It was exciting to hear of their plans to spend the summer up in Alaska working on the campground in exchange for free board, before returning home in the winter and then planning on doing it again the year after, and the year after that. The world was their oyster now, and with the motorhome they lived like turtles, with their home on their backs. There was talk of me putting the bike in the back of the motorhome and riding up with them to Anchorage, but as always it would have felt like cheating, as enjoyable as it would undoubtedly have been.

In preparation for the journey north I picked up a cheap pair of Wellington boots from the Walmart at the far end of town, along with a five-litre fuel can just in case the distances between gas stations were too far for what I could carry in the tanks. I also picked up waterproof fishing gloves in case of relentless rain, a survival blanket for the cold, spare oil, and some Tupperware boxes to keep all my electronic gear dry, as those Indian panniers were far from waterproof, especially with the number of tears in them now.

Otherwise, I just spent a few days hanging around the town, taking the bike down to the Alaska Highway sign to have a photograph with it, eating breakfast in a local diner where the chatty waitress would go around the tables endlessly re-filling coffee cups, like they do in the movies; the type of place locals dine every morning before heading off to work in their pickup trucks.

In another cafe I met a local girl named Andi, who gave me a walking tour of the town one evening, the pair of us walking for miles, from one end of town to the other. Andi was only nineteen years of age but she had a wise head on her shoulders and a strength about her personality that made me think she'll go far, and do well in life.

Andi was of First Nation descent, and we talked briefly about how that was, and how she saw the world, and what she'd encountered. Of course, the past always plays a part in the present, with it impossible to forget that her ancestors were here first, and the gold prospectors and other settlers came second. Attempts at reconciliation have recently been made. This to me is a good sign of man; that we can be unjust, and take what we like, but over time recognise our failures in doing that, and go some way to make amends, even if the clock can never be turned back completely. It's a start at least.

Finally came time to load up and head out of town, riding north along the Alaska Highway. I was daunted by the prospect of this. It felt like stepping on to a trail that you knew would take you through a very cold and lonely place. I believe that's why I stayed those few extra days. I was simply letting the pressure build until I could hold it back no longer, letting the inevitable explosion propel me out of town and along the first few miles of the road, like a rocket that had been lit by its own impatience at wishing to reach the sky.

Jack and Renee had left an hour or so earlier, the suggestion being that I go and see them on their campsite up in Anchorage, some 1,500 miles to the north of Dawson Creek, when I finally landed. I expected such a distance to take me no more than five days, as with nothing much to detour for, and no real attractions or distractions along the way, I would be able to cover a decent number of miles everyday, much as I'd done on the route through the Australian Outback; just keep heading for the horizon and count the miles as you go.

A short distance out of Dawson Creek I took a quick detour on to an old stretch of the original Alaska Highway (the route of the road has evolved over the years), in order to ride across the Kiskatinaw Bridge; one of the last remaining curved wooden bridges in the world. Built in 1942 and taking nine months to complete, it's also one of the longest, at 531 feet. The bridge was finally made redundant in 1978, when its weight limit of 25 tonnes was deemed insubstantial. The road was diverted a different way, and a new bridge was built.

The Kiskatinaw Bridge was a sight to behold, the way it organically emerged from one bank of this gentle valley – a white water river at the bottom – and across, in an arching manner, to the other side. Built out of wood, you're able to look over the side at all the girders and legs that hold it up from the valley floor. I didn't linger long, just time to take some photographs and savour the moment, remaining alert as I was still paranoid about bears, half expecting one to jump out of the bushes at any moment. Stupid really; bears can't cross bridges, can they?

What I remember most about this day, apart from the bridge, was the rain. It was relentless. For hour upon hour I was riding into it, with all of my waterproof clothing on, and because my helmet was open-faced, I still wore the handkerchief across my face, it bogging with water and proving almost impossible to breathe through at times, the material suctioned against my lips and my nose. I would like to say it was unpleasant, this long day in the cold rain, but somehow I enjoyed it; one of those masochistic battles with the road, a case of putting your head down and ploughing on through.

There is certainly something masochistic about these endeavours. They have to be hard or there wouldn't be a point in doing them. And if they become too easy then you do what you can – perhaps subconsciously – to make them hard again. Perhaps they are instead intended as periods of self punishment and self flagellation. This is the point that some people find difficult to understand, questioning why you would do such a thing. But I think sometimes you need that test, and that process to go through. The harder a journey is, the more you seem to get out of it. Twisted logic really.

I arrived that evening in the town of Fort Nelson (named after British naval hero Horatio Nelson and founded in 1805 as a fur trading post), having covered some 282 miles that day. I was cold and wet, looking for somewhere to sleep and being directed to a campsite at the top end of town. I was the only person in a tent; the others that night were all in motorhomes.

The campsite had a restaurant made out of old wooden beams, the inside like a nineteenth century saloon. For dinner I ordered poutine, a traditional Canadian dish consisting of chips, with chicken, smothered under a blanket of curdled cheese. It tasted worse than it sounds. I ate half of it, and saved the rest for breakfast.

It was cold in the tent that night. I slept in most of my clothes. The bike was parked close by outside, the Wellington boots upturned over the top of the wing mirrors to allow the water to drain out. I threw the tarpaulin over the bike to keep the sheepskin seat cover dry (the same one that I'd had since Caboolture), waking the next morning, crawling out into the cold air and warming myself with a coffee bought from the restaurant, while finishing the leftovers of last night's poutine.

The wilderness really set in from here on in. It was unimaginable to think what it must have been like back when they were carving out the road through this once uncharted wilderness. The rise and fall of the terrain, the wildlife, the mountains, the snow and the ice. Then the years that followed, the road improved but still not paved, people driving along this route in their 1970s cars and trucks. What an adventure that must have been; no mobile phones or sophisticated 4x4s. I gathered there were more gas stations and roadhouses back then, some of them visibly closed by the roadside now, slowly decomposing as nature retook its land. It was the same atmosphere as crossing the Australian Outback, another place I'd so dearly loved passing through.

Sixty miles out of Fort Nelson the road steadily climbs out of the valley you previously entered, rising to a point where a big gravel clearing has been made, with a wooden platform offering incredible views of the Muskwa River Valley below.

It was a spectacular sight, with a carpet of dark green fir trees in the foreground, only recently starting to take on some colour following a cold and brutal winter. Beyond that snow appears on the ground as the terrain on the other side of the valley increases in altitude, forming a crescendo of jagged mountains, met bluntly by a puffy grey and cloudy sky, the type you might see if snow loomed heavy in the air.

I shared this magical sight with several people who stopped that morning to see it for themselves: a couple in a car, pulling a massive trailer, relocating up to Alaska with all of their belongings; then another man travelling solo in an old German car.

This man was tall, wearing blue jeans, a checkered flannel shirt and a thick grey beard, easily in his seventies and with a very calm and easy-going manner about him. He told me how he lived in a cabin in the woods, deep in the heart of Alaska, and was now driving down to Seattle to visit his children, and their children.

He told me a story about a bear he encountered outside his cabin recently, it coming too close for comfort. The man went inside to get his rifle, the bear charged as he emerged, and the man brought it down with a single shot between the eyes. I stood and listened to the story, spellbound. It was a tale from a way of life that would sound so alien to most people, but one that had a certain appeal to it. I could have seen myself living up here for a while.

I think it's the vastness of it all; a real sense of entering the last frontier of man, a kinetic energy about everything you encounter and see, almost as though all those nice houses and cars, and everything you've worked for in your life, count for nothing up here, because it's just you, stood face to face with nature. And there's a certain enchantment in that. Alaska really does seem like the last bastion of the nomad, a place for those desperately scrambling to get away from the world.

Not many miles further along the road you come to Tetsa River Lodge, a place that promises the best cinnamon buns in the land. Sadly, the baker was just about to head out in his truck, meaning there were no buns to be bought. The lodge was just like so many rest stops up here: an old wooden building with a diner inside, some with a petrol pump outside, and a series of outhouses for chopped logs and machinery. Then nothing for another fifty miles.

The next one was Toad River Lodge, the ceiling of which was decorated with thousands of trucker hats, an age-old tradition it seems, started way back in sixties when the first trucker nailed his hat to the ceiling. I chatted with the waitress having downed a couple of hot coffees. She was a young Filipino girl, here to work for a few years before being granted full work rights to stay in America.

Much like the two guys back in the Midwest town of Carlinville (on the approach to St. Louis), I couldn't imagine what a culture shock that must have been; from South East Asia to the top end of Canada. Yet she seemed happy here, even staying through the brutal winter months, when there would have been such long periods of heavy snow and darkness, with few different faces passing through.

I continued on through what felt like an endless gorge, the road winding its way along the base of it, hugging a wall of loose rock and shale. There was a purple hue about the landscape, the trees without their fir appearing almost skeletal, and the countryside barren and bleak. There was an infrequent amount of traffic travelling in either direction, just the odd logging and pickup truck, still the endless need to keep one eye on the rear view mirror, just to be certain of there being no vehicles sneaking up from behind.

No matter how remote the terrain is, you never totally disconnect from the task at hand; you're always alert, always ready and reactive to the environment. You have to be, because it's just you up here; no backup, no mobile phone, no breakdown cover or local hospital. You can't afford to have an accident. And, touch wood, I hadn't had any of a serious nature so far, only those buses I'd found myself sandwiched between back in Indonesia. That had been a close call, but since then I had survived relatively unscathed.

The engine felt tired now. The bike felt old and weary, despite the new piston fitted back in Seattle. Poor old Dorothy. In a way, I think she was trying to relay messages to me. If she could talk I imagine she would have said, 'I've almost had enough now, when can we go home?' And I would have said, 'soon Dorothy, soon...'

The road fed me around a beautiful frozen lake, the edges of which were only just beginning to thaw. I stopped briefly to take a photograph. I reasoned that it would be nice to have someone standing next to me to share the moment, ordering a couple of hot chocolates at the next rest stop, going through the photographs taken, laughing about what we saw, and what we'd encountered. It made me wonder sometimes what I was gaining from all this, coming up here alone. But then I remembered; I was trying to find the end of the road, as elusive as that had been proving. It felt as though I was on my way to finding it. I just didn't know where it was just yet.

A pack of wild buffalo greeted me up ahead. They were mammoth things, with thick shabby brown coats, long curling horns and huge humps of fat behind their necks. I wasn't sure if they were dangerous or not. I'd heard moose could be, attacking for no reason and a more real and present danger than bears. Buffalo, however, I just wasn't sure and so rode forward with caution. A motorhome approached from the opposite direction, gently passing the herd. I used that as protection on one side, keeping an eye on the buffalo less than ten feet to my right, nodding at the occupants of the motorhome, and relieved to see the buffalo remain docile in my rear view mirror.

A little later I raced one, the beast initially over the other side of the roadside barrier, then hopping over it as I passed, so that it was now galloping right behind me along the road, thankfully not at a pace I couldn't outrun. I think it was just playing a game of chase, as I was with the rainbows that rose above me that afternoon, getting caught in rain showers that plagued the day. But everything was so crisp and blue, with thick green forest all around – a blanket of wilderness that I was slowly making my way through. Quite simply, it was brilliant out here.

Chapter Forty-Eight
The Yukon

I arrived that night in the town of Watson Lake, finding it to be a drab little place: one long wide street with a couple of motels and businesses on either side. I wouldn't have stopped here had it not been for the onset of nightfall. There was an RV park at the top end of town, operated by a man originally from Scotland who was not at all pleasant, not initially in any case, being quite blunt about the lack of anywhere else to camp in town.

He told me that to stay at his place I'd have to pay for a pitch on one of his powered motorhome sites. I asked if he'd do me a discount as I only had a one-man tent, but he wouldn't; those were just the rules. Reluctantly I took it, mainly because it had been a long day and I just needed somewhere to settle down for the night and I didn't much fancy bedding down with the bears, the moose and the buffalo.

My tent was set up against a bank of snow. I charged my laptop in the laundry area, sitting in the warmth for a while, before heading over the road to the gas station, only to find it attended by an Englishman out here working for the season. He told me about the problem with drugs and alcohol in the town, a consequence he assumed of the long dark winters, where people need something to turn to. And that's what they tend to turn to, causing massive social implications with no cure yet to be found.

Two other motorcyclists pulled up at the gas station as I paid for my evening snack of peppered beef jerky; a substance I was increasingly beginning to survive on out here. As both riders were on enduro bikes I thought I would introduce myself, and let them know about the campsite I was staying on, in case they needed somewhere to stay for the night. In response, one of them seemed to scowl at me, and then they just went about their business as though I wasn't even there. I caught that their accents were from overseas, I wasn't sure where, though I certainly didn't get a good vibe from them, so I left them to it and wandered up the road to check out Sign Post Forest.

This is Watson Lake's premier tourist attraction, and can be found on the roundabout at the top end of town. It is a strange phenomenon that started way back in 1942, when an American GI working on the Alaska Highway nailed up a sign with his name, the date, and his hometown on it. From there the trend spread, with there now thought to be as many as 80,000 signs, plaques and licence plates nailed to a forest of totem poles, set up in various expanding circles.

It really was an incredible sight, walking through the 'forest', reading the various messages and memos left by people who had passed through these parts over the last seventy years. Some just carried names and a date, others messages to loved ones, and even long deceased cats. Some messages were scratched into frying pans, written on planks of wood or any writable surface they could find. It made me wonder if the original GI was still alive, and if he'd been back to witness the phenomenon he'd unwittingly started. What a legacy that man had left, without even intending to do such a thing.

Having ridden west out of Watson Lake the following morning, it wasn't long before I was passing the junction where the Cassiar Highway joins the Alaska Highway. The Cassiar is the road I could have taken out of Prince George, a thousand miles ago. What many people do if they're on a return trip to Alaska, is take the Alaska Highway up and the Cassiar Highway back down, or vice versa, just to give them a change of scenery. I was glad I'd stuck to the main route. It was wild enough as it was, with just enough homesteads and stop-off towns to keep you company along the way.

This day was usual. Riding, eating, gas station and riding. I was heading to Alaska, and that's all that I had to do. I was overtaken at one point by another motorcyclist, riding a big Kawasaki trail bike. I waved to the rider as he passed and he waved back, fist pumping the air, his wild hair escaping the back of his helmet and a face of pure thrill. He and his bike slowly faded into nothing as they rocketed along the road, making me wonder who he was and where he was heading to. Another case of sonder perhaps, and certainly much more friendly than the two bikers from the night before.

Some 162 miles out of Watson Lake the road began to descend into the wide expanse of a valley, a great river running through the heart of it. Spanning the river was a sturdy metal bridge, of great length, green in colour, and no doubt surfaced with the same metal grids that covered all the bridges up here. I assume they are to prevent icing, but on a motorbike they are a nightmare to ride across as your front wheel skips and meanders from one groove of the metal grid to the next, making it hard to ride in a straight line.

Before riding down to the bridge I sat up on the rise, a gravel pull-off giving views of the river basin below, with an information board explaining that the small hamlet of buildings on the far side of the riverbank was the community of Teslin, an ancient Indian Reserve – home of the Tlingit First Nation – and a trading post established way back in 1903. You could see why they would build a trading post here; on a bend in the river, shadowed by the mountains around, perfect for hunting and trapping, which apparently is still done by members of the Tlingit First Nation who still live out here.

I stood on a rock to take better pictures of the view before me, starting to feel a real chill in the air now, the temperature certainly dropping in the 1,500 miles I'd been riding since leaving Seattle. I was now in the Yukon Territory, having crossed the border between here and British Columbia not far out of Watson Lake.

The Yukon is the smallest of Canada's three federal territories, with Whitehorse the territorial capital and Yukon's only city. Long before the arrival of Europeans, central and northern Yukon was populated by First Nations people. Coastal and inland First Nations had extensive trading networks. European incursions into the area only began early in the 19th century with the fur trade, followed by missionaries and the Western Union Telegraph Expedition. By the 1870s and 1880s gold miners began to arrive. The territory's population of 33,000 live in an area the size of Sweden, making it barely populated at all.

I rode down towards the community of Teslin, across the bridge of doom, wobbling and weaving along that metal grid, ready to stick a leg out should I need to. A homestead had been built on the other side of the river, offering a pod of petrol pumps, a small museum and a busy little diner. It was only 2pm and the perfect spot for a rest break after a full morning on the road. Filling up with gas, I met a man with a van load of motorcycles heading down to America, who was kind enough to buy me a coffee having heard all about where this little red bike had come from. He seemed enthralled, having owned a bike like this during his childhood. It gave him the chance to reminisce.

Inside the homestead I also met Calvin, a 24 year old from Tennessee, riding down from Alaska on a KLR650, the same sort of bike that had passed me earlier in the day. Calvin was a handsome chap, square jaw, southern drawl, and as polite as they come.

He had ridden up to Alaska at the end of the previous year, leaving his bike there while he went home and worked on his family's farm in Tennessee. He'd recently returned to Alaska, collected his bike, and was now heading back south, towards Seattle, where he planned on loading the bike on to a cargo boat and sailing it west to Russia. From there he would ride across Russia, also through Mongolia, heading in the direction of Europe.

We spent an age talking about his trip and the time frame he had, which wasn't so long, but he was certainly making the most of the time that he did have. I gave him my email address and told him that if he ever needed anything in England, or just wanted to drop by, that I should be back by the time he makes it there.

Odd to see how the world is connected in that sense; how Calvin can be going around it in one direction, while I go back in the other, and a little later we both end up at the same spot; making you realise just how small the world is, or at least how interconnected and accessible most parts of it are.

It was here that I also met Seth, who turned out to be the guy that overtook me earlier in the day, 'yopping' and hollering as he did so. Off the bike, Seth was a tall and strapping twenty-something; long, curly hair with plenty of volume, kept beneath a dusty old train driver's hat. He also wore a set of old dusty dungarees and had the appearance of a beatnik vagabond, the type that might previously have hitched a ride across America on the rail carts.

He too was from the south, or at least sounded like he was, a real long drawl and a carefree manner. Seth was just one of those people who commands the attention of any room he enters, explaining how he was heading up to Alaska to work on a fishing boat for the summer and planning on sleeping on the beach in a tent the whole time. He was something of a hippy and a nomad at heart, but in many ways all three of us were that day; me, Seth and Calvin, sat around the table drinking hot coffee in this pleasant Yukon community of Teslin.

We talked about my trip, and their trips, and about life on the road, and what had brought us here. The hours flew by, we got through some coffee, everyone trying and failing to flirt with the waitress, who was attractive and didn't she know it. We finally all conceded that none of us wished to ride any further that day and that maybe we should just set up camp in Teslin. Calvin and Seth had both wild camped through much of Alaska and the Yukon, just heading off into the forest and pitching a tent. With all the talk of bears it was not something I'd ever thought of doing, and I admired their recklessness greatly.

It was suggested that we all go off and wild camp this night, but with a campsite behind the homestead, with views across a frozen lake, I talked them into camping there instead, ten dollars covering the lot of us.

I suppose I was at the opposite end of my adventure to what they were. They were on the leading edge of it, their hearts and souls full of fuel, so camping wild was very much a part of their spirit, whereas I felt like I was nearing the end of my adventure and didn't need the wilderness quite so much, hence why I was happy to stay on a campsite. Besides, I was a little older than they were, and a great deal wearier.

We set up our tents as close to the lake as we could get them, only a low timber fence and a short stretch of soggy marshland and we could have been swimming, though with the mist descending and the light leaving the sky, it would have been a very cold swim. It was at this point that two more bikes arrived, the pair of them pulling into the campsite and heading over in our direction. I recognised them from the night before; the two unfriendly guys who had scowled at me at the gas station.

They turned out to be Israeli soldiers, on leave from the army and spending their extended break on a motorcycle trip around Alaska. They joined us in putting up their tents down by the lake. I wasn't so keen to have them join us at first, but what can you say? Half the problem was my own prejudice. I'd encountered Israeli travellers before, mainly up in the north of India, where many of them seem to head having completed their two years of compulsory military training, which to me seemed to make them militant, and exclusionary, never really mingling with anyone else.

It turned out to be a great evening. The Israeli soldiers, whose names I now don't remember, had bought a huge fresh salmon from a fisherman earlier in the day, wrapped in paper, storing it in one of their pannier sacks. They also carried broccoli, sweet potatoes, ranch dressing, and a whole assortment of spices in a rack, all in their motorcycle panniers. They were kind enough to share their food, and having cooked it over a roaring log fire we all sat down with plates of grub much better than any I'd eaten in a long time.

I got the impression that they didn't think much of me either, not at first in any case. At times they came across as quite intimidating, and dismissive of me travelling on the shit bike that I was. They would joke and laugh about me in Hebrew, and I didn't like the vibe very much. Finally they asked where I'd come from on it, and when I told them Australia they didn't believe me. But when I finally managed to convince them it was true, they discovered a new-found respect for me, and just wanted to hear how I'd done it. Strange how they had no time for me until that point.

In return, they told stories of how, during their time in the army, they'd been sent to guard the border with Palestine after people had tried to sneak through it the previous nights. The following night the soldiers claimed they were ready for them, gloating that they'd gunned down and killed the people who'd tried to come through. For me, living a life relatively free of violence, it was like hearing a story about a different world, one that I couldn't comprehend, despite my journey across half of it.

It reminded me of something the assistant in the army surplus store, back in Seattle, had told me when I was picking up supplies for this journey north. He'd said to me, following a quip I made about the necessity of war for keeping his shop well stocked, that, 'You can't have peace without war,' or, 'without war, you can't have peace.' One of the two…

His comment stopped me in my tracks and had me question whether what he said was true or not. And I couldn't help but conclude that maybe it was, as perverse as that might sound. To enjoy peace, we must have war. I'd be less inclined to agree with him were it not for the fact that, despite knowing how awful wars are, we still seem to engage in them, and find appetite for them, whether they be wars on a national scale, or even those we encounter in relationships, or in our own heads. Without war things would be stable, and I don't think that is man's inherent state. We seem to crave change and forward motion, and forward motion seems to bring about conflict, and so we pit ourselves against one another (or against ourselves). There is also good money to be made from war, whether it be at national or corporate level, or at the army surplus store selling cast-offs. That's not to say I agree with any of this. It's more just what I've come to accept, though not readily.

The following morning we all crawled out of our sleeping bags and lazily got up and packed. There didn't seem any urgency to this day, no desire to take off in any direction. Coffee helped perk us up, and by 11am we were all set to hit the road, apart from the two Israeli chaps, who were going to stay an extra day and chill out in Teslin. Calvin was heading south, in the direction of Seattle, whereas Seth and I were heading north, in the direction of Alaska.

It had been a great experience meeting them all that evening, making me question the way I'd been travelling the last 33,000 miles, and wondering if perhaps I ought to slow down a bit, and do things in a more relaxed manner, as they were doing. I'd certainly raced across the world, desperate to either go, or to get there. Now I saw how others travelled, and I quite liked the look of it.

As it was, Seth and I decided to ride together for a while, perhaps as far as Skagway, some 150 miles to the west. It was like riding with Vermin all over again, expecting him to get fed up after five minutes and come racing past telling me he'll see me when I eventually get there. But in fairness to Seth, he rode alongside for a good few hours, travelling at less than thirty miles per hour for long periods of time, simply because of the wind and the inclines that really pushed us back.

It was great to have some company on the road though; to have someone in your rear view mirror to point things out to, or to pull over and chat to when you want to find a hot coffee. Equally, someone else in the frame to photograph, instead of just taking pictures of you and the bike, which I often tended to do.

Seth did finally get fed up, and about seventy miles out of Skagway pulled over to tell me he would go ahead and see me at the destination some time later that evening. I said that was absolutely fine, it allowing me to relax a little, as ultimately I do tend to grow quite tense if I feel that I am holding someone up. I watched as the black dot of Seth and his bike grew smaller and smaller, before disappearing from sight all together. Back alone, in this vast empty wilderness.

I was tired and weary now, running on fumes, running on empty. I'd thought much about where this journey might end and whether or not I'd make it up to Anchorage or to Prudhoe Bay at the very top of Alaska. Part of me thought that I should, given that I was already up this way, and the other part of me couldn't give a damn, because I was fast approaching the point where I finally felt that I'd ridden far enough, and to ride any further would only have been to say that I had done. It was a conundrum that was beginning to plague my thoughts as I rode.

I hit a junction where the Alaska Highway carries straight ahead and the road to Skagway veers off to the left, along Tagish Road, with Skagway some fifty miles at the end of it. To carry on going straight would take me to the town of Whitehorse, but for whatever reason I felt that left to

459

Skagway was the right way to go, perhaps for no other reason than to catch up with Seth again.

The road now wound through the forest. I remember it being beautifully surfaced, and sheltered from the wind. After a decent distance you cross a river, passing through the community of Tagish, where summer businesses were starting to prepare for the onslaught of visitors from the south; a few restaurants, a bed and breakfast, and a campsite.

A little further along I arrived at the slightly bigger community town of Carcross, or Caribou Crossing as it was originally known. The town was once a fishing and hunting camp for Inland Tlingit and Tagish people, until the Klondike Gold Rush of the late nineteenth century changed the face of it, and the name of it, forever.

The town was now a haven for tourists out of Skagway, ferried out on buses to have a look around the replica buildings of the past. What a strange development the town had seen; from First Nation land, to be claimed by gold prospectors, and now to be swamped by the trade of tourism, the gold now being brought *to* the town in the form of tourist buses, rather than taken *away* from it in wagons.

I ran into Seth here, grabbing a coffee and a cake with him from the local German bakery. The ladies in there made a real fuss of us. I guess we were a novelty act, two desperadoes on motorbikes, in tatty old clothes and a reckless abandon. Normally the bakery would be busy with tourists on organised tours, but this was mid-afternoon, and so most of them would have been back on their tourist coaches, returning to Skagway. We met a nomadic traveller here, pedalling on a bicycle from town to town, everything he owned in bags and boxes on the bike, a bit like the gold prospector I met back in Pahrump. I felt for the man. It looked like he needed some help, though he probably would say the same about us.

Seth rode off once more into the distance, it now just 65 miles to Skagway. I'll never forget that afternoon of riding. It's fair to say both me and Dorothy were knackered. She felt tired and fatigued, barely able to haul us up these hills, and I'd long since stopped getting off and pushing. The wind was at our face, the rocks were to our right, and the vast expanse of those icy cold lakes dominated the views to the left. Then the road would climb and climb, snow by the roadside thickening, almost floor to ceiling high in some places. Fortunately it was dry and cold, a blue sky horizon, then the Canadian border post, surprisingly unattended, meaning that we could ride into the no-man's-land between Canada and America without anyone even stopping us.

To say that Skagway is in Alaska is something of a technicality, because when you look on the map it looks more likely to be part of Canada, but that's just the way the borders were formed. Still, at the top of the snow-covered pass, in the midst of no-man's-land, you are suddenly greeted by a sign declaring your passage into Alaska. It was a fantastic sight: Alaska, that place I'd half-heartedly set out to conquer when embarking on that trip across America. I knew I'd make it to San Francisco, but I was never quite sure I would make it this far north. But I was here, feeling a huge sigh of relief, and a little bit of weight lifting from my shoulders.

A pair of girls stopped to have their photo taken with the sign. We took one another's pictures and then they left, soon to be replaced by a young chap named Sean. Sean was only in his twenties, driving a battered old Toyota saloon car, loaded to the brim with camping gear, the boot full of dry foods, as that summer he planned on going off-grid, hiking solo into Alaska's various National Parks and heading off *Into The Wild* for a while, which, as anyone who has seen that movie or read the book will know, is a potential pathway to misery and doom.

Sean was up for it through, and in front of that big Alaska sign we both posed, smiling like Cheshire cats. I admired Sean a lot, he was at the foot of a great adventure, and planning on sleeping in his car in Skagway that night, such was his meagre budget.

The border post into America lay not far beyond this. I was asked the usual sequence of questions: who I was, where I was going, when I was going home, and how long I planned on being in America. I told the man that I had to be back in England in two weeks time, that I had a return flight home and that for now I was just heading to Skagway for a look around. He seemed satisfied with this and waved me on my way. From here it was downhill all the way into Skagway, the point at which this adventure finally comes to an end.

Chapter Forty-Nine
Skagway

If you look down at your outspread fingers, imagining them to be the land, and the air around them to be the water, then you will find Skagway right in the crease of where two fingers meet. The neighbouring town of Dyea is in the next crease along, but it now lies abandoned, almost vanished without trace, after the deep water port of Skagway became the most prominent town in the area way back at the turn of the twentieth century, back when the Klondike Gold Rush struck, making Dyea redundant.

The area was previously inhabited by the Tlingit people from prehistoric times, living here for thousands of years. Then the Klondike Gold Rush occurred in the late nineteenth century, bringing hordes of prospectors heading to the gold fields another 500 miles to the north. Skagway emerged to supply the rush and served as a drop-off point for steamboats bringing the prospectors up from San Francisco and Seattle. At the height of the gold rush, as many as 1,000 prospectors would pass through the town each week, many of them failing to return, such was the brutal nature of the landscape that faced them. Two books by Jack London, *The Call of the Wild* and *White Fang*, give an insight into this period and are well worth a read.

It was hard to imagine, as I rode into town on this old motorbike, that little more than a hundred years before this was a lawless place, 'little better than hell on earth,' as one person described Skagway at the time.

And now, in the space of one long lifetime, it had evolved into a peaceful, quaint, and immensely pretty town, with just 900 people living there year round. A further 900,000 souls visit on day trips every year, with an endless flow of cruise ships docking in the harbour, disembarking their cargo of passengers to spend the day wandering around the shops, or heading off on day excursions, before getting back aboard and sailing off.

I don't know what it was about the town, but when I got here, I felt like I'd made it. I felt like I'd finally 'arrived'. And despite intentions to move on the following day, I instead stayed an entire week, right up to the point at which I needed to leave. The reason I stayed so long is because I felt at peace here, and no longer felt the need to keep running to the next place. I think, finally, I'd exhausted myself of that, and was just content now to enjoy the place the road had brought me to. It almost felt like I'd been riding the last thirty-odd thousand miles solely in search of Skagway, and it was good to have finally made it here.

I stayed at the Alaskan Sojourn Hostel, in actual fact the beautiful home of Janilyn and Gary, which they just happened to have opened up to passing waifs and strays. The wooden house, with a big glass-fronted veranda, stood on a corner, eight blocks back from the harbour, with a big tree in the garden, and a front door that was always open; a system devised so that if you arrived without having made a booking, then you could see if there was a bunk available, put your name down for it, and check in, even if no one else was home. That alone was enough to set it aside as a place you knew you could relax.

Seth was also in town, staying on an old friend's couch, just a few blocks further out than the hostel. He too planned on staying just a few days yet ended up staying for a week as well. It was something to do with the weather further north, which meant that he was in no hurry to get up to his fishing boat duties outside of Anchorage. Instead, the pair of us hung out that week, getting to know the locals, wandering the streets like two weary old amigos from out of town.

It's said that there are two stories in life. The first, a boy leaves his village. And the second, a man walks into town. I guess that's what it felt like for us two wandering hillbillies.

We'd wander down to the docks to watch the cruise liners sail in and out, or we'd go for a beer in a bar called Red Onion, decked out like a saloon you might see in a vintage western movie, the waitresses dressed up in period clothes of petticoats and garters. It was more authentic than it sounds.

Skagway itself still consisted of the same wooden buildings that would have been there from the start, some of them brightly coloured, one of them covered with white sticks, nailed to the building in various patterns. The first three or four blocks back from the harbour were predominately made up of jewellery or gift shops, but after that it was a mix of everything, with some great little cafes and bakeries, and even a shop devoted to Sarah Palin, though sadly I was no longer wearing the bracelet given to me by Jeanie and Gerald, having lost it back in England.

Seth and I somehow found ourselves invited to the free showing for locals of the town's long standing 'Days of 98' musical production. It exists as a nod to the town's past, telling the story of the legendary Soapy Smith, a scoundrel and racketeer who ran the town until he was shot dead in 1898, hence the name of the act. It was a brilliant show, held in the town's old theatre, on chairs that felt like they too dated back a century.

There was one main actor playing Soapy Smith, and three buxom girls playing the whores that were around him at the time. Popcorn was served, and the theatre whooped and cheered.

It was whilst watching the play that we met a team of young people – most of them in their early twenties – who all worked on the White Pass Railway as tour guides and ticket sellers. The train line was originally built to send supplies to the gold fields in the north, but was now used to take passengers from the cruise ships on a day trip to the top of the mountain, and then back down again, at a cost of around $120, something me and Seth could never have afforded.

Having been taken pity on, we were invited to a complimentary ride on the steam train the next day, which proved to be one of the highlights of this entire adventure.

The train line snaked back up the mountain I'd ridden down a few days prior, up towards the border-crossing into Canada, and then back down again. The track passed through numerous dark tunnels, and across rickety old railway bridges made of wood. The snow grew thicker the higher we climbed, the train and all its carriages so long that on the sweeping corners you could look back and see the rear carriage of the train, way off in the distance, steam billowing from the top, and the sound of the whistle ringing out across the valley.

Most people sat inside in the vintage carriages looking out at the views from behind polished glass. Seth and I stood instead out on the deck at the back of the carriage, exposed to the fresh air, able to reach out and touch the snow banks as we passed between them.

Seth had brought a flask of coffee and a bottle of whisky, which he poured into the coffee and drank until he was drunk. This brought him to song, singing old western tunes and ditties at the top of his voice, much to the amusement, or perhaps annoyance, of all those in earshot. Not one for bringing undue attention to myself, I grew embarrassed and in the end had to demand that he calmed down and stopped 'yopping' at the top of his voice. At one point he even got a young Chinese lad 'yopping', and everyone else who came to the back of the train, he would try to get them to do a 'yop' or a 'yeehaa', which he performed relentlessly, until the whole mountain shook.

He was such a crazy character, raised as a Mormon, now borderline alcoholic, no doubt running from his own demons on that bike of his. He'd previously not ridden a bike; just thinking it would be a good idea and buying one to ride all the way up to Alaska. Later, in town, he stole a tin of sardines from the grocery store, and made a point of making sure I saw him. It was a strange thing to do. And I think he did it because he was trying to push me away, because I liked the guy. We got on well, and I think somewhere, deep down in his subconscious, there was a part of him that just didn't like being liked. But I told him that, and that I wasn't bothered about the stealing of the mackerel, because I really liked Seth, loved him in a way, not in the *Brokeback Mountain* sense, just in my admiration for the way that he was, and I cherished the time I got to spend with him in Skagway. He made Skagway what it was.

I also spent some time with Sean, the guy I'd met back up at the border.

He was another nut case, explaining how he'd bought a raft that folded down into a backpack – called a packraft – and that his plan was to hike out into the wilderness for days on end, then find a river, inflate the raft, and float back down to where he'd parked his car. And then move on to the next spot.

I later saw some of his photographs on Facebook; a man on top of a mountain, with the biggest smile I've ever seen on anyone. Then he met a girl, hiking with her for a while, and from what I can gather he really did have the most amazing of summers. I too met someone up here, a girl by the name of Danielle, who worked on the railway line that had taken us to the top of the mountain. It was a pleasant but brief romance of the road. Wave hello, and say goodbye.

Now it was a case of figuring out how to get home to England from here, as I was due back in just over a week to start the job on the magazine. Of course I felt like going AWOL and just not going back, perhaps turning around and riding all the way down to Argentina, as that had been my original plan. But I didn't have the energy or the desire to do that. Or the money. Indeed I was spent, worn out from the road I'd been riding for so long. No, the more time I spent in Skagway, the more I knew that this was as far I was going, and to hell with riding any further.

Besides, to have pushed on to Anchorage, or Fairbanks, or Prudhoe Bay, would involve stepping once again into the real unknown, with no certainty as to what I'd be able to do with the bike, as the quote I'd got for shipping it out of Anchorage had been an incredible three thousand English pounds, and I couldn't really afford that. Neither could I have brought myself to abandon the bike out here either. It needed to come home with me, for sentiment if nothing else.

That left one main option, and that was to take the four-day ferry from Skagway all the way back down to Seattle, travelling through the inside passage, along the coastline of Alaska, and then Canada, arriving in Seattle, where from there I knew I could quite easily – and much more cheaply – put the bike on a boat back to England and fly there myself. Geographically, it would be going back on myself, but psychologically it would still be moving forward (still running towards the light I suppose), if that makes much sense.

Actually, it was an easier decision to make than I thought it would be. After all, Alaska would still be there next year, and the year after that, and if I'm to do it, I would like to do it properly – learning something from the way Seth, Calvin and the two Israelis travelled – taking it a bit steadier, enjoying it more, exploring it more, and I just didn't have time to do that this time around.

It was then just a case of waiting for the ferry to show up, enjoying the time in Skagway that I was left with; hanging out with Seth and with Sean, even gate crashing a wedding and listening to Gary and Janilyn's son, Lucas, play some amazing self-written songs on guitar. He was a carpenter by trade but pinned to give it all up in search of a career in music. What can you say to that, other than, 'go on, you have to give this a go, you're too good not to.' And I hope by now that he has.

***

There was a ferry sailing on the seventh day of my stay in Skagway, giving me just enough time to travel down the coast, arrive in Seattle, sort out the shipping, and then get myself home in time for the job in England to start. It would be pushing it fine, but it was doable, and I'd realised by now that if you set your sights on something, then somehow, almost without fail, it'll work out in the end.

Strange how the world seems to work like that; with no rhyme or reason, sometimes with just a dash of magic, and those angels and fairies helping you on your way. How many more I'd met on this adventure across America. If life is a fairytale, then these angels and fairies are the characters that guide you on your way, your quest not quite possible without them. And who can say life isn't a fairytale, not when all of us believe in heroes, villains and monsters, at least to some degree.

In my case, I had not rescued the maiden on this mission, but I had slew many dragons, and passed through many enchanted lands, discovering many people afraid of their neighbours, and the village beyond. I had met people who had given me knowledge and gifts, who had pointed me in the right direction and come to my aid when I needed it most.

This is perhaps the same quest as all of us are on in life, with it only the backdrop that changes. Mine had been the road across the world, my transport a motorbike. But the nature of the quest is the same; to find answers and hopefully contentment. We all seem to be in search of those things in one way or another. We are all running towards our own version of the light, however that voyage happens to manifest. I certainly wish you all the very best on your journeys.

As for the remainder of my voyage, as the ferry gently pulled away from the docks, I stood out on deck and waved Skagway goodbye, certain that I would miss the place, and most of all the people that I'd met there. I remember it to be a beautiful day, with a vibrant blue sky, and it stayed like that for almost the entirety of those four days at sea.

It really was quite astounding, cruising south, along the coast of Alaska, with the mainland to the left, and a chain of islands to the right, guarding you from the open waters of the ocean. Occasionally we'd stop at towns to pick up other passengers, even Juneau, the capital of Alaska, which can't be accessed by land, only by the sea, these ferries the lifeblood of the state.

The best time was at night, when you could sit at the front of the boat, looking out of the windows ahead to where the full moon hung in the sky, chasing it through the night, it casting reflective glows across the water, often as still as a lake. The lights would be dimmed. Other passengers might be sitting nearby, but everyone would be silent, the faint sound of the engine, the faint sense of movement, the lot of us just staring out at the moon and the endless water ahead. And then in the morning the sun would rise, and out on deck we would all gather again, looking out at this enchanting snow-capped land.

I could have slept out on deck, on the sun loungers provided. This is a popular option for those on a tight budget, as the ferry itself wasn't cheap; the best part of a thousand dollars. Instead, I booked a tiny cabin, paying another few hundred dollars (credit card, overdraft, by this time I just didn't care) for the privilege of being able to shut the door behind me, lie on the bed, read a book, have a nap. It was just what I needed having spent so long exposed on the road. All the while Dorothy languished in the hold beneath me, strapped down beside the cars and the lorries, those old Indian pannier sacks hinting at quite a story to be told.

***

I disembarked in Bellingham, ninety miles to the north of Seattle, as this was the closest place to the city you could get off. Also disembarking was a lady in her seventies, about to ride a converted Harley Davidson – now with three wheels – on what she planned to be a three-month tour of the United States. This lady made me think of Gary, the Old Minister, Snow Cat and all the other adventurers of senior years, still out there, doing their thing, not allowing old age to stop them. What a brave thing to be doing, and I wished her well as we went our separate ways.

From Bellingham I rode south along the coast, taking my time, in no rush to get there, winding through pretty little villages and along the water's edge. It was strange now not to be heading towards Alaska. At times I wondered if I'd done the right thing by not pushing on to Anchorage or to Prudhoe Bay, but as I now know only too well, it's far harder to stop than it is to carry on. And it was time to stop. My whole body ached for it.

In Seattle I called round to see Jon and Natalie, who kindly offered to let me camp in their garden for a few days. Without Jon and Natalie, I don't know if this adventure would even have been possible. It was them who provided the base I needed to get this off the ground and I owe them both tremendously.

As for getting the bike back to England, I contacted Giles, the man who had organised the flying of the bike from London to New York in the first place. He told me it would be much cheaper to send it by boat, so that's what we agreed, it looking likely to cost around £900 by the time I was done. My dad kindly offered to help me out with this one, as I think secretly he was as attached to Dorothy as I was, and he certainly wouldn't have wanted me leaving her there either.

She certainly had an adventure in store; being picked up by a courier van, driven down to LA, loaded on to a boat, sailed down the Pacific Coast until she reached the Panama Canal, through that, and then across the Atlantic Ocean, arriving in England in an anticipated eight to ten weeks time. I on the other hand needed to fly home, leaving the bike in the capable hands of Jon and Natalie, who made sure she got picked up by the delivery guy sometime during the next few days.

As my return flight was out of Anchorage (that's where I thought I'd end up when I booked it) ironically I needed to fly up there first, then catch the plane that would take me home to England, via Iceland, meaning that it was a bit of slog getting home that day.

It was a strange sensation flying back to England, back to my flat, back to my stray cat, back to the end of an adventure. Thankfully it had all fallen into place, and whilst Alaska wasn't quite the euphoric victory I thought it would be, it had done what it needed to do. It had ticked that box, crossed it off the list, which meant that I could go home without anything on the list for a while. I could then stand still for a bit, which I did, starting that job and getting stuck straight into it, putting together a magazine about bikes and people who are leaving their own comfort zones.

Dorothy turned up a few months later. I went to collect her from the docks to the east of London, finding her in a warehouse much like the one I'd left her in all the way back in Indonesia, when trying to get her across to Malaysia.

I look at her and wonder if she has any adventures left in her, and I'm not so sure she has. Then I look at me, and ask, do I have any adventures left in me? And again, I'm not so sure I have. This journey from Sydney to Alaska, a distance of almost 35,000 miles, at an average speed of 37mph, had certainly opened my eyes to the world, and to my own reflection in it. Though in a way, I'd only just scratched the surface, there still so much to see and to learn, though perhaps just not for the time being at least.

Have I stopped running? I guess that is the key question. And the answer to that is probably no. All I've done is learnt how to control that running, and be in charge of it, and run only when the time is right. I certainly have no regrets now, not really. Things have worked out the way they have for the best. Mandy seems happy, and I'm getting there, certainly not punching myself in the face or attacking wooden sheds with pitchforks. Though that darkness will always be a part of me. It's what propels me. And in the future, I'm probably going to be needing that again. In the meantime thanks for riding with me. See you on the road.